SIMULATION PROGRAMMING
LANGUAGES

Proceedings of the

IFIP Working Conference on
Simulation Programming Languages

Edited by

J. N. BUXTON

C-E-I-R Ltd., London

1968

NORTH-HOLLAND PUBLISHING COMPANY - AMSTERDAM

Library of Congress Catalog Card Number 68–21424

PRINTED IN THE NETHERLANDS

PREFACE

In May, 1967, a Working Conference on Simulation Programming Languages was held at the Lysebu Hotel near Oslo under the auspices of Technical Committee 2 of the International Federation for Information Processing. In this volume, the proceedings of that meeting are made available.

This was the third Working Conference in a series of such meetings organized by TC 2 to discuss specific topics in programming language work, and the same principles were followed in its organization as in its predecessors. Attendance was limited by invitation and a group of some 50 recognised experts in the field or in related areas such as general purpose language design accepted invitations to the meeting. Copies of technical papers were distributed in advance of the meeting. About half of the time in the eight formal sessions was spent in discussion.

The conference was opened on the 22nd May with welcoming addresses by Mr. A. W. Owe (chairman of the Norwegian Council for Scientific and Industrial Research), Dr. L. Monrad-Krohn (Norwegian Society for Electronic Information Processing) and Prof. H. Zemanek (chairman of TC 2). The meeting closed with a banquet at the Hotel Bristol in Oslo on the 26th May, at which Mr. J. N. Buxton gave the closing address: in accordance with precedent, the text is given in the Proceedings.

This volume contains the technical papers presented to the meeting and the discussion which took place during the formal sessions; the equally interesting discussions which took place over meals and in the evenings cannot, of course, be included. With the exception that a few trivial errors in typing or translation have been corrected, the papers have not been subjected to any alterations by the Editor and they, therefore, stand effectively as the authors left them. The discussions, on the other hand, have been extensively edited. Most of the text reproduced here is approximately verbatim, subject to the removal of noise words, glaring redundancies and personal abuse (Note: the impersonal insults, for example, about somebody else's programming language, have been retained.) A few sections which were either completely redundant, entirely meaningless or beyond the Editor's comprehension, have been removed.

All references made to other works in the papers have been grouped together in one Bibliography, in the alphabetical order of Authors. One additional bibliography remains in the body of the proceedings; a chronological collections of papers on continuous simulation provided by Brennan.

It remains only to acknowledge the help of those who made the conference possible. The organizing committee consisted of O-J. Dahl (chairman), J. N. Buxton, A. Caracciolo, K. Čulík, P. J. Kiviat, H. S. Krasnow and T. B. Steel Jr. They were most ably assisted in the local arrangements by H. Thorgersen (conference secretary), Irene Siguenza, Else Falch, Lisbeth Hjort and F. O. Falch. N. Teufelhart put his extensive experience of organizing previous conferences at the Committee's disposal and assisted in running the Secretariat during the conference; this was most welcome. The scientific secretaries, to whom the Editor in particular is most grateful, were D. Belsnes, H. Hegna, P. M. Kjeldaas, S. Kubosch, A. Lunde, B. Myhrhaug and K. S. Skog.

Substantial support in financial and other resources was given to the Conference by the Norwegian Computing Centre, the Norwegian Society for Electronic Information Processing, the Norwegian Council for Scientific and Industrial Research, the Norwegian School of Business, Economics and Administration and IFIP itself. The Rank Xerox company kindly provided copying services during the Conference.

The editor would like to express his appreciation to the Directors of C-E-I-R Limited for the support of the Company, and for the use of its resources during the preparation of this volume.

CONTENTS

THE PROCESS VIEW
AND MANAGEMENT SYSTEMS

HOWARD S. KRASNOW

IBM, Advanced Systems Development Division,
Yorktown Heights, New York, USA

Abstract: The development of simulation languages has made available a variety of powerful capabilities for model building and experimentation. These include the capability to freely structure the components and the behavior of a model; to control dynamic behavior through the use of either state- or time-dependent events; and to specify behavior modules (processes) of extensive generality with the aid of dynamic referencing techniques. Modeling is essentially descriptive, and experimentation involves one form of activation of a description. It is suggested that in an analogous fashion some of the processes in a well defined system can be actually performed (automated).

An experimental, process-oriented simulation system and its implementation are introduced. The extensions necessary to employ this approach in management systems are then discussed.

1. INTRODUCTION

Discrete simulation languages have been developed to facilitate the modeling and the simulation of a wide range of dynamic systems. The conceptual orientation of these languages provides a framework for the user of very considerable power in simulation applications. This power depends, in practice, upon the internal organization of the language processor.

It is suggested that a language suitable for simulation may be capable of generalization for a far broader span of use - that the capability to describe systems is closely related to the capability to organize systems. The techniques that have been employed in implementing simulation systems may then provide the foundation for supporting this enlarged capability.

These possibilities will be explored in the context of a specific simulation language and its experimental processor. The process view of this language and the resulting organization of its processor are first discussed. The extendability of this view toward "management systems" is then outlined and a possible approach to its implementation in the broadened context is suggested.

1

2. A PROCESS VIEW FOR SIMULATION

A process-oriented simulation language is discussed at length
in [6] and [113]. For the purpose at hand, it can be briefly summarized as follows:

Simulation consists of the description of a system (i.e., construction of a model), the description of an experiment to be conducted with the model, the carrying out of the experiment and the
analysis of results. The essential features of the language are descriptive, and are appropriate to both the modeling and the experimental aspects of the simulation activity.

Description requires the specification of the components and behavior of a system or experiment. It involves the identification of
each type of entity which may be contained in the model and the
group of attributes which represent that type of entity. Attributes
may take as value the name of an entity, as well as a number or a
character string. Arbitrary and hierarchical groupings of entities
are possible, and the type of any entity may be readily determined.

The behavior of a system is the collective behavior of its processes. A process starts, takes place over a span of time, and
terminates. While active, it changes the state of the model by modifying attribute values of selected entities, by creating, destroying, or regrouping entities, and by starting, terminating, commu-
nicating or otherwise interacting with selected processes. The
state changes which occur while a given process is in control constitute an event. Any entity for which behavior has been specified
is in fact a process. Processes may, therefore, be manipulated
and referenced in the same manner as other entities.

The keynote of this simulation language is modularity. An entity
is a module whose structure has been specified. Such modules may
be replicated and organized at will. Similarly, a process is a
module whose structure and behavior have been specified. These
modules may likewise be replicated and organized. Indirect referencing, through the use of name-valued attributes, facilitates the
construction of general purpose modules, since references can be
evaluated dynamically and need not be constrained to entities of a
single type.

3. THE CONTROL OF SIMULATED PROCESSES

The processor for this simulation language consists of two
phases, a translation phase and a run-time execution phase. The
syntax-driven translator produces intermediate code for each type

of process whose behavior has been specified. However, since all data referencing is dynamic, a set of data descriptions, or proto-types, is also established for each type of entity specified. The translator also features a syntax macro facility [86] which permits the construction of macros defined in source language or in terms of previously defined macros. The macro variables are syntactic units (e.g., "expression", "data reference") of the source language. With this facility, the user may in effect extend or modify the source language or redesign it to meet the needs of a particular group of entity and process types with which he is concerned.

The execution phase implements the state changes called for by the translated processes under the central control of a simulation algorithm. The dynamic nature of the referencing makes possible a clean separation between program (behavior) and data (status). New types of entities may be added with minimum modification of the behavior description, and vice versa. Prototype data is read automatically in conjunction with data references. This organiza-tion makes possible a high degree of modularity in the user's pro-gram. For example, a single process description may be used in sequence to modify totally different sets of data.

Communication and interaction between processes is accom-plished by process-control statements in the language. To illus-trate the mechanism that has been used, the following two state-ments will be discussed:

1. START ⟨process-type⟩ AFTER ⟨expression⟩
2. WAIT CHANGE ⟨entity. attribute⟩

Statement (1) typifies the ability to introduce time-dependent events into a model; it initiates a process of the specified type and sched-ules it to start. Statement (2) is representative of the facility for dealing with state-dependent events; it causes the suspension of the current process until assignment is made to the specified attribute. In this particular language, this is accomplished by an automatic signaling device.

The implementation of these statements requires the use of cer-tain standard attributes for each process, such as TIME; PRIOR-ITY; WAIT_FLAG. The START statement assigns a relative time value to TIME; PRIORITY is assigned by the user; and the WAIT CHANGE statement sets the WAIT_FLAG. Scheduled processes ap-pear on a schedule list. Processes with relative time equal to zero and WAIT_FLAG not set appear on a ready list ranked by PRIOR-ITY. The first process on the ready list (the current process) re-ceives and maintains control until it executes a control statement. If the control statement causes a time-dependent delay, the refer-enced process is placed on the schedule list (e.g., statement (1)). If it causes a state-dependent delay (e.g., statement (2)), the pro-

cess itself is removed and effectively appears on a WAIT list, with
its WAIT_FLAG set. WAIT lists are associated with the prototypes
for each type of entity, and incorporate the specific data reference
for which each process is waiting. Upon assignment to the specified attribute, a signal is automatically generated, i.e., the WAIT_
FLAG attribute of the waiting process is reset, and the process is
returned to the ready list.

4. THE PROCESS VIEW FOR "MANAGEMENT SYSTEMS"

We now consider the extension of the process view from a simulated environment to a real environment. The system of interest is
extensive, open, and not necessarily fully organized, e.g., the
operations of a business firm. The computing system is visualized
as an integral part of the firm, performing those processes which
can be economically automated and interacting freely with those
which are not. Such a capability is often loosely termed a "management system", when postulated with respect to business operations.

The notion of status description is appropriate for defining the
structure of the data base for the firm. The simulation concepts of
entity-attribute are to some extent merely transliterations of the
familiar data processing concepts of record and field. However,
in traditional data processing these ideas are applied in an entirely
static manner, with facilities for structural change provided apart
from the normal mode of operation. In the proposed environment,
a far greater capability for change and growth would be provided.
As in simulation, some structural changes could be achieved dynamically by constructing arbitrary groupings (files) of entities. More
basic changes could be achieved by modifying the status description
to include new or revised entity types. As noted previously, a considerable degree of change is possible without the need for extensive program modification.

The ability to describe concurrent, diverse activity in the real
world in terms of a collection of interrelated processes is the essence of discrete simulation. It is proposed that a role for the
computer is to perform any of these real processes for which it is
qualified, i.e., those processes concerned with the storage and
processing of information. The sequence of development is first
the description (design) of the firm and then the assignment of processes to the facilities (e.g., computer) best equipped to handle
them. The notion of a process as something that takes place over
time, that changes the state of the system (e.g., by updating a data
base), and that communicates and interacts with other processes
remains valid.

There are several significant differences between this environment and the simulation environment. One key distinction is that all process activity is not necessarily programmed. Some processes take place entirely outside of the confines of the machine; some processes engage in a mix of external and internal activity; and finally some processes involve only computing activity *. A second major distinction is that all processes take place in real time, rather than in simulated time. The simulation concept of an event, which causes state changes instantaneously with respect to simulated time, does not exist (although some entirely internal processes may approach that ideal).

The simulation capability to define events as either state-dependent or time-dependent has an obvious application in the extended context. Consider some simple examples:

> "When gross laboratory expenditures have exceeded $X, only purchase requisitions approved by the general manager may be processed."

In this case, the activity of a procurement process is dependent upon the state of the system. The procurement process may be internal, with data supplied from outside; or perhaps it is initiated externally with partially programmed activity. Either way, control is being exercised in an indirect but broadly effective manner.

> "Each week, all department managers having product responsibility are to be advised of sales levels for their respective products during the past week."

This implies the existence of a process associated with each department manager, much of whose activity is probably external. Communication is achieved in accordance with a predetermined schedule.

An important need in the type of environment under discussion is the ability to provide a flexible interface between those processes carried out under program control (internal) and those performed external to the computer. It seems likely that this interface will evolve and change as the needs of the business and the understanding of the processes change. Furthermore, one can visualize a broad range of semiautomatic processes in which control is retained by a user who requests the performance of non-repeating sequences of automatic processes. Terminal access could provide the vehicle for such usage.

The ability to separate the task of building a model from that of

---

* Subsequently referred to as external, semiautomatic, and internal or automated processes respectively.

conducting an experiment with a model also carries over in the difference between the structuring of a system and its use. As with
simulation, it is necessary to be able to modify or add structure
readily and with a minimum impact upon unrelated parts of the
system (model). (Although most current simulation systems do not
provide it, the ability to perform this function in an on-line mode
appears to be desirable in both the simulation context and the extended environment under discussion.)

One attractive feature of a system motivated by a process concept would be the ease with which simulation studies might be
linked to the actual system. Similar, if not identical, status descriptions could be supplied to the simulation processor. Some of
the programmed processes could be incorporated into the model.
Other simulation processes could be substituted for their counterparts. Data for model initialization might be extracted and condensed automatically from active files. The entire activity of simulation would constitute one of the processes in the actual system.

Finally, the high degree of modularity provided by such a system would serve as the foundation for efficient operation. The firm
could standardize on commonly used structures and internal activities, for shared use by all.

5. THE CONTROL OF AUTOMATED PROCESSES

If the process view is relevant to the performance of system
activity in a "management system" context, it is plausible to consider the applicability of the simulation mechanism discussed
above for translation and control in this environment. The organization of a system into two phases again seems to be appropriate.
The translation phase would generate extensive prototype information concerning entity types defined to the system by its users. In
addition to recording the internal structure of each type of entity,
and providing the basis for dynamic referencing of entities, the
prototypes would also indicate the nature of file organization for
such entities. This mechanism would provide the data system with
flexibility for change and modification comparable to that enjoyed
by simulation users.

A capability for extending or modifying the source language
would also be a desirable feature of the translation phase, as it is
in the simulation context. A macro facility similar to that defined
for the simulation system would permit considerable specialization
of terminology and function to suit the specific requirements of the
firm.

The central issue, of course, concerns the internal control

over processes which the user has chosen to incorporate in the "automatic" sector of the firm (carried out by the execution phase). The activity of such processes can be classified, in a fashion similar to that of simulated processes, as follows:

1. Modify attribute values of specified entities
2. Modify structure by adding, deleting or regrouping entities
3. Communicate and interact with other processes, either as a function of time or of system state
4. Communicate with external processes (users).

Activities (1) and (2) would employ the simulation concepts of dynamic referencing to introduce a high degree of modularity into the system. General purpose processes capable of referencing a variety of types of entities, as well as different entities of the same type, may be utilized.

The question of control is directly related to activities (3) and (4) which involve communication and interaction. The basic philosophy, motivated by the simulation approach, is that the currently active process maintains absolute control while it is active, relinquishing control as soon as it terminates an active phase *. An active phase is terminated by an explicit process control statement. For purposes of illustration, consider the following set of control statements:

READ/WRITE ⟨file⟩
START ⟨process-type⟩ AFTER ⟨expression⟩
WAIT CHANGE ⟨entity. attribute⟩
SIGNAL ⟨process⟩

The READ/WRITE statements relinquish control for the performance of input-output operations. These may be considered as subprocesses of the calling process for which specialized hardware control is already provided. The START statement accomplishes in real time somewhat the same action as its simulation counterpart. However, in the absence of capability for performing parallel internal activity, the system can only guarantee that it will undertake the scheduled process some time after the passage of the required time interval (i.e., as soon as it can get around to it), but not necessarily at precisely the desired time. The WAIT CHANGE statement suspends the current process until an assignment is made to the specified attribute. The SIGNAL statement does not relinquish control immediately, but sends a signal to a waiting process.

The control algorithm would operate upon, in essence, two lists. The first would be a list of processes ready to become active, i.e.,

---

* An apparent exception concerns the handling of terminal input in an on-line mode, discussed below. However, this is not viewed as a significant transfer of control.

processes for which all of the conditions necessary for activation
have been satisfied. The discipline for sequencing processes on
this list is a subject for study, but does not affect the general approach. For simplicity, assume a first-in, first-out procedure.
The first process on the list is the current (active) process. When
its active phase terminates, it is transferred to the other list, or
destroyed. The second list (which would probably be implemented
as an extended set of lists), contains all waiting processes. All
such processes may be considered to be awaiting one or more signals which will be generated as a result of particular system states.
Some of these signals are initiated by hardware, specifically timer
and I/O interrupts; others are initiated by the software under program control. The latter group includes signals sent by an explicit
SIGNAL statement, as well as signals generated automatically by
assignments to specified variables. Upon receipt of the required
signals, the waiting process is transferred to the ready list for
subsequent activation.

It is possible to imagine a rigid separation between those processes which have been consigned to the machine and external processes. The internal processes then constitute a more or less
closed subsystem within the firm. A more realistic view, however,
visualizes a fluid boundary characterized by extensive communication between internal and external processes, i.e., the internal
subsystem is quite open. Users, interfacing with the internal system through terminals, can be considered as semiautomatic processes. A sequence of commands from the terminal is analogous
to the activity specification of a process, except that in this case the
activity sequence is determined on-line directly by the user. He
communicates with processes already in the system, initiating or
controlling action with respect to entities of interest, and exchanging data. He selects, from an available repertoire of generalized
processes (modules), those appropriate to the task at hand, and then
bids the machine to carry them out upon data of his own choosing.
He does not ordinarily enter into extended conversation with the internal system, unless dealing with a process that requires it.

The introduction of such an on-line capability does not significantly alter the approach to internal control. Terminals could be
serviced by the simple expedient of a timed read-out cycle. The
process for examining terminal input would, however, require
special treatment to assure prompt servicing. This could be a-
chieved, for example, by introducing a separate signal category
associated with terminal input. Receipt of this signal (probably a
hardware interrupt) would cause immediate, but temporary, interruption of the current process to allow standardized, minimal
handling of the input. One process would be started for the input

received from each terminal and placed on the ready list. Control would then return to the current process. Substantive response to terminal requests would take place when the associated processes became active.

It is apparent that this form of internal control does not establish any guaranteed level of service to users. In particular, the introduction of processes with lengthy active phases would cause a very slow response. The essential point is that the machine is available to perform certain processes needed to conduct the business of the firm, and that its suitability for any given task is subject to evaluation. The internal control mechanism does *not* attempt to administer the system - a management responsibility. Administration is a separate process of the firm which establishes priorities of use and service; which determines the rights and privileges of different users; which monitors internal processes and determines what actions to take under different forms of overload. From the viewpoint of the firm, there is nothing unique in this. Management is accustomed to allocating scarce resources under complex and conflicting conditions. This administrative process need not be automated in order to utilize the resources of the computer in the service of the firm. To the contrary, it seems likely that this will be an external or semiautomatic process for a long time to come. With experience, the firm may be able to more fully automate this decision process. However, the prospect of providing a general purpose, fully automatic administrative control appears to be very remote.

6. CONCLUSION

The evolution of simulation languages has introduced descriptive capabilities of great power and utility. The possibility of applying such capabilities in the actual construction of information systems offers considerable appeal. This will likely be increasingly attractive as "management systems" emerge, characterized by the availability of structural as well as operating data about the business, by multiple modes of access to the data for a wide variety of purposes, and by the sharing of data and services among many parts of the organization.

The techniques employed in implementing simulation languages may also prove relevant in this broadened context. If not entirely adequate, they certainly offer an excellent point of departure for future development.

ACKNOWLEDGMENT

The author wishes to thank Robert J. Parente for his valuable assistance and helpful criticism in the preparation of this paper.

DISCUSSION

Laski:

Of course we can describe management systems by languages of the kind that we have used in simulation systems and languages - but I don't see it being done. There are difficult problems, and there are solutions, but where are they being applied?

Krasnow:

I am not suggesting that they are applied here, or that the answers to the problems are here. I am suggesting primarily that these are questions to be addressed which have not really been addressed in the past. There seems to be a lot of talk about management systems; people talk about wanting to incorporate more structural data of the firm in the computer, to keep track more completely of what is going on. It seems to me that most of this discussion is in the context of data processing as it has existed in the past. All I am suggesting here is that a somewhat different view has emerged in simulation. This view would seem to be a highly fruitful one when you start trying to do more than simply process data within the firm - when in fact you try to get a comprehensive system within the computer so that you can achieve at least some degree of automatic control.

Caracciolo:

About parallel and quasi-parallel programming: I believe that from a simulation point of view one can in a sense identify a parallel and quasi-parallel operation, but in a real time situation I think that this distinction should be clarified.

Krasnow:

If one wishes to relate to a real world activity for purposes of controlling it, then clearly there is a great deal of real parallel activity going on. To view this, in a program, as processes

which are proceeding in parallel seems to me to be appropriate.
The synchronizing of these processes can not be done in precisely
the same manner as in the real world. In simulation, in the quasi-
parallel mode, you hold up one operation while proceeding with another. Clearly this cannot be done in the real world. On the other
hand one can certainly introduce activity which is state-dependent;
one can certainly say, "I want this process to take place, I want
this kind of a decision, this kind of a policy to be applied", when
the state of the system is thus - and - so. A state-dependent event
may no longer be an event in the simulation sense, but state-dependent activity is nevertheless appropriate in this kind of environment.

With time-dependent situations one might wish to specify the
real times at which activities are to occur, and one may have difficulty assuring that they take place at exactly these points of time.
One may have to settle for approximate times, probably depending
on when the system can mobilize the resources for an activity of
this priority. So there are constraints and there are differences
but I think that the basic approach is appropriate.

Caracciolo:

The second point is this. I guess from what you say that you can
produce the same sort of description of external components of a
system for simulation and for interaction in a real time environment. I would like to ask you whether it is really true that the same
sort of description is equally useful for both.

Krasnow:

I would suggest that substantially the same kind of description
should be appropriate. I think this is a question that might be worth
some discussion. It seems to me that if you are specifying a simulation your description is likely to be somewhat different from that
used when you describe for other purposes. But the method you use
for describing need not be different.

Caracciolo:

My third question is whether in management systems it is also
useful to do some partial simulation in order to make decisions. In
a management system you have thrown out part of the simulation,
and I want to ask you if it is not better to retain a complete simulation capability of the system in order to assist you in forecasting
decisions.

Krasnow:

I do not at all mean to rule simulation out in this kind of situation, but simulation therein becomes a process within the total organization, as part of the information processing for management decisions. One of the advantages here is that if one really had a comprehensive description of the organization that one was working with, then to simulate would become a much easier task, because either that description or a portion of that description could support the simulation model as well as the actual data with which the organization is dealing. It would then be possible to perform simulations which may change the direction of the actual operation by their results affecting the actual data base. That kind of overlap is particularly attractive.

Nygaard:

I think that Krasnow is perfectly right when he says that the simulation approach and the concepts from simulation languages will be essential when you create management systems in future. In fact I think that in future we will require of general programming languages that they have simulation capabilities. We are going to use them both for creating management systems and for creating real-time control systems. The reasons are the following. One of the main problems about such systems is that they are very complex and it is absolutely necessary that we have good concepts for organizing or thinking of such systems.

If we have a good description, then we can organize a good program - if you have a lousy description then you also tend to make a lousy program.

Another characteristic of such systems is that they are constantly under change, and if you produce them in the way you do today, you are going to be tied down to programs which are not easy to modify. You must free yourself to some extent. I suggest that we work on such systems in certain stages. First, we use the simulation capability to evaluate the whole system. Then we may have an intermediate stage where we have some components simulated - and then we have the system where the whole thing is moved into real time. I think we will find the need to have techniques for taking such compound programs and removing the excess coding resulting from the many-level development. I think this is a very fascinating area for work in the future.

ON LINE, INCREMENTAL SIMULATION

MARTIN GREENBERGER * and MALCOLM JONES

Massachusetts Institute of Technology,
Cambridge, Massachusetts 02139, *USA*

Abstract: The availability for the past several years of a time-sharing system at MIT's Project MAC made possible the implementation of an experimental on-line, simulation system called OPS-3. An improved time-sharing system is now under development at Project MAC. Adopting features of this system and using the experience gained from OPS-3, a new incremental simulation system called OPS-4 has been designed. Its motivation and characteristics are described.

1. INTRODUCTION

The essence of simulation is imitation or role-playing. One entity - the device performing the simulation - is made to assume the nature of another entity - the phenomenon being simulated. Simulation differs from direct experimentation in that the phenomenon under study is usually not a part of the simulation.

An on-line simulation system allows both the user and the simulation device to cooperate and share the task of performing the simulation. It does this by providing facilities for the user to interact with the simulation device so that they may both play active roles in the simulation process as it is occurring. Thus, the user may perform some of the simulation functions himself and the simulation device perform the remaining ones. Alternately, the user may act only as a monitor and observe, verify and record data or modify and redirect the simulation when it strays erroneously from the desired path [51, 52, 88]. An on-line simulation system also allows the actual phenomenon being simulated to become a part of the simulation.

On-line simulation is not new. Many people have been simulating on-line with analog computers for years. Simulations which evolve physical models are often conducted with user on-line. Both management gaming and war gaming are limited forms of on-line simulations. However, the on-line, interactive use of a digital

* Now at The Johns Hopkins University, Baltimore, Md. 21218.

computer to build, modify, test and run simulations incrementally is new.

Advances in hardware and software technology have made this possible. The cost of producing electronic components has decreased to the point that a user can now afford to have his own digital computer (e.g., he can buy a PDP-8S for approximately $10,000). He can observe, and participate in a simulation by manipulating his model directly from the computer console just as he could with an analog computer. With large scale computers the same on-line interaction is also possible. The technique called time-sharing allows one large computer to dynamically reallocate its resources so that users sitting at remote consoles attached to this large central computer feel as if they have a computer of moderate capacity all to themselves [129,164]. With these advances it is now possible to provide any user who wishes to simulate using a digital computer the same or greater degree of involvement in the simulation process as that obtained by a user accustomed to simulating with an analog computer.

It is with this environment in mind - the interactive mode of using either a small digital computer, or a large time-shared one - that the term on-line simulation is used in this paper. The term incremental simulation is defined to mean the building, testing and validating of a model piece by piece. This has always been the recommended method, but difficult to effect in a batch processing environment. On-line simulation systems now make incremental simulation more easily realizable.

The terms, event and activity are used frequently in the literature and throughout this paper [6, 84]. An event is some action which changes the state of the simulation by modifying the simulation data base, and/or scheduling or cancelling the execution of other events in the system. An important aspect of an event is that it occurs at a specific point in simulated time and is instantaneous. An activity is a sequence of related events which are separated by specified intervals of simulated time. Thus, an activity exists over a period of simulated time.

Simulation is sometimes characterized as a three-stage process. First, a descriptive model of the phenomenon is built. Then the model is tested. Finally, the completed model is exercised and, by inference, conclusions are drawn about the behavior of the real phenomenon being studied.

In reality no sharp line should exist between the first two stages. Ideally, the model building and testing stages are repeated many times and constantly interact with each other. In some instances, there is no formal final running stage, since by the time the model is fully debugged the user has obtained such a clear understanding of the phenomenon under study that it is not necessary to exercise the model any further.

The goal of an incremental simulation system is to completely remove the distinction between the building and testing phases by allowing the user to interact *continuously* with his model. He should be able to experiment with his model, either in whole or in part, at any point during its development. He should be able to change any portion of his model at any time and immediately test the effect of these changes. To allow this flexibility an appropriate language in which a user may easily specify his model and a simulation system that allows complete interaction with the model and the ability to easily restructure it must be provided. Neither is sufficient by itself.

2. SIMULATION LANGUAGES

An adequate language is the first concern. But, in designing the language the environment in which it operates - the simulation system - must be constantly kept in mind. For example, a language designed for an on-line environment should include facilities for allowing the user to directly communicate with a model as it is running. The type of debugging facilities provided in an on-line simulation system may take advantage of this communication and therefore substantially differ from those provided in an off-line simulation system. The language should reflect this difference of environment. Present simulation languages designed for use in the off-line batch processing environment are unsuitable for on-line simulation.

3. OPS-3

Since the fall of 1963 the compatible time-sharing system (CTSS) [164] developed by the MIT Computation Center has been running on a modified IBM 7094 at Project MAC. CTSS allows 30 people to simultaneously use the 7094 with almost no restrictions as to what they may do. Over twenty different languages, such as FORTRAN II and IV, MAD, FAP, AED, LISP, SLIP, COMIT, SNOBOL, etc. are available to users of CTSS. However, most of these languages were not specifically designed for on-line use.

Starting in the spring of 1964 a group led by Professor Greenberger set out to design and implement a language and system for on-line use. The result of that effort is the present OPS-3 system [50], a subsystem of CTSS which extends the facilities of CTSS to provide the user with a flexible method of an on-line programming and model building.

The simulation system available in OPS-3 was specifically designed for on-line use [52]. (It is the only simulation system to our knowledge that was designed for on-line use.) The following features of OPS-3 are particularly significant:

1. It is easy to modify the model structure at any time and no compilation or reloading of programs is required.
2. Specification of data structures and initialization of data in OPS-3 is done dynamically and is easily specified.
3. Complete or partial reinitialization of the model is simple and completely under the user's control.
4. The scheduling mechanism - called the Agenda - may be examined and/or modified by the user at any time.
5. The debugging and tracing facilities are comprehensive, flexible and easy to use.
6. A general algebraic language with implicit array operations is available, although the control statements in it are limited.
7. Communication with subroutines written in any language is simple and allows the basic features of OPS-3 to be easily expanded or shaped to the user's tastes.

OPS-3 is largely an interpretive language (the MADKOP feature to allow interpretively executed routines to be compiled is incomplete), and consequently execution speed is very slow. The present OPS-3 also suffers from a lack of statistics-collecting routines; has a limited variety of data entities; and seriously limits the amount of core space available for both program and data. Also the syntax used in some of the language statements is sometimes awkward and inconsistent *.

4. A NEW TIME-SHARING COMPUTER

The new time-sharing system called Multics which is now being implemented on a (two-processor memory-centered) GE 645 at Project MAC is intended as a major improvement of CTSS [21, 31, 32, 46, 109, 124, 153]. More than just an upgrading of CTSS, it incor-

---

* Since OPS-3 is a modularly constructed system, many of these deficiencies could be corrected and missing features could be added. However, the lack of core space available in CTSS prevents adding any new features to the present implementation. The basic OPS-3 system uses 24k of the 32k of core available to a user. The SCHED, DRAW and TAB operators used in simulations require almost another 2k of core. Thus, the user is left with only 6.8k of core space for his own programs and data storage.

porates a new philosophy of memory addressing. In Multics logical
sections are specified as segments. A single user may have available up to 2^{18} segments of 2^{18} words each. The physical core
memory contains 16 million words. To accommodate this much
programming, a technique called paging is employed. Each segment is subdivided into pages 64 or 1024 words long. The Multics
system keeps in core memory only as many pages of a segment as
it needs. New pages are brought into core as required, with pages
that have not recently been referenced removed, if necessary.

The segmentation scheme allows users to share programs written as pure procedures. Several people may use the same program
simultaneously in Multics, while keeping only their data segments
unique. In contrast, if 3 people are concurrently using the OPS-3
system in CTSS, 3 separate copies of OPS-3 are maintained by
CTSS. Multics gives users access to certain procedure segments
of the supervisor, this simplifying the writing of sophisticated user
systems. Eventually Multics will allow a user to specify parallel
processing of procedures, a feature which could be very useful in
simulations.

5. A NEW SIMULATION LANGUAGE

A new language and system for incremental simulation specifically designed to operate in a time-shared environment has been
specified by Jones [70]. It is called OPS-4. It borrows concepts
from existing simulation languages [20, 27, 28, 29, 69, 73, 75, 76, 98,
112, 147, 160, 161, 163]. The following is a summary of the important features.
1. The PL/1 language is the basic language of OPS-4 and provides
   a general algebraic and data handling facility [166].
2. OPS-4 is specifically designed to encourage a user to build a
   model incrementally and test the partial model before all the
   pieces have been completed.
3. The world view of OPS-4 encompasses both material- and flow-
   oriented models, machine- and entity-oriented models, or models combining both views [77, 151]. Both activities and events
   may be represented [6, 84].
4. Special data types known as sets, queues, and tables are available in OPS-4 in addition to the normal data types of PL/1.
   There is no limitation on the number or size of any data types.
5. It includes statements to specify the generation of random deviates from popular distributions.
6. Communication among program elements and variables in the
   model can be controlled, but is not restricted.

7. Restructuring of the data base does not require the recompilation of procedures. The normal mode of execution is interpretative.

8. The status of a model may be saved at any point and time by executing a single statement.

9. It is easy at any point during the simulation to reinitialize partly or completely both the system's and user's data base and reset system time so that the simulation may be restarted or a series of simulation runs easily executed. The model may be restored to a previously saved state and thus rolled back to previous points in simulated time.

10. The user has flexible controls to specify the exact order in which events are executed during simulation.

11. No important part of the simulation system is hidden from the user. He has direct access to and the ability to modify every element of the simulation from his console.

12. Extensive debugging and tracing features are available, and they are easy to use.

13. It is easy to modify the structure of a model without recompilation.

14. Flexible means are provided for specifying the starting and stopping points or duration of a simulation run.

15. Individual components of the model can be independently tested, even if embedded in larger modules.

16. The user can interrupt a model at any point during the execution phase, redirect its path, examine, and change the values of variables, then continue the simulation from the point of interruption.

17. In unusual situations, such as when an attempt is made to move time backwards, the user is given the benefit of doubt and the simulation is not interrupted. However, a flag is set.

18. There are comprehensive facilities for collecting statistics.

19. Only the structure and mode of initial data inputs in procedures usually need to be declared by the user. The structure and mode of most data objects resulting from a computation is inferred by the rules of the computation.

20. Immediate on-line diagnostic explanations are provided when an error is detected during the running of the model. The length and detail of these messages are under user control.

21. Debugged portions of a model may be compiled and run at full speed. Interpretive execution is used for sections of programs not yet checked out.

6. IMPLEMENTATION of OPS-4

OPS-4 has not yet been programmed. Its implementation will be in two phases. First, the conceptual framework of the OPS-3 system will be used as a base and will provide the required general algebraic language. Over a year's experience with OPS-3 has shown it to be well adapted for on-line use. However, OPS-4 will use the syntax of PL/1 throughout and will be substantially restructured and enlarged so that the deficiencies of OPS-3 as implemented in CTSS will be eliminated.

The second phase will consist of the implementation of an on-line conversational version of a subset of PL/1. This is an ambitious goal and perforce must await more experience with developing compilers for PL/1. All programming of OPS-4 itself will be done in PL/1. Experience using PL/1 at Project MAC to implement Multics has shown it to be a language well suited to the task of building programming systems which require complex data structures.

Since OPS-4 will be programmed in PL/1 it may be possible to transfer it to other machines (perhaps the IBM System 360 model 67) without a major recoding effort. Only machine-dependent and Multics modules would have to be changed. OPS-4 could also be implemented for a small stand-alone computer system and with a conversational computer language other than PL/1.

7. SIMULATION ESSENTIALS

Some of the features listed previously are absolutely necessary and are found in all simulation systems. Others are conveniences that are peculiar to the on-line environment. It is essential that every simulation system contain the following elements:

1. A mechanism for describing and manipulating the simulation data base. The data base may be partitioned in many ways, but the simplest division is between global data, which is accessible to all activities, and local data, which is accessible to only one activity. Many activities may be represented by the same procedure and differ only in their data base characteristics.

2. An activity sequencing mechanism. Simulation activities are different from normal subroutines since they conceptually operate in parallel. The standard subroutine call is not flexible enough to allow for the undeterministic flow of control between such quasi parallel activities. The transfer of control from one activity to another is a "sideways" transfer, not the standard hierarchical up or down transfer of control.

3. Special facilities for running and debugging a model. Many simulation programs have no fixed termination point. They can be
   run for variable periods of time. Special features are necessary
   for specifying the starting and stopping conditions of a simulation model. Also, because of the unpredictable order of activity
   sequencing, special debugging facilities are necessary for simulation systems.
4. Facilities for collecting statistical measures of a model's performance. Simulation models are constructed so that the user
   may learn something about a particular phenomenon. Often statistical measures are helpful to assess the functioning of the
   model in different environments.

8. LIMITATIONS OF MULTICS AND PL/1 FOR SIMULATION

Multics is faced with many of the same requirements as a simulation system. It must successfully direct the execution of many
processes, some dependent upon each other's actions, others independent of the other activities going on. Many of these processes
may be operated in parallel with each other. Also, Multics must
maintain global, or system wide, data bases which record the location, status, and description of every process and segment, both
active and inactive within the system. Multics must also continuously monitor the state of the system so that users may be properly billed for the resources they utilize. One is naturally led to ask,
"Can't the facilities available in Multics be used directly to provide the basis of a simulation system?" Unfortunately the answer
is no, for the following reasons:
1. Multics' scheduling system is not flexible enough for a general
   simulation language.
   A. Multics relies only on a computed priority for organizing its
      ready list; i.e. it is not possible for the scheduling process
      to use any process' attributes, such as scheduled execution
      time of processes already scheduled on the ready list.
   B. The conditional schedule mechanism is very limited. A
      Block-Wakeup system requires that Wakeup specifically
      know whom to wake up. This is fine for the conditional 'Wait
      for Event' of PL/1 but inadequate for the general

      'Wait until A = B or C > D'

   conditional allowed in OPS-4.
2. Multics' scheduling system maintains and manipulates far more
   information than is necessary just for scheduling simulation activities. Specifically, the majority of the information maintained

by the traffic controller in an Active Process Table is needed only for Multics and is extraneous for a general simulation system.

3. Multics does not automatically implement a standard lock mechanism which prevents user processes which share a common data base from getting in each other's way. It is left to the user to implement whatever mechanisms are necessary for maintaining and protecting shared data bases. The standard lock mechanism used by Multics is available but each user must implement it himself as necessary.

4. The initial version of Multics will not allow the user to have more than one working process, although Multics itself will use multiple processes.

A casual reading of the PL/1 manual might lead one to conclude that the PL/1 language is suitable as a simulation language [166]. However, study will show that it is not complete enough for simulation. The features for directing tasking are limited and, at the present time, not clear on such crucial matters as the sharing or independence of data bases by dependent tasks. Also, the data types in PL/1 are not as extensive as those needed in a simulation language. Furthermore, the sequencing methods available in PL/1 are not flexible enough.

Thus PL/1 and Multics by themselves do not provide all of the machinery necessary for an incremental simulation system. But they do provide a strong foundation.

10. AN OVERVIEW OF MULTICS

One of the central design features of Multics is that a user may have several processes working for him simultaneously *. Indeed, after a user has completed the Login procedure he has 3 processes automatically established for him. These are:

1. The overseer process which performs Login and Logout, handles user interrupts and oversees the other 2 processes.

---

* Saltzer defines a process as, "A process is a program in execution by a pseudo-processor. The internal tangible evidence of a process is a pseudo-processor stateword, which defines both the current state of execution of the process and the address space which is accessible to the processor" [124]. There is a one-to-one correspondence between processes and statewords, and also between processes and address spaces. Every process is identified with a descriptor segment which defines the address space of the process. Descriptor segments are not shared between processes, so there is a one-to-one correspondence between processes and descriptor segments. The stateword of a process includes a pointer to the descriptor segment of the process.

2. The device management process which is directly in charge of the particular console device being used, delivering an input string from it to the third process.
3. A working process which executes Multics commands and user programs as specified by the input string. At command level these strings are read by a procedure called the Listener, which hands over full command sequences to a procedure called the Shell. The Shell interprets the command sequence and calls the commands.

The working process also contains the Multics supervisory programs. A user may indicate by appropriate Multics commands that he wishes to have special versions of certain supervisor modules: e. g. a different scheduling mechanism, which always puts him at the top of the ready list; or a different typewriter management module which writes a verbatim copy of all typewriter input and output as files on secondary storage; or a private version of the PL/1 compiler which recognizes French rather than English keywords. If he has been allowed such freedom by the system administration, this flexibility is possible. Conversely, the administrative authorities might decree that only certain modules are to be used and only certain commands may be accessed by this user, thus restricting him to a subset of Multics available facilities *. This feature could be used to restrict the access of a student to specific programs, or to allow the Shell to be replaced by the OPS command. Thus, it would be possible to have a user automatically enter OPS-4 as soon as he completed the Login procedure.

11. MULTIPLE PROCESSES IN OPS-4

An important design decision relates to the freedom the user is given to specify asynchronous or synchronous processes in OPS-4. One of the major concerns of all current simulation systems is how to imitate simultaneity of events on a single processor computer. It would appear that Multics offers a solution to this problem. It does, but not a complete one. The traffic controller maps the actual hardware of the GE 645 (which is limited to 8 processors) into an indefinitely large number of pseudo-processors each capable of running one process at a time. Conceptually, the user may regard the pseudo-processors as operating in parallel with each other. In actuality, the amount of simultaneity is limited by the number of physical processors being used. Therefore, it will always be pos-

---

* This is currently done in a limited fashion in CTSS by an access vector which allows various system programmers to execute privileged commands not available to normal users.

sible for a user's model to create more simultaneous events than there are actual processors available to execute the events in parallel. Thus, sequencing rules will still be as important as they are in current simulation languages.

12. THE PROBLEM OF REPRODUCIBILITY

For example, consider a queueing model having several servers and separate queues for each server. The server processes and the arrival process are all conceptually occurring simultaneously. When an arrival occurs, it enters the queue which is the shortest. Hypothesize that there are two queues both of the same length and shorter than the queues for any of the other servers. Assume that these two servers finish serving both their requests simultaneously and that at the exact same instant a new arrival occurs. In which queue will the arrival be placed? The answer can certainly depend on the order in which the two server process and one arrival process actually are executed on the computer.

This element of irreproducibility offers both new problems and new possibilities. During the debugging stage it is a serious handicap. Reproducibility is essential if bugs are to be easily recreated so that they may eventually be eliminated. Conversely, once a model has been substantially debugged, the opportunity of actually observing the results of simultaneously interacting processes may add insight to the understanding of the model - especially if the element of non-reproducibility results in different model performance. It is analogous to reseeding the random number generator and seeing a different sequence of activities.

13. CONTROLLING PARALLELISM

This suggests that the user should be able to control whether simulation activities are executed sequentially or whether some of the activities are actually executed simultaneously. To provide this control OPS-4 will add a new attribute to activity declarations. The user may explicitly declare each activity to be either of type Sequential or Simultaneous. The default type will be Sequential. In addition, a global declaration of Sequential or Simultaneous may be invoked to cover all activities. However, the local declaration in each activity will always take precedence over the global declaration. Thus, certain activities may be executed sequentially or simultaneously with other activities, independent of whether all the other activities are being executed sequentially or simultaneously.

If the user declares activities to be simultaneous, he will have to program locks on the appropriate data bases, since OPS-4 will not do so in its initial implementation.

14. SPECIAL ASYNCHRONOUS PROCESSES IN OPS-4

OPS-4 will make use of the multi-processing capabilities of Multics when they are available for some peripheral processes which do not affect the execution of the central simulation. These are:
1. User communication and asynchronous interaction with the simulation to allow game playing and the like [157].
2. Asynchronous debugging monitors which allow the simulation to continue as trace results are simultaneously processed.
3. Statistics collecting and processing.
4. Memory compacting (or garbage collection) of list structures that have diffused throughout many pages of memory.
5. Asynchronous probes of the simulation data base with carefully designed inputs.

Each of these processes is essentially independent of the main simulation process. However, appropriate data base interlocks will have to be programmed to insure correct execution of all processes.

15. CONSTRUCTING A SIMULATION MODEL

The interactive features of OPS-4 allow a user to start building a model on the computer at a very early stage. The computer may then be used to help clarify and expand the formulation of the model from the very outset. The user is encouraged to build his model modularly so that it may easily be expanded in simple incremental steps. He may start at the inside and work out exploring the interactions of specific detailed functions, or else he may specify the entire structure in gross fashion and add detail as his understanding of the problem grows. Facilities are provided in OPS-4 to allow very unstructured problems to be described in three levels of specificity.

16. A MODEL IN OPS-4

The overall structure of an OPS-4 simulation model is rather simple, but quite different than the structure of a GPSS, SOL or

SIMULA program [28, 29, 75, 76, 160]. It is more akin to SIMCRIPT, as it is organized around the concept of indepenent, separately compiled activities, which are written as external procedures [98]. Each activity has its own local data base, and may share data with other, but not all other activities. In addition, there is a global data base which is available to all activities. Individual activities may be hierarchically structured using the features available to PL/1. In addition, groups of activities may form a hierarchical structure.

17. HIERARCHICAL MODELS

When studying a complex problem it is often helpful to subdivide the problem into parts. Each part may be further subdivided, and their parts subdivided again, ad infinitum, until a level of detail is reached that can be described and analyzed in simple terms. This is the technique that humans appear to use in solving difficult problems, and it has been mimicked with fair success by various computer programs attempting to demonstrate intelligent behavior [107, 134]. In fact, most complex computer programs are written in this hierarchical manner [141].

An interesting question is, "What is the route taken to write these hierarchically structured programs?" Is the whole hierarchical structure specified *a priori* and programmed starting at the detailed level, or does the structure grow in detail in parallel with the programming of increasingly detailed blocks? Historically, complicated programs such as the CTSS and Multics supervisors have been programmed using the former approach [123]. Often it turns out that many of the most interesting and important problems are at the higher levels of the program structure and must await testing until the majority of the programs have been written. When errors do arise at this level they may be very costly to correct, for they may require substantial restructuring of subcomponents of the system.

Simulation is often heralded as a solution to this problem. The suggestion is made that a simulation model can abstract the important high level interactions and focus of them, ignoring the detailed problems at lower levels. When the overall structure is completed, then the details can be added. To do this successfully requires that a model be constructed hierarchically. However, to exercise such models in conventional simulation systems requires that all they key pieces be specified and assembled before a run can be made. OPS-4 offers a new approach to this problem.

18. THREE TYPES OF PROGRAMS IN OPS-4

The OPS-4 system provides the user with three different modes of flexibility for specifying his model.
1. He may write an OPS-4 program, compile it, and then execute it.
2. He may write an OPS-4 program and execute it directly with no intermediate compilation phase.
3. He need not write a program at all, but may execute any previously written procedures, of either type 1 or 2, directly from the console.

Were it not for the idiosyncrasies of computers, which make them unable to converse directly in languages natural to the user, the first mode would not need to exist. The second is considerably more natural for a user than the first. Both require that a program - e. g. a specific sequence of actions - be formally stated and therefore they are fixed specifications. The third mode does not have this restriction. The user is not required to plan a sequence of actions in advance. He can improvise.

To distinguish between these three modes of specifications the following terms are used. The first is referred to as a compiled program. The second is called an uncompiled OPS-4 program. The third is known as a user portrayed program. All three are allowed to be intermixed in a simulation constructed in the OPS-4 system.

19. UNCOMPILED PROGRAMS

Most programmers have grown to accept the necessity of compiling a program before it can be executed. However, compilation is not a natural function included in specifying a model, and a user should not be constantly forced to think about it after every iteration of change to his model. Compilation is related to the efficiency of processor utilization. Therefore, the user should view compilation merely as a means of more effectively using a scarce resource, not as a function necessary to allow execution of a program. Even at this level, however, the user must weigh the benefits of decreased execution speed of a compiled program, versus the time take to compile the program. During the debugging and program testing phase it is not unusual for the compilation time to exceed by two or three orders of magnitude the program execution time. Thus, methods for executing uncompiled programs that are 10-20, or even 100 times slower than the execution of compiled programs meet a very definite need *. Cf course, an alternate approach is to attempt to shorten the compilation time. But this usually results in an unfortunate increase in execution time, because of the sloppy programs produced by the hasty compilation. (This is the approach taken in the design of the MAD Compiler [165].

20. USER PORTRAYED PROGRAMS

One of the attributes of a time-sharing system that has often been praised is the feature that a program may communicate with the user and ask for help. It has also been stated that a time-sharing system relieves the programmer of the need to write programs for contingencies that may rarely occur. This is true. In OPS-4, the user-portrayed program is used to provide both these options.

During the course of the construction of a model, any modules which the user realizes must be included in the model for completeness and accuracy, but which he is not interested in describing, or modules which he does not know how to completely describe at that particular time, may be defined as user portrayed programs. This allows the model description to be logically complete, but does not force the user to switch from his main area of interest to consider something of lesser importance. He is only required to be specific about the functions of the module when it is actually needed. At that time the environment of the situation is established and it may be helpful in suggesting what is the proper formulation of the program.

An alternate use of the user portrayed program is to allow the user, or anyone else, to participate directly in the simulation as it is running. This feature, together with the ability in Multics to direct output to, or receive input from several terminals allows OPS-4 to be conveniently used to specify interactive gaming models.

21. TWO APPROACHES TO MODELLING

How do we then start to build a model in OPS-4? We can start either at the detailed level of the individual modules and build up-

---

* Experiments performed by J.H. Morris, Jr. with the OPS-3 system showed that interpretive execution of OPS-3 programs ranged from 25-100 times slower than execution of the same program after it was translated to a machine program using the MADKOP translator. The OPS-3 system is quite inefficient, and the methods for executing OPS-4 programs should lower this figure considerably [36].

ward until we have constructed all the modules that are necessary
to completely specify the model, or we can start with a very abstract, simplified model and add detail as we find it necessary.
The first approach might be likened to that of building a computer.
The individual circuits are specified, they are combined into logical building blocks, the building blocks are combined into functional units, and the functional units are combined to complete the
whole computer. The second approach might be likened to building
a house. The outer structure is completed first and then the detail
is added. Both approaches have merit and both approaches can be
used in OPS-4.

22. ACTIVITIES AND EVENTS

Some languages, such as SIMSCRIPT, require that a model be
specified only in terms of discrete events [98]. That is, if we were
to model the action of a disk storage device in SIMSCRIPT we would
have one event that specified the beginning of the disk seek, and
which scheduled another event called the end of the disk seek. Such
artificiality is not necessary in OPS-4. Instead a Delay statement
may be used to specify the expiration of a certain amount of time
before the activity modelling the disk continues. This is much as
one would do in the SOL language [75, 76]. SOL, however, makes it
difficult to schedule events directly. Everything is oriented toward
the activity concept. All scheduling is done implicitly by the simulation system itself. In OPS-4 both the approach of SIMSCRIPT for
scheduling events directly and the implicit scheduling statements
are available. In OPS-4 an activity is described by writing a program which may define several events.

23. CONDITIONAL ACTIVITIES

OPS-4 allows the execution of an activity or event to be dependent on some condition in addition to the simple time dependency.
Two different classes of conditions are distinguished. The first is
identical to the event concept of PL/1 which is implemented in
Multics with the Block and Wakeup modules in the Traffic Controller and the use of an Event Table. One activity may send a signal
to any other interested events by the Set Event statement in PL/1
which declares that a specific named event has occurred. One or
more other events (or activities in OPS-4 parlance) may determine
if a specific event has occurred by the statement Note Event. Also,
an event may specifically 'Wait' for a specific named event to oc-

cur before proceeding. This type of conditional activation of activities is limited in generality, but it is implemented in a very efficient manner in Multics.

The second type of conditional execution of activities allows the
user to specify any relation between global and local variables as
the triggering statement. This type of scheduling is extremely
comprehensive, and subsumes the first type, since the Set Event
statement could be replaced by setting a switch which could be
tested in a Wait statement. Because of their generality, the testing
of these second type of conditional statements must be done continuously. Therefore, the execution speed of a simulation model having
many conditional statements of this latter type is quite slow.

24. THE INFORMATION FEATURE

Many times during the course of constructing a model, the user
may need to be refreshed about the exact details of how a particular
feature or statement in OPS-4 is used. OPS-4 will have available
an on-line information system which will describe how to use the
features of the OPS-4 system in sections of graduated detail. A
similar system has proved to be a very useful and important feature in the OPS-3 system. There will be a few differences, however, in this feature, called 'Info', in OPS-4, which are dictated
by experience using the Guide operator which supplies information
in OPS-3.

The basic different is that an Info request will only supply information about one subject at a time. When it reaches the last
section pertinent to the specified subject it will automatically return to normal execution. If there are one or more sections to a
specific subject, a carriage return will automatically continue with
the next section. If anything else is typed, Info will return to normal execution and deliver the typed line to be executed by OPS-4.
Furthermore, in addition to being able to indicate a specific section pertaining to a subject, a user may specify that he wishes to
see all the sections pertinent to a subject.

The Info system will also be implemented differently from the
Guide operator. It will allow the user to type, in natural English,
his requests for information about OPS-4. A program similar in
nature to ELIZA [156], will scan for key words in the sentence and
determine what information the user desires. A hash-coded index
of all subjects will be stored in the segment OPS. Index. This index will contain the address of the beginning of the first section of
each subject in the segment OPS. Information. The format of the
segment OPS. Information will be a tree-structure so that each

subject may have several sections, each of which have several subsections, etc. Facilities will be provided, as an integral part of OPS-4, to allow authorized users to revise the information contained in the segment OPS. Information and create a new OPS. Index segment. This authorization will be implemented as part of the access control information stored by Multics in the directory branch of these two segments.

DISCUSSION

Ross:

I have a general comment and I should like to have your feelings on it. I think the use of an on-line system is fine for debugging and for teaching but holds some real dangers if it is made an actual basic working tool of major production type simulations. It seems to me that it is all too easy to build in *ad hoc* changes to the system during production work, with the effect of producing the results the experimenter expects rather than those which would otherwise have emerged. It has to me somewhat the danger of statistics, where if you are a good statistician you can prove almost any *ad hoc* assumption that you wish merely by playing the game the way you wish to play it.

Jones:

I think I agree. We have thought quite strongly that first of all you should have essentially a compatible language available for what we call this on-line use and also available for running your final production program in the normal background or off-line environment. Certainly then you do have to specify very clearly your production simulation model because you are not going to be in contact to offer any *ad hoc* or any other type of advice to the system.

Gimpelson:

Do you actually intend to implement this? The specifications you have here are pretty fancy and require a team possibly comparable to the Project MAC team.

Jones:

Yes, we do, and we are right now planning on having something like four people working on it for what we hope may be two years and we think we can implement something in this time. I should say that we are strongly dependent on the stage of the MULTICS software itself (Laughter). We have hedged a little bit by saying that this system could be adapted to a small stand-alone computer and we might investigate that as a parallel activity. In fact that might turn out to be simpler than trying to implement a system of this sort in MULTICS. Many of the features that are specified in this paper were tried in a limited way in the present OPS system which is running on CTSS and that was not a massive effort at all. There were only two programmers who worked very hard for six months (and by very hard I mean they worked all night and slept during the day).

Conway:

I think it is very important that at this stage we define rather clearly what we mean by on-line simulation. In particular we have to distinguish whether this is necessary just for testing or whether it is seriously required during execution. If the on-line inter-active use is only necessary for testing there is no great difficulty in im- plementation. All you require is an interpreter or a compiler which is itself re-entrant. It does not really require time slicing to do line-by-line syntax checking and to do the testing that is required does not put the systems designers to any great strain. If on the other hand, you require interactive execution of the type that we discuss here, this is a problem several orders of magnitude more demanding. You require something like MULTICS or TSS to serve a number of users simultaneously.

The type of application that we have which is large in core de- mand, long in execution time and which makes very low density use of its data sets resembles list processing. This is a nightmare to people trying to define multi-access systems. This is the sort of thing they wake up in the middle of the night worrying about. We should have some mercy. They are having enough problems with rather conventional arithmetic processes without worrying about simulation so that unless it is really crucial that we have inter- active execution I think we should be much more modest in our de- mands. If we get only marginal utility for this enormous price of inter-active execution, let's not ask for it for at least another ma- chine generation until MULTICS and TSS have had a chance.

Laski:

I want to take issue with Ross and Conway about the need for in- ter-action and view of the simulation by the user during execution. In my experience, apart from relatively trivial simulations, where

one understands what one is simulating, and is merely concerned
with making a trivial statistical measurement, one is simulating
or model building in order to understand a system that is unknown.
Now if one's interaction is restricted to the program definition
stage, one may only evolve that understanding at the snapshot level.
Without interaction during execution I think one lacks a major capability in using simulation model building as a tool to understand
very complex systems.

Jones:

I think we have chosen to say that there is a clear point of departure between the model-building, testing and validation phase
and the actual running of the model. We feel that during the first
part, the model building, testing and validation, the interaction is
very important because you are trying to understand the consequences of this model that you are designing so that you can use
this understanding to be able to understand the system that you are
modelling. We have said that at some point in time this understanding is assumed to be complete and then you run this model
for standard statistical measures over a wide range of parameter
changes to the model. Now maybe that is, as I said, a naïve view.
Maybe the probing of the model and trying to gain further understanding of it never stops. However, we did feel during the initial
stages, the interaction and being on-line was very important, but
then after you would want to move perhaps to an off-line batch processing environment where you would have high efficiency of machine execution.

Ross:

I am surprised that Laski says that he disagrees with me because I think he was adding to the point that I was making, namely
that one must have an adequate model and that one obtains from
such a model results that one doesn't know rather than forcing into
the model ones original preconceived notions. But on the other
hand, coming back to Conway's point on the need for on-line access, I think very strongly, especially if one is talking about complex, highly structured and highly interactive problems, then it is
very important that you have a very fine control over the insertion
of probes and measurements and so forth so that you can in fact
learn from the model. If you have no way of learning except to see
whether it says "yes" or "no" at the end of a 15-hour computer run,
you haven't learned much from it. So I would put in a plea for interactive working, including the use of graphical displays and that
sort of thing so that coupling to the human during this monitoring
process can be in fact that much stronger.

GRAPHIC FORMS FOR
MODELING AND SIMULATION

Michael R. LACKNER
The Ford Foundation Advisory Planning Group,
Calcutta 16, *India*

1. INTRODUCTION

This paper suggests some graphic devices for use in conversational modeling and simulation. Conversational modeling was discussed briefly in a previous paper, [82] and the devices suggested here presume reliance on a process-oriented scheme for digital simulation that was described in another previous paper [83].

The use of graphic equipment deserves great attention by the developers of simulation languages since languages may be immensely enriched by graphic expression and because the very many possibilities invite chaotic development of competitive techniques. This paper does not attempt to suggest standard graphic forms or conventions, but it is intended to invite attention to the subject by suggesting some graphic devices to help form a simulation language resting on a particular simulation scheme.

In the general simulation scheme, the *behaviour space* of an object system is described by declaring entity types that may exist, and functions of those entity types that are necessary or possible; and classes in which the entity types may occur with necessary or possible functions of and relations among the classes. Graphic forms are suggested for these declarations to be made in conversational mode.

Definition of *behaviour-governing rules* is accomplished by specifying the conditions for and the changes that take place upon initiation, interruption, duration, or completion of any instance of the processes that are contemplated in the system.

Other graphic means are suggested for specifying the initial state of a model and still others for portraying model behaviour. In addition to the graphic forms traditionally used to describe various functions of data, forms peculiarly suited to the simulation schemes are proposed. The forms suggested are assumed to be well within the capabilities of existing or announced data processing equipment.

The simulation scheme itself has already been successfully implemented [78] *.

2. THE BASIC SIMULATION SCHEME

In the general simulation scheme, an object system is considered to consist entirely of entities that occur in various states and
come into or go out of existence through the operation of processes
that interact by their operation upon or sensitivity to the entities of
the system. The state of the system as a whole is described by the
sum of entity-states. All changes are attributable to the operation
of processes and occur with the initiation, the duration, the interruption or the completion of processes.

In a digital simulation model, processes are explicated by computer programs that specify procedures that generate, modify or
destroy records containing arithmetic or logical data and that insert
or remove them from various lists.

The notion of process is elaborated toward a more precise way
of thinking about and then expressing systems by introducing a pos-
tulate governing the interaction of processes: *processes operate independently except when beginning, when interrupted or when completing and interact only through their effects upon passive entities.*
This restricts the possible points of interaction among processes
and thus indicates the conditions under which sequences of instructions representing parts of individual processes may be executed
independently while maintaining valid representation of simultaneous
process operation. While processes may be conceived of as operating simultaneously and many separate instances of each process
may be operating at the same time, the operation of any one is so
constrained that one of its instances can only begin when and if an
instance of some other process begins, completes or is interrupted;
it may possibly be interrupted when any other process begins, completes or is interrupted; and its completion or interruption may
provoke the beginning, interruption or completion of some other
process. Furthermore, instances of the various processes interact
with one another only through otherwise passive entities. That is,
the conditions for process initiation, interruption or completion are
entirely identified by the states of entities other than processes; by
the states of those things upon which processes act or depend.

Table 1 relates object system events to their computer program
counterparts.

* I am grateful to Mrs. Patricia Kribs for her thoughtful comments on the
  draft of this paper.

Table 1

Object system event	Program counterpart
initiation of process	execution of subroutine that generates, modifies, or destroys discrete records of information or manipulates lists of such records to reflect initiation
duration of process	execution of subroutine that modifies time-dependent variables to reflect elapsed time
completion or inter-ruption of process	execution of subroutine that generates, modifies, or destroys discrete records of information or manipulates lists of such records to reflect cessation
generation of discrete object or information	generation of an information record and placement in a list or set of lists
destruction of discrete object or information	removal of record from list or set of lists
transition of informa-tion or object from situation to situation	transfer of record from list(s) to list(s)
modification of infor-mation or object	modification of record content

The correspondences shown in table 1 lend themselves to the sort of component-by-component analysis that is most practical in the cases of very large or complicated systems. For every process identified in the object system four subroutines must be supplied describing initiation, reaction, duration and completion of the process.

The general scheme relies on a fixed executive routine that uses lists of potential processes and lists of ongoing instances to control execution of various subroutines representing the four aspects of each process. The particulars of these four subroutines vary within an archetype.

The process initiation archetype includes a test to determine if the state of the model is such that an instance of the process must begin followed by modification of the model's state to reflect initiation. Operation of the executive routine is such that the process initiation subroutine is entered and re-entered each time an instance of any process is initiated, completed or interrupted so that as many instances of the process as conditions permit will be initiated. Each instance is represented by a list of the names of whatever passive entities are involved, the name of the process and the currently projected completion time of the instance.

INITIATION

For all potential processes:

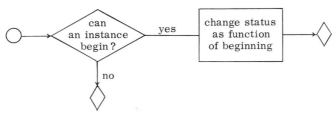

The process reaction archetype consists of a test that determines for any ongoing instance of the process whether or not it can
continue, and when it will complete given the current state of the
model. If the process instance is interrupted the instance record
is destroyed and the entities involved may be modified or placed in
different states to represent effects of interruption.
If the instance is to continue a new calculation of its completion
time is made based on the current state of the model.

REACTION

For all ongoing instances:

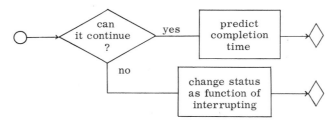

The process duration archetype modifies the state of the model
as a function of elapsed time. The process instance record is not
modified but variables of the entities named therein are modified
as a function of time.

(This simulation scheme attempts to encourage the modeller to
consider all aspects of a process and to relieve him of concern with
the details of other process-models while he is doing so. The integrity of the model, however, requires that a continuous change
- represented in the duration phase - capable of triggering the interruption or initiation of another process must first cause the
completion of the process producing the change unless the incremental change between events is insignificant. Otherwise the *initiation* or *reaction* phase of the other process might not be executed
when it should be.)

DURATION

For all ongoing instances:

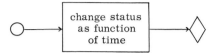

The process completion archetype modifies model state as a
function of completion of any process instance. The process instance record is destroyed and the entities involved are modified
or placed in different states to represent the effects of completion.

COMPLETION

For all completing instances:

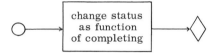

The executive routine is illustrated on next page together with
the four archetypical subroutines. The executive routine has four
phases corresponding to the phases of each process plus control
phases wherein model status is recorded and model timekeeping is
accomplished. A number of list processing devices are required
for practical implementation — a dynamic storage allocation facility,
for example, and operations such as priority insertion or deletion
from lists, intersection or union of 2 lists, etc. Various distribution sampling routines are also included for convenience.

Given the simulation scheme on next page modelling and simulation would proceed in conversational fashion as described below.

3. DECLARATION OF BEHAVIOUR SPACE

Declaration of behaviour space is achieved by specifying entity
types, possible class memberships of entities and relationships
among those classes. The modeller is assumed to be at a console
equipped with a teletype-like key-board for input and output of verbal information and with a CRT display and light pencil.

The modeller is first asked to declare all entities that may exist
in the object system. The names of entity types that may occur in
the course of operation of the model are supplied; both an abbreviation and a definition are given. The definition, furnished in ordinary

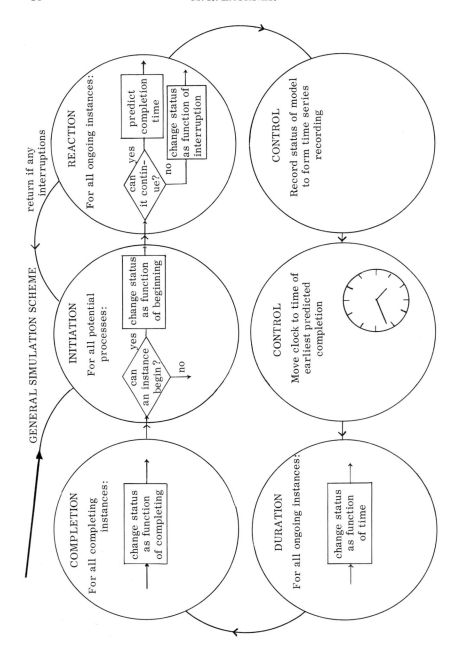

language, may thereafter be retrieved when desired but only the abbreviation is used for identification in further processing. Attributes
of the entity are also declared at this time; each is characterised in
reply to machine-generated queries so that the make-up of a proper
record type is implied.

The abbreviated name of each previously declared entity with its
natural-language definition is displayed, each in turn, and the following information is requested:

(a) Possible sequences of mutually exclusive class memberships
that the entity might attain. Abbreviations and definitions are
furnished as the names of classes are supplied and they are
added to a displayed list. Each class of a possible sequence
of classes is represented by a triangle, and a row of triangles
joined by straight lines is formed on the display scope.

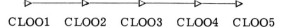

CLOO1   CLOO2   CLOO3   CLOO4   CLOO5

(b) Instructions for indicating the end of a sequence, the beginning
of a new sequence or a branch of a new sequence are displayed
on the scope. Previously identified sequences remain visible so
that branchings and joinings can be identified. For example:

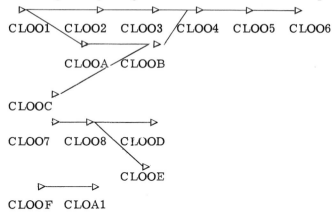

(c) For each possible sequence of mutually exclusive class memberships, other possible class memberships for the entity are indicated. Again the class names are added to the display list but
newly added classes are represented by long rectangles beneath
the displayed sequences.

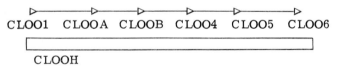

CLOO1   CLOOA   CLOOB   CLOO4   CLOO5   CLOO6

CLOOH

(d) If a mutually exclusive relationship exists between a class in
the sequence and a class represented by a rectangle the rectangle
can be broken by indicating the sequence class with the light pencil.

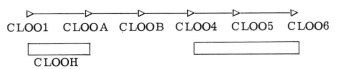

(e) For each class, the names of eligible entity types are requested.
All previously named entities are displayed so that they may be
identified by a light pencil indication or similar device. Previously given information is compared and contradictions are rectified.

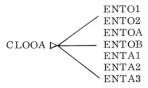

(f) Then limitations on class membership are requested; the limitations are defined by a single-valued function of current model
status. The formula, input by keyboard, is displayed and the
modeller may be supplied evaluations corresponding to hypothe-
tical sets of values if he chooses to supply them for the variables. For example:

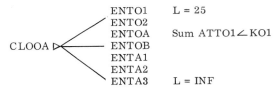

When contradictions are found between entity class memberships
identified by entity declarations and those identified by class declarations displays relevant to the situation are recalled and
must be altered to resolve conflicts.

4. DECLARATION OF BEHAVIOUR-GOVERNING RULES

Entity types, classes and class relationships having been declared, the behaviour-governing rules of the object system are now
declared by naming processes and specifying the operation of their
components.

For each class of each entity the name of the process responsible
for placing entities in the class and the process responsible for removing them from the class must be given. Both an abbreviation
and a natural language definition are supplied and the phase of the
process must be identified as initiation, interruption or completion.
The modeller indicates class transitions, entity creations and entity destructions by appropriate light pencil actions resulting in dotted
lines between named triangles for class transitions, left horizontal
lines for entity creations in the class, and right vertical lines for
entity destructions from the class. If a class relationship has been
previously identified as mutually exclusive, the dotted line is replaced by a solid line. More than one process or process phase may
be identified. For example:

───▷	or	▷───────▷	or	▷────────▷
CLOO1		CLOO1 CLOO2		CLOO1 CLO14
INIT, PROCA		COMP, PROCA		INTR, PROCA
		INTR, PROCB		

	or	▷◁	or	▷───────▷
		CLOO1		CLOOA CLOO1
		COMP, PROCB		COMP, PROCD

At this point a map of the object system is displayed. All classes
are represented as triangles and all class transitions are represented as dotted lines, if the classes are not necessarily mutually
exclusive, or as solid lines if the classes are necessarily mutually
exclusive. Double lines indicate entity transition may occur in
either direction. Entity creations and destructions are indicated as
above. For example:

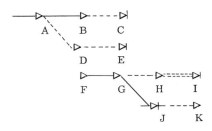

This map indicates that entities may be created in A and may
become members of D while still in A but members of B only if
losing membership in A. While members of G entities may gain

membership in I and vice versa. Entities may lose membership in
C, E, I or J without necessarily gaining membership in another
class. Entities may be created in J or may proceed to membership
in J from membership in G. No entities are created in F and no
members of other classes become members of F; thus if all original members of F become members of G. F will be empty. Similarly, entities remain in K, once having gained membership, because no process operates to remove them.

The accumulated supply of information now contains, by phase,
by process and by entity, the class transitions that occur or may
occur during model operation. For each previously named process
a full description of each of its four phases is now requested. The
name of the process is displayed and an archetype procedural flow
chart of each phase is displayed in sequence. Entity names and
entity class-to-class transfers previously identified with the phase
of the process are displayed. Classes, again, are represented by
triangles. For each phase the modeller must supply sufficient information to complete its definition.

The initiation phase requires definition of the test determining
whether or not any instance of the process can begin and a selection
function that identifies particular entities to be transferred from
class-to-class upon initiation of an instance of the process. For
each entity type that might be involved in the process instance a
light pencil is used to indicate the class memberships it must
possess and those it must not possess. It is understood that all
class tests for all entities must succeed before the selection algorithm joins particular entities in an instance of the process. For
each entity type, necessary class memberships are indicated by a
1 to the left of the class name, memberships precluding initiation
are indicated by a 0. For example:

ENTO1	ENTO3
1 CLOO1	1 CLOOB
CLOO2	0 CLOOC
0 CLOOA	1 CLAO1
	CLAO2

The reaction phase requires definition of the test determining
for each instance of the process whether or not it will continue. As
in the initiation phase, test components may be indicated by using a
light pencil to indicate the class memberships an entity must possess and class memberships the entity must not possess. These
indications are made for each entity involved in the process instance
and failure of any test for any entity is understood to mean failure
of the test. For each entity type involved in the process the modeller

indicates class transitions to take place on interruption. The modeller must also furnish a formula supplying time-to-completion as a function of current model status. As in other cases, the formula is displayed and evaluation may be had from hypothesized values of its variables.

The duration phase declarations require specification of formulas that supply values for any of the attributes of any of the entities involved in a process instance as a function of time and the current value of any other variable. The modeller may be presented with evaluations determined from hypothesized sets of variable values if he supplies them. *No* class transitions may be specified.

The completion phase is specified by sets of class transitions accounting for all entity types that might be involved in the process instance.

The model is now almost complete. Entity types and classes have been declared, and processes have been explicated. Output has not yet been fixed, however, and hard-copy outputs desired are identified by indicating whatever functions of the classes of entities are desired and supplying logical test formulae identifying the conditions for supplying the output. The classes are indicated by light pencil and so are available library recording functions and test formulae. These include graphic as well as verbal arrays of information, the graphic being a subset of the displays described below under graphic forms for simulation.

5. DECLARING AN INITIAL STATE

An initial state of the model is declared by identifying classes and entities to be inserted in them. The values of the entities' attributes may be supplied individually by keyboard or, having supplied the number of entities desired, the modeller may have their attribute values drawn from library distributions by supplying the necessary parameter values and pointing to a pictured distribution or perhaps he may draw the distribution. In any case the initial content of each class is displayed before simulation begins in the same manner as during the simulation if the modeller requests it.

The initial state declaration may be recovered and modified after simulation. The initial state declarations may also be preserved during modification of the behaviour-governing rules following one simulation phase and preceeding another.

6. GRAPHIC FORMS FOR SIMULATION

The modeller may specify various displays and conditions for

producing the displays. He indicates conditions as earlier; a map
of the system is displayed, the modeller indicates a set of classes
with a light pencil and this results in display of a list of entity types
for each of the classes. For each entity type the names of its attributes are also shown. The modeller than produces a formula specifying conditions for display as a function of entity attribute values
and characteristics of class memberships.

The modeller may then indicate one or more displays to be produced when the condition he has just specified is satisfied. Again
he begins with a map of the system and indicates classes with the
light pencil. Again the attributes of the entity types that may occur
in those classes are displayed. He may now choose from the library
of available displays.

For any class or class definable in terms of intersections or
unions of classes in the model: plots of one-way or two-way frequency distributions may be displayed for arithmetic functions of
the attribute values of members of the class. The range of values
of an arithmetic function of attribute values is shown as a bar broken
by a perpendicular line at the mean or median. The values of some
arithmetic function of attribute values of the class members are
sequenced according to positions in the class or ranked according
to some other arithmetic function of the attribute values; values
are represented by vertical bars from a horizontal base.

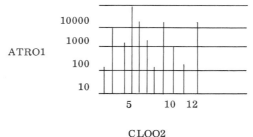

CLOO2

For any randomly chosen entity or formula - identified entity:
on a map of the system the classes in which the entity has membership may be indicated by superimposition of heavy border lines of
those classes. For any class of which the entity is a member the
position of the entity relative to other entities, ranked on the value
of an arithmetic function of its attribute values; the values are
represented by variable length vertical bars along a horizontal base
and the entity of interest is identified by a dot beneath it at the base.
A similar display may be had for the class of all entities of a given
entity type.

For any process the following displays may be had: the number
of instances of the process shown as a horizontal bar; the classes

containing entities involved in the process shown by heavy border
lines superimposed on the class triangles on a system map; the
entities involved in the process separated by entity type and ranked
according to predicted duration of process instance or according to
values of an arithmetic function of attribute values.

Any of the above displays may be viewed by the modeller for as
long as he desires while simulation is interrupted, or the modeller
may have a display remain and be modified while simulation proceeds. If he chooses the latter, the modeller may have the display
up-dated synchronously or asynchronously; that is, he may have the
display modified whenever a change in the model status occurs that
requires modification or he may superimpose on the model a condition that the display be modified and displayed at fixed intervals of
model time. Furthermore, in the latter case, the modeller may
require synchronisation of model time and real time according to
a prescribed scale, so that 30 seconds of real time corresponds to
one month of model time for instance. At a lower level of abstrac-
tion, "movies" could be produced by identifying pairs of attribute
values for deriving X, Y references and relative point locations,
and indicating pairs of points to be joined by lines.

7. SUMMARY

Some particular graphic forms have been suggested for conventional usage in constructing simulation models, and observing and
recording their operation. These forms would be elements of a
simulation language based on an already-implemented general simulation scheme [3]. Learning the language would mean learning the
scheme first and then the forms for describing behaviour space and
for defining behaviour-governing rules.

While the simulation scheme differs in many respects from
other general schemes it also has much in common with them.
Definition of behaviour space requires declaration of entity types
and their attributes in SIMSCRIPT [97, 98] which first used these
terms for what were called by other names in SIMPAC, GPSS,
CSL and others [81, 48, 15, 29, 148]. There is also close correspondence between the "classes" of this scheme and the "sets", "queues"
and "stores", etc., of others. Some common attention then might be
given to conventional graphic forms for describing behaviour space,
at least.

The definition of behaviour-governing rules might appear less
amenable to common development, but those elements concerned
with describing class transitions and membership changes are com-

mon to the conceptual bases of simulation schemes contemplating the generation, movement and destruction of discrete entities.

The graphic forms suggested here are obviously limited, and can easily be improved on. Any set will be rapidly obsoleted by hardware developments and user experience. But the question of what elements of a simulation language are best graphic and what elements are best verbal will remain an important question that ought to be given attention now.

DISCUSSION

Krasnow:

I would like to suggest, and I don't think you attempted to mini-mize this, that the essential problem is what to display and what to present given the capability of being able to present things in on-line fashion. The question of what form to present these in is essentially a secondary consideration. The problem of presenting information from a model would seem to be one area which can be handled by the notion of a process. The user should be able to define processes which are not operative in the sense of changing the state of the model but are simply operative for the purpose of observing the state of the model and displaying what has taken place or what is taking place. The attempt to pre-define exactly what is to be displayed and in what form is in a sense trying to pre-determine some processes for use within any model and I think that this is something that the user should do. The user should define his own observation processes and state what it is that he wishes to occur by using the facilities of the simulation language directly rather than a separate set of facilities for display.

Lackner:

Well, I think that is exactly what he does. I think it is important to separate the observation of that which is being simulated from the model which is being simulated. The model consists of the initiation, reaction, duration and completion phases, and recordings are specified by the user in the control phase. Unlike SIMSCRIPT for example or unlike the implied status of different blocks in GPSS, the recording of model status is logically separated from the modeling of the object system itself. This specification of what is to be recorded in the control phase is, I believe, in the correct logical place. It is done when everything has come to a rest between initiation and reaction phases of different processes and just prior to the clock being moved, so an accurate picture of the model status is available at that point.

I am not so sure what you mean when you say the user should use the facilities of simulation language directly. I think he does. I am using the term "language" to include the graphic as well as the verbal expression that he wants to have, and needs to have if he is going to interact usefully with the model and if he is going to avoid the mountains of paper that the traditional techniques of recording status produce.

Nicholls:

I think this subject is very important; it is not just a matter of what we are describing but of how easy these problems are to understand and the graphic display seems to be a very big help in understanding complex systems. I am sure these techniques will develop and need to be developed more as we understand more about complex systems. These include programming systems and programming languages as well as the physical systems which are usually simulated. If you start with the basic items which appear to be necessary, you have simple ideas of sets and sequences; these are certainly fundamental requirements in descriptive techniques and some elementary ways of putting these into graphical forms are by trees and by lists. But the interrelationships seem to be much more complex than can be handled by simple trees and simple lists, and it seems that we have a further difficulty introduced in this as in other simulation systems when we introduce time. How to represent time in a graphical system seems again to be a difficult and fairly fundamental question. Have you any comment about time and simultaneity and the possibility of representing that in graphical systems?

Lackner:

Well I am afraid that the ideas I have on representing time are pretty simple as I think the updating of a display is probably one of the most useful. I have indicated in the paper how movies can be produced, which is done, I think, at Bell Labs and other places where they use simulation to produce 35 mm film outputs. The representation of events in time, I think, is most naturally and very usefully shown by letting the picture of the model change as these events take place. That change might or might not be synchronous with change in the model and the model time could be scaled to real time to make things even easier to comprehend than they might be otherwise. I have touched on these very briefly here, but I think it is obvious how this can be accomplished with real time clocks and with the various devices available to us now.

The recording of events in time is only part of the question you are asking, I realise. The implications of sequence touch on the question of time and the prior dependencies of conditions again invite notions of time. I think that I can only say now that we need to pay a lot of attention to this, so we need to give some concerted thought to how to indicate time dependencies. Electrical and radio engineers have evolved ways of representing some of the dynamic characteristics of electronic systems but even so they have, I think, failed adequately to show time in any static way. So my answer is that I don't know of any static way to show time, and we need to show time in time.

Gimpelson:

I question whether or not methods of this sort are of value for real problems. I doubt that real technical problems could be described in a sufficiently small number of these symbols to make this useful. None of the problems that I've ever worked on, I think, could be put on any known scope. You'd need a whole wall of displays and therefore I wonder whether we should not restrict our attention to their use as teaching devices rather than technical useful devices.

Lackner:

I do not think we need to restrict ourselves to teaching devices at all. I'll confine myself to the question you asking about the scopes being large enough to show the entire map of the system. There are, I think, if we worry about it enough, ways of aggregating elements of a complicated system with lots of classes and lots of processes so that it can be shown at once on a single scope. Certainly it is possible to have a number of scopes all operating simultaneously showing different parts of the system and, of course, it's possible to use one scope to survey different parts of one big system without showing all of that system at one time. Even in very complex models, I think it's usually going to be true that for any given entity, the string of classes it might be a member of, can be confined to a single scope. If that's not the case, it's not so hard to scan along the string without showing everything that's a member.

Gimpelson:

My remark was based on our experience with a number of these automatic flowcharting programs that supposedly print out block diagrams or FORTRAN statements in diagrammatic form. People begin to use them on small programs to serve ends that become large and they end up with lines going miles down the print-out. People stop using them after a time and, in fact, in-experienced people stop using them very early in the game. I haven't seen any

of these automatic flowcharting systems in use after the initial
learning period. I wonder if anyone has any different experience?

Monrad-Krohn:

Have any of these ideas been implemented? I think in this area
a very useful thing would be for someone to try on an experimental
basis to see what can be made of these ideas, for instance, with a
display in a time-sharing situation. The closest approach I can
think of is that in the MAC system there's a facility for making
geometrical drawings on the display and then after you have drawn
one projection you can turn the model and have a look at if from
other view points. This is a very different area from simulation but
may be there is some connection, particularly with interactive simulations.

Lackner:

On this question of implementation I have said in the paper that
the basic simulation scheme has been implemented. As far as the
graphic forms to which I think your question was directed are concerned, I haven't had anything to do with implementing them and I
don't expect to for a while but I think someone ought to be implementing something along this line. I do agree that some of the
techniques used at MAC would be applicable here. For example,
if you have identified a sequence of class memberships in a particular form, it is perfectly possible for a transformation of that
picture to take place, under the logic of the model assembly program if you will, to show you a different aspect of its structure
from which you might gain some new understanding.

Steel:

I find Gimpelson's remarks preposterous. It strikes me that it
is the same thing as saying that we should not draw circuit diagrams
for part of a big computer because we don't have a big enough sheet
of paper to draw a diagram of the entire computer. It seems to me
that you've got to look at something big and complicated in pieces
and that, I believe, is precisely the kind of thing Lackner is talking
about. Now I gather your comment was that people don't find this
useful. That I find very strange and I would like more views on this
point.

Laski:

Lackner seems to me to be concerned, unlike other participants,
with what one wants to do and understanding what one wants to do
rather than doing what one can do. It seems to me very important
that this should be done and I think that he has lighted on something

pretty fundamental in the problems of the nature of our apprehension
of simulated reality - how we may best understand what is going on
in a simulation model or indeed in the kind of management process
system that Krasnow outlined. I've got a specific question on the
nature of the language, because I believe that this display system is
a language: initially you display static pictures, and eventually dynamic pictures by the computer to the human being. Should you close
the loop so that the human can also communicate with the computer?

The second point is, can we know what kind of display language
is the useful language, without some knowledge from human experimental psychology about how we apprehend information? A third
point: how immediately apprehensible should this communication
language be? If it's to be rich enough does it have to be learnt the
way English or American has to be learnt for 10 years before one
can use it.

Lackner:

On your first point on closing the loop, I think this is a very
interesting area. I've given only a very little thought to it but I
think it would be quite useful to do just exactly as you say, to allow
a modeler to express certain aspects of a model dynamically.

On the second point, having to understand human psychology,
yes or no - I don't know whether we could ever understand it anyway. I just think we have to experiment in the area. On the third
point, I think the answer is yes, it would need to be learned but
I don't see that it need take a long time.

Nygaard:

I tended initially at least, to agree with Gimpelson because if
you look at complex systems you find after you have worked with
them for a long time that the characteristics you want really to
study vary very much from system to system. And therefore to have
a simple graphic system which contains everything you need seems
to be rather difficult. On the other hand, I do think we should extend
our collection of tools with which we work on simulations. Let us
consider a program or model: it is split up perhaps into declarations, processes etc. One thing one would like to be able to do is
to have a collection of procedures which you insert at specified
points and which will give prints-outs which tell you something
about the system. Some of these are rather obvious but I think one
thing you need and which we have provided in the SIMULA tracing
system is the concept of what we call the "Process Descriptor".
If you use the statement "Write (X)" and X is a reference to a process, then you get printed out information on the state of this process. Another thing which is rather important here and for which

this inserting of output routines into the program is not sufficient, is the general development of the model. The important thing is, of course, the change of action from process to process and therefore we should like to have an automatic trace. We have provided a scheme in SIMULA whereby we can have a variety of modes of tracing.

The next problem is what kind of graphic representation could we provide in this connection to increase the rapid identification of the state of the system. I think that what we need is a combination of these kind of tools and these graphic tools which Lackner was talking about.

Jones:

To refer to the point made by Gimpelson, Steel and others, it seems that what you need is the ability to selectively aggregate this graphical display of your model. You certainly don't want to have to display at a detailed level all the blocks because naturally they won't fit and even if they could fit on the wall you couldn't comprehend them all simultaneously. You want to be able to choose to see some blocks in great detail because that is where your interest at the moment lies. Then you want to be able to aggregate many of the other blocks, but you don't want to have a uniform level of aggregation across the whole display. It doesn't do you any good to have one big block saying "That's the model" and it doesn't do any good to have 20 000 little circuit level diagrams. You've got to be able somehow to manipulate the display and control the aggregation of detail. We have tried in a non-graphical sense using line by line tracing to do this in the OPS system. It is difficult to do: you have to have all sorts of controls to allow the user to switch back and forth but it does provide some degree of control.

GENERAL DISCUSSION - SESSION 1

Strachey:

On the general point of communication and use of diagrams to aid in writing programs (and also, I suspect, simulations), I think it is important to realise that diagrams are not suitable for conveying complicated information. They are only suitable for conveying very simple information and we use block diagrams, flow diagrams and so on in order to simplify what we are doing. We do not try to put an entire problem on to one diagram. You cannot see it all at the one time. I think there is a very important way in which we think about complicated things and that is the hierarchical way. If we have got a whole system, we like to think of the overall system to start with and then break that down into smaller sections and consider those one at a time. I think it also very important that we should try and design languages which will enable us to work and think naturally in a hierarchical manner. What seems to me to be lacking in simulation languages is just this hierarchical structure which exists in ALGOL and general-purpose programming languages.

It is a great mistake to think that you have got to have access to everything from everything. If you do this you immediately get into a very complicated state and you cannot structure the problem in the way which is necessary to help human thought.

Ross:

I am probably the person who has had the most experience with graphics, having started in 1952, and so I feel I have to say something. With respect to Lackner's paper, I have very little specific to say except I feel that the actual graphic forms used in connection with simulation or other programming languages will have only slight relationship to those in the paper, not from a lack of foresight but because history seems to work that way. A comment was made earlier that hopefully we could learn about complex processes through the use of graphics; my experience has always been just the opposite. If you have a complex problem, sometimes you find that you have a graphical way of thinking about it which you wish to incorporate into your attack on that problem using a computer but you very seldom can go in the other direction of having beforehand enough knowledge of what you might do. Anybody can think about putting spots on a display scope and tickling them with light pens but it is quite a difficult step beyond that to talk about a graphical language.

I believe that there is no distinction whatsoever between a graphical language and a non-graphical or verbal language. I think these are just different mechanical forms of the same overall communication process and, in fact, we have over the years been designing the AED system precisely on this viewpoint using both kinds of language separately and together to good effect. I feel quite strongly that the problem we are really faced with, especially when it comes to complex systems, is not just a matter of simulation and not just a matter of graphics, but it is a matter of building knowledge and being explicit about what understanding we have developed. There was a nice word that Laski introduced that I want to end with. He introduced the term "apprehensible" when he said that that is exactly what we would like out of this mixture of verbal, graphic and man-machine communication. I think what you have to watch out for is the distinction between apprehensible and reprehensible because it is all too easy to distort and do things just for the sake of doing them.

Laski:

I just want to distinguish the conflict between apprehensibility and representability.

Knuth:

I would like to make two comments. One is directed to Lackner's paper: perhaps it is just my ignorance in the matter but I think the main feature that struck me about his paper was the following idea. The conventional way for drawing directed graphs on paper through the years has been to represent vertices as dots or boxes of some kind and then to have arrows between these boxes, and this is not particularly conducive to computer displays. On the other hand in Lackner's paper we see that if we make the boxes a triangular shape, it is now no longer necessary to put arrows on the lines connecting them because the place at which they enter or leave the box indicates the direction. This, I think can be a valuable notational technique for graphical displays.

Turning to the general discussions of papers, I just wanted to say a little about Jones's paper which I meant to say earlier this morning. He distinguished between creation of the model, which is what the OPS system is specially intended for, and the later running of the production form of the model. I would like to express the point of view that the second phase is quite unimportant. To me, the entire advantage of simulation is just the setting up of the model itself

in the first place and the misuse of simulation is to try to get something out of the answers that you get after you have it running.

For example, take a steel mill situation. I believe that anybody
who has to sit down and actually express the model of the steel
mill, in terms of exactly what goes on, will learn infinitely more
than they will ever learn trying actually to use this model later on.
To my mind the creation of the model is the central problem in
simulation and I am sure that anyone who has ever tried this realises that this is the most critical bottle neck in the use of simulation.

If you ever do this with an on-line system you are for ever
spoiled for doing it any other way. On-line programming has somehow enhanced simulation programming by a much greater degree
than it enhances more typical numerical analysis programming. I
think on-line working is almost necessary for developing complex
models. The main point I want to make is that perhaps simulation
languages should not include output statements except of course for
when you are debugging.

Krasnow:

I just wanted to make a brief comment concerning hierarchical
descriptions and simulation languages. It seems to me that one of
the central motivations in going to the notion of process, is to make
possible a much more general description in a hierarchical sense
than is possible with general purpose languages where the hierar-
chies are rather constrained.

You want to talk about parallel processes, and one of the things
that characterizes the process is that you can think in terms of
sub-processes and structures of processes in ever greater detail.
This is also one of the things that makes the possibility of display
feasible in the sense that Jones was talking about, looking at higher
level processes without the detail of all the subordinate processes
which are contained within a higher level process. As far as I know,
the only programming structures that permit this are those in simulation languages. It seems to me a very difficult thing to do with a
conventional general-purpose system.

Buxton:

I am reminded by Knuth's comments about a conversation I had
with Dr. Tocher many years ago. I succeeded with some difficulty
in proving to him that a simulation system which I was at the time
working on was in one small respect a little bit faster than Dr.
Tocher's own simulation system. He instantly countered this by
pointing out to me that any simulation that got to the execution stage

was in fact a dismal failure, and all the useful information came
out in the course of writing the program. When you had done that
you understood the entire system anyway, and so maybe simulation systems should never even get into execution.

Skousen:

I do not agree with the idea that simulation languages should not
have input and output statements. My experience is that we can distinguish simulation problems into those involving human decisions
and those you can describe without human decisions.

For the first kind, where we try to describe what human beings
are doing, I think it is right: we do not need input/output statements, but for the second group of problems we do need them. I
have myself worked with elevator systems, lift systems - it is very
useful to get results in these cases because you know everything
that is in the system and results are really meaningful.

Hutchinson:

I don't think that there are many of us that would disagree with
the paraphrasing of Hemmings statement that "the purpose of modelling is insight and not numbers", but on the other hand it does
seem to me that we might break the use of simulation down into a
couple of areas. One is for management type problems and the
other possibly is for problems in the research area. It is nice that
the modeller gains this understanding but frequently, as for example
in steel mills, it is the manager who is going to be responsible for
implementing these decisions who needs this understanding.

I am concerned about the fact that there is less use being made
of simulation as a problem-solving device than possibly is warranted
by the tremendous power which is available through the use of the
computer in this manner. Possibly we as researchers and scientists
have failed in this very area of making this understanding available
to the people who have to implement and be responsible for the decisions and for using this tool. Maybe it goes back to the philosophical question of whether a tree falling in the woods makes a sound
or not: if we do this research and are then unable to communicate
the results and the strategies to the managers, or the people who
are responsible for this decision making, we have failed to make
the work useful.

Garwick:

I must say I hear many very strange views here and one of these,
which obviously nobody really meant, is to say that the only important thing in simulation is to produce the model and when you've done

that there is no point in proceeding and you do not have to do production runs. Well, I have done some simulation in my time too by writing war games for NATO and I would say that it was the output of all these war games that was productive and interesting and not the model building. The other point I would make is that I agree absolutely with Strachey that we do have to work in the hierarchical way. We are able in English to have a certain parenthetical structure but not with very deep levels: I think that to go rather deep in level can only be done in German.

If you look at the way you go about proving some complicated theory in mathematics, you don't start with the entire problem and develop pages after pages of mathematics. Nobody would be able to follow the proof. What you do is to develop various lemmas and subtheorems and you end up with the theorem itself. It is only by splitting a problem up into subsystems that you are able to grasp all its complications. If you try to explain everything in English, which we do in a complicated program, nobody would be able to understand what we are talking about.

Ross:

I too am in favour of hierarchy, motherhood, brotherhood and so forth; however this comment is in direct response to your plea for some comments about the need for input and output. As Jones mentioned, there has been relatively little work on simulation as such at MIT; this is both true and false depending on the department.

For example, we have tried many times to set up chemical process design studies by combining electrical engineers, for work on the control theory, with chemical engineers. Now each time they get a problem bounded and defined and get the group together, they set about designing the system which will lead in effect to the simulation which will then supply the control. The electrical engineers go off into their corner to work up the instrumentation and programs and so forth and come back when they are halfway done to have another meeting with the chemical engineers. At this point the chemical engineers say, "in the meantime, from the understanding that we have obtained from the analysis work we can now save 20% rather than the 3% which the fine automatic controls would give us" so that the whole problem disappears. So, in the case of chemical engineering, this idea of the model building being the important thing does seem very much to be true. On the other hand in the strict field of electrical engineering and when it comes to analysis of electronic circuits and so forth, we have built quite a number of systems which do use graphics for both input and output for doing non-linear circuit analysis. In this case those who build the system get the same benefit of understanding but on the other hand there is a whole line-up of actual users who do want the output. These are the people who are actually going to design circuits on the basis of these simulations.

Laski:

I want to bring this issue of hierarchy into the centre of our attention. I find myself when concerned with modelling systems dissatisfied with the inadequacy of ALGOL and the traditional algorithmic languages. I feel that the notion of hierarchy, as in these languages it affects the data, which comes out of nowhere when the block is entered and goes into the unknown when the block is left, is unsuitable for the modelling in parallel processes of the external world. I feel very sympathetic to the notion of control and hierarchy and knowing what one is doing. I think I understand how one could have data which is external to the block in which is created and in which access to this data is available under controls given by the way in which it is specified. I feel this to be essential to the problem of parallel processes operating on a data base and I feel the need for a clear understanding here which is in some way less trivial than the hierarchy notion of access and existence of data that exists within the algorithmic languages.

Strachey:

To add one point immediately to what Laski has just been saying, I think the important thing about hierarchical structure is not in the structure of the data so much as in the structure of the processes or the procedures. There is a curious feature in ALGOL, which he has been complaining about, and that is that there is a hierarchy in the use of names; that is to say there is a nesting block structure in the use of names which is very rigid and quite useful, but by some curious coincidence this is used to control the extent of the existence of the objects defined. They come into existence when they are defined to start with at the beginning of a block and they disappear when you leave the block. Now there is no theoretical reason why these two things should be connected at all. The extent of a variable and its scope are two completely different concepts and it is purely fortuitous, I think, that they happen to coincide in ALGOL. I can quite imagine languages in which they do not coincide but in which the data structure exists outside the block in which it is constructed. Quite what the consequences of this will be in the design of languages I am not quite sure at the moment.

There is just one other point - graphical displays are not always capable of describing everything that you want. It is a commonly held fallacy that you can describe all programs by means of flow diagrams. I have a very simple ALGOL procedure here whose body consists of two statements, which cannot be described by a flow diagram:

<u>begin</u>:

    <u>procedure</u> R (<u>integer</u> K, <u>label</u> L, M) <u>value</u> K, L, M

    <u>begin</u> <u>if</u> K ⩾ 0 <u>then</u> R (K-1, M, N);

            N: <u>goto</u> L;

    <u>end</u>

    - - - - - - - - - -

    R (99, P, Q);

    P: - - - - - - - - -

    Q: - - - - - - - - -   <u>end</u>

Consider this call to R with parameters 99, P and Q. First of all it is quite difficult to find out what would happen and secondly I do not want to draw a flow diagram of it.

Steel:

I would like to come back for a moment to this question of never executing a simulation because we learn all we need to learn by setting up the model. There is an instance in some simulation work that we are doing concerned with the modelling of entrances and exits to limited access highways. In the course of designing the model we obtained a fundamental insight. If automobiles get too close together they collide. In the course of running the model we discovered some little details about how wide the lanes should be to keep this situation from happening. It is not always the case that the numbers that you get out of running a model are of no value.

Dahl:

There has been much talk about hierarchy and I sympathize very much with that notion. Now there is another notion which is of the same kind but perhaps not exactly the same. When it comes to understanding very complicated phenomena, it is useful to try to reduce the complicated and difficult things, to things which are less difficult. To be specific, suppose you want to grasp a system which goes on in real time and involves parallel activities. One useful thing that you can do in order to understand that system in a better way, is to split that system up into parallel processes and think of each process at a time. The essential thing here is that each process will be a sequential sequence of events and it is much easier to think sequentially about subsections of the system than to think of a complicated system where everything happens at once. I am not sure that this notion has anything to do with hierarchy but it is still very useful.

Laski:

I sympathize with Dahl and his wish to keep private within individual cooperating processes the data that they use. I do not believe this to be possible. I believe that processes must cooperate using external data whose existence in time is longer than that of the scope of the block in which the data is created. I believe this to be necessary for the management of the data base whether in real or simulated time. It is necessary to have a God sitting on my right hand to manage this data for me as the primary universe within which my processes operate. Now what I'm not sure about is whether there is a unity or a trinity or a hierarchy of Gods to sit on my right hand and whether these data bases have themselves a hierarchical structure.

Dahl:

Evidently it is, in general, impossible to divide a system into processes which are not interconnected. So in addition to processes as individuals there must be something to connect them but some of the activities taking place inside a process will be strictly local and so you have at least achieved something by isolating them. One other point; as long as you are within one sequential process, I think that the conventional programming languages like ALGOL which have proved very useful for sequential programming are in fact adequate. The main concept in ALGOL for breaking up a large problem is that of a procedure; the procedure concept corresponds to the concept of a sub-problem and the sub-problem concept may still be an important one within one single process.

Caracciolo:

I would like to come back for a moment to the question of actually running simulations. Although I agree essentially that model making and system understanding is usually the most important issue, it seems to me that what has been said is somewhat too strong. I would like first to remark that in a sense experimental runs with outputs are necessary just for testing the model while building the model itself. Then going back to the first paper read this morning, I believe also that simulation may be used as a part

of decision processes in management and in that case they should
also be run. I would also add that actual simulation may be useful
for comparing models and finding corrollation between system
parameters and the system behaviour and I think for this purpose
one has actually to run the model.

Nicholls:

I think that whether the universe as a whole is hierarchical, is
a philosophical, perhaps a religious problem but at the level at
which we handle objects of data, I think they are very often not
hierarchical. We are in danger of making the mistake of taking
something which is easy to handle, which undoubtedly hierarchical
objects are, as being the only subject worthy of study. Certainly
it is harder to deal with non-hierarchical objects but I believe these
are more representative of many of the objects we have to deal with
in the universe at the level on which we have to deal with them. I
make a plea for non-hierarchical data and non-hierarchical control
mechanisms even if at the moment we don't understand how to handle
them very well.

Lackner:

On the question of hierarchy I would like just to point out that
the flow chart I used in my paper expresses the hierarchy which I
think is extremely useful and quite sensible in simulation modelling
at the present time. Secondly, I would like to thank Knuth for pointing out that I might have found a neater way to draw a directed
graph than used heretofor. The point I was trying to make is that
directed graphs and circles and squares and triangles and other
primitive graphic symbols need to stand for something and I am
suggesting that the arrangements of triangles and dotted and solid
lines I was using represent class transition and classes respectively. Thirdly, and I think perhaps most important, the question
of the hopelessness of using graphics to study the complex systems
and situations needs to be answered. If you told anyone wiring a
plugboard machine some 10 or 15 years ago that some day verbal
language was going to be able to do what he was doing, I don't think
he would have believed you. We have spent an insignificant number
of man-years on the development of graphic languages for expressing system relationships, whereas there have been by now thousands
of man years spent on the development of verbal computer languages.

ON A SIMULATION LANGUAGE
COMPLETELY DEFINED ONTO THE
PROGRAMMING LANGUAGE PL/1

Luigi PETRONE
Olivetti General Electric, Milano, Italy

Abstract: This paper presents some results obtained by undertaking the project of defining a simulation language based on PL/1. This language is called SPL; it is derived essentially from SIMULA and, to a lesser extent, from SOL. Two defining methods are presented. The first one, based primarily on the tasking concept of PL/1, is discussed in full. Of the second only a general idea is given. A preliminary investigation on the relations between parallel and quasi-parallel programming is also carried out.

1. INTRODUCTION

One of the fundamental problems involved in the programming language theory is the formal definition of semantics. There are two well known and distinct ways of doing this: the first consists of presenting a machine (abstract or real) that will react to the strings of a language A. The description of the machine state transitions settles the problem of defining the meaning of language A. The second method consists of providing an algorithm T translating A into a second language B. If the meaning of B is known, then the meaning of A will also be known.

If the language B is such that the algorithm T can be written in B, then we may say that the problem of defining the semantics of A has been *completely* reduced to that of B's semantics.

The problem of expressing a language in terms of another is thus of a precise conceptual interest. From a practical standpoint, the situation is, however, somewhat different. It is not sufficient in fact to be able to rely on a theoretical possibility of translation. The algorithm T must also be simple and the running of the translated text not too time-consuming. Hence, the reference language must contain more than just the integer arithmetic, although the latter does theoretically enable it to claim to be "universal".

The new wave of general purpose algorithmic languages, i.e.

PL/1 [166] and the forthcoming ALGOL X, are dissimilar in style
but are both multipurpose languages. They contain a large number
of devices, such as integer arithmetic, string manipulation, record and files handling and even multiprocessing (at least PL/1). It
is, therefore, likely that the translation algorithm will not be unduly
complicated. Moreover, the great richness of these languages (especially PL/1), leads us to avoid extending them further for the purpose of solving particular problems (such as formula manipulation,
system simulation, etc.).

2. THE SPL LANGUAGE

SPL is an acronym for Simulation Programming Language and
is a language created neither as a pure extension of PL/1 nor as a
collection of PL/1 procedures. SPL has been designed with a particular aim in mind - that of having a preprocessor, written in PL/1,
that translates it into PL/1. These are the reasons why we say that
SPL is *completely defined* onto PL/1. Understanding of PL/1 implies full understanding of SPL *.

The practical consequences of this approach are obvious: any
machine for which a PL/1 compiler is available, automatically gets
SPL at no extra cost. The theoretical consequences have already
been emphasized, i.e. the desire to cut down the number of primitive concepts existing in the programming language area.

In fact, the PL/1 multiprocessing capability has given us the
opportunity to discuss the relations between parallel and quasi-
parallel programming.

Since it is not certain that PL/1 has added a stable and conclu-
sive asset, the SPL language is for the moment still only in the
experimental stage and both its translating algorithm T and the
resulting PL/1 text have not yet been checked on any PL/1 implementation.

3. SOME CONDITIONS FOR SPL

There is a drawback in our approach, namely an increase in
compilation time owing to the twin translation: SPL → PL/1 and
PL/1 → machine-code. In order to keep this increase within reasonable limits, it has been necessary to accept some conditions for
SPL. The most important of these is that, whenever possible, a

---

* From some points of view PL/1 is not the ideal language for this purpose
  since its defining rules are not simple and allow for many exceptions.

piece of SPL text, recognized as belonging to PL/1 - i.e. not containing symbols of the extension SPL - must have itself as its translation into PL/1. In other words, translation, in those cases, has to coincide with the identical transformation (merely copying).

Since, naturally, all the expressions (arithmetic, string etc.) have been kept in SPL, this implies their non manipulation and the reduction of compiling to the following phases:

1. parsing of SPL text ;
2. processing of declarations and specific SPL statements only (like ACTIVATE, WAIT, SEIZE...) with the mere copying of the involved expressions.

We have investigated two implementations of SPL: A and B. Implementation A has a greater appeal for us for it constitutes the direct application of the discussion on parallel and quasi-parallel programming. In addition, A is of course less expensive from the point of view of the SPL preprocessor. Implementation B is based completely on the use of programmed allocation and in particular of the based variables concept. The programmed interrupt of PL/1 has also been widely employed in the two implementations.

4. PARALLEL VERSUS QUASI-PARALLEL PROGRAMMING

Let us discuss now some aspects of quasi-parallel programming (or, briefly, QP programming), as defined in [25] (see also [26]), in connection with the parallel programming. We shall, however, confine our examination to the particular type of parallel programming of which the *tasking* of PL/1 is a representative element.

A program P of an algorithmic language defines a sequence of elementary actions performed by an automaton. We say that the program P defines within P a "time relation" or an "order" between these actions.

In PL/1 a procedure P may call another procedure S_1 *with a task option*. In this case, P is called the *attaching task* and S_1 the *attached task* and the action of calling is said to *create* a *new* task. Both tasks, when created, are executed *asynchronously*.

This does not necessarily imply that the actions of these two tasks will be executed simultaneously, but only that one does not know which time relation will hold between them. Both tasks cause their successive actions to proceed independently so that it will therefore usually be necessary to arrange two independent stacks for their implementations.

PL/1 provides some devices to synchronize the actions of two tasks: the *wait statements*. Normally, an EVENT variable E is associated with the completion of a task S_1 and, somewhere after the point calling the task S_1, within the attaching task P, a WAIT (E) statement is written. This causes all the S_1 actions to precede all those which in P follow the action of WAIT (E). This pattern is usually used when P and S_1 happen to use peripheral units of the computer; we are not interested in it, here.

Another, more general, synchronizing technique still uses EVENT variables I_1, I_2, ... But these variables are set to "1"B or "0"B, by program. A WAIT (I_γ) statement blocks a task if $I_\gamma =$ "0"B, and reactivates it only when $I_\gamma =$ "1"B. As we shall see later, this enables us to construct very general timing routines.

In the QP-programming, the most challenging example of which so far is the SIMULA language, at any given moment of (computer) time *, several processes may have been activated, but one and only one is actually progressing. Scheduling of successive active phases of the other processes is left to the choice of the programmer, who makes use of a few fixed list-handling algorithms.

To the QP-programming "process" concept we shall counter the parallel programming "task" concept. In both cases, the same piece of code is shared by several processes or tasks. In both cases, within each process (or task), the generality of ALGOL 60 is available (that is: begin and procedure blocks nesting, recursive calls of procedures, etc.). This circumstance may require the building up of a separate stack for each individual process (or task).

If we can construct within the parallel programming (PL/1 in particular), any synchronizing mechanism (in particular that of SIMULA), we shall be in a position to state that the QP-programming may be considered a particular case of the parallel programming. However, it is our impression that PL/1 has not been designed with the objective in mind of using it as a QP-programming language. It is, therefore, possible that the uses to which we shall be putting the PL/1 synchronizing devices, may not lead to efficient object codes. However, we do not have data with which to pass judgement on this. Nevertheless we feel that our attempt is of interest for two reasons:

a) to present a serious application of PL/1 multiprocessing features;

b) to determine elements for a preliminary study in order to design a language equipped with a multiprocessing capability, but also able to use this capability for QP-programming purposes.

This study, for instance, could reveal that it is necessary to bring to light some, now hidden, devices through which the machine

---

* In this set-up simulated time plays a completely secondary role. It is nothing more than one of the parameters which happen to be used for ranking certain objects in an ordered set: the time set.

operating environment interacts with the PL/1 tasking. Let us quote the possibility of referencing a task [26], or that of gaining access to the queues concealed behind the PL/1 EVENT variables.

5. A SYNCHRONIZATION METHOD

Let $S_0, S_1, \ldots, S_N$ be $N+1$ tasks, which for preliminary purposes only, we shall assume as defined by distinct procedures, and let $E_0, E_1, \ldots, E_N$ be $N+1$ distinct EVENT variables. Let us assume that any WAIT statement occurring in the procedure which defines S_i ($i = 0, \ldots, N$), is of the WAIT (E_i) type only. Then, every time the variable E_i is set equal to "0"B, the task S_i, and this only, is blocked until such time as E_i is set to "1"B. The task S_i may be said to be *synchronized on* the variable E_i.

Let us now assume that whenever a WAIT statement occurs in the procedure defining S_i ($i = 1, \ldots, N$), it appears only in the pattern:

$$\text{EVENT}(E_i) = \text{"0"B}, \ \text{EVENT}(E_0) = \text{"1"B}, \ \text{WAIT}(E_i) \ .$$

This means that S_i is blocked and S_0 is activated. If, in the procedure defining S_0, the WAIT statements appear as follows

$$\text{EVENT}(E_0) = \text{"0"B}; \ \text{EVENT}(E_i) = \text{"1"B}; \ \text{WAIT}(E_0) \ ;$$

and if initially only one task is active, then we may say that S_0 is a synchronizer of the tasks $S_1, \ldots, S_N$ by means of the EVENT variables $E_1, \ldots, E_n$.

We put in evidence that at any given moment of time one - and only one - task is progressing. Moreover, for a given scheduling $S_{r(1)}, S_{r(2)}, S_{r(3)}, \ldots$ to occur, it is sufficient for the succession $r(1), r(2), r(3), \ldots$ to be computable and accessible to task S_0, the synchronizer.

In order to eliminate the restriction that the procedures defining the tasks are distinct, it is sufficient to associate a based structure with each task, and to give, as a parameter *, the value of a pointer referencing the structure, at the time of creating the task.

---

* The parameter transmission must obviously be made by value since the same piece of PL/1 text, which performs the task call may be executed several times as in the simple example:

LABEL: CALL ACT(I+J, I) TASK K(I) EVENT E(I);
        I = F(I);
        IF B(I) THEN GO TO LABEL;

The PL/1 dummy mechanism is unable to preserve the correct value of the argument $I+J$. The PL/1 task naming mechanism is also of limited use. We shall therefore not be using it here and reference to tasks will be made indirectly through the associated system record.

The EVENT variable, synchronizing the task, must be an element of this structure (that we shall call system record later) and reference to a task will be made through the chain

$$\text{pointer} \rightarrow \text{structure (EVENT variable)} \rightarrow \text{task.}$$

6. HAZARDS AND WAIT UNTIL STATEMENTS

The PL/1 statement WAIT(E) is conceptually similar to the SOL statement WAIT UNTIL E, where E is a boolean. It would therefore seem that the SPL WAIT UNTIL statements are not difficult to implement in PL/1. This is not the case. The difficulty lies in their synchronization with the timer routine.

In fact, the simplest solution for the SPL preprocessor is achieved through an asynchronous definition of the reactivation process. This fact engenders a situation which - to borrow a term from the theory of asynchronous sequential circuits - we have called *hazard*. A hazard occurs when the final state of a system subjected to the actions of several concurrent processes is correctly defined, *regardless of the order* of the processes execution.

If, however, some of these processes do not happen to be elementary (atomic), but are instead made up of a sequence of elementary processes, then the result is undefined in the case of a non elementary process being interrupted by another and so on *.

Interrupts of this kind frequently occur in a multiprocessing environment when more than one processor is available (and task is considered equivalent to the "job"). See also section 13.

7. IMPLEMENTATION A

Here we are proposing a scheme for an implementation of SPL, based primarily on the tasking concept of PL/1. This scheme is not unique, of course. A fair knowledge of the PL/1 defining report is assumed of the reader. For a definition of SPL concepts, see the attached appendix. If G is an SPL text, we shall indicate its translation in PL/1 by $T(G)$.

---

* This situation seems different to that treated by Caracciolo in [17], in his definition of incompatible processes. The concept of elementary process is not invariant in respect to the descripting frame. What is considered an elementary process in Markov Algorithms theory or in a mental model of the real world is no longer such in a Turing machine or in SPL and vice versa.

8. MAIN BLOCK

The main SPL block is translated into a PL/1 external procedure, which we shall refer to as the main task and call MAIN.

A typical system record SYS-RECORD (see appendix) is structured as follows

CLASS	PRED	SUCC	EVENT	TIME	STATE	PRIORITY	EXOG.	ENDOG.

in correspondence to the PL/1 declaration:

DECLARE 1 SYS-RECORD CONTROLLED (SYS-P),

        2 DUMMY ,

                3 CLASS FIXED (h) ,

                3 (PRED, SUCC) POINTER ,

                3 PROC-EVENT EVENT INITIAL '0'B ,

                3 TIME x,

                3 STATE BIT (1) ,

                3 Y ,

        2 W ;

        2 Z ;

where h, the number of digits necessary to represent classes, is
determined by the preprocessor, x (TIME type and precision) is
taken from the user's system definition, Y may or may not appear
(depending on the user) and W and Z are parameters and attributes
(exogenous and endogenous) declarations. There are, of course, as
many different system record declarations as there are activity
declarations. As we shall see later, we need to declare each system record SYS-RECORD twice: the first time, in the MAIN, the
second time in the PL/1 procedure body that is the translation of
the ACTIVITY associated to the SYS-RECORD. These two structure
declarations differ only in regard to the names of their elements.
We shall prefix a $ sign to the names of the elements of the MAIN
declaration.

The system record associated to MAIN consists of the hidden
attributes only (it has no exogenous or endogenous attributes). It
is declared only once: in MAIN. In fact, all items local to MAIN
are accessible from the interior of any activity or procedure block.

9. ACTIVITY BLOCKS

An ACTIVITY block Z is translated into a PL/1 procedure block, labelled Z, that will be *called with a task option.* In addition, a certain structure declaration will be inserted in MAIN. The PL/1 parameter mechanism will be used only to transmit the value of the pointer pointing to the particular system record, associated to the process of class Z.

The procedure Z declaration is inserted in MAIN, of course. For example, the following SPL declaration

ACTIVITY Z (X1, X2); DECLARE X1 POINTER, X2 FLOAT, G FIXED;

> BEGIN;

> DECLARE B (100) FLOAT CONTROLLED X1;

> S; END Z;

where S is any sequence of SPL statements, will be translated into

> Z: PROCEDURE (P); DECLARE P POINTER;

> R; SYS-P = P;

> WAIT (PROC-EVENT); PROC-EVENT = "0"B;

> DECLARE B (100) FLOAT CONTROLLED X1;

> T(S);

> END Z;

where $T(S)$ is the SPL translation of S and R is the declaration of the system record:

DECLARE 1 SYS-REC CONTROLLED (SYS-P), 2 HIDDEN-ATTR

LIKE DUMMY, 2X1 POINTER, 2X2 FLOAT, 2 G FIXED;

An analogous structure declaration, but with all the names preceded by the dollar sign $, will be inserted in the main block MAIN.

We recall that, in this case, $X1$ and $X2$ are the exogenous attributes of Z, while G is an endogenous attribute of Z.

Note that any data declaration, internal to the main BEGIN block of activity Z, is *left unchanged* by the translating algorithm T.

10. INVARIANTS

The translating algorithm T leaves invariant the following syntactical categories:

a) expressions other than generative expressions;

b) procedure and begin blocks. This means that any contained SPL statement S_i is replaced by its counterpart $T(S)$ (this definition is, in fact, a recursive definition);

c) any data declaration with the exception of sets;

d) IF, GO TO, CALL ... statements;

e) I/O statements.

Declarations of entities within BEGIN or PROCEDURE blocks are translated by substitution of the identifier ENTITY with the hidden attributes substructure (see section 4). The translation of the entity declarations that are in the heading of MAIN is more complicated.

To each global variable declaration two EVENT variables will be associated, see later in section 13.

11. GENERATIVE EXPRESSIONS

A generative expression NEW Z (ADDR(B), 3.4) is translated into

a) an action creating a new generation of the system record associated with the activity Z (see section 5); this generation is retrieved by means of the pointer MAIN-POINTER;

b) an action assigning the values "ADDR(B)" and "3.4" to the exogenous elements of Z'; actions a) and b) may be synthetized in a procedure call;

c) the statement: CALL Z (MAIN-POINTER) PRIORITY (1); where MAIN-POINTER is the pointer pointing to Z'. The priority option is here irrelevant, its main purpose is to indicate that the procedure is *called with a task option.*

If the computer environment has sufficient resources (more than one processors), phase b), that is, the prologue of procedure Z can be executed in parallel with the action following the evaluation of the expression NEW Z(ADDR(B), 3.4). After completing its prologue, the newly-created task will stop waiting for the EVENT variable PROC-EVENT to become "1"B.

This EVENT variable will become "1"B, if and when an active phase of Z is entered.

12. SEQUENCING STATEMENTS

The statement ACTIVATE X is translated into the following sequence of statements *:
  i) an action which will put the system record referenced by X at the top of the CL list;
 ii) EVENT (X → $PROC-EVENT) = "1"B;
     the process referenced by X is activated;
iii) WAIT (PROC-EVENT);
     the process which is actually executing the statement ACTI-VATE X now suspends its action waiting for its synchronizing variable PROC-EVENT to become "1"B;
 iv) EVENT (PROC-EVENT) = "0"B;
     now, after the past passive phase, control is given back to here. "Let us set at "0"B our synchronizing variable" (this is the process point of view!).

The statement ACTIVATE X DELAY T_1 is translated into one single procedure call which, according to the ranking criteria defined by the user (priority etc.), properly inserts the system record referenced by X into the set TS, with a time reference equal to "TIME+T_1".

The statement WAIT is translated into

CALL REMOVE (CURRENT, CL);

IF EMPTY(CL) THEN CURRENT = FIRST (TS); ELSE CURRENT = FIRST (CL);

EVENT (SIGNAL) = "1"B;

WAIT (PROC-EVENT); EVENT (PROC-EVENT) = "0"B;

Here is the central point of implementation A. SIGNAL is an event variable, declared in MAIN. SIGNAL controls the processing of the TIMER routine, a procedure called with a task option at the beginning of simulation. Each generation of PROC-EVENT, which is an element of the system record, controls the processing of the task associated with the particular generation of this system record. While the TIMER routine resumes control, as an effect of the signal issued by EVENT (SIGNAL) = "1"B, the task will be waiting on PROC-EVENT.

---

* Any assignment of value to an EVENT variable has to be made through the pseudo-variable function EVENT. See the PL/1 report.

The TIMER task is always progressing "between" any two active phases (or perhaps different processes), except in the case of direct sequencing, as we have already seen, and when interrupts on global for wait until statements (see section 13) occur.

The TIMER routine cycles on itself, each cycle ending in a WAIT (SIGNAL); its purpose is to pick up the first element of *CL* or, if *CL* is empty, of *TS*, and give control to it.

Here is the sequence of the main statements of TIMER:

LAB: EVENT (SIGNAL) = "0"B;

   IF EMPTY(CL) THEN IF EMPTY(TS) CALL SIMULATION-STOP;

   ELSE Y = FIRST(TS); ELSE Y = FIRST(CL);

   EVENT (Y → $PROC-EVENT) = "1"B;

   WAIT(SIGNAL);

   GO TO LAB;

The statement WAIT(T) has the same translation of WAIT with the sole addition of the statement

CALL T-RANK (CURRENT);

after "CALL REMOVE (CURRENT)";

The procedure T-RANK inserts the system record referenced by its sole parameter into the *TS* set, according to the criteria fixed by the user.

13. A "HAZARD" SITUATION

The translation of the statement

WAIT UNTIL B(GA, . . . , GZ) ;

according to the first of the two SPL possible interpretations (see Appendix, sect. A.9), may be performed in several ways. The most straightforward of these would associate each global variable with a list which is scanned throughout every time the associated global changes in value. This method is not simple from the preprocessor point of view.

Here, however, we shall examine an asynchronous implementation which, while requiring little or nothing from the SPL → PL/1 preprocessor, will throw some light on the peculiar problems of the multiprocessing environment; these are similar to the problems encountered in the theory of asynchronous circuits (races, hazards, etc.). The proposed solution suffers from certain limitations which are described at the end of this section.

In order to translate the statement

WAIT UNTIL B (GA, GB, . . . , GZ);

where GA, GB, . . . , GZ are the global variables occurring in the expression B, the following actions must be taken during compilation of the MAIN heading:

a) with every global variable GA occurring in at least one WAIT UNTIL statement, two event variables, EV-GA and DRIVER--OF-A, are associated;

    a1) if the global variable GA happens to be declared BIT(1), then the associated event variable can actually be identified with GA, i.e. the global GA is declared with an event attribute;

b) for each global variable GA satisfying condition a), the following piece of code is inserted in MAIN:

ON CHECK(GA) BEGIN;

EVENT (DRIVER-OF-A) = "0"B;

EVENT(EV-GA) = "1"B;

WAIT(DRIVER-OF-A);

END;

This code gives rise to an interrupt whenever GA changes its value. In the case of an interrupt, the variable DRIVER-OF-A is set at "0"B, all the tasks waiting for EV-GA to change are asynchronously reactivated, and a setting of DRIVER-OF-A at "1"B is awaited.

c) Finally, statement (1) is translated into

SWITCH = 1;

LAB1: IF B (GA, . . . , GZ) THEN BEGIN;

       IF SWITCH = 1 THEN T(WAIT(0));

       ELSE BEGIN; CALL PARALLEL-WAIT-ZERO(SYS-P);

       IF ¬DRIVER-OF-A THEN EVENT(DRIVER-OF-A)="1"B;

       . . . . .

       IF ¬DRIVER-OF-Z THEN EVENT(DRIVER-OF-Z)="1"B;

       END;

       GO TO LAB2; END;

ELSE BEGIN;

      SWITCH = 2;

      IF ¬ DRIVER-OF-A THEN EVENT(DRIVER-OF-A)="1"B;

      . . . . .

      IF ¬ DRIVER-OF-Z THEN EVENT(DRIVER-OF-Z)="1"B;

      WAIT (EV-GA, . . . , EV-GZ) 1;

      IF EV-GA THEN EVENT (EV-GA) = "0"B;

      . . . . .

      IF EV-GZ THEN EVENT (EV-GZ) = "0"B;

      GO TO LAB1; END;

LAB 2:;

This code sets out to avoid, whenever possible, the unnecessary assignments of value to the event variables, an operation which we believe to be time consuming.

Drastic simplifications occur if the global variables $GA, \dots, GZ$ happen to satisfy point a1). In this case, if one translates any left occurrence of $GA, \dots, GZ$ into the expression EVENT(GA), EVENT(GZ), respectively, then the code under b) is not required and, for instance, translation of * WAIT UNTIL(GA | GB) is the following PL/1 text:

WAIT(GA, GB)1; CALL PARALLEL-WAIT-ZERO;

Another substantial simplification is obtained, of course, if the SPL 1 preprocessor is able to insert this PL/1 statement

EVENT(EV-global) = "1"B

after any assignment statement in which a global occurs on the left side and after any CALL statement which happens to have a global variable as one of its arguments.

The statement "T(WAIT(0)); " stands for the translation of the SPL statement WAIT(0).

The ELSE clause of the statement labelled LAB1 may possibly be executed in parallel by more than one task at a time, whereas CURRENT refers to another process (= task, in our implementation). Thus, if we want to perform the action of inserting the system record into the TS set, we may not use T(WAIT(0)).

The procedure PARALLEL-ZERO(SYS-P) is the equivalent of T(WAIT(0)) in which CURRENT is replaced by a correct value; this

---

* The infix boolean operator "or" is represented in PL/1 by the symbol " | ".

value is available under the local name SYS-P within the activity and is transmitted as a parameter to PARALLEL-WAIT-ZERO.

The procedure PARALLEL-WAIT-ZERO will be executed in a substantially hazard situation. It, in fact, attempts to insert a system record in the unique TS set.

But several PARALLEL-WAIT-ZERO may be operating in parallel. The order through which these procedures are executed is of no significance; what does matter is that their actions must not be interlaced.

The result is defined only in the highly frequent cases of:

a) there being only one processor in the operating environment where, in addition, the interrupts of a task to hand over control to another task occur only by a request to use peripheral units or on program command;

or, equivalently:

b) software facilities exist which compel the environment to simulate the situation as per a).

The condition established also ensures a correct conclusion of the "race" which may arise between the task S which sets to "1"B the event variables EV-GA,..., EV-GZ and the tasks T_i which are waiting for these variables to change values.

The statements which in the code c) precede the statement "WAIT(EV-GA,..., EV-GZ) 1; " reactivate, in cases where B is false, the task S described in code b).

If the task S, which has just been reactivated, starts off and is executed before the T_i local control reaches the statement "WAIT(EV-GA,..., EV-GZ) 1; ", then any value changes of the variables $GA,..., GZ$ would not be detected by one of the task T_i.

14. ALLOCATION OF SYSTEM RECORDS

Since, in PL/1, all storage allocated within a task is destroyed when that task is completed, a special mechanism to allocate and free system records has been devised. To each system record class a task (together with a synchronizing variable) is associated. This task, created at the beginning of simulation, will last until the end. Each reactivation of this task will be performed through an event assignment to the synchronizing variable and will cause allocation or returning of storage of the associate class. Communication from the task requiring storage and the task creating it will be through the value of a variable of the pointer type, pointing to the relevant record.

15. IMPLEMENTATION

We shall only give here some general criteria we have followed in implementation B.

An ACTIVITY block Z is still translated into a procedure block Z'. But Z' will be called without a task option. Z is likely to be executed concurrently by several processes so that no local space may be assigned to it. The local space of the activity Z will be organized as a based PL/1 structure: one structure for each block which sets up a nomenclature level. The structure is allocated at the entrance and freed at the exit of a block.

The variable space, local to the outermost block, i.e. the "attributes" space, is organized more or less as the system record of implementation A. Among the hidden attributes there is now an integer defining the reactivation point and, if necessary, a pointer pointing to the structure of an internal BEGIN block (if activated).

There will be two ways of entering a BEGIN or a PROCEDURE block: i.e. in *"first activation"* and in *"reactivation"*. In first activation, the space (= structure) is allocated, whereas in reactivation it is retrieved by reassigning to the implicit structure pointer the value stored as a hidden attribute of the structure associated with the lower level block. In fact, structures associated with the different levels of nomenclature are organized in a list, the *process* list. The first element in a process list is the process system record. The process list works as a stack for the corresponding process. But this applies only to the declared variables and not to the dummies. Consequently it is not legal to define and call functions whose bodies contain SPL extension statement.

An active phase of a process is translated into an execution of the procedure associated with the process class.

The action of making passive a process (resulting from the execution of a sequencing statement) is translated into the setting of the re-entry point integer and the execution of a RETURN to the TIMER routine.

The main program is now the TIMER routine. It is a piece of PL/1 text that is inserted in the main block of the SPL model.

This implementation makes use, within BEGIN and PROCEDURE blocks, of programmed allocation only (neither the static nor the automatic "storage classes" are used).

Interrogative sequencing (WAIT UNTIL statements) is implemented through ad hoc lists. At this point the PL/1 "cell" concept becomes useful again in defining two structural possibilities within system records.

Here again, as in implementation A, the programmed allocation concept is fundamental (especially the base structure).

The unique PL/1 feature of the implicit pointer of a based variable, has enabled us to simulate any number of parallel stacks without altering the manner in which the variables are named within the BEGIN or PROCEDURE blocks.

Acknowledgements. The author is indebted to Jack Merner of General Electric for an enlightening discussion on the subject matter of this paper.

APPENDIX

A.1. *The* SPL *language*

The SPL design has been strongly influenced by that of SIMULA and, to a lesser extent, by SOL [76]. Thus, in many instances, we shall be limiting our description to those points in which it deviates from the SIMULA model. Moreover, almost the all terminology used here has been taken from Dahl [25].

Since SPL is imbedded in PL/1, its syntax and style will certainly follow the PL/1 pattern. However, PL/1 is too wide a language to allow any of the PL/1 features to be included in SPL. There is no doubt, for instance, that no compile time processing will be allowed within SPL. But there will be other restrictions which lack of space prevents us from mentioning in full.

To follow this description, a full knowledge of SIMULA is required of the reader.

A.2. *The* SPL *model*

A simulation model written in SPL acts as a PL/1 external procedure; it may interact with other PL/1 external procedures, but it has to be independently preprocessed by an SPL compiler. An SPL model consists of an optional part: i.e. the System Definition, followed by an SPL block.

In the present version of the System Definition the user may define the general features of the System. For instance, he may declare the system time-functions as returning a fixed or floating quantity with any precision (compatible with the existing PL/1 implementation). He may want the existence of a priority concept for activities and processes and, if so, he may specify type (integer or float) and precision.

An SPL block consists of a heading followed by a BEGIN main block. The heading consists of the declaration of global devices: i.e. stores; facilities, global variables, sets. The BEGIN main block consists of the activities and procedure declarations, followed by any SPL statement (other than activity block statements).

A.3. *The process concept*

The process concept is basically similar to the corresponding SIMULA concept. A process has its own *local data, operation rule* and *local control*. Local control (here we differ from SIMULA) is always defined for a generated process.

Processes belong to classes, called *activities*.

A process is described by an *activity declaration*, which is similar to a PL/1 procedure declaration. An activity declaration consists of an ACTIVITY statement

ACTIVITY activity-name (parameter-list);

followed by a heading and a BEGIN block. The heading contains parameter specification and declaration of items which are local to the process but also accessible to other processes through the mechanism of *remote accessing*.

These items, together with the parameters, are called *process attributes*.

A.4. *Data types*

Data may be of the following types:
a) arithmetic, i.e. fixed point, floating point, real, imaginary;
b) string: i.e. character string, bit string;
c) pointer;
d) label;
e) set;
The process parameters may not be of label type. Data may be organized in arrays and the PL/1 array expressions are allowed.

The parameters of an activity are transmitted by value, without exception. This is not a restriction since pointer data exist.

The expression

NEW activity-name (argument-list)

will invoke a new generation of process with the replacement of the parameters by the arguments and creation of a local control point. The value of the expression is a reference to the process (i.e. a pointer).

The local control point is positioned at the entrance to the BEGIN block. A sequencing statement will cause the local control point to move forward, following the instructions of the BEGIN block.

Certain sequencing statements cause action of a process to stand while awaiting the positive effect of other scheduling statements issued by the same or, perhaps, other processes. Interrupts may occur if the process alters the state of global variables.

When the local control reaches the END of the main block of the activity declaration (or it executes a GO TO statement out of the

activity block), the process leaves the system and its data structure is destroyed.

The BEGIN block of an ACTIVITY declaration may contain any
SPL statement (other than ACTIVITY declaration). BEGIN blocks
and procedure block may be nested to any depth; each block establishes a scope for the identifiers declared within the block (according to PL/1 conventions).

If an activity has no operation rule, we shall call it an ENTITY.
The declaration of an entity is similar to a PL/1 structure declaration. Here is an example

DECLARE 1 L ENTITY, 2 B BIT (1), 2 C FIXED, 2 D POINTER;

The expression NEW L ("1"B, 3, ADDR (R)) generates a new entity
of class L and has, as a value, a pointer pointing to it. An entity
is a process with a null scope for its attributes. Since accessing of
ENTITY attributes is always from the outside, the entity, as an independent concept, has been introduced in order to facilitate accessing.

Different generations of entities are retrieved by means of pointers.

For instance, if, in relation to the above entity declaration, we
write:

$$T = NEW\ L\ ("1"B, 3, ADDR\ (R));$$

$$S = NEW\ L\ ("0"B, 4, T);$$

then the expressions "$T \rightarrow C$" and "$S \rightarrow C$" have the values "3" and "4"
respectively. If there is any danger of ambiguity, field names may
be qualified as in PL/1:

$$T \rightarrow L.\ C;$$

Entities may be declared in the heading of the SPL block or within
the body of procedure or activity declarations. In the former case
the scope is the entire SPL block and attributes may be accessed
from any point. In the latter case the scope is reduced to the en-
compassing block and, moreover, no generative expression is allowed; their declarations only serve for the purpose of computing
off-sets of fields within system records.

We use the term *system record* to indicate in general the accessible data structure of a process or the data structure of an
entity. In a system record there are other attributes than those
specified by the programmer: i.e., the system attributes. These
are 1) for an entity; the type (or class), the predecessor and successor; and 2) for a process: in addition to the foregoing, we have
also the time reference, state (1 bit), and, if desired, the priority

attribute *.   When time reference is not used, a pointer P may take its place (this is accomplished through the CELL mechanism of PL/1).

Whereas a process dies when its local control reaches certain specific points of its operation rules, an entity is destroyed by the action of the statement:

DESTROY X;

or

DESTROY X OF A;

X being a pointer and A a class. In both cases an error condition is raised if X is not an entity; in the latter case if X does not belong to class A.

A.5. *Sets*

Processes and entities may be members of sets, but of only one set at a time. This, at first, may seem a serious drawback. But we know of very few examples where a process belongs to more than one set at the same time. However, in case of necessity, the programmer may still define a referencing entity which points to the given process (or entity) and belongs to a second set. Thus any reference to a process or an entity in SPL is direct and the SIMULA element concept is not provided by the system.

Sets are declared as variables or arrays in the heading of the SPL block or of any activity declaration. An SPL set is, like a SIMULA set, a cyclic sequence of element: i.e. the system records (processes or entities). A particular type of a system record - the set HEAD - is always present in a set. Its predecessor is the last element of the set and its successor, the first element.

A set of elementary set functions is provided with the same meaning as the corresponding SIMULA set: SUC(X), FIRST (S), LAST (S), = PRED (HEAD (S)), EMPTY (S), EXIST (X). EMPTY (S) may be used in connection with wait until statements.

A.6. *Global devices*

The global concepts are derived from SOL, but the underlying philosophy is different. They are considered only as a useful short-writing for some standard list manipulations.

A.7. *Global variables and sets*

Global variables and sets have to be declared in the heading of

---

* There may exist other hidden attributes: in implementation A the Event variable PROC-EVENT, in implementation B the integer defining the re-entry point and a pointer pointing to the second element of the stack-list.

the SPL block. They may be accessed from any point of an SPL block.

Boolean * functions defined on them may occur in wait-until statements.

A.8. *Facilities and stores*

A facility is a global element, defined as in SOL. Only one process at time may have control of a facility. Control is requested (released) by execution of SEIZE (RELEASE) statements.

A process may request control of more than one facility; that is, SEIZE and RELEASE statements may be nested or interlaced to any depth. An interpretation may be given, but requires some cautions. We will not discuss it here. A facility F may be in two states: busy or not busy. Correspondingly we have the boolean function BUSY (F).

Again, the definition of busy states requires certain precautions (in relation to interrupts).

When a process takes the control of a facility, even if an interrupt occurs, it enters in a *blocked state* (see later).

The STORE concept is identical to the corresponding SOL concept. ENTER and LEAVE statements are defined as in [76]. A store S may be empty, not empty, full, not full; in correspondence we have two boolean functions, EMPTY (S), FULL (S).

A.9. *Sequencing*

Processes and their system records are associated in such a strict way that we will often identify a process with its own system record.

System records that correspond to processes may be members of two principal sets: the *current list CL*, and the *time set TS*; the latter set is partially ordered according to the value of one or two parameters: priority and time. Other conventions make TS a totally ordered set. The union of CL and TS is called the *sequencing set SQS*.

When the currently active process reaches a standing point, the timer routine picks up the first element of CL and gives the control to the associated process which will then move forward (beyond its previous standing point). If CL is empty, the timer routine will put the first element of TS into CL and acts as above.

The CL list is build up as consequence of *direct sequencing* whereas the TS set is handled by other sequencing statements. Direct sequencing puts an element at the top of CL list. The CL list acts as a push-down store under sequencing operations (not under set operations as REMOVE, etc.).

---

* "Boolean" means a quantity declared BIT (1).

The value returned by the TIME (or CURRENT) function is made equal to the time reference of (or pointer pointing to) the element on the top of the CL list.

The sequencing statements are

a) WAIT   The current process will enter a standing phase (see PASSIVATE of SIMULA); its system record is taken out of CL.

b) WAIT(T) T is an expression. This statement will remove the current process from CL and insert it in SQS with a time reference equal to "T+TIME". The statement WAIT(0) will allow the execution of other events having the same time-reference but higher priority than the current one.

- ACTIVATE X AT T;

- ACTIVATE DELAY T;

- ACTIVATE X;

These statements operate as in SIMULA (except for the SQS ranking criterion which takes also in account the priority, when it exists) and have effect even if X is already in SQS. (The elimination of the element and event concepts of SIMULA has greatly reduced the sequencing statements list.)

- WAIT UNTIL(B)

Where B is an expression. For this statement to have a sense B must involve global variables.

For instance   WAIT UNTIL (BUSY (A)) or
WAIT UNTIL (A > 0)

There exist two interpretations:

a) WAIT UNTIL(B) is considered to be equivalent to an implicit determination of time, i.e., it is considered absolutely equivalent to

$$\text{WAIT UNTIL TIME} = T_1$$

where T_1 is the system time to which B first happens to be true (the only condition being that reactivation must not occur before the active phase of the process which made B true). This implies that if B is true, a WAIT(0) statement is executed.

b) As in a) but an interrupt will occur immediately after the computing step which made B true to give control to the process that was waiting for B. No WAIT(0) statement is executed if B *was* true.

The user chose one of these two interpretations in the system definition.

- SEIZE, RELEASE, ENTER, LEAVE.

Lack of space prevents us to discuss these features here. We, however, closely follow the SOL report.

A.10. *Remote accessing*

A connection group has the format

$$\text{WHEN X OF Z THEN } S_1; \quad \text{ELSE } S_2;$$

where S_1 and S_2 are any statements (but S_1 may not be a connection group). Within S_1 the attributes of process X of class Z may be accessed through their local names prefixed by a $ sign. For instance, the following statement

$$\text{WHEN X OF Z THEN } \$B=B;$$

would update the attribute B of process X with the value of the same attribute of the current process (it is assumed that CURRENT belongs to class Z). Labels of the connected process are not accessible.

An error condition is raised if the process referenced by X is in a blocked state.

A.11. *Blocked state*

A process is in a blocked state if
a) it is executing a WAIT UNTIL statement, or
b) it is controlling a FACILITY, or
c) it is in an interrupted state (after having had control of a facility).

It is illegal to try to connect a blocked process or to change its set membership.

Here is the SPL transcription of the example at the end of SIMULA manual [28]

```
SPL SYSTEM; DECLARE TIME FLOAT; NO PRIORITY;

BEGIN; DECLARE (POPULATION, NR-DEAD (4:10), NR-UNIN-
        FECTED, U1, U2) FIXED (7, 0), (P, MORTALITY (4:10))
        FLOAT, (DEAD, CURED) SET, REF POINTER;
        ACTIVITY INFECTED-PERSON; DECLARE DAY FIXED (7,0);
            NR-UNINFECTED = NR-UNINFECTED - 1; WAIT (3);
            DO DAY=4 TO 10;
            IF DRAW (MORTALITY (DAY), U1) THEN BEGIN;
```

```
          CALL INCLUDE (CURRENT, DEAD); WAIT; END;
          ELSE WAIT (1); END;
          CALL INCLUDE (CURRENT, CURED);
     END;
GET LIST (POPULATION, U1, U2, P, MORTALITY);
NR-UNINFECTED = POPULATION;
INFECT: ACTIVATE NEW INFECTED-PERSON;
WAIT (NEGEXP (P, U2));
IF NR-UNINFECTED > 0 THEN GO TO INFECT;
WAIT (11);
PUT LIST (POPULATION, CARDINAL (DEAD), CARDINAL (CURED));
REF = HEAD (DEAD);
DO REF = SUC (REF) WHILE EXIST (REF);
WHEN REF OF INFECTED-PERSON THEN BEGIN;
          NR-DEAD ($DAY) = NR-DEAD ($DAY)+1;
          ACTIVATE REF; END;
PUT LIST (POPULATION, NR-DEAD);
END SPL;
```

There is no essential difference between the foregoing program and the one shown in the SIMULA manual. The only noticeable difference lies in the fact that the process destroying here is not automatic; a process vanishes only if its local control performs a stop instruction. In our example the statement "ACTIVATE REF; " had to be introduced in order to reactivate the processes, elements of the set DEAD, which then carry out the instruction "END; " and die.

If the statement "ACTIVATE REF; " was not inserted, all the records (and associated tasks) would be destroyed (or terminated) only at the end of the simulation main program.

DISCUSSION

Molnar:

If we have two pointers pointing to the same process or entity, what would be the value of the other pointer when the process terminates?

Petrone:

First of all, processes are not destroyed - processes naturally die when the operating rule reaches its end point so the question is linked only to entities. If I destroy the entities I think that the meaning is the same as in PL/1 that is, its effect is undefined.

Nygaard:

I just want to follow up Molnar's question here because you may find any number of pointers to any object regardless of its being an entity or a process, being terminated or active or suspended. Now, if you allow the statement "Destroy (X)" where X is one of the pointers then of course the store which is allocated to this will now be allocated to other things. If you try to activate it, if you refer to one of its attributes via some other pointer the program goes to hell and you don't know why. You can't trace it and this is a very bad thing.

Petrone:

That's the policy of PL/1 - in PL/1 you have no control over records and you may reference a record in a very different way from the way it was initially intended when created and that may cause trouble. From my point of view, my emphasis was not on PL/1 data handling but it was to relate two different concepts - parallel programming and quasi-parallel programming. We had available only PL/1 and so we used it.

Hoare:

I get the impression from remarks in this paper that in the design of a language based on PL/1 the designer felt that in many cases he was struggling against the language which he had chosen.

Petrone:

No, this is not so: there is only one remark which states that unfortunately PL/1 allows too many exceptions and we had to find out personally where they apply. We found it not too difficult to build on PL/1.

Laski:

At the risk of appearing trivial and referring to problems that everybody understands and knows well I want to point out that when you have data type "reference", i.e. data that may refer to records or to conceptual objects or what have you, you have always the problem to know what to do when you destroy these objects - how you are to interpret the reference data that may be left behind. It seems to me that no language and no system has yet managed to get a clean solution that gives adequate freedom to the user and adequate efficiency to those who are still concerned with real machines.

Hutchinson:

I think two general issues are being raised here. Firstly, how much protection should the language give to the user? you can't protect him against himself completely and also give him complete freedom to do what he wants, you see. The second question is, who should be doing the simulations anyhow? - which I am sure belongs to the general session.

Nygaard:

A question on this language: you have based it upon PL/1 and you have utilised certain features of PL/1, mainly the task concept. Is the task concept implemented in any PL/1 compiler and if not when can we expect to see it implemented?

Petrone:

I know what is happening in my company - where a PL/1 compiler has been made but I don't think that tasking has been implemented.

If in the future different languages would decide to handle parallel programming, it should be done with the quasi-parallel programming in mind. Many connections exist between these two concepts. Parallel programming is the case in which you may have many different tasks progressing at once. In quasi-parallel programming you have only one task and a very strict synchronizing method to decide which of the many procedures have to be active at that moment and which will be the next one to be active. In the multi-programming environment you have a set of many tasks and in the quasi-parallel programming you have a set of one; amongst the set of many in the multi-programming environment you do not know the time relation.

AS: AN ALGOL SIMULATION LANGUAGE

R. D. PARSLOW

Brunel University, Acton, London W.3, U.K.

1. INTRODUCTION

In order to simulate the working of a dynamic system we have to build a mathematical model suitable for running on a computer. The difficulties involved in writing the description of such a system are exaggerated by the restrictions imposed by the computer, but these are considerably eased if a high level language (FORTRAN, ALGOL or PL/1) is used. Even with a high level language the program can be long and highly complex and although syntactic errors are fairly easy to correct, the debugging of logical errors can be highly time consuming. Many of the processes of simulation are basic to most programs and these can be organised into subroutines or ALGOL procedures and assembled in a standard package so that they can be incorporated in the user's program.

The real difficulties involved in simulation however are of an organizational nature and it is helpful to provide the user with a framework so that he can write simulations to a standard pattern. The use of a framework has other advantages in that the housekeeping and general organization of the run can be accomplished automatically, and monitoring facilities are more easily obtained.

There are many disadvantages to such a method: the object program is usually inefficient in machine time and space which is of considerable importance when one considers the length and number of runs necessary, and the framework can act as a straight-jacket into which the model must be forced. These objections have to be balanced against the enormous saving in user's time by aid in organization, writing, debugging and monitoring, and it is the job of the language writer to minimise the snags.

AS (ref. [59]), the language described in this paper, not only enables the user to write in ALGOL using the procedures of a package but, since these procedures contain no machine code instructions, the package can be easily adapted to any machine capable of accepting ALGOL.

The method of operation is based on the work of K. D. Tocher [150]

It incorporates an hierarchical structure to facilitate faster updating of time and includes automatically the time taken in transport and all other housekeeping requirements.

An attempt has been made to keep the terms of the language compatible with other simulation languages [15, 28, 77, 158].

2. SAMPLING FROM RANDOM DISTRIBUTIONS

Simulation uses Monte Carlo techniques because the variables which we wish to investigate are compounded from distributions in such a complex fashion that analysis is completely impractical. To use the technique we determine, by observation, the distribution of each variable in the system and whenever it is needed in the simulation, we choose a random sample from this distribution. The prime tool of this technique is a random number generator which will give a uniform random sample between 0 and 1. By comparing this value with the cumulative relative frequency of the distribution we determine the required sample value. A true random number generator would be of no value in simulation studies since the runs could not be repeated and we usually require repeats of the runs with variations in the system parameters. We therefore attempt to produce pseudo-random numbers, i.e. numbers which are produced to a formula but which appear random and satisfy certain tests. As has been emphasised by Page (ref. [50]) and Tocher (ref. [61]) the large number of runs and the enormous number of calls for random samples makes it of vital importance that the generator should produce random numbers of long periodic cycle, uniformly distributed with low serial correlation for reasonably high orders.

To obtain a true picture of the effect of a given set of system parameters, we need to be able to repeat runs with different random numbers, but when we wish to determine the effect of varying each of the system parameters, we need to be able to repeat the set of runs with the same stream of random numbers that were used previously for each variable. The language should therefore provide several random streams, which are not necessarily reset to their initial values for repeated runs.

The random number generator used in AS has been revised many times and the method now being considered involves a shuffled Lehmer congruence suggested by Maclaren and Marsaglia [94]. The distributions available are uniform, negative exponential, negative binomial, Poisson, binomial, binomial proportion, and normal. It is also possible to sample from a distribution determined by the user.

3. MONITORING

The need for adequate monitoring facilities for the program
developer and the manager has been fully stated by P. J. Kiviat [14].
In AS, the debugging of syntactic errors is covered by procedures
incorporated in the ALGOL compiler. To eradicate logical errors,
monitoring facilities are provided by two procedures 'alarm' and
'ask'. 'alarm' is used throughout the package of procedures to in-
form the user if some fault has developed in the program. The point
of failure is given together with simulation time and the present
value of all variables in the simulation. 'ask' is a boolean procedure which provides optional facilities (usually used to obtain output). It operates in conjunction with a global variable 'askq' whose
value is provided from data. If askq is exactly divisible by a specified integer parameter of ask, then ask is *true* otherwise it takes
the value *false*. If the procedure parameter is given different prime
values in different sections of the program, optional output is obtained by choosing as the value of askq the product of the primes
of the parameters in the calls selected. Each procedure contains
a call of 'ask' with parameter 2, so that any even value of askq
will output the name of every procedure of the package as it is
entered.

4. THE MATRIX

The elements manipulated during the simulation are known as
'entities' and each entity has its attributes stored in the cells of
one row of a matrix. The contents of these cells may be altered by
the 'activities' of the simulation. The entities must be grouped into
one or more 'pools', which may contain a homogeneous set of entities or may contain entities grouped for housekeeping convenience
in the simulation. The pools themselves may be grouped forming an
hierarchical structure which is of considerable value in the speedy
operation of the program.
Most entities are time dependent and are known as 'ents' but
others, named 'depots', merely serve as records or represent
stores.
An activity which is set to operate on a particular entity at some
predetermined time is known as a bound activity, 'b act' while one
which requires the availability of several entities is a conditional
activity, 'c act'.
Each 'b act', 'c act', 'ent' and 'depot' is given a row of the matrix. The layout of the matrix is given in fig. 1 and the purpose of
the columns of cells will be described during the paper. The pres-

Sheet No. . . . .

SIMULATION. . . . .

No.	place	pool	totim	totop	ran d	ran c	ran b	ran a	enter	time	ready	Name	No.
1													1
2													2
3													3
4													4
5													5
6													6
7													7
8													8
9													9
10													0

Fig. 1. The matrix.

ent state of the cells of the matrix may be obtained by a call of the procedure 'matrix', which may also be used with 'ask' as an additional monitoring aid.

5. CHANGING THE STATE OF THE MODEL

A fundamental action of almost all activities is the 'committal' of entities, i.e. the determination of the duration of the activity and the alteration of the state of each of the entities involved. When an entity has been committed, it is made unavailable for other tasks, by changing the value of the 'ready' cell to zero. The time when the entity will have completed the task is recorded in its 'time' cell, and, if the entity is engaged to enter a bound activity at that time, the number of this 'b act' is put in its 'enter' cell. These changes are reflected in the cells of the appropriate pools: the ready cell records the number of available members of the pool; the time cell contains the time at which the first working entity of the pool will become available, and the row number of this entity appears in the enter cell.

The procedure 'commit' considerably simplifies the description of these changes in the cells, since it requires only the specification of the row number of the entity, the number of any 'b act' to which it is to be subsequently engaged, its final location, and the random parameters. When called, the procedure first ensures that the row number is within the correct range and that the entity is available. It then determines the committal time using 'random' and ensures that the value is non-negative. If the row specified as a parameter gives the number of a pool, a search is made through the pool to find an available entity. The entity is committed as specified by the random parameters, and then the pool of the entity has its cell states upvalued. Two side effects are the recording in the 'totop' and 'totim' cells of the entity and its pools the total number of operations in which they have been concerned, and the total time for which they have been committed.

The cells of an entity row may be used to store the committal parameters, with 'ran a' containing the type of distribution to be sampled, 'ran b' and 'ran c' containing distribution parameters such as mean and standard deviation, 'ran d' the random stream, and 'place' the location when the task is completed. They can then be invoked in 'commit' by calling 'recommit' but if an entity is likely to be engaged in many activities the committal parameters can be stored in the cells of the b act row and the call could then be 'b act recommit'.

The matrix of AS has been described earlier; the initial frame-

work for the setting of the values in the cells is managed by two
procedures 'prepare' and 'rerun'. 'prepare', organises the random
streams, delineates the rows for b acts, c acts, pools, ents and
depots, records the ents or pools required for c acts and their subsequent engagement to b acts, in arrays 'key' and 'key enter', and
sets up the two dimensional array, 'movetime', giving the time
to move between locations. 'rerun' sets, or resets, the values in
the cells for the beginning of each run. To initiate the simulation
processes, values may be set into the cells of the matrix by using
procedures 'setrow', 'copyrow', and 'setcommit'.

6. THE PHASE STRUCTURE

The procedure 'next' is the most important in the package as it
controls the cycles of four phases of the simulation, and is called
at the end of each activity block of the user's program. The basic
phase is the *T-phase* in which simulation time, TIME, is advanced.
This is accomplished by first finding the time of the next event, i.e.
the least value in the time cells of all the working entities. To scan
the time cells of all the entity rows would be extremely wasteful,
so use is made of the grouping of the time dependent entities into
pools. The time cell of each pool row contains the time of the next
event concerning a member of the pool. (The row number of this
member is stored in the enter cell.) The search is therefore restricted to the highest level of pool. The value of TIME being found
it is now possible to enter the next phase, the *B-phase* of the simulation, a second scan of the entities, in which all bound activities
now due are entered, and incidentally those working entities which
have completed their time of committal, but are not engaged to a
bound activity, are made available. If a number of events are due
to occur within a short time of each other, the whole phase structure would have to be repeated for each, even though their separate
operation is not vital to the simulation. It has therefore been ar-
ranged for a value of 'tolerance' to be read in as data and for all
events occurring within this tolerance of TIME to be treated during
this rescan, without materially affecting the simulation.

At the termination of this phase the *C-phase* can begin and 'next'
causes transfer to the start of the first conditional activity, after
organising that the following entry to it shall restart the *T-phase*.
The entry to each of these activities requires a test of the conditions
of the activity by a boolean procedure 'c act'. This procedure not
only checks the availability of the key entities, after searches
through pools if necessary, but also records in the array 'key act'
the row numbers of the entities found. If the activity can be entered

these entities can be committed most easily by the call of 'c act commit' or, if the parameters required for the committal have been stored in the c act row, by a simpler call of 'c act recommit'. If no side effects are required, the activity of the program need only consist of one line, e.g. *if* c act (4) *then* c act recommit (4). If the required entities are not available for the activity then the *A-phase*, a subdivision of the C-phase, can be entered in which two procedures 'able' and 'assemble' are involved. 'able' tests whether a non available entity will be available at the termination of its present task; if so 'assemble' marks it so that only the specified c act can use it and ensures that the entity is in the correct location. In the case where a pool has been requested a search is made for that entity which can be assembled first taking account of time required for movement to the location. The call of 'next' at the end of the c act block returns the simulation to the T-phase.

7. HISTOGRAMS

Apart from the collection of data in the totop and totim cells, information about distributions can be accumulated using a package of histogram procedures. The histogram arrays are declared dynamically and sizes are fixed from data.

'Hm prepare' prepares an empty histogram from parameters giving the lowest class, the class interval, and the number of classes

'Hm set'   sets a value into a histogram a given number of times

'Hm add'   adds one histogram into another a given number of times

'Hm in'   replaces one histogram by another

'Hm output'   prints out the histogram

'Hm analyse' analyses a histogram giving: number of points; mean; standard deviation; skewness; kurtosis; coefficient of variation; lower quartile; median; upper quartile; and mode

'Hm random'   allows a random sample to be taken from the histogram specified.

8. CURRENT DEVELOPMENT

AS is under continuous revision to provide better facilities for the user. At present the developments are concerned with a better random number generator and further distributions. The speed of operation is of secondary consideration, since the main purpose of

AS is to provide a method of getting simulations working quickly. To obtain more efficient computer runs the procedures may be translated into machine code, and if the same program is to be a library item it may be worth writing the whole program in machine code using the methods of AS. However it is to be hoped that with more efficient ALGOL compilers this will be unnecessary.

ACKNOWLEDGEMENTS

I am extremely grateful to Dr. Tocher for detailed explanations of the methods of operation of G. S. P. on which AS is based, and for suggestions in the development of the language. The program was written for the KDF9 at the National Physical Laboratory and I received great assistance during development from the members of the Mathematics Division and in particular from R. Healey, who was responsible for many of the procedures. The work in altering the program to Elliott ALGOL for running on ATLAS has been possible through the aid of R. F. A. Hopgood and A. G. Bell of Chilton ATLAS.

APPENDIX

Example
The loading bay of a factory which operates as follows:
1. For 3 hours large crates arrive at the loading bay. The time between crate arrivals is 2 min plus a delay time distributed negative exponentially with mean $\frac{1}{2}$ min.
2. 4 cranes remove the crates taking time distributed normally with mean 10 min and standard deviation 2 min.

The activities which will be necessary for the simulation are:

bound activities	1. arrival of crates
	2. stopping the arrival of crates
	3. outputting the results
conditional activities	1. loading

The entities involved in these activities will be:

time dependent entities	1-4 Cranes
	5. entity to initiate b act 1
	6. entity to initiate b act 2
	7. entity to initiate b act 3
depots	1. loading bay.

The 4 cranes can be combined into one pool and the other 3 time dependent entities could be combined into another, but since the scanning time can be shortened if rarely called entities are kept together in a separate pool, we arrange the pools as follows:
1. pool of cranes
2. pool of single entity which initiates the arrival of crates
3. pool of remainder of time dependent entities
We assemble this information on the matrix sheet. 'b acts', 'c acts', 'pools', 'ents' and 'depots' must be given in that order and all members of a pool must be in consecutive rows.

row number

	1.	arrival
b acts	2.	session end
	3.	results
c acts	4.	loading
	5.	cranes pool
pools	6.	crate pool
	7.	remainder pool
	8.	crane 1
	9.	crane 2
	10.	crane 3
ents	11.	crane 4
	12.	arrival trigger
	13.	close trigger
	14.	results trigger
depot	15.	loading bay

We now have the row numbers for reference in writing the program. We begin by declaring a *switch*, act, whose elements are the labels of the b acts, in order, and then the label of the first c act (the only one in our case).

We then set the initial values of the cells.

We set row 4 for c act loading by specifying every cell:

set row (4, 1, 1, 0, 0, 0, fast normal, 10, 2, 1, 0, 1);

To have 4 cranes available

ready [5]: = 4;

We arrange for the initiation of a bound activity by utilising a time dependent entity as a trigger, so that when the committal time of the entity expires the bound activity is entered.

The parameters used by random in committing row 12 (arrival trigger) will be used many times so we write them into the row cells as well as committing it by using

set commit (12, 1, negexp, . 5, 2, 1, 1);

i.e. activity 1 (crate arrival) will enter at a future time found by making a random selection from a negative exponential distribution of mean . 5 min and adding 2 min (random stream 1 being used). Crates will be delivered to location 1.

To end the session we use row 13 to trigger activity 2 in 180 minutes by

commit (13, 2,   180,   1);

activity 2 will stop crates arriving so that we will deal with any backlog present without addition.

We do not want the results output (activity 3) until we are sure the loading bay is clear so we delay entry to the activity until long after all other activities have ceased. We choose 1000 min after simulation begins by

commit (14, 3,   1000,   1);

To ensure that the loading bay is empty at the start we put

ready [15] : = 0;

since the ready cell of a depot gives the number of items available in the depot i.e. in our case the number of crates awaiting loading.

The various activities need to operate as follows

arrival: (triggered by entity 12)
              will add 1 to the crates in the loading bay (row 15) and since the 'enter' cell of a depot is not used by the simulator we utilise the enter cell of row 15 to record the largest number of crates ever in the bay. The trigger will be reset by recommitting entity 12.

session
   end: (triggered by entity 13)
              to stop crates arriving we need only change ready [1] from 1 to 0 so that activity 1 (crate arrival) will not be entered again.

results: (triggered by entity 14)
              we need to output a message giving the number of the run and then all the information we need can most easily be obtained by using 'matrix'.
              We call rerun and conditionally return to the beginning of the user's program.

loading: consists of checking whether loading can take place i.e. a crate and a crane available in the right place. If load-

ing is possible the relevant entities are committed by
'c act recommit' and another check made.

The initial stage and all activities entered during a simulation must
end with

goto act [next];

We also need to call prepare, to set up the simulation and fix
the time at which it starts.

The program must be preceded by a label 'start' and terminated
by 2 *extra ends*.

The program now reads:

prepare;

start:TIME := 540;

begin comment dispatch;

switch act := cratearrival, sessionend, results, loading;
setrow (4, 1, 1, 0, 0, 0, fast normal, 10, 2, 1, 0, 1);
ready [5] := 4;
setcommit (12, 1, negexp, . 5, 2, 1, 1);
commit (13, 2, 180, 1);
commit (14, 3, 1000, 1);
ready [15] := 0;
goto act [next];

cratearrival: begin ready [15] := ready [15] + 1;
if ready [15] > enter [15] then enter [15] := ready [1
recommit (12, 1);
goto act [next];
end;

sessionend:ready [1] := 0;
goto act [next];

results: print "*l*3' RESULTS OF RUN NUMBER', sameline, run;
matrix;
rerun; if runs > 0 then goto start else stop;

loading: if cact(4) then
begin cactrecommit(4)
goto loading
end;
goto act [next];

end dispatch;
end procedures;
end AS;

Table 1
Output from first run of program

RESULTS OF RUN NUMBER 1

NO	READY	TIME	ENTER	TOTOP	TOTIM	RAN A	RAN B	RAN C	RAN D	POOL	PLACE
1	0	1.0000000	0	0	.00000000	0	.00000000	1.0000000	1	0	1
2	1	1.0000000	0	0	.00000000	0	.00000000	1.0000000	1	0	1
3	1	1.0000000	0	0	.00000000	0	.00000000	1.0000000	1	0	1
4	1	1.0000000	0	71	709.88911	8	10.000000	2.0000000	1	0	1
5	4	$5.000_{10}+08$	0	71	709.88911	0	.00000000	1.0000000	1	8	11
6	1	$5.000_{10}+08$	0	72	182.45770	0	.00000000	1.0000000	1	12	12
7	2	1540.0000	14	2	1180.0000	0	.00000000	1.0000000	1	13	14
8	1	729.23313	0	17	176.17877	0	.00000000	1.0000000	1	5	1
9	1	726.27752	0	17	171.68797	0	.00000000	1.0000000	1	5	1
10	1	728.66053	0	20	181.31606	0	.00000000	1.0000000	1	5	1
11	1	728.05628	0	17	180.70629	0	.00000000	1.0000000	1	5	1
12	1	722.45770	0	72	182.45770	2	.50000000	2.0000000	1	6	1
13	1	720.00000	0	1	180.00000	0	.00000000	1.0000000	1	7	1
14	1	1540.0000	3	1	1000.0000	0	.00000000	1.0000000	1	7	1
15	0	1.0000000	3	71	.00000000	0	.00000000	1.0000000	1	0	1

The data needed (see DATA REQUIRED)

1 for q ask (not used)
. 1 for tolerance: = . 1
10 for runs
3 for b acts
1 for c acts
2 for maxents
3 for pools
7 for ents
1 for depot
1 for ranstream
1 for Hm number
0 for Hm classes
1 places
0 for starting value of random stream
2 entities needed for loading 5 to enter 0 and 15 to enter 0
for first pool entities   8 to 11
for second pool entities 12 to 12
for third pool entities   13 to 14

no more data needed

The state of the matrix at the end of a run is given in table 1.

DISCUSSION

Nygaard:

All the time you refer to the importance of creating a scheme
which is easy to understand for the user. I must say that I think
we all very much sympathise with this and I think this has been a
basic motive for most of the work which has been going on. I regard it as your best point, but I don't think it's a very original one.

Parslow:

No, what I was trying to say was that we seem to be getting more
interested in designing the languages than in thinking how the users
can use them. By keeping yourself to ALGOL as a basis you get to
a situation where you know there are certain extensions that you
would like to add but you force yourself not to do them because they
would in fact make life more difficult for the user.

Strachey:

I would like to enlist the support of the participants - I am trying to design a new language which is for matrix algebra. It's to be specially easy for the user to understand. Of course, naturally when we come to multiplication - like addition, it will be done as element by element. However, I have certain difficulties because there are some problems that I don't seem to be able to do!

Now, it seems to me that it's all very well saying that we want to make languages easier for the user. The important thing about a language is that it is only easier for the user if it naturally re- flects the important concepts. The thing about matrix algebra is that it is rather difficult to learn when you first start. It has a very unnatural way of doing things. However, it does turn out to be the best way, and the same is true about programming languages, not only simulation languages, but about all types.

To think that it is possible to make a rather difficult operation like programming simple for the uninitiated is, I think, a great mistake. You can't do even relatively much simpler operations like playing the violin without some teaching.

Parslow:

I can only comment with Shaw that Cleopatra refused to spend four years learning philosophy in order to play the harp. She wanted actually to do something rather than learn how it should be done.

Caracciolo:

Could you make a comparison between the power of your way of putting things and for instance, Simula. Another way of putting this question: do you think that all problems in which, for instance, the set concept assumes a basic importance can be as easily done in your system?

Parslow:

There are difficulties here with the set concept and, in fact, you finish up by doing something which is very artificial. But at least you always have to do it in this particular way and you get a program which, even though rather badly expressed, does, in fact, operate.

As to a comparison with Simula, I know of no easy way to make such comparisons.

Conway:

I'd like to add to this question of languages that have been devel- oped for the ease of the user. Matrix algebra, for instance, might

be a good example - it's certainly natural, no argument on that -
but it seems to me that you would not spend much time arguing
whether curly brackets or square brackets should be used to en-
close the arrays, or whether capital letters or lower case letters
should be used. I think we are involved in this sort of problem in
some of these languages - we ask the user to take care of lot of
details of punctuation of syntax and we elevate them to the same
rank in the description of the language as the basic concepts which
are important to the process itself. In SIMSCRIPT for example,
the language with which I am most familiar, the user is asked to
do a lot of declaring of forms that have to do with packing. These
have nothing to do with his problems, they are strictly for machine
efficiency. I think we have gone too far in this way and unless somehow we find an order of magnitude reduction in the effort to describe
processes in these languages, they are just not going to be used except by people who devise the languages - us - or by professionals.
These languages are sufficiently esoteric and arcane that people
cannot pick them up and put them down and return to them after six
months and have any facility in using them. This has restricted the
amount of use of these languages to much less than the real opportunity that they represent.

Parslow:

Yes, this is why I used ALGOL. If there's a better language
which lets us leave out all these semi-colons, I'd be only too happy
to use it. Seriously, I think one should take a high-level language
which is in popular use and just use this high-level language without
any additions to it as a simulation language. It doesn't matter much
what the language is as long as they don't need to learn something
new in order to learn how to simulate.

Buxton:

This is a problem which has become more and more apparent to
me over the last year or so and which this discussion has put into
quite strong relief. I used to agree with Strachey in this respect -
that I had an impression that programming was, in fact, only for
the highly intelligent and that the use of computers was in practice
restricted to that sort of person. A lot of our language design, I
think reflects that this viewpoint is widely but unconciously held by
a great many of the professionals in the field. Parslow's suggestion
is that the vast majority of programmers are not of top ability and
should be provided with and constrained to use simple tools in simple
ways. I think this raises a most serious problem for us; who are
computers actually for? Should we be aiding the use of computers
by people who are not trained computer specialists?

SLANG-COMPUTER DESCRIPTION AND SIMULATION-ORIENTED EXPERIMENTAL PROGRAMMING LANGUAGE

L. A. KALINICHENKO

Ukrainian Academy of Sciences, Institute of Cybernetics,
Kiev 28, USSR

SLANG (Simulation LANGuage) is a programming language which is intended to be used as a source language in the experimental programming system whose primary goal is the simplification of the simulation process at the early stage of the design of the computer systems.

The experimental nature of the language is the first reason for its name.

The second reason is that the SLANG incorporates several features which are characteristic for different general purpose system simulation languages and are of great importance for describing and simulating the computer systems.

The paper defines several requirements for the simulation language arising at the early stage of computer system design:

1. The language must include a convenient tool for describing creation processes of flows of nonuniform requests and of servicing the latter.

2. Proceeding from the necessity of description of some processes characteristic to monitor algorithms of computer systems (e.g. scheduler) the language should have a means making it possible to construct and process list structures, item of which being a single request.

3. The simulation language is considered to be not only a simulation tool but a tool of the first stage of the formalized system description. For this reason the description of a system in the language should be brief and convenient.

From this standpoint a comparative analysis of existing languages of the system simulation is further brought about, whereupon a grounded choice of the SLANG language means is effected.

1. INTRODUCTION

Up-to-date multiprogramming computers, complexes of computers, information-control systems (henceforth referred to as CMS - computing machines and systems) are characterized by a great number of devices for storage, processing and transfer of data, operation of which is overlapped. Different information flows generated by input data currents entering CMS circulate among the CMS components.

The following basic characteristics of CMS must be defined at the initial stage of CMS design:
(a) set and principal parameters of CMS components,
(b) configuration of communications among CMS components,
(c) number of control levels of different processes,
(d) priority system for various data flows.

In doing so it should be borne in mind that CMS incorporates a number of control elements (e.g. monitor) establishing an optimum service order inside different processes, the control elements being such that depending on the state of the system a reconstruction may occur: Change in configuration of communications, in the number of control levels, in priorities and algorithms of operation of the control elements proper.

Consequently, the choice of basic characteristic of CMS cannot be accomplished without the choice of operation algorithms of the control elements. To state the problem of designing the CMS optimal in a sense of some index of effectiveness (e.g. possessing a minimum cost of the effective speed [47] is possible only if they are considered jointly.

One of the most important task of the initial stage of CMS design is the construction of the CMS mathematical model. Some of the current methods of obtaining the formalized descriptions of complex systems are given in [14].

Since in constructing the mathematical model it is not always possible to obtain analytic relations completely characterizing the CMS behaviour, the statistical simulation methods are called for the system evaluation in the course of analysis.

2. MAIN REQUIREMENTS TO THE LANGUAGE OF DESCRIPTION AND SIMULATION OF CMS

The experience shows that when the machine language is used for the system description in the process of simulation the time consumed by development and debugging of a program considerably exceeds the time required for stating the problem in analysing. Prob-

lem-oriented languages (e.g. ALGOL) are inconvenient for description of systems. Moreover their usage leads to less effective programs what is inadmissible for simulation.

This conditions the necessity of developing special languages
oriented on easing the interaction between the designer and a computer during the simulation of CMS.

The main requirements to such languages are:

1. According to [14] the process of formalization of the system
under investigation consists of the following stages: Drawing up of
a nonformalized description of a process, building of the formalized scheme and construction of the mathematical model.

Some changes in this sequence may take place when simulation
language is used. That is, the description of a system in simulation language should always follow the nonformalized description.
Such a step can be considered as a first stage of formalization.
The advisability of the step (even if the formalization process will
continue) consists in that in the process of description the essential
features of the CMS are revealed which might be omitted in the informal description.

Upon completion of the CMS description in the simulation language the attempt of applying the analytic or numerical methods of
computation to the whole CMS model or to some processes occurring
in CMS can be made.

Hence, it follows that one of the main requirements to the simulation language as a tool of the first stage of formalization is that
the language must include a set of means leading to a brief and convenient description of models of real processes.

2. The input information of CMS may be considered as the nonuniform input request flow, each request being characterized by the
moment of arrival and a set of parameters. Every request may be
considered as a multidimensional vector.

It is essential that in servicing an input request new requests
having new parameters may appear at different phases in CMS.

The next requirement then reads: The language must include
a convenient tool for describing the creation processes of flows
of nonuniform requests.

3. Proceeding from the necessity of description of some processes characteristic for CMS control algorithms (monitor algorithms
in particular) the language should have means allowing to construct
and process list structures, elements of which being individual requests.

The expediency of incorporating the explicit list structures into
the CMS simulation language becomes understandable, for instance,
in connection with the necessity of describing the scheduling algorithms in which there is a need for means of formation and pro-

cessing of arbitrary sequences of nonuniform requests during the schedule construction.

4. Finally, the CMS simulation language should contain convenient tools for gathering statistics in simulating and means for stating arbitrary distribution functions of random variables.

The subsequent part of the paper is devoted to the choice of means of the SLANG language, which meets the requirements given above.

3. A BRIEF COMPARATIVE ANALYSIS OF THE CURRENT SIMULATION LANGUAGE OF SYSTEMS

A number of programming languages oriented towards the description and simulation of complex systems have been invented by now. GPSS II [35], GPSS III [55], SIMSCRIPT [98], SOL [76], SIMULA [28] can be considered as examples of rather developed languages.

In spite of the difference of terminology the listed languages have very much in common in their core.

First of all, all of these languages are oriented towards the description of discrete event systems [28].

The feature of operation of such systems is the creation of new requests in the process of one input request servicing, nonuniformity of requests and overlapping of the servicing processes at different phases. Just this feature determines the basic peculiarity of information keeping in simulation languages, implying the creation and disappearance of arbitrary data structures (ADS) containing the values of request parameters at any moment.

Such an organization of data structures is used in all above languages, the difference between such structures being only the restrictions imposed by the languages on the permissible classes of request parameters.

Simulation languages imply the existence of connection between ADS and operation rules representing the algorithms of behaviour of some parts of the system and expressed by means of tools of the language procedure part. Every ADS may be considered as moving through the system description program being at a definite point of it at any moment.

In some languages with a distinct declaration part (SOL, SIMULA) it proved convenient to separate syntactically operation rules corresponding to the processes of servincing the uniform requests.

Thus, the system description in the language is represented by several processes describing the actions associated with the uniform request servicing, the syntactical separation of individual processes being made by the designer naturally so that the separated operation rules correspond to certain actual processes occurring in the system.

Some languages (e.g., GPSS II, III, SOL) include special object with fixed characteristics similar to characteristics of components of many real systems.

For instance, objects named facilities and stores are tools for describing time-shared and space-shared components of real systems correspondingly.

Such languages do not require the explicit description of processes of request servicing by any facility or store. All operations on queue formation, priority keeping, pre-emptive servicing are defined by semantics of the language and their execution is a duty of an appropriate interpretive system constructing and processing the necessary lists.

Such possibilities of languages are especially useful in the case when the language is used as a tool for the first formalized system description.

At the same time such automation introduces a certain rigidity and restricts a set of systems conveniently described in the language.

Other languages (e.g., SIMSCRIPT, SIMULA) include lists and list processing tools explicitly due to which the flexibility of the language increases but the size of program increases considerably.

Thus the main differences of the languages consists in:

(a) Different restrictions imposed on arbitrary data structures.

(b) Different flexibility in communication among different procecces and ADS.

(c) Different characteristics of the procedural part of the languages.

(d) Different means for description of the processes of request servicing (in some languages such operations are provided for by semantics, in others - they have to be programmed explicitly).

4. THE CHOICE OF MEANS USED BY SLANG LANGUAGE

The comparative analysis of the current simulation languages and experimental programming of the processes characteristic for CMS have shown that SIMSCRIPT- and SIMULA-languages possess rather flexible set of means. However, the description of CMS models in these languages appears to be much more cumbersome and less natural than, e.g., in SOL-language provided that it is possible to use automatism inherent in this language.

Keeping in mind the importance of natural and brief coding in

formalized system description and similarity of special objects
used in SOL-language to the objects which are the components of
CMS, the use of SOL-language is the base of SLANG was found
to be convenient. This choice was assisted by the fact that for the
experimental language (taking into account its orientation and the
necessity of reducing the job during implementation) it is expedient
to use the language with a simpler procedural part.

Development of SLANG was going in the direction of elimination
of restrictions inherent in SOL-language, which were detected during the experimental programming.

The informal description of the principal differences between
SLANG- and SOL-languages is given below. In the case when the
means used by SLANG-language coincide with the means of other
languages the appropriate references are made.

4.1. *Exchange transactions among processes*

SLANG offers an opportunity to organize interaction among
processes by means of exchange transactions.

A transaction belonging to the other process can be formed
with the help of a generative expression included in the start statement or the one used as an element expression (see 2. Means for
list processing).

⟨generative expression⟩ ::= new ⟨ process identifier ⟩

⟨actual parameter part⟩

⟨start statement⟩::= ⟨generative expression⟩ to ⟨label⟩

Any label in the program is accessible from the inside of the
start statement. This gives an opportunity to start any part of any
process by a given transaction.

Process description is changed in connection with the new form
of the start statement. Local variables are divided into two groups:
exogenous and endogenous.

⟨process description⟩ ::= ⟨process heading⟩

  begin ⟨process declaration list⟩ ; ⟨ statement list⟩

    end

⟨process heading⟩ ::= process ⟨ process identifier ⟩

        ⟨formal parameter part⟩ ; ⟨specification part⟩

The values of exogenous parameters are determined during the
creation of a transaction and calculation of actual parameters of
the generative expression.

All substitutions of parameters are made by value.

4.2. *Means of list processing*

One of the most substantial means incorporated in SLANG for the purpose of improving the flexibility of control of transaction movement in the system are lists and list processing.

List processing technique in the SLANG language in its basic is analogous to the similar means in SIMULA.

Language is provided with:

(a) Global objects types *list* and *element* (*set* and *element* - SIMULA analogs).

(b) Local variables type *element*.

(c) Element expressions and several special functions and procedures for list processing.

⟨element expression⟩ ::= ⟨element name⟩|

⟨function designator⟩|current| none |

   ⟨generative expression⟩

The semantics of the introduced concepts is the same as in SIMULA. (It is worth-while to note that an element in SLANG is a reference to a transaction.)

The following special function designators having the values of *element* type are used in the language:

suc(X)   defines the element which is the successor of the element *X* in a list.

pred(X)   defines the element which is the predecessor of the element *X* in a list.

create(X)   denotes a new element having the same reference to a transaction as the element which is a value of the element expression *X*.

(proc(X)   is an analogous function designator in SUMULA).

head(R)   defines an element which is the head of the list *R*.

Boolean expression applying to elements is completely analogous to the corresponding basic expressions of SIMULA.

As a standard procedure statements for list manipulation the following procedure statements are used:

link(X, Y)   includes element *Y* in a list between *X* and its predecessor.

unlink(X, Y) removes element *Y* from a list and predecessor and successor of *Y* becomes adjacent element in a list.

In connection with the appearance of the means for creation of transaction references in the language the set of possible transaction states has changed.

(a) Transaction moving through the program is in active state.

(b) While interrupted or stayed in one of the following statements (wait, seize, enter, wait until, find, assemble) the transaction is in a waiting state.

(c) Transaction is passive when it is not in a waiting state and is not active.

A transaction is removed from the system if it is in a passive state and if it has no references by means of elements.

The meaning of cancel statement is also changed: It makes the current transaction passive and defines its reactivation point - the next statement in the process.

The standard procedure

$$\text{activate } (\langle \text{element expression} \rangle)$$

activates the passive transaction referred to by an element which is the value of an element expression. In the case when the generative expression is used as an actual parameter of the procedure "activate" a new transaction is activated which starts from the first statement of the corresponding process.

The transaction being activated begins execution of the *wait* 0 statement the insertion of which is implied directly ahead of the statement defined by the reactivation point or before the first statement of the process.

4.3. *Connection*

The presence in the language of the possibility for creating references allows to have an access to local variables of other transactions.

For that purpose the connection statement (analogous by its idea to the SIMULA connection statement) is included in the language and provided with the following syntax:

$\langle$ connection statement $\rangle$ ::=

for $\langle$ element expression $\rangle$ do $\langle$ statement $\rangle$

Since SLANG does not imply the feasibility of using the same identifier for some different purposes in a program the utilization of a more complex construction specifying the identifier of the process defining the local variables used in the connected statement turned out to be useless.

The connected statement is considered to be inserted into description of the process defined by the transaction referred to be an element which is the value of an element expression calculated.

4.4. *Synchronization of processes*

In spite of introduction into SLANG of lists and means for their processing the means for synchronization of concurrent processes were retained and expanded to some degree, namely, the wait until statement was retained and assemble and find statements were incorporated.

The language is equipped by such elements for two reasons. First, in some cases such statements reduce the program size considerably making the description more natural which is essential for the formalized system description.

On the other hand it is interesting to retain in one language two different approaches to the control of the event sequencing to compare their effectiveness in practice.

Find statement is used for programming the algorithms of choosing a certain system object (from a set of objects) satisfying the conditions given.

⟨ find statement ⟩ ::=

find ⟨ array identifier ⟩ [⟨ list of identifiers of indexes ⟩], ⟨ relation ⟩

Find statement determines the values of indexes of the first item in array for which the relation becomes true. Variables, identifiers of which are members of a list of identifiers of indexes obtain values corresponding to the item. The items of an array are tried in a lexicographical order.

In the case when there is no item in an array for which the relation becomes true, the current transaction state is changed from active to wait state. The transaction will remain in this state until not less than one item of array provides the relation value to be true.

For example, there are n identical facilities in a system and a request may use any of the facilities which are not engaged. If all facilities are engaged, the request waits for releasing any one of them.

The searching process of the free facility can be described as follows:

find A[i], A[i] not busy;

(it is assumed that A is a global object introduced by a declaration *facility* A[n];).

Find statement may be augmented by otherwise clause:

⟨ otherwise clause ⟩ ::= otherwise ⟨ statement ⟩

In this case when the necessary item is not found the transaction remains active and executes the statement in an otherwise clause.

In future, it is intended to expand the possibilities of the find

statement. In particular, the opportunity of searching for a necessary element in a list will be given.

Assemble statement is another means of synchronization of concurrent processes.

In the time of creation every transaction acquires an identification mark coinciding with the identification mark of the transaction
which is active when the generative expression is executed. In each
moment of simulated time there are some sets of transaction having the same identification marks in the system. Creation of a new
set is achieved by means of supplement statement, which adds a
current transaction to a new set of transactions which is not inter-
sected with others.

⟨supplement statement⟩ ::= new set

⟨assemble statement⟩::= assemble· ⟨arithmetic expression⟩

The value of arithmetic expression in the assemble statement
determines the number of branches to be synchronized. When the
first transaction belonging to some set reaches the assemble statement it stops and waits for entering into this statement of the other
transactions of the same set, the number of which is equal to the
value of an arithmetic expression in the assemble statement obtained by the first transaction minus one. Each transaction entered
the assemble statement after the first one is subjected to operations
of the cancel statement.

Upon completion of assemblage of all branches the first transaction is activated and continues its movement.

One and the same assemble statement can take part in assembl-
ing the groups of transactions pertaining to different sets simultaneously.

4.5. *New function designators*

The list of standard function of SLANG-language is expanded by:
control (⟨facility name⟩) which has the control strength of the transaction occupying the given facility as a value; and queue (⟨facility
name⟩) which has the queue length of the facility as a value.

Such functions simplify the determination of states in which the
facilities of the system are at a given time moment.

4.6. *Input statement*

The input statement is used for the assigning of initial values to
the global variables and arrays type *real, integer or Boolean.*

⟨input statement⟩ ::=

input ⟨list of identifiers⟩

The input statement may occur in a program only once - immediately after the global declarations and is executed just before the
beginning of the simulation run.

There is a possibility of determining the length of global arrays
dimensions during the execution of an input statement.

Thus the change of a simulated system during the experimentation is simplified.

4.7. *Debugging aids*

The debugging system determines a fixed set of such changes
in the state of the system being simulated which will enable to give
an appropriate printout.

In the language there are means which allow to determine for
every transaction in a system the subsets of the changes in the state
of the system at which it is necessary to give a printout. Besides,
for the debugging purpose the standard procedures are introduced
permitting to obtain information about the transactions which are
in the statement wait, wait until, find, in the queue to any facility
or store at any time moment.

In conclusion, an example of a system description in SLANG
is given.

5. THE EXAMPLE OF A SYSTEM DESCRIPTION IN SLANG

Consider a computer in a time-sharing mode of operation (fig. 1).

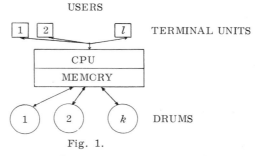

Fig. 1.

Users come up to terminal units at random time moments. Intervals at which the users come up are assumed to be exponentially
distributed. The mean of this interval is equal IUA. The distribution of the number of users' interactions with the computer carried
out during the period of users' staying at the terminal unit and the
distribution of the memory volume required by users' job are assumed to be known. The corresponding distributions are represented
by arrays INT and JV.

(Drawing from such distributions can be performed by a function distr(A) supplying values distributed in accordance with the cumulative distribution function which is obtained by linear interpolation in a equidistant table defined by array A).

In a model the values of the number of interactions (NI) and job volume (VOL) are determined at the time of user's arrival. In the case when at the moment of user's arrival all terminal units are engaged, the user stands in a queue and waits until any of the terminal units becomes free.

After occupying the terminal unit the user's interaction with the computer begins. In every interaction the required central processing unit (CPU) service time is assumed to be exponentially distributed and has a mean T.

On obtaining the answer of the computer the user decides whether to leave the terminal unit or to go on interacting. In the case of continuation the user "thinks" in the course of random interval of time the length of which has an exponential distribution with mean THT and then repeats the interaction.

In every interaction the computer allots its time to the user in fixed quanta q.

To get the next quantum of time the user enters the queue waiting for the necessary space in a core memory (MEMORY).

Then the request for job loading from the drum is generated. It is assumed here that the user's job with equal probability is placed on any drum (DRUM[1], DRUM[2]... DRUM[K]).

After loading from the drum the user's job is moved into the queue to get the quantum of time from the computer (CPU).

On getting the quantum the job is placed into drum and the space in the core memory is freed.

If the user's servicing is completed he receives the answer from the computer. Otherwise the cycle is repeated.

In regard to the process representing the data exchange with the drum it is assumed that exchange with each drum can be performed by means of individual channel. Therefore the request queues are organized separately for each drum. The period when the drum is engaged is composed of the search time (it is assumed to be equal to a half revolution time $T/2$) and the exchange time $t \times WN$, where t is time of one word exchange, WN is number of words in a job.

1. begin integer a, b, d, e, f, k, IUA, IT, s, l, t, T, INT[a],

2.   JV[b], THT;

3.   facility CPU, DRUM[k];

4.   store   TU, 1, MEMORY, s;

5. begin TAB (d step e until f);

6.   input (a, b, t, T, d, e, f, k, IUA, IT, INT, JV, THT, s, l);

7.   process USER(NI, VOL); integer NI, VOL;

8. begin

9.   M:new USER (distr(INT), distr(JV)) to M1;

10.   wait exponent (IUA); go to M;

11.   M1: enter TU;

12.   M2: new QUANTUM (exponent(IT), VOL, time,

13.   current) to SERV; cancel;

14.   NI: = NI - 1; if NI ≠ 0 then

15. begin wait exponent (THT); go to M2 end;

16.   leave TU

17. end   USER;

18. process QUANTUM(ST, CORE, T, REF);

19.   integer ST, CORE, T; element REF;

20. begin cancel;

21.   SERV: enter MEMORY, CORE;

22.   new ACCESS (CORE, current, 1:k) to D;

23.   cancel;

24.   seize CPU; a:= if q > ST else q;

25.   ST:=ST-a;   wait a;

26.   release CPU;

27.   new ACCESS (CORE, current, 1:k) to D;

28.   cancel;

29.   leave MEMORY, CORE;

30. if ST ≠ 0 then go to SERV;

31.   tabulate time - T in TAB;

32.   activate (REF)

33. end QUANTUM;

34.   process ACCESS (WN, REF1, DN);

35.   integer WN, DN; element REF 1;

36. begin cancel;

37. D: seize DRUM [DN];

38.   wait T/2 + t × WN;

39.   release DRUM [DN];

40.   activate (REF1)

41. end ACCESS

42. end

     comments

line 4.   In the model terminal units (TU) are represented by store
           owing to which the user's queue description is simplified.
           l = quantity of terminal units, s = capacity of core memory.
line 5.   Table TAB is used for gathering statistics about the time
           when user waits at the terminal unit.
line 6.   The input statement reads the values of listed variables
           before the beginning of simulation. At the input time the
           length of arrays INT, JV, DRUM, intervals and the length
           of table TAB are determined.
line 7.   Process USER (lines 7-17) describes user's behaviour in
           the system.
lines 9 to 10. Here the generation of a new user takes place.
line 11.   The search for free terminal unit and the queue to termi-
           nal units are represented by *enter* statement.
line 12.   The user's interaction with the computer is initiated by
           the start statement. The created transaction contains a
           reference to the current transaction and is transferred
           into another process.
           The moment of request generation (*time*) is stored in the
           transaction. The transaction which represents the user
           is transferred into the passive state.
line 14.   On obtaining the answer from the computer (procedure
           statement activate in line 32) the necessity of further in-
           teraction is determined.
line 15.   Wait statement introduces a delay corresponding to the
           "thinking" time.
line 16.   The user leaves the terminal unit.
line 18.   Process QUANTUM (lines 18 through 33) describes the
           behaviour of the computer which services the user's re-
           quest.

Every transaction has the following parameters:
ST = time required from computer for servicing in a
given interaction, CORE = number of memory cells
occupied by the given user, T = moment of interaction
initiation, REF = reference to a process USER transaction waiting for service completion.

line 21. The queue of users' requests for memory space is formed
by means of enter statement.

line 22. Here the request for job loading from the drum is created.
The drum number is determined from equal probability
distribution $(1:k)$.

line 23. The transaction is transferred into the passive state and
waits for activation at the completion of job loading (line
40).

line 27. The request for job writing to the drum is created here.

line 29. Leave statement is executed by the transaction upon its
activation after completion of the job writing on the drum.

line 31. The value of the answer waiting time is tabulated in TAB.

line 34. Process ACCESS (lines 34 through 41) describes the data
exchange with the drum.

Each transaction in the process is characterized by param
eters:

WN = number of words in the job,

REFI = reference to the transaction waiting for data
exchange completion,

DN = drum number.

DISCUSSION

Nygaard:

I met Kalinichenko in Kiev last fall and my impression was that
he considers SLANG as suitable for a reasonably small computer -
and I should like to know if any of the Soviet delegation knows
whether he or others intend to implement SLANG on the BESM 6
computer which is the likely choice for the Institute of Cybernetics
in Kiev. Is it intended for implementation on a large scale computer?

Beliakov:

This is not impossible.

Knuth:

I can say for myself that I believe Kalinichenko has made a very good analysis of the deficiencies of the SOL language, and he put in features which were intended specifically to overcome some deficiencies in that language.

SIMULATION PROGRAMMING LANGUAGES - NORTH-HOLLAND (1968)

SIMULATION OF DISCRETE
INFORMATION SYSTEMS

M. I. NECHEPURENKO, A. H. HAIRUTDINOV and G. V. SHABROV

*Computing Centre, USSR Academy of Sciences,
Siberian Division, Novosibirsk 90, USSR*

Abstract: This paper gives a short account of a DIS language specialized in description and time simulation of physical systems for discrete information processing. The term "system" will be used for physical objects. The term "scheme" will be used for their abstract models.

1. SCHEMES, BLOCKS, PROCESSES

A scheme description is a description of a fixed totality of algorithmic processes in their development and interaction. The groups of the scheme processes termed "blocks" correspond to the real autonomous functional devices of the information system, and the block input/output information corresponds to the physical poles of the devices.

The real communication lines of the system are represented in the scheme by corresponding identification of the block input/output information. The variable "time" representing the current time of the system life is related with the scheme.

Interaction between the processes from different blocks take place only through the input/output information of the corresponding blocks.

In addition to the input $I_i[k]$ information and the output information $I_0[k]$, a local information $I_l[k]$ is related with the block $B[k]$.

Conceptions of a state and an event are related with the processes. A final set of the process states is fixed for each process. The process can be in two phases: active and passive. In the active phase the process $\Pi[j]$ is resultative, that is, it can transform the input and local information of a block and change its state $Z[j]$. The active phase of the process is executed instantaneously: a set of the time instants of activity of every execution forms a discrete sequence of points on the time axis. The active phase of a process is termed an event.

Thus each process (hence a joint process of the scheme as well) is a system of discrete events according to the terminology used in [28].

If the process $\Pi[j]$ is in the passive phase the following objects are related with it: $t[j]$ is a time label (a planned time instant of the nearest event in a system $0 \leqslant t[j] \leqslant +\infty$), and $B[j](I_l[k]I_i[k]$, time) is a Boolean expression (value) which stirs the process to activity independently of the value of $t[j]$.

The value of $t[j]$ and the expression (value) of $B[j](.\,,.\,,.\,)$ are fixed after an event execution in the process.

The process of a block can interact directly: one (active) process can stop another process, i.e. fix for it $t[j] = +\infty$ and $B[j] \equiv$ *false*, or it can stir the stopped process to avtivity, i.e. it can fix for it $t[j] =$ time or $B[j] = true$.

The variable "time" (a standard identifier) is related to a totality of the scheme processes. This variable is the scheme model time.

A process development order is assumed to be based on the principle "all consequences are realized after overall execution of the event in which causes have arised". This prevents possible contradictions in the actions coinciding in one event and eliminates the dependence of the process developments on the order of their realization in stimulating.

The processes in a scheme develop and interact according to the events.

Suppose that the value "time" has been defined at some stage of the development of a joint process and there are processes in which events are fixed for the time instant "time". Following is the sequence of realization of these events and further development of the processes:

1) The active process algorithms transforming the block output and local information are realized

$$(I_l[k], I_o[k]): = A[j, Z[j]](I_l[k], I_i[k]) . \tag{1}$$

A new value assignment is realized after accomplishment of all the fixed events.

New states of the active processes are defined

$$Z[j]: = S[j, Z[j]](I_l[k], I_i[k]) . \tag{2}$$

The old values are used in the right hand sides of (1) and (2).

The processes which should be started or stopped are marked.

2) New time marks are calculated for the active processes

$$t[j]: = T[j, Z[j]](I_l[k], I_o[k], \text{ time}) \tag{3}$$

and the functions

$$B[j]: = B[j, Z[j]] \tag{4}$$

are fixed. If naturally we assume that (3) is independent of the choice of the time count origin we come to

$$t[j]: = \text{time} + D[j, Z[j]](I_l[k], I_o[k]) . \tag{5}$$

The new values obtained at step 1) are used in the right hand sides of (4) and (5).

3) The process interaction statements are realized, i.e. $t[j]$ and $B[j]$ are changed for the processes marked at step 1).

4) If there are processes with $t[j]$ = time or $B[j](I_l[k], I_i[k], \text{time})$ = *true* we go to step 1), otherwise we calculate time = min $t[j]$, in this way stirring to activity the processes with t = time, and then we go to step 1).

2. LANGUAGE FOR THE TIME SIMULATION OF SCHEMES

The description of the DIS language principal structures given below is based on the ALGOL-60 conceptions. The ALGOL conceptions are enclosed in the brackets ⟨ ⟩. The double brackets ⟪ ⟫ are used for the newly introduced conceptions.

The DIS description of the simulation program of the scheme (which is a full time model of the scheme) implies that the model description (that of a simulated object) is separated from the task description for the experiment with the model. In the model description the description of its network (i.e. the block structure and the permanent information connections) is separated from that of the block operation algorithms.

⟪simulation program⟫:: =
    test
    ⟪scheme or block description⟫
    ⟪experiment description⟫
    end

⟪scheme or block description⟫
    ⟪scheme description⟫|
    ⟪block description⟫

2.1. *Scheme description*

⟪scheme description⟫ :: =
    <u>scheme</u> ⟨identifier⟩
    ⟨formal parameter part⟩
    ⟪input part⟫
    ⟪output part⟫
    ⟪parameter and scheme variable description part⟫
    ⟪subscheme description part⟫
    <u>subscheme</u> ⟪subscheme part⟫
    <u>network</u> ⟪network description⟫
    <u>end</u>

Scheme parameters may be given values in the experiment description and/or in the structure description of the scheme into which the given scheme enters as a subscheme.

As usual

⟨formal parameter part⟩ :: =
    ⟨empty⟩ | (⟪identifier list⟫)
⟪identifier list⟫ :: =
    ⟪identifier⟫|
⟪identifier list⟫, ⟨identifier⟩

A scheme parameter may be either a scalar (i.e. a variable of *Boolean, real* and *integer* type) or a one-dimensional array. The type and structure of the scheme parameters are described in the parameter and scheme variable description part.

Scheme input and output parts are of the form:

⟪input part⟫ :: = ⟨empty⟩ |
    <u>input</u> (⟪identifier list⟫)
⟪output part⟫ :: = ⟨empty⟩ |
    <u>output</u> (⟪identifier list⟫)

The variables which form the input (output) information of the scheme are enumerated in the scheme input (output) parts, the type and structure of these variables being described in the parameter and scheme variable description part.

The parameter and scheme variable description part is an ALGOL description of a simple variable type and a description of arrays.

A subsheme description part is an enumeration (without special delimiters) of the scheme or block description where the blocks from the described scheme:

⟪subscheme description part⟫ :: =
    ⟪scheme or block description⟫ |
    ⟪subscheme description part⟫
    ⟪scheme or block description⟫

Actually the kinds of subschemes and blocks are enumerated in the subscheme description part. The kind is indicated by a corresponding identifier.

The scheme structure description contains a list of individual representatives forming the described scheme.

⟪subscheme part⟫ :: =
    ⟪subscheme title⟫ |
    ⟪cyclic subscheme list⟫ |
        begin ⟪subscheme list⟫ end

⟪subscheme list⟫ :: =
    ⟪subscheme part⟫ |
    ⟪subscheme list⟫ ;
    ⟪subscheme part⟫

⟪subscheme title⟫ :: =
    ⟨identifier⟩
    ⟨actual parameter part⟩

It is assumed that the actual parameter part has the structure identical to the formal parameter part (which is described in the corresponding subscheme description).

The cyclic subscheme list is of the form:

⟪cyclic subscheme list⟫ :: =
    for ⟨variable⟩: = ⟨for list⟩ form
    ⟪subscheme part⟫

Correspondence between the input and output information on the one hand and its subschemes on the other hand is postulated in the network description.

The input (output) information of the scheme is regulated in the input (output) part in a natural manner and it can be considered as a vector, i.e. a one-dimensional regulated array of (generally speaking, many-typed) scalar variables of the *Boolean, integer* and *real* types. We consider a scalar variable as a one-dimensional vector.

The subschemes forming the described scheme are regulated in the subscheme part. This makes it possible to refer, for example, to the nth member of the subscheme, the type of which is described in the subscheme description part and which has a fixed identifier, by means of the structure

⟨identifier⟩ number n

If the scheme contains only one member of the subscheme of the given type, then instead of the reference

⟨identifier⟩ number 1

one may simply use

⟨identifier⟩

Thus we define

《reference to subscheme》 :: =
    ⟨identifier⟩ |
    ⟨identifier⟩ number 《copy number》
《copy number》 :: = variable

Here the variable is of an *integer* type.

In accordance with the subscheme regulation we suppose that all the input and output information of the scheme and its subschemes is regulated as follows:

It is possible to address the inputs and outputs of the scheme from its description by means of the identifiers which are enumerated in the input and output parts.

The following structures are based on the regulation of the scheme external information and make it possible to address the scheme input and output parts:

《standard identifier of inputs and outputs》 :: =
    input scheme | output scheme |
    input 《reference to subscheme》 |
    output 《reference to subscheme》 |
    input network | output network

The following conception is used generally with references to the scalar variable parts:

⟪reference to vector⟫ :: =
   ⟪composite expression⟫|
   ⟪distinguishing expression⟫

⟪composite expression⟫ :: =
   ⟪simple composite expression⟫|
   ⟪cyclic composite expression⟫

⟪simple composite expression⟫ :: =
   ⟨identifier⟩|
   ⟪standard identifier of inputs and outputs⟫|
   (⟪totality of references to vector⟫)

⟪totality of references to vector⟫ ::=
   ⟪reference to vector⟫|
   ⟪totality of references to vector⟫ ,
   ⟪reference to vector⟫

⟪cyclic composite expression⟫ :: =
   <u>for</u> ⟨variable⟩: = ⟨for list⟩ <u>form</u>
   ⟪reference to vector⟫

The simplest form of the distinguishing expression is

$$(A)[P]$$

where A is a reference to vector and P is an arithmetic expression. If vector A is described as an array of the $n \geqslant p$ dimension, then $(A)[p]$ is a scalar quantity which (as pointed out above) is considered as a one-dimensional array (vector). If A is not a cyclic composite expression, then the structure $A[p]$ is used instead of $(A)[p]$. If α is a scalar the reference $[1]$ is equivalent to α. In particular, if A is an arbitrary vector, then $(A)[p][1]$ is equivalent to $(A)[p]$.

Evidently, the reference A to the vector described as an n-dimensional array is equivalent to the use of the cyclic composite expression

<u>for</u> i: = 1 <u>step</u> 1 <u>until</u> n <u>form</u> $(A)[i]$.

Both in the cyclic composite expression and in the for list one may use the brief enumerations in the ⟨for list⟩ by employing three points (this structure is accepted in the ALPHA language [159] which is an extension of the ALGOL-60 language). Thus, for example, if A is an n-dimensional vector, then the cyclic expression

<u>for</u> i: = p <u>step</u> 1 <u>until</u> q <u>form</u> $(A)[i]$

for $1 \leqslant p \leqslant q \leqslant n$ is equivalent to

$$((A)[p], \ldots, (A)[q])$$

and

$$\underline{\text{for}} \; i: = p, \ldots, q \; \underline{\text{form}} \; (A)[i] \; .$$

A network description is a totality of the information identification statements:

《network description》 :: =
  《identification statement》|
  《cyclic indentification statement》|
  begin 《identification statement list》 end

《identification statement》 :: =
  《reference to vector》 ─ 《reference to vector》

《cyclic identification statement》
  for ⟨variable⟩: = ⟨for list⟩ do
  《network description》

《identification statement list》 :: =
  《network description》|
  《identification statement list》 ;
  《network description》

The direction of the pointer   is interpreted as the direction of the corresponding connection line. In the identification statement it is possible to use the identification vector which is not described in the parameter and scheme variable description part. These vectors are localized in the network description. The identification statement in which they occur in the left hand side may simultaneously be considered as their description. Every such vector may occur only once in the left hand sides of the identification statements which form the network description.

2.2. Block description

《block description》 :: =
  block ⟨identifier⟩
  ⟨formal parameter part⟩
  《input part》
  《output part》
  《block parameter and variable description part》
  《block body》
  end

The block parameter and variable description part differs from the scheme parameter and variable description part in that the scheme may contain the description of the block local information $l_1[k]$ (see section 1).

The block body is a totality of the labelled descriptions of its processes (that is, algorithmic processes).

An algorithm process is described in the ALPHA language (the language of the ALGOL type) [159]. The description of the algorithmic process is given in a labelled block form. The statement list is supplemented with the synchronization statements. Each algorithmic process $\Pi[j]$ involves the conception of its state $Z[j]$. The state $Z[j]$ defines the first event statement which is planned in $\Pi[j]$. The statement of the internal synchronization process is the one which completes the event. The statement following that of internal synchronization is the statement of the next event.

The total form of the statement of the internal synchronization process is:

wait while φ or wait ψ ,

where φ is a Boolean expression and ψ is an arithmetic expression. φ an ψ depend on the input and local block variables. φ is allowed to depend on "time".

The statement (6) realizes the operations (4) and (5)

$$B[j] = \varphi , \qquad t[j] = \text{time} + \psi .$$

In case of the improper value ψ ($\psi = +\infty$) we may use the statement

wait while φ

which is equivalent to

wait while φ or wait $(+\infty)$

When φ is a Boolean *false* value we may introduce the brief record

wait ψ

which is equivalent to

wait while false of wait ψ .

If $\psi = +\infty$ we may use for this statement the record

cancel

which, obviously, is equivalent to

wait whith false

It is easy to see that the following statements are equivalent

<u>wait</u> <u>while</u> <u>true</u> <u>or</u> <u>wait</u> ψ
<u>wait</u> <u>while</u> φ <u>or</u> <u>wait</u> 0
<u>wait</u> <u>while</u> <u>true</u>
<u>wait</u> 0

There are two types of the external synchronization statements. The statement which stops another process $\Pi[j]$ labelled M is

<u>cancel</u> M .

As a result of its application the following assignments take place (at the third step of the event development in the scheme):

$$B[j]: = \underline{false}$$
$$t[j]: = +\infty$$

The operator which stirs to activity the process $\Pi[j]$ labelled M is either

<u>jump</u> M

or

<u>continue</u> M .

The events prescribed in the process $\Pi[j]$ has, as its first statement, either the initial statement of the process algorithm (in case of <u>jump</u>) or the first statement of the event before which $\Pi[j]$ has been stopped (in case of <u>continue</u>). One is allowed to use compound labels. As a result of the operation of the statement jump the following assignments take place (at the third step of the event development in the scheme):

$$B[j]: = \underline{true}$$
$$t[j]: = \text{time} .$$

2.3. *Experiment description*

⟪experiment description⟫ :: =
  ⟪initial value block⟫
  ⟪block of the statistic data collection and processing⟫ .

The input and output variables of the scheme and the subscheme are used as variables (of the experiment) in the experiment description.
The reference to the input and output variables and parameters of the described scheme is

⟪reference to vector⟫ .

The reference to the input, output and local variables of the sub-schemes contains a compound reference (in accordance with the hierarchic structure of the scheme) to the subscheme as well as the reference to the corresponding vector:

《compound reference to subscheme》 :: =
    《reference to subscheme》|
    《compound reference to subscheme》 .
    《reference to subscheme》 .

Thus we have

    《reference to variable   :: =
    《reference to vector》|
    《compound reference to subscheme》.
    《reference to vector》 .

The initial block is constructed by analogy with an ALGOL block. Besides the following references to variables and initial value assignment statements are used:

    《reference to variable》 = 《value》 .

Here 《value》 is a one-dimensional value array.

The block of the statistic data collection and processing is constructed by analogy with an ALGOL block too. Besides one uses references to variables and standard identifier "time" (the scheme model time). In this block the transition to the statement stop (of the input language of the ALPHA translator) corresponds to the completion of the simulation program operation.

The initial value block is performed at the beginning of the simulation program operation.

The block of the statistic data collection and processing is performed after completion of each event.

2.4. *Standard procedures*

Standard procedures for pseudorandom numbers, array regulations, histogram processing and formation are introduced for the sake of a compact entry of the processes and statements of the statistic data collection and processing. The standard procedure list contains, in particular, appropriate procedures of the SIMULA language [28]. In addition to the standard procedures, it is possible to use the standard blocks and to design an appropriate standard block list.

3. DISCUSSION

When working out the DIS language we followed the principal that a language for the description of the discrete information systems should be a block general algorithmic language which would allow a visual description of a block structure and permanent information connections in the system. None of the known simulation languages possesses the above properties, though it should be stressed that some of them, especially such as SIMCRIPT [98], SIMULA [28], MAD (supplemented to a simulation language) [127] and GPSS [35] have had an undoubtedly significant influence upon our work.

At the same time we ought to point out two disadvantages of the DIS language, as they are important for the general purpose of simulation. These are:

1) The block *test* is not intended to be used as the ALGOL language block (thus, the DIS language which uses all means of the ALGOL language is not its extension).

2) In course of a single simulation program run the number of the processes in the scheme described in the DIS language remains permanent (an essential restriction as compared with SIMULA [28].

DISCUSSION

Nygaard:

Maybe I should make some comments upon this language and tell you a little about the background for this work. As you know, it has been developed at the Computing Centre in the Academic City of Novasibirsk. The background here is that they are intending to develop an information system - a whole computer system - to serve the whole Academic City. They are first going to work on alternative experimental set-ups, and it is rather important for them to be able to simulate these. They have presently a rather small computer, the BESM 3. They decided to make a special purpose simulation language which could be of use in this work.

They also have some alternative systems they want to analyse, which can be described by the structure which is imposed by this language. The people over there are completely aware of what they want, they want to analyse a special type of structure, and they have created something which is rather easy to implement and can be run efficiently on the computer they have at hand.

Carracciolo:

I have not exactly understood the time mechanism. Could you add some words about this?

Lavrow :

There is a special time variable which controls each process. When a process is carried out the time variable $t(j)$ which is bound to this process is assigned a new value.

Knuth :

There are two conditions for being active; one is the time value and the other is a Boolean condition, and the time advance is to the next event.

GENERAL DISCUSSION - SESSION 2

Knuth:

I think a very appropriate topic to start the general discussion is this: what sort of things are to be done in the design of languages and simulation languages in particular? We all know that the design of languages is very difficult and is an activity which involves many different phases - and we are trying to find the best way to solve it. We have about 20 goals in mind, and we cannot achieve any one of them without denying some of the others.

The points which were raised earlier were whether we should design for the unsophisticated programmer and whether we should try to protect the programmer from making any possible errors. I think these are two issues which should cause some discussion.

Hutchinson:

I would like to add one more question - who should be doing the simulations anyhow?

Steel:

I should like to speak on this point about Buxton's inexperienced programmers - there is a serious point here in trying to make these languages easy to use, that does not require the assumption that we are trying to make them so that they can be used by the ill-prepared. Let me take an example outside of programming where simple notation made a vast difference in the ability of people to rapidly learn and assimilate a concept, and that is the notation of tensor calculus. Prior to introduction of that notation one could still talk about the concepts of tensors, but it was very difficult to do, it was difficult to explain, it was hard for people to learn. Now the introduction of special notation and special conventions that were natural to the subject in no way meant that all of a sudden tensor calculus was open to all and sundry, but it did mean that those people who needed to use it, could far more rapidly learn and far more easily remember many of the pertinent notions and could more effectively work with it. It seems to me these are the kind of criteria that we want to look for in language designing; to make it easy for the people who do have to use it, rather than having a lot of extraneous material so that only some sort of priesthood spending their lives to learn special conventions can use it.

Strachey:

It seems to me that in general there are two completely different things that you want to do in designing languages. The first is
to provide power in the language; to provide the facilities which do
naturally and simply the things which are powerful and natural and
simple, like the tensor calculus. And you want to make this easy,
in the sense that they can be done naturally in the language. The
powerful concepts should correspond to constructs in the language.
That is one thing.

The other thing is concerned with the introduction of new ideas
such as the use of block structure. Whenever you come across a
new idea from the outside, it is very difficult to understand. It is
very difficult to understand for about a year or two, until you have
been using it, then suddenly you can not understand why you did not
understand before and you can not understand why somebody else
does not understand it. If it is a good concept it becomes a necessary concept. Take as an example the use of conditional expressions; this is natural to about half the programmers working at present and quite unnatural to the others.

The interesting thing is that when you provide a really new power
in a language, to begin with people say, "we do not want it". Then
after a very short time they can not imagine using a language that
has not got it.

On quite a different level of seriousness, but with much greater
impact, is what I call the problem of syntatic decoration of a language i.e. whether you put in semicolons, whether you use gram-
matical forms, heavily underlined words, begins and ends, curly
brackets etc. This stuff, which Landin christened "syntatic sugar"
though sometimes I would prefer to say "syntatic vinegar" - this
level of importance is clearly of no mathematical interest. It is,
however, the thing that strikes the beginner who first comes to the
language most heavily. The fact that you always have to put in semicolons is one of the most irritating things in Algol. The fact that
there are a lot of irrational things that have to be done in some
fixed order is another.

I think most programming language designers do not spend nearly
enough time seeking the convenience of the man who is going to
write the program in this sort of minor, unimportant syntatic way.
The ends of lines should be the ends of statements if they obviously
are the ends of statements. If you want to write "unless" instead of
"if not", you should be able to do so. You should be able to write
reasonable approximations. There should be flexibility, the language should be natural. People do not remember the regulations
exactly, only approximately. In that sort of way it seems possible,
without changing the nature of the language, to make it more convenient.

I think that simply leaving out difficult ideas is not the right way
- not the right thing to do with the language to make it easier to use.
If you do not understand the difficult ideas there is no reason why
you should use them.

Knuth:

I think you miss the point - the most important thing in the programming language is the name. A language will not succeed without a good name. I have recently invented a very good name and
now I am looking for a suitable language.

Dahl:

I have a very small comment on what Mr. Strachey said. I am a
firm believer in a strong syntax and the syntax should be thought
about very seriously by the designer of a language. I do not think
that it is wise to have too much freedom within the syntax for the
programmers, because they will develop rather different styles
and then communication becomes not so easy. It is much easier to
communicate if you force programmers into the same syntax.

Knuth:

So we have now the issue whether there should be one obvious
way to write something or whether there should be many equivalent
ways.

Brennan:

I come really as a representative of the continuous system simulation field and certainly with no credentials in the discrete area.
But listening today I come away with the feeling that if a priesthood
exists, it is more likely to be in the discrete field than in the continuous. In our field we had such a priesthood; for complicated
problems one had to belong to the exclusive group in order to use
an analogue computer well. In reaction to this we have had to make
the effort to design languages which the ordinary, technically
trained person, engineer or scientist, could use, many of whom
would in fact resent the title of "programmer". I question whether
or not the discrete field would not benefit from having been burned
as we were. I sense that the priesthood is still strongly supported
here?

Laski:

I want to distinquish between the words apprehension and apprehensibility. I am worried about any kind of discrimination I can

make in program text that does not have a meaning. If two pieces
of program text look different whether in lay-out or in use of words,
I am worried unless I can clearly know whether or not they are the
same in intended content. Furthermore I do not like stuttering, I
do not like saying anything twice, - and if I mark anything by layout, I do not want to mark it by signs like stars or semicolons.

Steel:

The opposing lines seem to be drawing up here, Laski and Dahl
on one side, and, believe it or not, Strachey and I on the other side.
I can claim to be somewhat of an expert on this point, having served
as editor of the proceedings of a previous conference of this sort
which Strachey attended. I believe he and I communicate very well,
but I can assure you that our syntax is wide apart.

Seriously, the question of syntax having to be the same does not
apply to people-to-people communication. I think the very fact that
we are all sitting around the table here is evidence enough that we
do not need that kind of careful layout to understand each other. I
believe that Laski's point was that all of this ought to be spelled out
carefully - if that is what he means, I agree with him. You have to
define carefully what you mean. For example, I do not think that
we would accept for a synonym for "go to" something like "please,
machine, would you be kind enough to go to this label".

Laski:

I would like to add that the CPL language is defined using a canonical form and then local conventions translatable into this form
can be specified. I believe this way is a proper way to bring convenient flexibility of syntax into languages. You need a still point
somewhere in the turning world.

Nygaard:

I am going to leave the subject of notation and go back to the
question of a general language versus special purpose languages
in simulation: I think we have to realize that when we use simulation we want to use it on a very wide range of phenomena, and they
may be utterly different. Just compare the system of an epidemic
which is spreading through a social system with a queuing situation
with a fixed number of queues and services. These need completely
different instructions. And therefore you must have a very wide
range of features which you can model with your language.

Another thing is that the operational groupings in systems, e.g.
in a factory, are very complicated. One of the advantages of simulation is that we can make our own model to fit the real situation,

instead of simplifying the situation to suit the model. Therefore you must have great power in formulating things inside the system and this introduces a definite need for general purpose languages in simulation.

Then we turn to the question of making special purpose areas simple. But we have a very large number of different types of systems, so if we should create a special purpose language for each of these areas, I think that we would be in trouble. Also, a person using a simple system soon becomes dissatisfied and wants more power. Should he first learn one simple technique and then a more powerful one later? I think that it is better to take another approach, namely to try to introduce the possibility of creating dialects within the general languages. You should provide means so that you easily can define highly aggregated concepts, data types, procedures etc.

Then you have the situation that for the people who want to use simple dialects all the terms of the highly aggregated concepts can be used. So as they need more power, they can, inside this dialect, have the power of the general language. I think this will be possible, and I think this is something which will prove to be very useful in the future.

Caracciolo:

My remark is very similar to one which has been made by Nygaard. A simulation language seems to me especially valuable from a conceptional point of view, as an aid to the model designer. It seems generally possible to reduce simulation language features to another sequencial language. However, generally speaking a problem-oriented language seems to me to have two values; a conceptual value for identifying the basic concepts relating to a given field of applications, and a value as a useful tool for people having actually to write many similar problems.

I would also add a remark on the concept of dialect. I would say, this is not what we should like, but rather we would prefer what might be called self-defining features in the language, i.e. providing in a language means for defining special concepts to be used within the language. This is actually a feature which is being considered by general purpose programming language designers but it has a long way to go. We might achieve the point when all special problem-oriented languages could be considered to be defined within a very general system.

I would simply add a final remark, that an important point seems to me to find some means for comparing the powerfulness and naturalness of the various simulation languages with respect to the type of systems to be modelled and simulated.

Conway:

I would like to say something back on syntatic sugar. In 1962 a group at Cornell implemented a compiler and processer for a language, trying to see mostly out of curiosity how far one could go in building a very tolerant system. We took a very simple syntax just to make our problems easier and then built a processer that would tolerate almost anything. You could feed it any punctuation you liked and any spelling of the key words. There were only two rules. One was that the compiler always produced executable code; there was nothing you could do to it to cause it to quit. Secondly, that with anything it did it had to output a sufficient description. This was intended for student jobs with short run times so that there was no great loss of computer time.

There were really two strategies built in this. One was a simple list of synonyms; by going through other languages we picked up many of the synonyms and took them in, so that you could have your choice. The other was that there was room for some of the obvious mistakes in spelling and key punching to be rectified, such as wrong shift uses and character transpositions.

This was intended for a neophyte programmer but it turned out after a while even experienced programmers would use the system. We thought originally that people would be weaned away from it into one of the senior languages, but on the contrary people stayed with it longer than we had intended. Senior people who went off to the cold cruel world of FORTRAN were annoyed by the ridiculous things that FORTRAN would do to them, when they mis-spelled the word "dimension" or made some other simple error.

The frequency with which correct assumptions were made by the compiler was surprisingly high; something in the neighbourhood of 50% of the syntatic errors were corrected by the system itself. If you measured the success of programmers by noting the number of approaches that they had to make to the machine in order to get successful execution, this too is reduced by a factor of about 2.

Strachey:

Firstly, about general or special purpose languages. This argument is now raging in the language design field. Some ten to fifteen years ago it was raging in the machine design field. Then it became perfectly obvious that a special purpose machine was merely a badly designed general purpose machine with a few extra instructions put in. It was badly designed because it was designed by people who did not know how to design machines but were particularly interested in that problem area.

This leads me to the second point, about self-extending languages, or languages which allow the user to extend his language. Designing programming languages is a highly specialized task and very few people who use computers know very much about designing the languages. I do not think they are required to do so. I do not think it is a good idea to expect users to be able to design their languages or to extend their languages in a self-consistent or logical way.

Since Laski mentioned CPL and what it does about syntactic sugar, I think I have an excuse to say what actually happens in CPL. There is a canonical form of CPL in the same way as ALGOL had a reference set. Unfortunately, the ALGOL authors never bothered to make the publication set usable and took too much care to make the reference set usable. Nobody has ever described canonical CPL as usable. A canonical CPL program is pretty difficult to write; it consists of a long string of small integers.

In the preprocessor all the problems about recognizing names and brackets and things like that have been done; all the syntactic sugar has been removed. There are various implemented preprocessors and there are local implementation rules about translating from an implementation alphabet to the canonical form. These rules include rules about how to interpret lay-out, because lay-out is important. To anyone who thinks it is not I recommend that they write - say - three pages of ordinary high-school algebra as current text with no gaps and semicolons between the equations and see if they understand it.

It is important to realize that the local version or local alphabet can have an influence on the language which is much deeper than you expect. For example, how you recognize identifiers is certainly determined or influenced by whether you have upper case as well as lower case letters. Whether you allow juxtaposition in your language to mean multiplication or whether you insist on inserting a multiplication sign will probably depend on whether you have upper case and lower case letters.

This sort of thing is not part of the central core of the language, it is part of the syntatic sugar. It is very important to realize this. The publication language should take advantage of the fact that when you print something, you have a very large character set, much larger than anything that we have on any computer. And we should take advantage of the fact that it is possible for printers to put signs not only in a straight line but all over the paper. I think that the publication version of a language should be designed to make it as easy as possible to understand the parenthetical structure of programs, which is often the hardest thing to understand.

Knuth:

I believe tensor calculus is largely based on syntactic sugar; the usefulness of it is in the layout. You want syntax not only designed to be a way of expressing the concepts so that the computer can read them; it should also help you visualize what is going on, whenever possible.

Petrone:

I am against flexibility in the syntax of languages for man to man communication. If one likes to put flexibility in a computer one may build up a private preprocesser which translates into a standard way of expressing things from ones own private language. But until the time comes when man to man communication will be facilitated by machines, one has to rely on a fixed way of expressing things, in order to facilitate the task of people.

These private preprocessers are very simple to make - there is no problem with them.

Lackner:

This reference a few minutes ago about simulation languages called us back a little from this talk about syntax and other things which really apply to almost any language. I would be grateful if tomorrow one of the chairman might redirect us toward essential differences - if there really are any, between simulation languages and other programming languages. I think there is a difference, and I think it lies in the concepts, which we try to develop in order to make the description easier than they would be otherwise.

Laski:

Some time ago FORTRAN was called a problem oriented language; now it is understood. At the moment the so-called simulation languages - which is a bastard term - are called problem oriented languages. That is because the outside programming community does not yet understand the important contribution this stream of understanding can make to the general problem of expressing the way in which we can describe processes. It is my opinion that in the distant future this conference will be shown to have been misnamed.

Knuth:

I feel that the only real difference between simulations and other problems is the fact that simulations tend to be a little more complex and therefore we have to be more careful about what we are doing, and also this idea of quasi processes shows up more often in this sort of application. However, it is certainly not true that languages such as we are discussing here are only applicable to the simulation of discrete systems. The main reason why I personally am interested in this conference is the fact that I believe in the generality of the types of programming constructions that are being used and discussed here. I think that every computer programmer should have a repertoire for a very wide range of application.

On the other hand it is true that the discussion we have been going through has been directed toward programming language design in general. I do think really that it is an important purpose of conferences, that serious problems of the day should be discussed at them.

Garwick:

We have heard a lot here about the high priests of programming, and we have heard about neophytes, and there is hope for some sort of middle class too. But Nygaard and myself are both interested in producing a language in which one can express an incredible number of things. Nygaard thinks that if one simplifies a language, the user will soon want something better. He could not be more mistaken. Has he ever seen a FORTRAN programmer change to anything else? Not even IBM is going to get rid of FORTRAN. I would say that at least 80% of all programmers program in FORTRAN - and I do not think that we will ever get past it. Computers 50 years from now will still depend on FORTRAN.

Bauknecht:

I think we have not to forget one aspect. This is effectiveness. We are talking about simulation languages, but we have computers with limited core storage available and we have limited computer running time for our simulation problems. So we may have a lot of good simulation languages, but I think we must look at the implementations so that we can do effective simulation problems.

Caracciolo:

Strachey said that we cannot expect any programmer to be capable of designing a language well, which is obviously true. The aim of including self-defining features in programming languages is not to have every programmer writing in his own language, but to provide a basic language to which certain general tools may be added by highly qualified groups. Therefore I think that the possibility of introducing self-defining features is one of the most essential roads in programming language development.

Hutchinson:

I think like most of the rest of us I am for flexibility in languages
to the extent that it is good. I think the real problem is what is good
and what is bad, and we have not talked about the criteria by which
a language should be judged. The overall objective is probably increasing understanding to help us in our problem solving activities.
The first area that we can talk about is that of problem definition,
programming, checking, data collection and analysis of results.
The fact that these are perhaps separate and distinct activities
does not mean that they can not all be done by the same person. I
see no particular reason why any one particular language should be
ideal for all these different activities. I should like to hear the other participants talk about what the different languages have to offer
in the different areas. Possibly the most important point is the
problem of the definition area because here we have people who
are trying to describe their problems sufficiently clearly to a person who is able to write the solution down, so that the machine can
transfer the information from one person to another. We spend almost all our time talking about the transferring of the problem from
the person to the machine, not from person to person, which seems
to be even a weaker link.

Nygaard:

I wish to remark on the problem of dialects within the general
purpose languages. The situation is that FORTRAN is a limited language which is not at all intended for the wide range of use which
we need in simulation. Therefore this language does not contain the
basic components which we need when we want to describe a wider
class of systems, and therefore it is not possible, of course, to
extend it. But in the future we are going to have languages which
have had from the start the general framework. The question is
just the opposite - it is how to structure this general language into
a number of different problem areas.

I might say to Lackner, who thinks simulation languages are
different from other programming languages, that I think that when
we describe an execution of any algorithm, we are in fact performing a simulation. We have described a certain sequence of actions
and we introduce this inside the computer. When we write a simulation, we usually think of time dependent discrete event systems,
we describe them and we perform them inside the computer.

There are many border line cases here. When we started creating simulation languages, we started on time dependent discrete
event systems, and we gave them all the tools needed. Then we
worked out that the problem in languages is that we want to describe

wider and wider classes of systems, so we wanted to have much
more flexible block structure, and simulation languages now provide this. I think most of us now tend to regard our efforts as
creating very general program languages and then injecting in
these extra facilities for structuring and writing sequencing
schemes, which make them what we would earlier have called
special languages.

Lackner:

I should like to reply quite briefly to Nygaard. If I understand
you right, you are saying that simulation languages are another
generation of languages which are more capable of expressing
things that were originally going to be expressed by earlier languages. To a certain degree I agree with that, but I think the simulation languages specifically are able to tackle two problems which
do not arise if we simply want to program a computer to produce a
report of some kind or to solve a numerical problem. These two
problems are the representation of simultaneous activity and of
continuous activity. You do not need a facility for handling those
problems in most programs.

Knuth:

In the first place I think perhaps the most important example of
programs using simultaneity is the idea of operating systems and
programming of these, but even on a simpler level there is the concept of co-routines, which was independently discovered by several
people and used in the writing of compilers in 1958-59. You consider a program, in a simple case, to be composed of two parts,
each of which is operating in quasi-parallel with the other. It would
be impossible to express this concept of co-routines in any natural
way in FORTRAN or ALGOL, but on the other hand in the case of
SIMULA in particular this becomes very natural.

As a further example, I could cite the geometry theorem proving
program, which is an old artificial intelligence routine. Another
example is a parsing algorithm for context-free languages given by
Floyd in his survey paper on programming languages in the IEEE
transactions where he describes the algorithm in terms of a corporation and men hiring and firing other people. This is another algorithm that you cannot express using the recursion in ALGOL, but
on the other hand in SIMULA it becomes very natural.

In many cases, in other words, we have repeated routines that
are not like sub-routines. You do not just start them out with some
parameters and wait until they exit and then stop. This is some evidence to support my belief that the constructions of simulation lan-

guages do not specifically apply only to the type of thing that you first think of with respect to discrete simulation.

Ross:

Thank you for providing a nice string of illustrations to the points that I want to make. Coming back to the question of extending a language, I should like to introduce a distinction between extending a language and augmenting a language. If you merely add more syntatic sugar or synonyms and macro expansions - things that are strictly syntatic - we regard that as augmenting the language. Only if you get in and actually add something new to the scope of the language itself; only in that case would we think of it as actually extending the language. I think this is a very worthwhile distinction to make and one which we have been using ourselves in our work for quite a while. It is really by augmenting languages that we make them user oriented. We do not expect the average programmer to be able to extend a language but he may very well be able to augment it in simple ways which are useful to him.

I have one other point that has come up a couple of times; the fact that the end of line or tabulation is just as good as a semi-colon. I agree heartily and I believe that any lexicographic processor which starts off the translation of a language should be written in such a way that these things which show us position on the page as well as the marks on the page should be significant. We lay great store in the other direction of the output layout from a system. We even have a print algorithm in the AED system which prints out our programs showing structure by indenting the phrase structure and parenthesis matching and so forth and we find this extremely useful; so much so that we almost never write a flow diagram. You can greatly enhance the communicability between people by having programs properly formatted and the computer can do this for you automatically if you build it into your system.

Nicholls:

I am glad that we have got back to what I think is the theme of the Conference - which I think is "What is the problem of simulation and what are the primitive operations we need in simulation that can not be expressed in terms of other operations in a language?" I think this is the central difficulty and I do not think we have got a good answer to it yet. It seems that some generality in data representation is one primitive and some means of expressing parallel or quasi-parallel operations is another. I think it does need some time to discover what are the primitives.

I think that the whole of the other issue, namely the syntactic side, deals very largely with the question of who are the users, which was another question which was raised earlier on in the meeting. It is here that you study the convenience and the practicality of a language. To some extent I think you can also deal with the question of discipline in syntax; syntax is the way in which you can control the forms that you can write and you can attain some of the discipline that some people seem to be in favour of and some people seem to be against.

Skousen:

I am concerned with the education of students and how we can teach the students about simulation.

We have a particular installation in our school, and we do not know which installation the students will go to when they leave the school. So, I wonder, if what we should teach is a kind of problem solving attitude? We might have some primitive solution method or system which we can give the students and then we can illustrate this primitive system using the languages implemented on the installation we have now. We have many languages and we also have to live with these languages in the future so I think it would be a very good thing if we came to such primitives.

Brennan:

I think it was Knuth who first made the comment that perhaps our manuals should always start with an example because it facilitates understanding. I think the same thing is certainly true in the education field. The way to educate students in the use of simulation is to have the students do a number of simulation examples. It makes very little difference what language they use as far as their understanding of the technique is concerned; by the time they get out of school, we shall have invented six more languages anyhow!

DO WE NEED ALL THESE LANGUAGES?

JAN V. GARWICK
KIRA, *Kjeller per Lilleström, Norway*

1. INTRODUCTION

Programming languages were developed shortly after the construction of the first electronic computer. The first type of language, which incidentally is in use even today, was the assembly
language. These languages are not in any way general purpose,
they are intimately connected to one computer or line of computers.
The second type or generation of languages were the problem oriented languages. As there are a large number of problem areas
and different languages designers disagrees on the best language
for a specific type of problems, the number of second generation
languages is enormous and their number is rapidly increasing. The
obvious solution to the problem of reducing all these languages to
reasonable proportions is to produce a general purpose language.
The only published effort in this direction is PL/1, which, however,
attracks the problem in the spirit of the second generation language
by including all the features the designers thought anybody could
possibly require. The result is, as one can expect, very messy.
It is furthermore obvious that there always will turn up applications
where the built-in features are either insufficient or at least unsuitable.
The proper way to design a language seems to construct a framework of basic principles which can be increased as much as needed
by the programmer, not by the language designer.

2. HISTORY OF GPL

The insufficiency of second generation languages was recognized
among others by Peter Z. Ingerman, Peter Lucas, Thomas B. Steel
Jr. and the author at a meeting of the IFIP WG 2.1 in Princeton in
May 1965. A sketch of a better language was presented to the other
members of the group, but it did not create much interest. We then
decided to do it alone and an ACM subcommittee with me as chairman was formed with the objective of creating a third generation

language. Aside from the original members of the group ideas from
J. McCarthy, P. A. Hoare, N. Wirth and others have been included.
Whereas a large number of people have contributed directly or indirectly, only the present author can be held responsible for the
result.

A conference on simulation is obviously not the right forum to
present a new type of programming language, it is furthermore a
little premature to publish all the ramifications of the language now.
In this paper I will therefore only describe enough to give a fair understanding of what GPL is, but hardly enough to permit its use in
other than fairly simple cases.

3. THE DESIGN OF GPL

In any language one must first discuss the entities upon which it
operates, then the operations which can be performed upon these
entities. Because GPL permits both the data types and the operations upon them to be declared by the programmer and as the language is extremely recursively defined fig. 1 gives an indication of
the way the full language is defined. Going from top to bottom one
sees the various main elements of the language. Inside each box
are fields naming syntactical entities so far not defined. Arrows
points back showing when they are defined. We will, however, as
previously stated not discuss all these boxes in detail.

3.1. *Basic types*

The basic types of data are real (floating point) numbers, signed
integers and bit patterns (bytes). They are all equipped with a precision indicator which, if it is omitted, has a default value. In
PBF * notation we have

$$\langle\text{basic item}\rangle :: = \underline{\text{real}} \langle\text{precision indicator}\rangle |$$
$$\underline{\text{byte}} \langle\text{precision indicator}\rangle |$$
$$\underline{\text{integer}} \langle\text{precision indicator}\rangle$$
$$\langle\text{precision indicator}\rangle :: = \langle\text{empty}\rangle | (\langle\text{unsigned integer}\rangle)$$

The precision indicator gives a minimum precision in decimals for
real and an exact precision in bits for byte and integer.

More complex data types are built up from the basic ones.

A general data type can be of three subtypes: a data block, corresponding to Hoares records, an array or a pointer to any of
these. Specifically we have

* PBF means Paniani-Backus Form. Paniani was a Persian scholar who
  about the year 600 BC described Sanscrit in what today is denoted BNF.
  I am indebted to P. Z. Ingerman for this note.

⟨variable type⟩ :: = ⟨pointer list⟩⟨item⟩
⟨pointer list :: = ⟨empty⟩ | ⟨pointer list⟩ ptr
⟨item⟩ :: = ⟨basic item⟩ | ⟨block type⟩ | ⟨array type⟩ | ptr none

⟨block type⟩ :: = ⟨symbol⟩
⟨array type⟩ :: = ⟨symbol⟩

⟨array declaration⟩ :: = array ⟨array type⟩ of ⟨variable type⟩

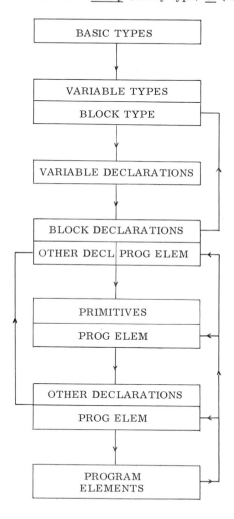

Fig. 1. The structure of GPL

A pointer (<u>ptr</u>) serves both as "address variables" and as "call by name". One can obviously have a pointer to a pointer etc. In the combination "<u>ptr none</u>" the ptr is a call by name of a program element of type <u>none</u>, i.e., one which does not deliver a value; a statement in ALGOL 60.

The declaration of array types is shown, the declaration of block types is more complex and will be discussed later.

A few array decalarations are

> <u>array</u> <u>vector</u> <u>of</u> <u>real</u>
> <u>array</u> <u>matrix</u> <u>of</u> <u>vector</u>
> <u>array</u> <u>string</u> <u>of</u> <u>byte</u> (8)
> <u>array</u> <u>switch</u> <u>of</u> <u>ptre</u> <u>none</u>

All arrays are one dimensional, so a two dimensional "array" is an array of arrays.

A variable is declared quite simply by

$$\langle \text{variable declaration} \rangle :: = \langle \text{variable type} \rangle \langle \text{variable list} \rangle$$

where variable list as usual consists of identifiers separated by commas.

If a variable is of pointer type or array type it is at declaration time preset to a <u>null</u> value. One can therefore not write

> vector a ;   5.3 → a[5]

because the vector is not yet created, one only has created a variable "a" capable of pointing to a vector.

3.2. *Blocks*

Blocks are used both to hold data and to form "subroutines". We will here only give a very simplified syntax for blocks which only takes care of the first function (and also leaves out synonymous blocks).

> $\langle \text{block declaration} \rangle :: = \underline{\text{block}} \langle \text{block type} \rangle | \langle \text{block body} \rangle |$
>
> $\langle \text{block body} \rangle :: = \langle \text{variable declaration} \rangle |$
> $\qquad\qquad\quad \langle \text{block body} \rangle ; \langle \text{variable declaration} \rangle$

In its full generality blocks can contain other declarations and program elements (statements and expressions in ALGOL 60) and the block may have a value which is produced when the block is executed.

Some samples of blocks are

> <u>block</u> <u>complex</u> {<u>real</u> real, imag}
> <u>block</u> <u>lim</u>   {<u>integer</u> (24) lower, upper}
> <u>block</u> <u>node</u>   {<u>ptr</u> <u>node</u> left, right; <u>real</u> data}
> <u>block</u> <u>Boolean</u> {<u>byte</u> (1) B}

We see that complex numbers (as well as three dimensional vectors or any other special data structure) is definable by the programmer. Later we will see that operations upon these structures are definable. The lim block is used in connection with arrays. The precision 24 is implementation dependent.

3.3. *Primitives*

The definition of primitives relies heavily upon the as yet undefined concept program element. Program elements are, however, the same as statements and expressions in ALGOL 60 and it is impossible to define them in PBF.

Primitives are somewhat similar to primaries in ALGOL 60. Variables and constants are primitives. A block is a primitive. The form of block we are primarily interested in are unnamed blocks which consist of an opening and a closing curly bracket with a block body between. The block body consists of declaration and program elements, the latter may be labelled. We will not give the exact definition here, but only state that if any program element inside the block delivers a value, the dynamically last such value is the value of the block. Possible blocks are

$$\{i+1 \rightarrow i; \quad a[i]\}$$
$$\{a[i]; \quad i-1 \rightarrow i\}$$

Here in both cases $a[i]$ is the value of the block and $i \pm 1 \rightarrow i$ are side effects.

Very important primitives are the pointer elements and the array elements. These elements create storage space as a side effect. Their values are pointers (array pointers) to the created storage. The syntax for these elements is

⟨pointer element⟩ :: =	⟨block type⟩(⟨program element list⟩)
⟨array element⟩ :: =	⟨array type⟩(⟨limits⟩ ⟨replication⟩)
⟨limits⟩ :: =	⟨lim element⟩
⟨replication⟩ ::	⟨empty⟩ | : ⟨program element list⟩ | , ⟨controlled variable⟩ : ⟨program element⟩
⟨program element list⟩ :: =	⟨program element⟩ | ⟨program element list⟩, ⟨program element⟩
⟨controlled variable⟩ :: =	⟨identifier⟩

The controlled variable is an identifier declared by the array element and existing only inside it.

The use of these elements can be seen from some examples

<u>ptr</u> <u>complex</u> x; <u>complex</u> $(0,1) \rightarrow x$

If x had been declared as <u>complex</u> x, the rule for assignment of a pointer element to a non pointer element would have been invoked, this rule will be described later.

<u>matrix</u> x ; <u>matrix</u> $(\underline{\lim}(1, n),\ i: \underline{vector}\ (\underline{\lim}\ 1, i))) \rightarrow x$

x is now a non preset triangular matrix.

It is seen that when an array is created, the limits are always given. These limits are, however, not fixed in the same way as the limits of arrays in ALGOL 60 are. The lower limit is indeed fixed, but the upper limit is automatically extended if reference is made to an element with higher index than the upper limit. An absolutely empty array has the upper limit one less than the lower limit. The actual limits of an array, i.e. the lower limit and the larger of the preset upper limit and the highest index used so far, can be obtained by the "procedure" bound. In our previous example we have

bound $(x) = \underline{\lim}\ (1, n)$ and bound $(x[3]) = \underline{\lim}\ (1, 3)$

Procedure elements may in their simplest form look like ALGOL 60 procedures, but the actual parameters can only be program elements. This excludes e.g. procedure names. The equivalence of a procedure name must be achieved through Jensens device, but this is somewhat easier in GPL than in ALGOL 60.

Simple primitives are the go to element (exactly as in ALGOL 60), the dummy element (again as in ALGOL 60) and the comment element. The latter can be considered as a sort of dummy element.

A program element enclosed in parenthesis is a primitive with the usual meaning of giving the sequence in which elements are evaluated.

A primitive followed by a subscript list within square brackets means indexing if the primitive is an array, exactly as in ALGOL 60.

An important primitive is one with the syntax

⟨variable name⟩ (⟨program element⟩)

This assumes that the program element is a block or a pointer to a block and that inside this block there is declared a variable with the variable name. We may e.g. have the primitive

real (<u>complex</u> (p, q) + <u>complex</u> $(r, s))$

its value would be $p + r$ if complex addition is defined in the usual way.

<u>null</u> is a primitive which can be assigned to any variable of array type or pointer type. It makes the data pointed to inaccessible if there are no other pointers pointing to the same data.

Finally we will mention the pointer quotes ' and '. If they surround a program element, the value becomes a pointer to this element. In some special cases they are put in automatically, but we will not go into this refinement here.

We will remark that a pointer element not only points to a variable (block, program element of type <u>none</u> etc.) but also to the block in which this variable is imbedded, this has, as we will see later some very important consequences.

A further remark is that we now can give a loose definition of program elements. They consist of primitives joined by and operated upon by operators, but so far operators have not been defined.

3.4. *Procedure declarations*

For the purpose of this conference it is unnecessary to give the complete definition of procedures. A simplified syntax is

⟨procedure declaration⟩:: = <u>procedure</u> ⟨procedure indent⟩
                                    ⟨parameter part⟩ ⟨general element⟩
⟨procedure ident⟩:: = ⟨identifier⟩
⟨parameter part⟩:: = ⟨empty⟩|(⟨formal parameter list⟩)
⟨formal parameter list⟩:: = ⟨formal parameter⟩|
                                    ⟨formal parameter list⟩,
                                    ⟨formal parameter⟩
⟨formal parameter⟩:: = ⟨identifier⟩
⟨general element⟩:: = ⟨body element⟩|⟨iff list⟩
⟨body element⟩:: = ⟨proc type⟩ <u>to be</u> ⟨program element⟩|
                         <u>macro</u> ⟨program element⟩
⟨iff list⟩:: = ⟨iff element⟩|⟨iff list⟩ ⟨iff element⟩
⟨iff element⟩:: = <u>iff</u> ⟨iff condition⟩ <u>take</u> ⟨general element⟩
⟨iff condition⟩:: = ⟨iff secondary⟩|⟨iff condition⟩∨⟨iff secondary⟩
⟨iff secondary⟩:: = ⟨iff primary⟩|⟨iff secondary⟩∧⟨iff primary⟩
⟨iff primary⟩:: = (⟨iff condition⟩)|⟨type specification⟩
⟨type specification⟩:: = ⟨type⟩⟨formal parameter list⟩
⟨type⟩:: = ⟨ptr list⟩ ⟨spec type⟩
⟨spec type⟩:: = <u>real</u> | <u>long real</u> | <u>integer</u> | <u>byte</u> | ⟨block type⟩|
                     ⟨array type⟩ | <u>none</u>

The fairly complex "iff list" replaces the specifications in ALGOL 60. A procedure may have parameters of varying types with the same or different bodies depending upon the types. One may consider the specifications in the iff list as a question about the types of the actual parameters in a procedure call. The type <u>long real</u> is a question to the compiler whether the parameter in question was stored in single or double length precision. As declarations only give a precision in decimals, it is the compiler which decides whether a single or a double length variable results.

All the actual parameters are by the compiler surrounded by ptr brackets (' ') and these are evaluated every time the parameter is referred to inside the procedure body. This corresponds exactly to the ALGOL 60 "call by name" feature. If, however, the actual parameter already had more pointers than the formal parameter, so many pointers are evaluated that only one extra is left which is then evaluated when the parameter is used. Procedure bodies can either be in the form of "subroutines" in which case the type of the result must be given, or as a macro. In the latter case no extra pointers appear and a straight copying of the body takes place. The actual parameters surrounded by parenthesis are inserted for the formal ones. Macro's can of course never call themselves recursively.

3.5. *Operator declarations*

A very important property of GPL is the ability to declare operators. The meaning of an operator depends upon the symbol used to indicate the operator and the type of the operands.

The actual parameters of a procedure is given by the parameters enclosed by parentheses (in the simplified version given here); for operators the actual parameters are given by the priorities of the operators in a way which is well known.

The syntax of operator declaration is:

⟨operator declaration⟩:: = operator ⟨operand⟩ ⟨operator⟩
⟨operand⟩ ⟨priority⟩; ⟨general element⟩
⟨operand⟩:: = ⟨empty⟩ | ⟨formal parameter⟩
⟨operator⟩:: = ⟨symbol⟩
⟨priority⟩:: = priority ⟨unsigned integer⟩

The priority is lowest for the assignment operator →.
An example of an operator declaration is

operator $a \times b$ priority 30;
iff complex a take
{iff complex b take complex to be
complex (real(a) × real(b) - imag(a) × imag(b),
real(a) × imag(b) × imag(a) × real(b))
iff real $b \vee$ long real $b \vee$ integer b take complex to be
complex (real (a) × b, imag(a) × b)}
iff complex $b \wedge$ (real $a \vee$ long real $a \vee$ integer a) take macro $b \times a$

This declaration defines all types of complex multiplication, there are in all 7 different declarations. Observe that the last set is only seemingly recursive.

3.6. *Input, output and formating*

GPL has two other types of declarations namely code declarations used by input output and radix declarations used by formating and for the definition of constants. We will not discuss these further.

4. THE CONSTRUCTION OF A PRACTICAL LANGUAGE

The language described so far can not be used for the simplest calculations. The reason is that we have given a method of extending a language, but we have no operators or procedures with which to describe the extension. Furthermore we have left the concept symbol floating rather loosely. The latter can be dealt with by saying that the standard arithmetic operators +, - etc. are symbols and that any underlined collection of characters (whatever thay may be) is a symbol. Only the code declaration gives the exact definition.

In order to get a start in the language we therefore need a set of basic operators and basic procedures.

The operators do of course include arithmetic operations between reals, long reals and integers. (Division of one integer by another has the same meaning as the ALGOL 60.) For type conversion we need fix, float etc. It is in fact an interesting exercise to find the minimum number of operators needed to produce an *efficient* language. The assignment operator can assign any type to a variable of the same type, but the two operands need not have the same number of pointers. If they differ, the one with the largest number of pointers is evaluated until the number is the same. Relational operators give results of type Boolean.

It is seen that conditional elements, repetitive elements etc. are not defined in the language. This is because they are definable in the full language (but not in the subset described here). When we use such constructions in examples they are assumed to have their conventional meaning.

Some very useful operators are $\pm$, $-$, $\underline{x}$ and $/$ which operate upon reals and give as result long reals.

After the basic operators (and procedures for I/O) have been defined, a much larger set of standard operators and procedures can be defined in terms of them. The set of basic and standard operators will constitute a very useful general purpose language which over 90% of all programmers will be satisfied with. For special purposes, further extensions are of course possible.

5. THE USE OF GPL

It is believed that it is hard to find applications from system

programming to commercial data handling which can not be simply
and efficiently programmed in GPL.

There are, however, two reasons for using other languages. One
is the large number of programs already written in other languages,
the other is that it will take a very long time (if it is at all possible)
to train all programmers to use this new language.

Because of its enormous generality, nearly all other languages
can, however, be considered as subsets of GPL if differences in
syntax is taken into account and a set of special data declarations,
operators, procedures etc. are added. It should therefore be possible to write, in GPL, a preprocessor which translates e. g.
FORTRAN into GPL and then compiles the resulting program. The
same approach can be taken by language designers who for one
reason or another does not want to use the GPL syntax, he can
limit himself to a syntax translator, a usually very simple job,
giving, again usually, a very fast program.

It is also seen that this approach gives an enormous economy
when a new computer shall be "broken in". Only a minor part of
the GPL compiler need be rewritten, the rest is done by boot-
strapping.

6. SAMPLE PROGRAMS

Our first example is from numerical analysis and consists of
the solution of n linear equations with m right hand sides. The
equations are contained in the $n \times (n+m)$ matrix a. It is assumed
that all lower limits are 1. The procedure "solve" will triangulize
the coefficient part of the matrix and replace the right hand sides
by the solutions.

```
procedure solve (a); iff matrix a take none to be
{integer n, tot; matrix A; a → A;
comment this corresponds to calling the array pointer a by
value;
upper (bound (A)) → n; upper (bound (A[1])) → tot;
integer i, j, k; vector row, row 1;
real (15) work; real pivot;

for i eq 1 step 1 until n do
    {A[i] → row;
for j eq i step 1 until n do
    {A[j] → row 1; row 1[i] → work;
for k eq 1 step 1 until i-1 do
    work - row 1[k] x A[k, i] → work;
    work → row 1[i];
real max; 0 → max; i → k;
for j eq i step 1 until n do
```

```
if abs A[j, i] >max then {abs A[j, i] → max; j → k};
if k ≠ i then {A[k] → A[i]; row → A[k]; A[i] → row ;
comment this was the row interchange;
for j eq i+1 step 1 until tot do
    {row [j] → work;
for k eq 1 step 1 until i-1 do
    work - row [k] x A[k, i] → work;
    work / pivot → row [j]}};
comment the forward solution is now done;
for i eq n-1 step -1 until 1 do
    {A[i] → row;
for j eq n+1 step 1 until tot do
    {row [j] → work;
for k eq i+1 step 1 until n do
    work - row [k] x A[k, j] → work;
    work → row [j]}};
comment the back substitutions are done}
```

The following points merit observation

a) By using the auximiary vector-variables row and row 1 the amount of indexing is appreciably reduced.

b) The row interchanges consist of the interchange of two vector variables, not of all the individual elements.

c) By using the multiplying operator x and declaring work to have a high precision, the scalar products are evaluated to higher than normal precision thereby reducing the rounding errors.

Our second example is more in line with the theme of the present conference. It contains the nucleus of an event directed simulation process.

```
{block event {real time; ptr event link; ptr none action};
ptr event head; real T; 0 → T;
comment head heads the sorted list of upcoming events,
T holds the simulation time;
procedure create (t, a); iff real t ∧ ptr none a take none to be
{comment this procedure will insert the action a in the event
list at relative time t i.e. absolute time t+T;
real time; t+T → time;
if head = null then event (time, null, a) → head else
if time (head) > time then event (time, head, a) → head else
{ptr event temp; head → temp;
L: if link (temp) = null then event (time, null, a) →
link (temp) else
if time (link (temp)) < time then {link (temp) → temp; go to
L} else
event (time, link (temp), a) → link (temp)}};
comment the following piece of program causes events to be
executed. The initial go to is to skip it at entry to the pro-
```

gram;
go to Q; ptr event aux;
next event: if head = null then go to finish else
{head → aux; link (head) → head; time (aux) → T;
action (aux); go to next event}; Q:
comment the following procedure can be inserted in any program causing a simulated time delay t;
procedure wait (t); iff real t take none to be
{create (t, 'go to L'); go to next event; L :}
comment here follows other standardprocedures and the
program proper}

The most interesting observation here is the effect of storing the
ptr none 'go to L' in the event list. Because this pointer not only
contains a pointer to the program element "go to L", but also a
pointer to the surrounding data structure at the time the ptr was
created, this data is not lost even if we are leaving the middle of
a procedure. When this pointer is executed in "next event" the data
structure is again made accessible and the program reentered as if
it had never been left.

7. CONCLUSION

So far we have no practical experience with GPL because no
compiler exists yet. Several experimental programs like the ones
in the previous paragraph have, however, been written. So far it
has proved very practical. A simple feature of the language, not
described in this short paper, permits the programmer to have the
same amount of control over variables as he has in an assembly
language while still using a higher level language which can be tay-
lor-made to his special application.

A compiler for the CDC 3600 is well under way. Experience with
this compiler shows that it will not be particularly long, about the
same as a normal ALGOL 60 compiler, and probably quite fast.
The logic of the compiler is, however, vastly more complex than
other compilers I have been in touch with. There are few "run time
programs" required, but one of them is a garbage collector. This
has been written. It contains two superimposed learning programs
and requires considerably less than 1/10 second for each collection.

I do of course not claim that GPL is the only possible third generation language, nor that it is the best possible, but I do claim that
it is a significant advance over the existing second generation languages.

Note added in proof. Since this paper was written GPL has undergone
several changes. Up to date information is obtainable from the author at
Control Data Corporation, 3145 Porter Drive, Palo Alto, Cal. 94304.

DISCUSSION

Buxton:

I think I am of the school, as Garwick obviously is, which believes that there is nothing special about simulation programming languages. Simulations are just hard problems which often call for complicated data and parallel operations, and therefore to present this sort of language at a simulation programming conference is, I think, entirely proper. Now I suspect that other people may not agree.

I agree entirely with Garwick's attempt to move in the direction of a third generation of programming languages and I think this is the correct step for us to take in the present programming language mess-up. I suggest there are possibly two fundamental qualities which the 3rd generation language is likely to display. In one of these I am in agreement with Garwick; I think also that we must have a return towards simplicity in programming languages. I think we have to get away from the dinosaurs of the programming world of which there are a few splendid examples lumbering around at present. We have got to return to some very fundamental simplicity.

What I am much more doubtful about is whether, having returned to this simplicity, we should try to offer power to the user by permitting him to make fundamental extensions to the language when he has got it in the way Garwick suggests; that is, by allowing him to define his own implicit operators. I doubt that this can be correct. My feeling is that the defining of operators is an extremely specialised study which only programming language designers can really undertake and therefore what I doubt is whether a language of this type can be applied to general everyday programming. I think the method of extension is probably disastrously wrong for use by 99% of programmers.

Garwick:

I could not agree more. 99% of programmers are completely unqualified to extend the language but if we do not have extendability, you will obviously have a different language on each machine. There is one language now completely independent of any machine and, as we now have in the Communications of the ACM an ALGOL algorithm section, there could very well be a similar section for defining types and defining operators done by the people who are qualified to do it and which can be used by the less qualified programmers.

Steel:

My comment was somewhat spiked by Buxton's remarks so I will
allude to an earlier remark of Buxton's about the less than monu-
mentally bright programmers. The thing that concerns me here is
the problem of teaching this language or some piece of it to a large
number of people. This is all well and good as a device for the experts; by experts of course I mean the set of people in this room,
but we have to keep in mind the fact that there are a great many
people who are presumably going to use languages. Lord knows our
schools are doing their best to make every graduate a programmer
of some sort and I am concerned about how one can take this language, describe it in relatively simple terms and make it available
for use by large numbers of people in such a way that they are not
going to get into all kind of trouble by defining operators that they
could not possibly comprehend.

Garwick:

This is of course a real problem. Theoretically it is easier to
explain these languages than say even FORTRAN because they have
fewer rules in them, but that is pure theory. Practice is very different. There is however no difficulty in constructing a sub-set.
First of all we do not describe the declaration of operators. Secondly all procedures look like FORTRAN procedures with a few
small changes. Furthermore we never tell about pointers. That is,
everything looks as though it is a complex number, there is never
a pointer to a record or anything like that. Now you have something
of the simplicity of FORTRAN but you can build into it just the types
you want and it could be just the FORTRAN types for all I know.
This subset will have the additional slight advantages that you can
call procedures recursively but of course none of the programmers
you have in mind here know what a recursive procedure is. I would
furthermore supply these users with a quite big set of built-in procedures. So by selecting a proper sub-set, by adding the proper set
of predesigned procedures and operators and types, I think the
problem can be solved.

Laski:

Unlike Buxton I believe that simulation languages are an extension of ALGOL-like languages rather than a mere augmentation,
to use the useful terminology introduced by Ross. It seems to me
that a mechanism is being provided here to augment a primitive
language, which is splendid provided that, even augmented, this
primitive language is adequate for the nature of the algorithms that
one wishes to describe.

It seems to me that it is unproven and I suspect is false to say that the ideas of simulation languages such as SIMULA will be interpretable in GPL and it seems to me that the proof lies with the proponent.

Garwick:

I will of course first state that well-known theorem that ALGOL is not an ALGOL-like language. This was some surprise to Ginsburg when he found it out.

Secondly, Laski may of course have his opinion. Mine is different.

Laski:

It seems to me that verification is a proper action to prove the validity of your opinion. Without verification the case can be at best undecided. I do not think it is undecidable.

Krasnow:

I hope that this very interesting point can be further debated at a later time.

CLASS AND SUBCLASS DECLARATIONS

OLE-JOHAN DAHL and KRISTEN NYGAARD
Norwegian Computing Center, Oslo, Norway

1. INTRODUCTION

A central idea of some programming languages [28,57,58] is to provide protection for the user against (inadvertantly) making meaningless data references. The effects of such errors are implementation dependent and can not be determined by reasoning within the programming language itself. This makes debugging difficult and impractical.

Security in this sense is particularly important in a list processing environment, where data are dynamically allocated and de-allocated, and the user has explicit access to data addresses (pointers, reference values, element values). To provide security it is necessary to have an automatic de-allocation mechanism (reference count, garbage collection). It is convenient to restrict operations on pointers to storage and retrieval. New pointer values are generated by allocation of storage space, pointing to the allocated space. The problem remains of correct interpretation of data referenced relative to user specified pointers, or checking the validity of assumptions inherent in such referencing. E.g. to speak of "A of X" is meaningful, only if there is an A among the data pointed to by X.

The record concept proposed by Hoare and Wirth [58] provides full security combined with good runtime efficiency. Most of the necessary checking can be performed at compile time. There is, however, a considerable expense in flexibility. The values of reference variables and procedures must be restricted by declaration to range over records belonging to a stated class. This is highly impractical.

The connection mechanism of SIMULA combines full security with greater flexibility at a certain expense in convenience and run time efficiency. The user is forced, by the syntax of the connection statement, to determine at run time the class of a referenced data structure (process) before access to the data is possible.

The subclass concept of Hoare [59] is an attempt to overcome the difficulties mentioned above, and to facilitate the manipulation of data structures, which are partly similar, partly distinct. This paper presents another approach to subclasses, and some applications of this approach.

2. CLASSES

The class concept introduced is a remodelling of the record class concept proposed by Hoare. The notation is an extension of the ALGOL 60 syntax. A prefix notation is introduced to define subclasses organized in a hierarchical tree structure. The members of a class are called objects. Objects belonging to the same class have similar data structures. The members of a subclass are compound objects, which have a prefix part and a main part. The prefix part of a compound object has a structure similar to objects belonging to some higher level class. It can itself be a compound object.

The figure below indicates the structure of a class hierarchy and of the corresponding objects. A capital letter denotes a class. The corresponding lower case letter denotes the data comprising the main part of an object belonging to that class.

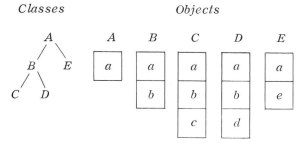

B, C, D, E are subclasses of *A*; *C* and *D* are sublasses of *B*.

2.1. *Syntax*

⟨class id.⟩ :: = ⟨identifier⟩
⟨prefix⟩:: = ⟨class id.⟩
⟨class body⟩:: = ⟨statement⟩
⟨main part⟩:: = <u>class</u> ⟨class id.⟩ ⟨formal parameter part⟩;
        ⟨specification part⟩ ⟨class body⟩
⟨class declaration⟩:: = ⟨main part⟩|⟨prefix⟩ ⟨main part⟩

2.2. *Semantics*

An object is an instance of a class declaration. Different instances of the same declaration are said to belong to class C, where C is the class identifier. If the class body does not take the form of an unlabelled block, it acts as if enclosed in an implicit block. The parameters and the quantities declared local to the outermost block of the class body are called the attributes of an object. The attributes can be referenced locally from within the class body, or nonlocally by a mechanism called remote acessing (5).

The parameters are transmitted by value. One possible use of the statements of the class body may be to initialize attribute values.

A prefixed class declaration represents the result of concatenating the declaration referenced by the prefix and the main part. The concatenation is recursively defined by the following rules.

1) The formal parameter lists of the former and the latter are concatenated to form one parameter list.

2) The specification parts are juxtaposed.

3) A combined class body is formed, which is a block, whose block head contains the attribute declarations of the prefix body and the main body. The block tail contains the statements of the prefix body followed by those of the main body.

The attributes of the main part are not accessible from within the prefix body, except by remote accessing. The attributes of the prefix are acessible as ordinary local quantities from within the body of the main part.

The object class represented by a prefixed class declaration is a subclass of the class denoted by the prefix. Subclasses can be nested to any depth by using prefixed class identifiers as prefixes to other class declarations.

Let A_0 be any class. If A_0 is prefixed, we will denote this prefix by A_1. The prefix of A_1 (if any) will be denoted by A_2 etc. The sequence

$$A_1, A_2, \ldots$$

will be called the "prefix sequence" of A_0. It follows from the syntax that if A_i and A_j both have A_k as prefix, they have identical prefix sequences.

It will be required that all prefix sequences are finite. (This excludes multiple occurrence of any class A_i in a prefix sequence.) Let

$$A_1, A_2 \ldots, A_n$$

be the prefix sequence of A_0. We shall say that the class A_i is "included in A_j" if $0 \leq i \leq j \leq n$.

3. OBJECT REFERENCES

Reference values in the sense of [59] are introduced, in a slightly modified form.

3.1. *Reference types*

3.1.1. *Syntax*

$\langle$type$\rangle$ :: = $\langle$ALGOL type$\rangle$ | ref | ref $\langle$qualification$\rangle$
$\langle$qualification$\rangle$ :: = ($\langle$class id.$\rangle$)

3.1.2. *Semantics*

Associated with each object is a unique value of type ref, which is said to reference or point to the object. A reference value may, by qualifying a declaration or specification by a class identifier, be required to refer to objects belonging to either this class or any of its subclasses. In addition the value of any item of type reference is restricted to objects belonging to classes whose declarations are statically visible from the declaration or specification of the item.

The reference value none is a permissible value for any reference item, regardless of its qualification.

3.2. *Reference Expressions*

3.2.1. *Syntax*

$\langle$simple ref. expr.$\rangle$ :: = none |$\langle$variable$\rangle$|$\langle$function designator$\rangle$|
$\langle$object designator$\rangle$|$\langle$local reference$\rangle$
$\langle$ref. expr.$\rangle$ :: = $\langle$simple ref. expr.$\rangle$| if $\langle$Boolean expr.$\rangle$ then
$\langle$simple ref. expr.$\rangle$ else $\langle$ref. expr.$\rangle$
$\langle$object designator$\rangle$ :: = $\langle$class id.$\rangle$ $\langle$actual parameter part$\rangle$
$\langle$local reference$\rangle$ :: = this $\langle$class id.$\rangle$

3.2.2. *Semantics*

A reference expression is a rule for computing a reference value. Thereby reference is made to an object, except if the value is none, which is a reference to "no object".

i) *Qualification*. A variable or function designator is qualified according to its declaration or specification. An object designator or local reference is qualified by the stated class identifier. The expression none is not qualified.

No qualification will be regarded as qualification by a universal class, which includes all declared classes.

ii) *Object generation*. As the result of evaluating an object designator an object of the stated class is generated. The class body is executed. The value of the object designator is a reference to the generated object. The life span of the object is limited by that of its reference value.

iii) *Local reference*. A local reference "this C" is a meaningful expression within the class body of the class C or of any subclass of C. Its value is a reference to the current instance of the class declaration (object).

Within a connection block (5.2) connecting an object of class C or a subclass of C the expression "this C" is a reference to the connected object.

The general rule is that a local reference refers to the object, whose attributes are local to the smallest enclosing block, and which belongs to a class included in the one specified. If there is no such object, the expression is illegal.

4. REFERENCE OPERATIONS

4.1. *Assignment*

4.1.1. *Syntax*

⟨reference assignment⟩ :: = ⟨variable⟩: = ⟨reference expr.⟩|
⟨variable⟩: = ⟨reference assignment⟩

4.1.2. *Semantics*

Let the left and right hand sides be qualified by Cl and Cr, respectively, and let the value of the right hand side be a reference to an object of class Cv. The legality and effect of the statement depends on the relations that hold between these classes.

Case 1. Cl includes Cr: The statement is legal, and the assignment is carried out.

Case 2. Cl is a subclass of Cr: The statement is legal, and the assignment is carried out if Cl includes Cv, or if the value is none. If Cl does not include Cv, the effect of the statement is undefined (cf. 6.1).

Case 3. Cl and Cr satisfy neither of the above relations: The statement is illegal.

The following additional rule is considered: The statement is legal only if the declaration of the left hand item (variable, array or ⟨type⟩ procedure) is within the scope of the class identifier Cr

and all its subclasses. (The scope is in this case defined after having effected all concatenations implied by prefixes.)

This rule would have the following consequences.

1) Accessible reference values are limited to pointers to objects,
whose attributes are accessible by remote referencing (5).

2) Classes represented by declarations local to different instances of the same block are kept separate.

3) Certain security problems are simplified.

4.2. *Relations*

4.2.1. *Syntax*

$\langle$relation$\rangle$:: = $\langle$ALGOL relation$\rangle$|
$\qquad\qquad$ $\langle$reference expr.$\rangle$ = $\langle$reference expr.$\rangle$|
$\qquad\qquad$ $\langle$reference expr.$\rangle$ ≠ $\langle$reference expr.$\rangle$|
$\qquad\qquad$ $\langle$reference expr.$\rangle$ is $\langle$class id.$\rangle$

4.2.2. *Semantics*

Two reference values are said to be equal if the point to the
same object, or if both are none. A relation "X is C" is true if
the object referenced by X belongs to the class C or to any of its
subclasses.

4.3. *For statements*

4.3.1. *Syntax*

$\langle$for list element$\rangle$:: = $\langle$ALGOL for list element$\rangle$|$\langle$reference expr.$\rangle$|
$\qquad\qquad$ $\langle$reference expr.$\rangle$ while $\langle$Boolean expr.$\rangle$

4.3.2. *Semantics*

The extended for statement will facilitate the scanning of list
structures.

5. ATTRIBUTE REFERENCING

An attribute of an object is identified completely by the following
items of information:

1) the value of a $\langle$reference expr.$\rangle$ identifying an object,

2) a $\langle$class id.$\rangle$ specifying a class, which includes that of the
object, and

3) the $\langle$identifier$\rangle$ of an attribute declared for objects of the
stated class.

The class identification, item 2, is implicit at run time in a
reference value, however, in order to obtain runtime efficiency

it is necessary that this information is available to the compiler.

For a local reference to an attribute, i.e. a reference from within the class body, items 1 and 2 are defined implicitly. Item 1 is a reference to the current instance (i.e. object), and item 2 is the class identifier of the class declaration.

Non-local (remote) referencing is either through remote identifiers or through connection. The former is an adaptation of the technique proposed in [57], the latter corresponds to the connection mechanism of SIMULA [28].

5.1. *Remote Identifiers*

5.1.1. *Syntax*

⟨remote identifier⟩ :: = ⟨reference expr.⟩ . ⟨identifier⟩
⟨identifier 1⟩ :: = ⟨identifier⟩ | ⟨remote identifier⟩

Replace the meta-variable ⟨identifier⟩ by ⟨identifier 1⟩ at appropriate places of the ALGOL syntax.

5.1.2. *Semantics*

A remote identifier identifies an attribute of an individual object. Item 2 above is defined by the qualification of the reference expression. If the latter has the value none, the meaning of the remote identifier is undefined (cf. 6.2).

5.2. *Connection*

5.2.1. *Syntax*

⟨connection block 1⟩ :: = ⟨statement⟩
⟨connection block 2⟩ :: = ⟨statement⟩
⟨connection clause⟩ :: = when ⟨class id.⟩ do ⟨connection block 1⟩
⟨otherwise clause⟩ :: = ⟨empty⟩ | otherwise ⟨connection block 2⟩
⟨connection part⟩ :: = ⟨connection clause⟩ |
              ⟨connection part⟩ ⟨connection clause⟩
⟨connection statement⟩ :: = inspect ⟨reference expr.⟩ do
              ⟨connection block 2⟩ |
              inspect ⟨reference expr.⟩
              ⟨connection part⟩ ⟨otherwise clause⟩

5.2.2. *Semantics*

The connection mechanism serves a double purpose:

1) To define item 1 above implicitly for attribute references within connection blocks. The reference expression of a connection statement is evaluated once and its value is stored. Within a connection block this value is said to reference the connected object. It can itself be accessed through a ⟨local reference⟩ (see section 3.2.2).

2) To discriminate on class membership at run time, thereby defining item 2 implicitly for attribute references within alternative connection blocks. Within a ⟨connection block 1⟩ item 2 is defined by the class identifier of the connection clause. Within a ⟨connection block 2⟩ it is defined by the qualification of the reference expression of the connection statement.

Attributes of a connected object are thus immediately accessible through their respective identifiers, as declared in the class declaration corresponding to item 2. These identifiers act as if they were declared local to the connection block. The meaning of such an identifier is undefined, if the corresponding ⟨local reference⟩ has the value none. This can only happen within a ⟨connection block 2⟩.

6. UNDEFINED CASES

In defining the semantics of a programming language the term "undefined" is a convenient stratagem for postponing difficult decisions concerning special cases for which no obvious interpretation exists. The most difficult ones are concerned with cases, which can only be recognized by runtime checking.

One choice is to forbid offending special cases. The user must arrange his program in such a way that they do not occur, if necessary by explicit checking. For security the compiled program must contain implicit checks, which to some extent will duplicate the former. Failure of a check results in program termination and an error message. The implicit checking thus represents a useful debugging aid, and, subject to the implementor's foresight, it can be turned off for a "bugfree" program (if such a thing exists).

Another choice is to define ad hoc, but "reasonable" standard behaviours in difficult special cases. This can make the language much more easy to use. The programmer need not test explicitly for special cases, provided that the given ad hoc rule is appropriate in each situation. However, the language then has no implicit debugging aid for locating unforeseen special cases (for which the standard rules are not appropriate).

In the preceding sections the term undefined has been used three times in connection with two essentially different special cases.

6.1. *Conflicting reference assignment*
Section 4.1.2, case 2, Cl does not include Cv: The suggested standard behaviour is to assign the value none.

6.2. *Non-existing attributes*

Sections 5.1.2 and 5.2.2: The evaluation of an attribute reference, whose item 1 is equal to <u>none</u>, should cause an error printout and program termination. Notice that this trap will ultimately catch most unforeseen instances of case 6.1.

7. EXAMPLES

The class and subclass concepts are intended to be general aids to data structuring and referencing. However, certain widely used classes might well be included as specialized features of the programming language.

As an example the classes defined below may serve to manipulate circular lists of objects by standard procedures. The objects of a list may have different data structures. The "element" and "set" concepts of SIMULA will be available as special cases in a slightly modified form.

```
class linkage; begin ref (linkage) suc, pred; end linkage;
linkage class link; begin
    procedure out; if suc ≠ none then
        begin pred. suc: = suc; suc. pred: = pred;
            suc: = pred: = none end out;
    procedure into (L); ref (list) L;
        begin if suc ≠ none then out;
            suc: = L; pred: = suc. pred;
            suc. pred: = pred. suc: = this linkage end into;
    end link;
linkage class list;
    begin suc: = pred: = this linkage end list;
```

Any object prefixed by "link" can go in and out of circular lists. If *X* is a reference expression qualified by link or a subclass of link, whose value is different from <u>none</u>, the statements

$$X.\ \text{into}\ (L) \qquad \text{and} \qquad X.\ \text{out}$$

are meaningful, where *L* is a reference to a list.

Examples of user defined subclasses are:

```
link class car (license number, weight);
    integer license number; real weight; . . . ;
car class truck (load); ref (list) load; . . . ;
car class bus (capacity); integer capacity;
    begin ref (person) array passenger [1 : capacity] . . . end;
list class bridge; begin real load; . . . end;
```

Multiple list memberships may be implemented by means of auxiliary objects.

> link <u>class</u> element (*X*); <u>ref</u> *X*;;

A circular list of element objects is analogous to a "set" in SIMULA. The declaration "<u>set</u> *S*" of SIMULA is imitated by "<u>ref</u> (list) *S*" followed by the statement "*S*: = list".

The following are examples of procedures closely similar to the corresponding ones of SIMULA.

> <u>procedure</u> include (*X*, *S*); <u>value</u> *X*; <u>ref</u> *X*; <u>ref</u> (list) *S*;
> <u>if</u> *X* ≠ <u>none</u> <u>then</u> element (*X*). into (*S*);
> <u>ref</u> (linkage) <u>procedure</u> suc (*X*); <u>value</u> *X*; <u>ref</u> (linkage) *X*;
>   suc: = <u>if</u> *X* ≠ <u>none</u> <u>then</u> *X*. suc <u>else</u> <u>none</u>;
> <u>ref</u> (link) <u>procedure</u> first (*S*); <u>ref</u> (list) *S*;
>   first: = *S*. suc;
> Boolean <u>procedure</u> empty (*S*); value *S*; <u>ref</u> (list) *S*;
>   empty: = *S*. suc = *S*;

Notice that for an empty list *S* "suc (*S*)" is equal to *S*, whereas "first (*S*)" is equal to <u>none</u>. This is a result of rule 6.1 and the fact that the two functions have different qualifications.

8. EXTENSIONS

8.1. *Prefixed Blocks*

8.1.1. *Syntax*

> ⟨prefixed block⟩:: = ⟨block prefix⟩ ⟨main block⟩
> ⟨block prefix⟩:: = ⟨object designator⟩
> ⟨main block :: = ⟨unlabelled block⟩
> ⟨block⟩ :: = ⟨ALGOL block⟩|⟨prefixed block⟩
>   ⟨label⟩:⟨prefixed block⟩

8.1.2. *Semantics*

A prefixed block is the result of concatenating (2.2) an instance of a class declaration and the main block. The formal parameters of the former are given initial values as specified by the actual parameters of the block prefix. The latter are evaluated at entry into the prefixed block.

8.2. *Concatenation*

The following extensions of the concepts of class body and concatenation give increased flexibility.

8.2.1. *Syntax*

$\langle$class body$\rangle$:: $= \langle$statement$\rangle | \langle$split body$\rangle$

$\langle$split body$\rangle$:: $= \langle$block head$\rangle;\langle$part 1$\rangle$ inner; $\langle$part 2$\rangle$

$\langle$part 1$\rangle$ :: $= \langle$empty$\rangle|\langle$statement$\rangle;\langle$part 1$\rangle$

$\langle$part 2$\rangle$ :: $= \langle$compound tail$\rangle$

8.2.2. *Semantics*

If the class body of a prefix is a split body, concatenation is defined as follows: the compound tail of the resulting class body consists of part 1 of the prefix body, followed by the statements of the main body, followed by part 2 of the prefix body. If the main body is a split body, the result of the concatenation is itself a split body.

For an object, whose class body is a split body, the symbol inner represents a dummy statement. A class body must not be a prefixed block.

8.3. *Virtual quantities*

The parameters to a class declaration are called by value. Call by name is difficult to implement with full security and good efficiency. The main difficulty is concerned with the definition of the dynamic scope of the actual parameter corresponding to the formal name parameter. It is felt that the cost of an unrestricted call by name mechanism would in general be out of proportion to its gain.

The virtual quantities described below represent another approach to call by name in class declarations. The mechanism provides access at one prefix level of the prefix sequence of an object to quantities declared local to the object at lower prefix levels.

8.3.1. *Syntax*

$\langle$class declaration$\rangle$:: $= \langle$prefix$\rangle\langle$class declarator$\rangle\langle$class id.$\rangle$
$\qquad\qquad\qquad\quad \langle$formal parameter part$\rangle$;
$\qquad\qquad\qquad\quad \langle$specification part$\rangle\langle$virtual part$\rangle$
$\qquad\qquad\qquad\quad \langle$class body$\rangle$

$\langle$virtual part$\rangle$:: $= \langle$empty$\rangle|$virtual: $\langle$specification part$\rangle$

8.3.2. *Semantics*

The identifiers of a $\langle$virtual part$\rangle$ should not otherwise occur in the heading or in the block head of the class body. Let $A_1,\ldots,A_n$ be the prefix sequence of A_0 and let X be an identifier occurring in the $\langle$virtual part$\rangle$ of A_i. If X identifies a parameter of A_j or a quantity declared local to the body of A_j, $j < i$, then for an object of class A_0 identity is established between the virtual quantity X and the quantity X local to A_j.

If there is no A_j, $j < i$, for which X is local, a reference to the virtual quantity X of the object constitutes a run time error (in analogy with 6.2).

8.3.3. *Example*

```
class A; virtual: real X, Y, Z; . . . ;
A class B(X, Y); real X, Y; . . . ;
A class C(Y, Z); real Y, Z; . . . ;
A class D(Z, X); real Z, X; . . . ;
ref (A) Q;
```

The attribute reference $Q. X$ is meaningful if Q refers to an object of class B or D. Notice that all three subclasses contain objects with only two attributes.

8.4. *Example*

As an example on the use of the extended class concept we shall define some aspects of the SIMULA concepts "process", "main program", and "SIMULA block".

Quasi-parallel sequencing is defined in terms of three basic procedures, which operate on a system variable SV. SV is an implied and hidden attribute of every object, and may informally be characterized as a variable of "type label". Its value is either null or a program point [5]. SV of a class object initially contains the "exit" information which refers back to the object designator. SV of a prefixed block has the initial value null. The three basic procedures are:

1) detach. The value of SV is recorded, and a new value, called a reactivation point, is assigned referring to the next statement in sequence. Control proceeds to the point referenced by the old value of SV. The effect is undefined if the latter is null.

2) resume(X); ref X. A new value is assigned to SV referring to the next statement in sequence. Control proceeds to the point referenced by SV of the object X. The effect is undefined if $X. SV$ is null or if X is none. null is assigned to $X. SV$.

3) goto(X); ref X. Control proceeds to the point referenced by SV of the object X. The effect is undefined if $X. SV$ is null or if X is none. null is assigned to $X. SV$.

```
class SIMULA; begin
    ref(process)current;
    class process; begin ref(process)nextev; real evtime;
        detach; inner; current: = nextev; goto(nextev)end;
    procedure schedule(X, T); ref(process)X; real T;
            begin X. evtime: = T; ----------- end;
```

```
process class main program; begin
     L: resume(this SIMULA); go to L end;
  schedule(main program, 0)end SIMULA;
```

The "sequencing set" of SIMULA is here represented by a simple chain of processes, starting at "current", and linked by the attribute "nextev". The "schedule" procedure will insert the referenced process at the correct position in the chain, according to the assigned time value. The details have been omitted here.

The "main program" object is used to represent the SIMULA object within its own sequencing set.

Most of the sequencing mechanisms of SIMULA can, except for the special syntax, be declared as procedures local to the SIMULA class body.

Examples:

```
     procedure passivate; begin current: =current. nextev;
                                 resume(current)end;
     procedure activate($X$); ref $X$; inspect $X$ when process do
       if nextev = none then
       begin nextev: =current; evtime: =current. evtime;
             current: =this process; resume(current)end;
     procedure hold($T$); real $T$; inspect current do
        begin current: =nextev; schedule(this process, evtime+$T$);
           resume(current)end;
```

Notice that the construction "process class" can be regarded as a definition of the symbol "activity" of SIMULA. This definition is not entirely satisfactory, because one would like to apply the prefix mechanism to the activity declarations themselves.

9. CONCLUSION

The authors have for some time been working on a new version of the SIMULA language, tentatively named SIMULA 67. A compiler for this language is now being programmed and others are planned. The first compiler should be working by the end of this year.

As a part of this work the class concept and the prefix mechanism have been developed and explored. The original purpose was to create classes and subclasses of data structures and processes. Another useful possibility is to use the class concept to protect whole families of data, procedures, and subordinate classes. Such families can be called in by prefixes. Thereby language "dialects" oriented towards special problem areas can be defined in a convenient way. The administrative problems in making user defined classes generally available are important and should not be overlooked.

Some areas of application of the class concept have been illustrated in the preceding sections, others have not yet been explored.
An interesting area is input/output. In ALGOL the procedure is the
only means for handling I/0. However, a procedure instance is generated by the call, and does not survive this call. Continued existence, and existence in parallel versions is wanted for buffers and
data defining external layout, etc. System classes, which include
the declarations of local I/0 procedures, may prove useful.

The SIMULA 67 will be frozen in June this year, and the current
plan is to include the class and reference mechanisms described in
sections 2-6. Class prefixes should be permitted for activity declarations. The "element" and "set" concepts of SIMULA will be replaced by appropriate system defined classes. Additional standard
classes may be included.

SIMULA is a true extension of ALGOL 60. This property will
very probably be preserved in SIMULA 67.

DISCUSSION

Garwick:

This language has been designed with a very specific line of
thought just as GPL has been designed with a very specific line.
Dahl's line is different from mine. His overriding consideration
has been security. My effort has always been security but not to
the same degree. I think that Dahl has gone too far in this respect
and thereby lost quite a number of facilities, especially a thing like
the "call by name". He can of course use a reference to a variable;
this corresponds very closely to the FORTRAN type of "call by address", as opposed to the call by name in ALGOL and so for instance he can not use Jensens device. As you know in GPL, I use
pointers. A pointer is not the same as a reference; it is a more
general concept. So I think the loss of facilities here is a little too
much to take for the sake of security.

The "virtuals" seem to be very closely corresponding to the
"externals" in FORTRAN or assembly languages. But you see first
of all you can only access things which belong to the same complex
structure and secondly it seems to me that it is pretty hard to get
type declarations for these procedures. You have to have declared
the type of the value of the procedure and the type of parameters. In
the example given the procedures seem to be parameterless and
they do not deliver any value for the function. So I would like to
know how Dahl would take care of that.

Dahl:

We think of SIMULA as an extension of ALGOL 60. We therefore provide exactly the same kind of specification for a virtual quantity as you would do for a formal parameter. You can write <u>procedure</u> *P*; <u>real</u> <u>procedure</u> *Q*; <u>array</u> *A*; and so forth.

I would much have preferred to specify the formal parameters of *P* within the virtual specification of *P* itself. Then, of course, alternative actual declarations in subclasses could have been simplified by omitting much of the procedure heading. This would have made it possible to check at compile time the actual parameters of a call for a virtual procedure. But in order to be consistent with ALGOL 60, we decided not to do it in this way.

The virtual quantities are in many ways similar to ALGOL's name parameters, but not quite as powerful. It turns out that there is no analogy to Jensen's device. This, I feel, is a good thing, because I hate to implement Jensen's device. It is awful.

If you specify a virtual <u>real</u> *X*, then you have the option to provide an actual declaration <u>real</u> *X* in a subclass. But you cannot declare a real expression for *X*. So, if you specify a quantity which looks like a variable, you can only provide an actual quantity which is a variable. This concept seems more clean to me than the call by name of ALGOL.

To begin with, the whole concept of virtual variables seemed to be superfluous because there was nothing more to say about a virtual variable than what had already been said in the specification. But there is: you can say whether or not it actually exists. A virtual variable *X* takes no space in the data record of an object if there is no actual declaration of *X* at any subclass level of the object. Therefore you can use the device for saving space, or for increasing the flexibility in attribute referencing without wasting space. If you access any virtual quantity out of turn, the implementation can catch you and give a run time error message. It is a problem similar to the "null" problem.

Strachey:

Supposing you had classes *C* and *D*, could you then define procedures *P* in both and if so, if you defined one in *C* and one in *D*, both being called *P*, which one would win? Do the scopes go the reverse way from the ordinary scopes or do they go the same way?

Dahl:

Thank you for reminding me of the problem which exists here. The concatenation rule states that declarations given at different prefix levels are brought together into a single block head. Name conflicts in a concatenated block head are regarded as errors of the same kind as redeclarations in an ordinary ALGOL block head.

However, if there is a "name conflict" between a declared quantity and a virtual one, identity is established between the two, if the declaration and specification "match".

Strachey:

The other thing I was going to ask about is whether you have thought about the question of achieving security, not by making it impossible to refer to any thing which has gone away but by making it impossible to cause anything which is referred to, to go away. That is to say, by keeping an account of the number of pointers or references to each record, which is one of the methods of garbage collection and only letting it go away when this count reaches zero. The curious thing is this is generally faster than garbage collection.

Dahl:

We have made some experiments on that recently which suggest that it may not be faster.

Strachey:

Anyway, have you thought of this as an alternative method for providing security?

Dahl:

Evidently an actual parameter called by name is represented at run-time by a pointer of some kind, and you could achieve security by instructing the garbage collector to follow such pointers in addition to stored reference values. But then the price you pay for the call by name is much higher than for instance in ALGOL, where data referenced by any parameter has to be retained for other reasons. In my view, a call by name mechanism for classes would be a convenient device which would invite a programmer to entirely misuse the computer - by writing programs where no data can ever be de-allocated and without realizing it.

Petrone:

My first question was covered by Strachey but I now have another question which has arisen from his question. I am asking you whether the call by name mechanism was already present in the old SIMULA in the array case. And did you use it in garbage collection on arrays?

Dahl:

That is quite correct. There is a pointer from the object to the array, and the garbage collector will follow it. The reason why we did that is that an array is usually a big thing, which it is reasonable to regard as a separate object.

It is not reasonable to give a small thing like a real variable an independent existence, because that may cause very severe fragmentation of the store. Fragmentation is a disaster if you do not have a compacting scheme, and if you have one the fragmentation will tend to increase the time for each garbage collection and also the frequency of calling for it.

Petrone:

Your concatenation mechanism expresses the possibility of generating families of activity declarations - I am speaking now in terms of your old SIMULA - and the virtual mechanism seems to be a restricted call by name of quantities declared within such a family. Maybe it would be better to restrict the call by name to within an activity block, so that an activity block is equivalent to an ALGOL program with the full call by name mechanism available for procedures.

Dahl:

SIMULA in new and old versions has the complete call by name mechanism for parameters to procedures. You could also have name parameters to classes at no extra cost if you restricted any actual parameter called by name to be computable within the block enclosing the referenced class declaration. That is, it must only reference quantities which are local to that block or to outer blocks. But this is a rather unpleasant restriction considering that an actual parameter may be part of a generating expression occurring deep down in a block hierarchy.

TWO PROPOSALS
TOWARDS DISCRETE MODELLING

JOHN G. LASKI
London, U.K.

1. INTRODUCTION

This work has two concerns, constructive and destructive. The destructive is to expunge the term "simulation language" from our vocabulary. The constructive is to present two independent facilities that may be of some value to the simulation builder.

The first is a language of commands to sequence in real or simulated time activities of interacting parallel processes. This may be added to whatever model-building language is used to express these activities.

The commands are of four kinds: those that suspend a process and express the conditions that must hold before its next activity may begin; those that may effect the status of other processes; those that mediate between processes which require shared resources; those that give a particular process control of the access to particular data. This last is required only when more than one process is in parallel execution in real time; i.e., when there is more than one processor or the single processor multiprograms that have access to this data controlled other than by means of these commands. Finally, since we are interested in simulation, there is a system-provided simulated-time-advancing process in terms of which some of these commands may take an application-oriented form.

The second and more important facility presented is a model-building language. I do not give the commands or predicates, the manipulation and enquiry capabilities, since these can be as extensive or parsimonious as in any other programming language and for much the same reasons of individual taste. What I give is the declaration syntax that allows to be determined whether or not expressions, built up by application of attributes or functions to objects, are well-formed. Effectively, I am proposing a type of data-object adequate to a persistent model of the real word. I then provide a data-structure in which these objects can be interpreted. The motivation is to allow the model-builder to set things up so that he has brought into the syntax the kind of semantic discrimination that leads him to reject expressions like Wife(Mary) as meaningless nonsense. This wholesale cutting down on what are well-formed expressions has two advantages: firstly during the development and execution of programs such semantic errors are caught before they damage the model in unpredictable ways; we can check validity as is done by index-in-range checks on ALGOL arrays but more quickly, more discriminatingly and more meaningfully to the model builder. Secondly we need to allow for data to occupy just that space which it is meaningful to address; Wife(Mary) leads not to a fetch from store of a null value, but to a complaint along the access route that the expression is improper.

(A note on two uses of 'semantic' in this paper is needed. From the point of view of the model builder, 'semantic' is used for those formulae of the model whose sense or nonsense depends on the structure of the object system. Thus Father(Jim) ← Wife(Bill) is semantic nonsense. The proposed language has formal syntax for the model-builder, to make semantic distinctions of this kind syntactically ill-formed. From the point of view of the system implementer 'semantic' is used to refer to the interpretation of the formulae of the language in a certain data-structure. By extension, the data-structure exhibits the semantics of the language).

2. "SIMULATION LANGUAGE"

To stop the use of this term I must establish two things: there is no need to use it; using it does harm. A little history is in order. In the early sixties, it was seen that it would be useful for simulation-programming to add statistical sampling and output routines and what was variously described as a Timer, Cycler or Executive to the general facilities of a programming language. Unfortunately the languages available at that time were almost exclusively aimed at the natural expression of arithmetic on various kinds of number. To express the discrete structures we wished to model, more powerful indirect expressions, set expressions and commands, were found to be useful.

Simulation languages, therefore, were designed and implemented in which a discrete model-description language and a simulation executive were tied up together for the user.

I have elsewhere compared the power of the event and activity-simulation executives and their suitability for describing updating in various kinds of object systems. Process-based systems also can be categorised into event - or activity - based systems.

For example, SIMULA is purely event-based, whereas SOL, with its <u>wait until</u> predicate, requires simple activity-list technique to implement it. The system proposed below also allows dynamic control of sequencing within the activity list to tackle the dispatching problem when several processes are competing for available resources.

With the notable exception of CORC, the user has been required to make a simultaneous choice of simulation executive and discrete modeling language. This simultaneous choice is unnecessary. Consider the way in which the timing mechanism in these languages is implemented. One sees at once that, for example, CSL's T-cells, SIMULA's SQS, SIMSCRIPT's calendars are special examples of the data-objects that these systems allow, and it is very easy to simulate their executives and the effect of their special timing within themselves.

A stronger statement, however, applies. Any of these timing executives may be simulated in any of these languages, less efficiently perhaps, and perhaps having to be rewritten for each model if subroutine linking arrangements are a little weak. I have written an event-based system in CSL and I see no reason not to have an activity-list-based system coded in SIMSCRIPT, though the codings will be inefficient in each case.

The conclusion I draw from this is that there are two distinct concepts for which we want separate names: *discrete modeling languages* and *timing executive*. Put together a language and an executive and we get a *simulation system*.

The historically hallowed term "simulation language" has done positive damage by associating a unique timing executive, and therefore a unique approach to object-system-change, with a unique language and therefore a unique descriptive power. In future we should see modeling languages provided with every kind of timing executive.

We know that the predicates, commands and data structures in the simulation languages are powerful in any discrete, non-numeric, logically complex coding. Yet the outside programming community absorbs these concepts only slowly, believing them to be limited to this single application of simulation.

3. A SIMULATION DRIVER IN A PARALLEL PROCESS FRAMEWORK

A simulation driver will manage co-operative processes that co-operate through the advance of simulated time. Thus, if we have a co-operating process supervisor, we should be able to interpret the driver by providing a simulated-time advancing process, and replacing the simulation commands by commands that affect data referred to by the driver and commands to the co-operating process supervisor. In this way we can separate those concepts that are peculiar to the time-dependent nature of simulation and those that are general to the problems of co-operating processes.

We shall specify certain commands; first, a primitive group that co-operation may take place; second, additions that manage the dispatching problem of breaking ties according to priority rules in the shared-resource situation. We show how these can be interpreted in terms of the primitive commands with the help of a dispatch system process. We can then treat the simulation commands similarly.

The primitive commands are conceptually primitive; they are chosen for clarity of understanding rather than because they form a necessary set. Equally the dispatching extensions are not unique; other choices could be made in the compromise between user convenience and system simplicity. Finally, the way in which the extensions are interpreted is specified not for efficiency but for generality and clarity. Any implementation would depend on system timing for the precise way in which the coding should be made quite, quite different.

We consider processes consisting of the application of programs to data. Any process has as its name the name of its main program unless it was designated by a local name when it was launched. All coding given is informal and aimed at expressiveness.

'$\langle$name$\rangle$' stands for any occurrence of any expression that evaluates to a string when actual parameters have been substituted for free variables, and which can be the same as or distinct from another name.

$$\langle \text{namelist} \rangle :: = \langle \text{name} \rangle \langle, \langle \text{name} \rangle \rangle_0^*$$

The lower index on a bracketed syntactic form is the least number of times the form may appear, the upper the greatest; a missing index is 1. Thus $\langle \ldots \rangle$ means $\langle \ldots \rangle_1'$: otherwise nested BNF is used.

'$\langle$pred$\rangle$' stands for any occurrence of any expression that evaluates to <u>true</u> or <u>false</u> when actual parameters have been substituted for free variables. The primitive commands fall into two groups, the start/stop group and the blocking group.

The blocking groups are:

<u>dyke</u> $\langle \text{namelist} \rangle_0$
<u>undyke</u> $\langle\!\langle \text{namelist} \rangle | \underline{\text{all}} \rangle_0$
<u>seize</u> $\langle \text{namelist} \rangle$
<u>fix</u> $\langle \text{namelist} \rangle$
<u>release</u> $\langle \text{namelist} \rangle_0$

The start/stop groups are:

launch ⟨process⟩⟨called ⟨name⟩⟩$_0$ ⟨controlling namelist⟩⟩$_0$
suspend ⟨process⟩$_0$ ⟨restart ⟨procedure⟩⟩$_0$
activate ⟨process⟩ ⟨controlling ⟨namelist⟩⟩$_0$
end ⟨process⟩$_0$

any list of the above with and as separator.

The effect of a dyke command (which may also be spelt dijk) is
to mark off serially reusable sections of procedures. More precisely, if a process reaches a dyke command it may not continue in
real time unless any other process that has passed a dyke mentioning any name in the namelist has subsequently passed an undyke
mentioning that same name. An undyke without namelist cancels
the effect of the most recent dyke without namelist introduced in
this process. An 'undyke all' cancels the effect of every dyke introduced by this process.

A seize command is the data equivalent of the program dyke.
More precisely, if a process reaches a seize command, no other
process may read or write to the data named in ⟨namelist⟩ until it
is mentioned in the ⟨namelist⟩ of a release command. If any names
in ⟨namelist⟩ involve parameters, the commands apply to any data
accessed by evaluating them.

A fix command is weaker. More precisely, if a process reaches
a fix command, no process - including the one in which it appears -
may alter the data named in ⟨namelist⟩ until a release command has
mentioned this data. This lets a number of processes concurrently
fix some data which only can be written to when all these processes
are finished with it.

Data seized or fixed by a process can be released only by that
process or, alternatively, by a process subsequently launched or
activated by it and empowered to do so (see below).
Finally, if the release command has no namelist it is construed to
refer to all data which the process in which it occurs has seized or
fixed and retained power to release.

THESE COMMANDS CAN EASILY JAM SOLID ALL PROCESSES
IN THE MACHINE - THE USER IS WARNED.

The start/stop commands, by contrast, have obvious effects,
with the exception of the restart clause in the suspend command.
If no process name is provided they refer to the process in which
they occur. No assumptions are made about the actual time-se-
quence in which activated processes are performed. This is regarded as being in the province of the operating system rather than
that of the parallel process supervisor. (FIFO or by-the-authority-
of-their-owner are rules that might be employed.) The restart option is provided so as to enable one to specify a "fix-up" proce-

dure that must be completed before a given <u>suspended</u> process may be re-<u>activated</u> by the co-operating process supervisor †.

There may also be a special activate command whose exact forms depend in part, on hardware:

<u>on</u> ⟨condition⟩ <u>activate</u> process

We can consider such commands as being performed continuously in order to handle interrupts. We shall use a command of this kind later for the timing process of the simulation driver.

We now generalise to the despatching situation. We wish to be able to put a process to bed until a condition is satisfied. We wish to try to wake up a process only at times when the condition might have only just become satisfied. We may be able to wake up several processes simultaneously yet have priority conditions so that only a certain subset will be activated while the rest are put back to bed.

It is not clear to me what logical interface is required by the programmer to specify his requirements. I give some sequencing commands and an interpretation of them by a dispatch process in terms of the primitive commands. It seems to me, however, that the dispatching function is not a global system function acting asynchronously upon all processes that obtain, but rather a system utility that the programmer calls upon to mediate among several resource-sharing processes. This view has two consequences: one can see a tree of levels of global and local dispatching groups; these can be more or less general in the complexity of interaction they require, and hence in the efficiency of the dispatching process they permit. I hold tentatively a similar position on parallel-process supervisors to that which I certainly hold on simulation drivers: there is no "best buy" universal parallel-process supervisor but, rather, according to the logical complexity of the interaction, a "value for money" dispatcher to be picked from the library shelf. Here, the one I shall describe I have coded for clarity and generality in order to bring out the issues involved.

† It has been pointed out to me that there are problems in deciding both bind time for "procedure", and also in what block it shall be deemed to be from the point of view of associating L-values with names. It is defined in the *suspending* process, must have access to the status of the *suspended* process and is executed in the *restarting* process. An unsatisfactory solution is to consider it as operating in an "environmental" namespace external to the processes involved. Clearly the generalisation of hierarchical structure of naming (given by block-structure for the sequential process) to concurrent processes is far from obvious and this restart procedure will powerfully probe any rules put forward elsewhere for exceptions and inconsistencies.

Two new commands are required in the start/stop group:

suspend ⟨process⟩₀ ⟨in ⟨activelist⟩⟩₀ until ⟨predicate⟩⟩₀
⟨restart ⟨procedure⟩⟩₀
incite ⟨activlist⟩₀

A new group of commands, the priority group, is required:

prefer ⟨criterion⟩ ⟨in ⟨activlist⟩⟩₀
prefer ⟨activ⟩ ⟨to ⟨activ⟩⟩ *

where ⟨criterion⟩:: = ⟪max│min⟩ ⟨expression⟩⟩ │first│last│next│previous│any│random│ etc. Suspended processes are regarded as being in one or more activity groups according to those mentioned in any ⟨activlist⟩ in the command that suspended them. If 'in ⟨activlist⟩' was not present, the process is put in a special activity group, the "always group", if the until clause is also missing, the predicate of the suspend command is identically false; otherwise, in the absence of any until clause, the predicate is identically true. An incite command wakes up processes in the always group and in any activity group mentioned in its ⟨activlist⟩. It should be understood, of course, that expressions that evaluate to names of activity groups can appear. Further, these commands can be put together in an and list with other start/stop commands.

The prefer... to .... command controls Priority, which mediates between activity groups. The other prefer command controls Criterion (a) which mediates within an activity group; if no activity group is mentioned explicitly, the intended reference is to all activity groups. The activate command of the primitive group also removes the process from any activity group in which it was placed by the suspend command. The incite command is interpreted as:

for $a\epsilon$ ⟨activlist⟩ do Open (a) ⟵ true; launch dispatch;

Then dispatching is performed by:

let process Dispatch be reference Pred, Proc;
§ test New then do dyke Disp or do New --true;
 Aset ⟵ those $a\epsilon$ ActivityGroups such that Open(a);
 find $p\epsilon$ AlwaysGp such that Pred(p)
  ifany do § p from AlwaysGp; Proc(p); New ⟵ false;
    activate p; end and launch Dispatch §
 fix Priority, Criterion(a) such that $a\epsilon$ Aset;
 find $a\epsilon$ Aset with max Priority(a) such that
    [find $p\epsilon a$ such that Pred(p) with Criterion(a,p)]
  ifnone do § release Priority, Criterion(a) for $a\epsilon$ Aset;
     for $a\epsilon$ Aset do Open(a) ⟵ false;
     undyke Disp; end §
      ⟦final exit from dispatching process nest

release Priority, Criterion(a) for $a \epsilon$ Aset;
Proc(p); New ← false; activate p;
end and launch Dispatch §

Proc(p) will perform such changes to Priority, Criteria and Pred as are needed, since the process to be activated uses shared resources that inhibit activation of competing processes. A process can be inhibited from altering Priority, Criteria and Pred until dispatching is completed by including within its code the two commands:

dyke Disp; undyke Disp;

Notice that Proc may make Pred true where it was not before. This may be used when a suspended process has been blocking another.

An efficient coding would obviously depend on a craftier management of Aset and Open. Precisely how best to code depends both on what hard-ware there is and on the expected pattern of complexity; this should prove a fruitful field for simulation experiments.

We are now in a position to consider the simulation driver. This requires Driver, a process which manages activities either in terms of either an event calendar or T-cells. We will describe it in terms of a calendar, but will also assume the availability of functions:

When(p) where p is the name of a process or resource
When(e, n) where e is an entity and n is an integer.

For processes and resources When(p) evaluates to the epoch of some simulated time at which p will leave the calendar or last left it. Entities, unlike processes and resources, may appear multiply on the calendar and n, if ≥ 0, specifies the nth occurrence on the calendar, if < 0, the $-n$th to have been removed from the calendar. It may be helpful to think of resources and entities as degenerate processes (without activities).

The simulation commands fall into three groups: local, global, modificatory.

The local commands are:

wait ⟨expression⟩$_0$ ⟨restart⟩⟨procedure⟩⟩$_0$
wait until ⟨expression⟩ ⟨restart ⟨procedure⟩⟩$_0$
make ⟨⟨resources⟩|⟨entity⟩⟩ available after ⟨expression⟩
make ⟨⟨resource⟩|⟨entity⟩⟩ available at ⟨expression⟩

The global command is:

wait ⟨activlist⟩ ⟨until ⟨predicate⟩⟩$_0$ ⟨restart ⟨procedure⟩⟩$_0$

The modificatory commands are:

⟨delay | advance⟩ ⟪process⟫ | ⟨resource⟩ | ⟪entity⟩, ⟨expression⟫⟫
by ⟨expression⟩
retime ⟪process⟩ ⟨resource⟩ ⟪entity⟩, ⟨expression⟫⟫ for
⟨expression⟩
cancel ⟪process⟩ | ⟨resource⟩ | ⟪entity⟩, ⟨expression⟫⟫

The effect of the local commands on When and the Calendar is straightforward. The wait command also suspends the process in which it occurs and sets Local (p) ← true. The modificatory commands affect When, and if the process, resource or entity is on the Calendar, may change its position. If its When < Clock it is removed from the Calendar and Driver activated. The cancel command removes the process, resource or entity from the Calendar, if present, and sets When to infinity. Notice that retiming processes, resources and entities not in the Calendar to times in the simulated future does not enter them into the Calendar.

The global wait command suspends the process in which it occurs, and sets Local(p) ← false. If When(e) is mentioned in the Predicate, Tied(p, e) ← true. If no ⟨predicate⟩ appears Tied(p, e) ← true for all e. Proc is set to $e \epsilon$ Calendar do § Tied(p, e) ← false; procedure § and thus always occurs in the suspend command. We can now describe the simulation driver which is launched by an on command whenever all simulation activities are halted.

let process Driver be reference Proc, Pred;
   § dyke Drive; Disp ← false;
     Clock ← min When(e) for $e \epsilon$ Calendar;
     If Clock > SimFin do Terminate;
     while value of §e, result ← e, When(e) for $e \epsilon$ Calendar with
                            min When(e) § = Clock
               notice side-effect on e of block expression
       do §e from Calendar;
         for $p \epsilon$ HaltedProcesses such that $p=e$ or Tied(p, e) do
            test Local(p)
               then do §Local(p) ← false; Proc(p); activate p§
               or if Pred(p)
                  do test ActGp(p) = null
                      then do §Proc(p); activate p§
                      or do Open(ActGp(p)), Disp ← true §
    if Disp do activate Dispatch;
    undyke Drive; end §

Again, if an activity of a process changes Pred etc. in ways that should not occur until the time beat is concluded the command pair:

    dyke Drive; undyke Drive;

should appear.

The attentive reader will have observed that the essential distinction between <u>wait</u> and <u>suspend</u> is that, though both are synchronising operators, the one is effective in simulated and the other in real time.

4. SEMANTIC DISCRIMINATION IN PROGRAMMING SYNTAX

The notion of a record or plex of information associated with an entity or object of a given sort enables the beginning of a semantic-type theory to be a part of a programming language. For an entity of a given sort has a pattern of attributes that may not be used with entities of some other sort. Formally:

$\lambda x \, \text{Captain}(x)$

can be closed only by applying it to an entity of type 'ship' †

The λ-calculus formalism is not good enough. It would suggest that:

Captain(Oslo)

is a well-formed expression (wfe) whereas, of course, entities of the sort 'town' may not have the attribute Captain. 'Captain' can be thought of as a mapping from ships to men. I propose the following formalism:

> $\lambda'Df$. is a function which is defined on the domain D such that $\lambda'Dfd$, given an expression d that evaluates to an object O *of the domain D,* evaluates to the value of the expression obtained from f by substituting d for D wherever it occurs.

(1) Further $R\lambda'Df$ is an optional notation to signify that all expressions so obtained evaluate to objects of the domain R.

The need for semantic type-matching before application can yield a wfe. is not needed in, say, ALGOL 60 where all attributes are realised as vectors over a contiguous list of displacements, so that each semantic type has to have its objects "gödelised" into integers. Thus if Oslo were Town(5), Captain(Oslo) would evaluate to the captain of the fifth ship This simple semantic type-theory articulates well the notions of those systems in which an object is identified with a record. It is, however, not powerful enough to articulate many other object systems. Let me give three examples:

† I am assuming the reader's goodwill in these informal examples. There are to be no looking-glass tricks in our world-description to confuse us with multi-referent names (puns), or multi-named referents (synonyms). No army captains or shipmasters allowed.

a) Captain(Qnmary) is meaningful
   Captain(Tuga)   is meaningful
   Purser(Qnmary) is meaningful
   Purser(Tuga)   is nonsense

   Thus Captain and Purser have domains of application that have
   some objects in common, not others. Conversely, we may see
   this as two objects having some attributes in common, but not
   others.

b) Consider Distance(Oslo, London). Is this an attribute of Oslo?
   Or London? Clearly neither, in fact; Distance is an attribute defined over a domain whose extent is the symmetric logical
   square of the extent of towns.

c) Wife(Bill) is not meaningful early in the life of the object Bill,
   but when a man marries he acquires new attributes (relations).

The formalism (1) can be used to describe a semantic type-theory that accommodates these complexities if the type-matching evaluation rule is generalised to:

(2) $\lambda'Df$ is a function which is defined on the domain D such that,
    given an expression e that evaluates to an object O, *which
    can be shown to be defined in the domain* $D, \lambda'Dfe$ evaluates to
    the value of the expression obtained from f by substituting e
    for D wherever it occurs. Further $R\lambda'Df$ is an optional nota-
    tion to signify that all expressions so obtained evaluate to ob-
    jects of the domain R.

In order to discuss languages in which these ideas of semantic
type (1) and automatic type-transfer (2) appear, we begin with an
informal description that introduces some terminology, and will,
I hope, satisfy the reader that such languages will solve the problems above that are not dealt with in simple-semantic-type languages. We follow this with a fragment of syntax of two such languages. Only that part that enables one to say whether or not the
application or quantification of an expression involving a free variable yields a wfe is shown; the syntactic sugar of commands, predicates, etc., would be no different to that for a simple-semantic-
type language, and therefore is not relevant to our present concerns. Finally, we present data-structures which are possible,
and fairly efficient, implementation of these languages.

What we talk about are *objects*. Each object is of some *sort*. We
are also concerned with (families of) *attributes* and *prex* (defined
below) which are grouped together to be applicable over (explicit)
domains.

An attribute may properly be applied to an object, or an object tested for membership of a prex if and only if the object is presently defined in the relevant domain. Of course, this requires the domain to be a proper one for objects of this sort.

Notice the distinction between domains, which have attributes defined over them, and prex, which are merely agglomerations of objects. Implicit domains correspond to groups of attributes and prex that apply to combinations of objects, built up in ways to be described below.

Objects may be simultaneously defined in several domains. The sort of object thus determines in which domains the object may legally be defined.

It remains to discuss the relationship between the two equivalence-classes of objects introduced: 'of the same sort' and 'in the same domain of applicability'. The more general case is to allow several sorts of objects to be defined in any domain (many-many overlap). Suppose for example Men and Women are two such sorts. Then the domain of which "Father of" is an attribute would be a legal domain for each such sort. The restricted case is to require that the extent of a domain shall be contained within a single sort of objects (one-many overlap). In such a model, People would be a sort of object and each object of this sort would be defined, either in the domain of male attributes or in the domain of female attributes, according to sex.

The advantage of the general case is that it allows any sort of object to be examined with respect to attributes applicable to any domain. If, for example, the model has been set up with objects of distinct sorts, the restricted case would forever bar a domain of attributes being defined which could meaningfully apply to every sort of object. On the other hand, when considering a model of an object system whose structure is fixed, it is natural to think of the objects forming mutually orthogonal universes of discourse with no attributes in common, as is suggested by the relative adequacy of the simple-semantic-type models.

The simpler restricted case is probably adequate for simulation modeling. If objects that were originally seen as being of distinct sorts are suddenly seen as having in common a domain of attributes, then, on the next run, the declarations that structure the model can be recast to accord with the new insight. If, however, the model exists and persists in real time, this wholesale restructuring is not possible and, if I were restricted to having a domain of attributes apply to only a single sort of object, I should not feel safe unless I had only a single sort of objects in the model; after all, every real object has a mass, and it might be relevant to include mass as an attribute in the model. Thus for databanks, the more general structure is to be preferred.

Objects, of course, can be created and destroyed. They may also, during their lifetime, become defined or cease to be defined in any domain appropriate to what sort they are. If they are created without being defined in a domain, no attribute applies to them. Conversely, if they are destroyed, they cease to be defined in any domain.

Later, we will discuss the varying of what domains are appropriate to a given sort of objects, and of the family of attributes applicable in a given domain. Let us remark here that it presents interesting implementation problems and is probably better not admitted for simulation modelling. Again, however, I would not feel safe without the facility if my model were to be persistent in real time.

We now introduce the notion of implicit domains. These are the domains of families of attributes applicable not to the objects we have so far met taken singly, but to specific kinds of combinations of objects. For example, given two distinct domains D_1, D_2 there can be a domain - the <u>logical product</u> domain D, whose attributes could be applied to:

$$\hat{d}\,(d \equiv \{d_1, d_2\})\,, \quad d_1 \in D_1\,, \quad d_2 \in D_2$$

Where the notation $\{\ \ \}$ implies that the order of elements is not significant, that is $\{d_1, d_2\} \equiv \{d_2, d_1\}$. Clearly the logical product domain can also be built up from any number of domains, but those over which it is built must be distinct. Further, its scope lies within the scope of its component domains, where by scope is meant the extent in time of its existence.

5. THE SYNTAX OF DECLARATION COMMANDS

$\langle$stname$\rangle$:: $= \langle$dmname$\rangle$:: $= \langle$atname$\rangle$:: $= \langle$obname$\rangle$:: $= \langle$name$\rangle$
$\langle$stlist$\rangle$:: $= \langle$dmlist$\rangle$:: $= \langle$atlist$\rangle$:: $= \langle$oblist$\rangle$:: $= \langle$namelist$\rangle$

These definitions will allow us to talk about sorts, domains, attributes and objects. The commands that follow suffice to determine whether or not application and quantification expressions are "semantically" well-formed.

<u>sort</u> $\langle$stname$\rangle$ $\langle$<u>with domains</u> $\langle$dmlist$\rangle\rangle$
<u>destroy</u> $\langle$stname$\rangle$

$\langle$stname$\rangle$ is introduced, as the name of a sort of object; the objects of $\langle$stname$\rangle$ may be defined in any of the domains in $\langle$dmlist$\rangle$. The <u>destroy</u> command makes the objects of $\langle$stname$\rangle$ no longer available.

⟨define | loose⟩ ⟨dmlist⟩ over ⟨stname⟩
⟨new | destroy⟩ domains ⟨dmlist⟩

With these commands the allowable domains of ⟨stname⟩ may be
extended or diminished. In the case of the destroy command, any
implicit domains built from destroyed domains are destroyed.
Further the domains cease to be defined for any sort of object.
The define command is restricted to one sort of object in the restricted case.

⟨dmname⟩ logical product ⟨dmlist⟩
⟨dmname⟩ ⟪sym | dir⟩|⟨square, ⟨integer⟩⟫ ⟨dname⟩

These commands introduce implicit domains. The domains in
⟨dmlist⟩ must be distinct and already defined, as must be the domain on the right of the square commands.

⟨prex⟩ :: = ⟨set⟩|⟨list⟩|⟨stack⟩|⟨queue⟩|⟨ring⟩
⟨type1⟩:: = ⟨integer⟩|⟨real⟩|⟨complex⟩|⟨character⟩| ⟨bit ⟩|
          ⟨L-value⟩|⟨offset⟩|⟨prex⟩
⟨type2 :: = ⟨dmname⟩ ⟨type1⟩
⟨type⟩ :: = ⟨type2⟩| value of ⟨type2⟩ ⟨result block⟩

These syntactic types are given as examples only; it may well be
desirable to admit others. ⟨dmname⟩ can be called a semantic type
for the model. We now have the vocabulary to define how to interpret attributes defined to be applicable over domains. The ⟨type2⟩
are direct look-up; the ⟨result blocks⟩ describe an evaluation procedure. However, the latter "functions" are not seen as logically
distinct from "direct look-up evaluation" attributes.

attributes ⟨type, atname⟩* ⟨in ⟨dmname⟩⟫₀
⟨atlist⟩ ceases

These commands make attributes available over a domain, and
lose them.

create ⟨oblist⟩ in ⟨stname⟩ ⟪like | ⟨copy⟩ ⟪⟨oblist⟩|⟨obname⟩⟫|
        ⟨defined in ⟨dmlist⟩⟫₀
⟨oblist⟩ ⟨enters | leaves⟩ ⟨dmlist⟩
destroy ⟨oblist⟩

These commands introduce new objects into the system, vary which
domain they have attributes in, and cancel their existence. The domains referred to, of course, must be definable for objects of the
named sort. copy initialises each attribute of the new objects to the
same value as the objects from which they are copied; like is
weaker, merely defining the objects in precisely the same domains
without initialising the value of their attributes.

Quantified forms of such commands can be introduced. For example:

$s \in$ Hiredships <u>such that</u> Dwt(s) > Big <u>enter</u> Ownedships;

Notice that if 'Hiredships' is a prex, Dwt' is merely an attribute applicable over some domain spanning the objects of the domain on which 'Hiredships' is itself testable, whereas 'Ownedships' names a domain over the extent of which a family of attributes is applicable.

The fragment of syntax exhibited above is sufficient to allow it to be determined whether or not:

⟨atname⟩ (⟨expressionlist⟩)

is a wfe, which it will be if and only if the expression list evaluates a list of objects currently of the same domain as that which the attribute is applicable. A clever compiler, of course, can bind names to objects at compile time or arrange to have them bound at load time to save this explicit run-time type-interpretation. Apart from such semantic types, a useful language would also have to be salted with the traditional syntactic types such as real, numerically indexed arrays and prex with elements in a given domain, and sugared with assignment statements, conditional expression, quantification, and blocks.

6. IMPLEMENTATION IN A DATA STRUCTURE. THE RESTRICTED CASE

The data structure described below realises an interpretation of the declaration fragment given above for the restricted case. The general case follows. Clearly the layout of particular records and their interpretation depends in detail on what is convenient in any particular machine; whether or not particular -valued data is included depends on where the implementation stands in the space/ speed compromise.

The following records are used in the system:

Sort Descriptor

↓ S						
N	FLP	L	DDP	. . . .	DDP	. . . .

N: BCD name of S   )
FLP: Pointer to free list of DDP)   These fields are common
L: Length of S record   )   to all records
DDP: *L*-value of domain descriptor for domains currently definable for this sort of object.

Domain Descriptor

N	FLP	L	S	ADR	...	ADR	...

(with ↓ D marker above the S/ADR boundary)

S: *L*-value of owning sort descriptor if explicit null if implicit.
ADR: Attribute descriptor. This is made up of:
    ADR1: *L*-value of attribute name in system name table.
    ADR2: Type of attribute. This consists of:
        ADR21: Interpretation of attribute, e.g. real, predi-
              cate etc. or address of domain descriptor if
              semantic.
        ADR22: Width of attribute field.
        ADR23: Offset of attribute in data record.
        ADR24: Access routine.

Object

LB	LF	N	FLP	L	S	AR	...	AR

(with ↓ O marker above the S/AR boundary)

LB: *L*-value of 'backward' object of the same sort
LF: *L*-value of 'forward'   object of the same sort
    These provide an implicit prex (two-way list) whose extent is
    the object of this sort.
 S: *L*-value of sort description for this object.
AR: *L*-value of attribute record of this object in domain of corre-
    sponding DDP in sort descriptor; null if object not defined in
    this domain.

Attribute Record

LB	LF	N	FLP	L	O	D	V	...	V	...

(with ↓ A marker above the O/D boundary)

O: *L*-value of object of which this is an attribute record; null if it
    is an attribute record of an implicit domain.
D: *L*-value of domain descriptor of which this is an attribute rec-
    ord
V: Bit patterns giving value of attribute.

Attribute records of implicit domains are accessed via a reference
chain of attributes in the attribute records of the domains of which
they are compounded. For example, if:

    A <u>logical</u> <u>product</u> *B, C, D*;

then, in attribute records of domain B, there is a V, of type <u>offset</u>, that describes which V, of type offset, of the b (= <u>count</u> (<u>entent</u>(B))) such in each C-attribute of objects in domain O, shall be used to retrieve the correct V, of type L-value in each D-attribute record of domain D (there will be $b*c$ in each such record), so that one can retrieve the correct A-record of the $b*c*d$ possible.

Here is the first example of the use of FLP and L to manage storage, in the individual records, if the objects can be created and destroyed after loading. If L is not to be exceeded, certain limitations on the flexibility of declarations must be accepted.

Call a domain <u>static</u> if no element may enter or leave its extent.

Call a domain <u>bounded</u> if there can be predetermined a maximum to the number of objects in its extent.

Call a domain <u>dynamic</u> otherwise.

Then not more than one domain can be dynamic of those domains from which a logical product implicit domain is built up; no domain can be dynamic that is used to build up square domains.

Similar considerations impose restrictions on the dynamic use of statement like:

A <u>attribute</u> <u>real</u> B
<u>new domain</u> A <u>in</u> C

There are two ways of avoiding these restrictions if the evolution of the model cannot be constrained within them. Which is chosen depends on the hardware and software available. The first is to provide some form of two-dimensional addressing such as is only available in certain segmented virtual store machines. The second is to provide relocation mechanism to copy any record whose length is to be increased onto a larger record space. Pointers to this record, of course have to be reset. The store arrangements of systems like AED or L6 encourage this approach.

The management of space in records suggested here leads to practical problems in that, if attribute values, say, are to occupy the same space as those of a previous attribute that is no longer used, traces left behind can lead to unpredictable results. It seems well to have three states for positions in the records. Then, for example, '⟨attribute⟩ <u>ceases</u>' would set the ADR in the domain descriptor from 'in use' to 'deleted', launch some parallel process to set to null the corresponding V for all attribute records of the domain before returning the ADR space in the domain descriptor to the free list.

The implementation of the syntactic fragments given above to set up the required data-structure for any particular model in the restricted system and modify it as it evolves is now straightforward. It is, of course, necessary to have a table maintained to look

up the L-value of the record corresponding to any particular name
as in the implementation of any high-level programming language.
It remains to discuss how $\lambda'DfO$ is evaluated. Checking whether
this is a wfe. is required in general at run time, and is reasonably
efficient in the method shown. However, clever compilers perhaps
helped by advice from co-operative programmers, can arrange to
make the check earlier to increase the efficiency of the object code.

The interrelation of the various records is shown in fig. 1.

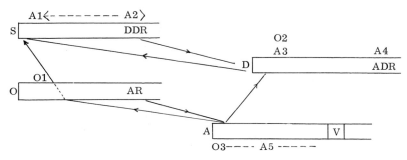

Fig. 1.

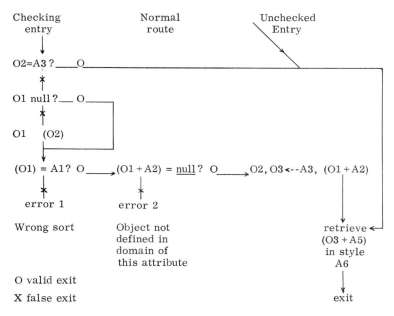

Fig. 2.

Suppose A to be a variable of type attribute, and O a variable of type object. Suppose their R-value to be the attribute and object shown in fig. 1. Then A is a record of six components:

A1: L-value of S
A2: Offset of DDR in S (= offset of AR in O)
A3: L-value of D (redundant since = (A1 + A2))
A4: A3+offset of ADR in D
A5: Offset of V in the A-records (redundant since = (A421))
A6: Accessing and interpretation conventions (= (A4.22) - (A4.24))

O is a record of three components:

O1: L-value of O or null
O2: L-value of D)
O3: L-value of A) for some defined D of O

The required application is best shown by the flow-diagram of fig. 2.

7. IMPLEMENTATION. THE GENERAL CASE

We now consider the general case where domains do not have an owning sort. We require to specify the data-structure, A, O and the application of A to O, which we shall do by comparison with the restricted case. The changes to the records in the data structure is comparatively slight. What we want, in effect, to be able to do is to have a 'domain' that is the logical product of 'the sort of object' and 'explicit domain of attributes' and applicable to which there is a single 'attribute' viz. the offset of the L-value of the attribute records for this domain in object records of this sort of object.

There is no Sort Descriptor needed. For each sort of object there is an offset value S which will be used in each Sort-Domain record. The Domain Descriptor, rather than pointing back to its owning Sort, yields the L-value of a Sort-Domain Descriptor.

Sort-Domain Descriptor

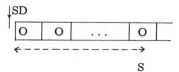

O: Offset of L-value of attribute record corresponding to this domain in objects of the sort S.

The Object record is unchanged save that the offset value S appears in the place where, in the restricted case, the L-value of the Sort Descriptor appeared.

We can now consider the application of the attribute A to the object O in the data-structure that implements the general system. Then A is a record of four components:

> A1: L-value of D
> A2: A1 + offset of ADR in D
> A3: Offset of V in A record (redundant since = (A2.21))
> A4: Accessing and interpretation convention
>   (= A4.22) - (A4.23))

O is the same record of three components as in the restricted case:

> O1: L-value of O or null
> O2: L-value of D)
> O3: L-value of A) for some defined D in O

The required application is shown by the flow-diagram of fig. 3.

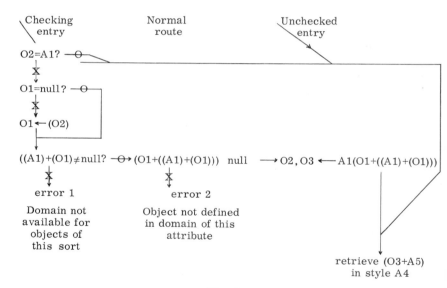

Fig. 3.

comment (A1)   = L-value of SD
       (O1)   = Offset value S for this object
therefore ((A1)+(O1)) = Where L-value of this domain is found in
                  this object descriptor.

ACKNOWLEDGEMENTS

Arguments of my friends, especially Alan Tritter and Gary Marliss, have added much to the clarity of the ideas, and their expression, expounded here.

The Support of the S. R. C. (Atlas Computer Laboratory) for this work is gratefully acknowledged.

DISCUSSION

Garwick:

I was wondering very much how the speaker was going to manage not to assign core store for something before he needed it. What he has done is to replace the problem of cluttering up the store with records you are not using by another and worse problem - namely store access. Here you have to have a series of pointers to run round and you have to interpret the description in order to find out what you are talking about at run time. As you very well know, core store is getting cheaper and cheaper practically day by day and they are not getting all that much faster. You are saving store at the cost of time - I think this is the wrong way round.

Laski:

I am sorry - I am going to say that I have not got my implementer's hat on. I'm concerned not with how one could implement particular fragments of such a system; I am concerned with the underlying ideas of what is needed in order to be able to talk about the world in the complexity that the world displays. No doubt, those damned engineers will design computers to do what is wanted if we are clear about what is wanted.

Ross:

I hope that Laski will accept my compliments on having the germination of a number of good ideas which have a very important role to play, but to me the most important thing - aside from reading the paper itself - about his comments was when he said, "Let us not use the word simulation language". When it comes to this question of implementation, much of what he has got sketched there could either be done interpretively at run time or at compile time and could go many different ways. I am more concerned to know if it is possible for you who think of yourselves as simulators to change for the sake of the rest of the world your terminology and just talk about rich language or complex problems - because there is really a vast population whom the world simulation scares away. I plead guilty to the same problem on another score - in that our own work is always labelled with "computer aided design" and every time we talk about it, we say "No - we are really talking about general complex problem solving".

I think we should get some better terminology than computer simulation or computer aided design.

Laski:

Can I put forward my suggestion which is 'Data Base Management' languages?

Ross:

May I say I think that would not be sufficient. I think it is "real life" or "richness" or "complexity" - somehow we have to catch those concepts in a word which will be meaningful to a much larger audience.

Lackner:

If I understand Laski's point of view as expressed in his paper and in his talk this morning, he wants a great deal of flexibility in that the user may more or less define his own scheme of simulation in so far as a driver for simulation is concerned. On the other hand - I am not sure he demands as much flexibility in the area of data structure and I think the emphasis should be reversed. I think a great deal of flexibility is necessary in the structuring of data so that the particular scheme he has shown would be one of many that would be open to an implementer of the simulation model. In cases where the data types tend to be very few and there are very many instances of the same type, advantage might be taken of the ability to have a scheme similar to this. In other cases, things like sentences are being developed and passed around through the model, and things which vary in length and vary in the number of attributes. In these cases, a scheme allowing and demanding more pointers, might be more useful.

Laski:

I would entirely agree with this. I regard my suggestion as a particular primitive kind of object that I think has a useful duration. I can think of others but I am very bothered by the whole problem of managing and cross-referencing such a structure. I do not understand the term 'file-structure'. I am trying to have a model of the external world that is in some way a natural one. Now, my suggestion is natural to some particular kinds of problems that have interested me. This does not exclude others being natural to the intuitions of other people.

A SIMULATION-ORIENTED MEMORY ALLOCATION ALGORITHM

R. J. PARENTE

IBM Advanced Systems Development Division
Yorktown Heights, New York, USA

Abstract. In implementing a simulation language, the method of allocating memory must be integrated with the internal data organization and referencing scheme. Thus, it has a strong influence on the structure of the language.

The algorithm that is presented is intended to support a data organization that provides for the referencing and manipulation of several types of records, where each type of record and its structure is defined by the user of the language. Separate lists of available records are constructed, dynamically, for each type of record. Thus, searching is usually avoided when a record is obtained or returned. "Garbage-collection" is semiautomatic in that the user must explicitly return records, but consolidation of available records is accomplished automatically when necessary. Implementation of a capability to collect records in sets is easily accomplished using the algorithm as a base.

Implementation of the algorithm as a package of FORTRAN functions is shown in an appendix.

1. INTRODUCTION

The design of any memory allocation algorithm must be based on some assumptions about its use. The algorithm that is presented is based on assumptions that appear to be valid within the context of a simulation language. It is for this reason that it is referred to as a "simulation-oriented" memory allocation algorithm.

In the development of processors for simulation languages, the use of list processing techniques in the implementation of facilities for manipulating sets and for handling transient data has become fairly standard practice. The list elements in the simulation systems differ from the list elements in list processing systems, such as SLIP [155] in that, normally, several types of list element exist, rather than a single type. This imposes on the supporting memory allocator the requirement that it must be capable of delivering and receiving list elements, hereafter referred to as records, containing different numbers of cells. The solution to the problem can be simplified, as in the original SIMSCRIPT [98] implementation, by arbitrarily selecting several fixed record lengths and by maintaining status information within each record.

In the design of the algorithm described below, one of the primary objectives was to eliminate the need for fixed record lengths. Other objectives were to avoid searching through lists whenever possible and to consolidate adjacent records only when necessary. The price that is paid to meet these objectives is the loss of space that is occupied by the memory allocator.

2. ASSUMPTIONS

The following assumptions have been made about the environment within which an implementation of the proposed algorithm must function:
1. Several types of record will be requested. All execution-time memory requirements will be satisfied by the memory allocator. This includes requests for a sufficient number of memory cells for a single record, a group of records, or a program.
2. With certain exceptions, the number of record types and their lengths can be determined prior to execution time. The exceptions result from the desire to allow certain dimensions to vary during execution.
3. The user can return records that are no longer needed.
4. The majority of requests will be for records containing two or more cells.

3. THE ALGORITHM

Let S be a group of M contiguous memory cells that are available for use.

Let V be a list of records, with each record containing two or more cells in S (fig. 1). The first cell in each record contains a link to the next record in the list or NULL, indicating the end of the list. The second cell in each record contains the length of the record.

Let U be a list of unit cell records, with each record containing a link to the next record in the list or NULL (fig. 2).

Let H be a sequence of N lists such that each $H(I)$ is a list of homogeneous records; also, let L be a sequence of lengths such that $L(I)$ is the length of each of the records in $H(I)$. The first cell in each record in list $H(I)$ contains a link to the next record in the list or NULL (fig. 3).

The records in list V are ordered with respect to their position

R.J. PARENTE

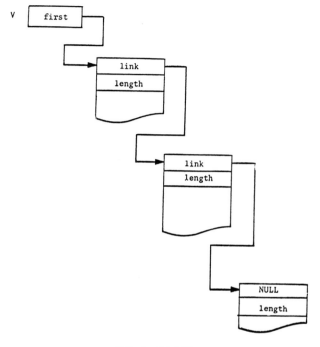

Fig. 1. List *V*.

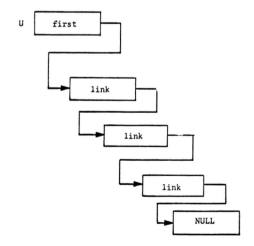

Fig. 2. List *U*.

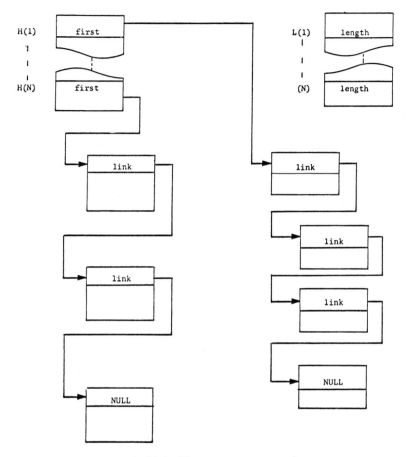

Fig. 3. List of homogeneous records.

in S; all other lists will be maintained as last-in, first-out queues. Initially, all of S is considered to be a single record of length M, in list V. All other lists are empty. L contains the lengths of the records in homogeneous lists.

The three basic functions to be considered are:
1. obtaining a record of length K,
2. returning a record, R, of length K, and
3. the consolidation of adjacent records into a single record.

When a request for a record of length K is received, an attempt is made to satisfy that request from one of the homogeneous lists.

If this is not possible, the request is satisfied from list V. When a record is returned, an attempt is made to return it to one of the homogeneous lists. If this is not possible the record is returned to list V. Consolidation occurs only when a request is received for a record of length K, and no record exists that contains K cells, or more than K cells.

The procedure for obtaining a record, R, of K cells is:
1. If K is equal to any $L(I)$, and the corresponding list $H(I)$ is not empty, then obtain R from $H(I)$.
2. If K is 1, and list U is not empty, then obtain R from U.
3. If K is not 1, and is not equal to any $L(I)$, or if the corresponding list, U or $H(I)$, is empty, then search list V for a record, T, with length, l, that is equal to or greater than K.
4. If T exists, and l is equal to K, then R is obtained by removing T from list V.
5. If T exists, and l is greater than K, then remove T from list V, form records R and r, where R contains K cells and r contains $(l\text{-}K)$ cells, and return r.
6. If T does not exist, then remove a record, Q, from any $H(I)$ for which the corresponding $L(I)$ is greater than K.
7. If Q exists, then form records R and r, where R contains K cells and r contains $(L(I)\text{-}K)$ cells, and return r.
8. If Q does not exist, then perform the consolidation function.

The procedure for returning a record, R, of K cells is as follows:
1. If K is 1, then enter R as the first record in list U.
2. If K is equal to any $L(I)$, enter R as the first record in list $H(I)$.
3. If K is not 1, and is not equal to any $L(I)$, then insert R into list V, ranked by its position in S.

The procedure for consolidating records that are adjacent, in S, is:
1. Return all records in lists $H(I)$ through $H(N)$ to list V.
2. Combine adjacent records into single records in list V.
3. If two successive records in list V are separated by a single cell, search list U for that cell and, if it is found, combine all three records into a single record in list V.

4. IMPLEMENTATION

The implementation of the algorithm that is shown in the appendix is entirely in FORTRAN. It treats S as a vector and each record identifier as an index in S. Such an implementation limits the length of S to the maximum subscript that is allowed by the FORTRAN processor. Also, the program shown in the appendix contains a crude sorting method for use during consolidation.

A different implementation, written in part or wholly in an assembly language, would remove the restrictions imposed by FORTRAN.

5. SUMMARY

An algorithm has been presented that allows the build-up of N homogeneous lists of available records. After the build-up takes place, a request for a record and the return of a record can be satisfied by simple manipulations involving the first record in a list. Provision is made for "abnormal" requests, i.e., requests for records that are not contained in any of the homogeneous lists, and for consolidating records.

6. APPENDIX

The FORTRAN program shown in this appendix is not intended as an optimal implementation, but rather as a supplemental description of the memory allocation algorithm that is presented. The program assumes that $L(1)$ is initialized to 1; thus, list $H(1)$ is list U.

```
      FUNCTION NEW (K)
      COMMON S(5000), V, H(25), L(25), N
      INTEGER S, V, H, L, N
c     DOES K MATCH WITH A LENGTH IN L
      DO 101 I = 1, N
      IF (L(I) - K) 101, 102, 101
 102     INDEX = I
         GO TO 103
 101     CONTINUE
         GO TO 105
c
c     IS LIST H(I) EMPTY
 103 IF (H(INDEX)) 104, 105, 104
c
c     OBTAIN R FROM H(I)
 104 J = H(INDEX)
      H(INDEX) = S(J)
      NEW = J
      RETURN
c
```

```
c     IS LIST V EMPTY
  105 IF (V) 108, 200, 108
c     CONSOLIDATE RECORDS
  106 CALL CONS (LGL)
      IF (LGL - K) 107, 105, 105
  107 STOP
c
c
c     IS THERE AN H(I) WITH RECORDS LARGER THAN K CELLS
  200 DO 201 I = 1, N
          IF (L(I) - K) 201, 201, 202
  202 INDEX = I
      GO TO 203
  201 CONTINUE
      GO TO 106
c
c     IS H(I) EMPTY
  203 IF (H(INDEX)) 204, 106, 204
c
c     SPLIT A RECORD FROM H(I)
  204 J = H(INDEX)
      H(INDEX) = S(J)
      CALL RTRN (J + K, L(INDEX) - K)
      NEW = J
      RETURN
c     IS THE FIRST RECORD IN V LARGER THAN K CELLS
  108 IF (S(V + 1) - K) 116, 114, 115
c
c     OBTAIN R FROM TOP OF V
  114 J = V
      V = S(V)
      NEW = J
      RETURN
c
c     SPLIT FIRST RECORD IN V
  115 J = V
      V = S(V)
      CALL RTRN (J + K, S(J + 1) - K)
      NEW = J
      RETURN
c
c     SEARCH LIST V
  116 LPT = V
      IPT = S(V)
  112 IF (IPT) 113, 200, 113
```

```
   113 IF (S(IPT + 1) - K) 111, 109, 110
c
c      REMOVE A RECORD FROM V
   109 S(LPT) = S(IPT)
       NEW = IPT
       RETURN
c      SPLIT A RECORD IN V
   110 S(LPT) = S(IPT)
       CALL RTRN (IPT + K, S(IPT + 1) - K)
       NEW = IPT
       RETURN
c
c      EXAMINE NEXT RECORD IN V
   111 LPT = IPT
       IPT = S(IPT)
       GO TO 112
c
c
       END
       SUBROUTINE RTRN (R, K)
       COMMON S(5000), V, H(25), L(25), N
       INTEGER S, V, H, L, N, R
       IF (K - 1) 100, 110, 100
   100 S(R + 1) = K
c
c      DOES K MATCH WITH A LENGTH IN L
   110 DO 101 I = 1, N
       IF (L(I) - K) 101, 102, 101
c
c      RETURN R TO H(I)
   102 S(R) = H(I)
       H(I) = R
       RETURN
   101 CONTINUE
c
c      INSERT R IN LIST V
       IF (V) 105, 104, 105
   105 IF (V - R) 103, 104, 104
c
c      RETURN R TO TOP OF V
   104 S(R) = V
       V = R
       RETURN
c      SEARCH R FOR INSERTION POINT
   103 LPT = V
```

```
      IPT = S(V)
  109 IF (IPT) 107, 106, 107
c
c    INSERT R
  106 S(LPT) = R
      S(R) = IPT
      RETURN
c
c
  107 IF (IPT - R) 108, 106, 106
  108 LPT = IPT
      IPT = S(IPT)
      GO TO 109
c
      END

      SUBROUTINE CONS (LGL)
      COMMON S(5000), V, H(25), L(25), N
      INTEGER S, V, H, L, N, U
      DO 101 I = 2, N
      K = L(I)
      L(I) = 0
  103 IF (H(I)) 102, 104, 102
  102 J = H(I)
      H(I) = S(J)
      CALL RTRN (J, K)
      GO TO 103
  104 L(I) = K
  101 CONTINUE
      IF (V) 202, 201, 202
  201 STOP
  202 IPT = V
      LGL = S(IPT + 1)
  211 LINK = S(IPT)
      LGTH = S(IPT + 1)
      IF (IPT) 203, 205, 203
  205 RETURN
  203 M = IPT + LGTH
      IF (LINK - M) 206, 204, 207
  204 S(IPT) = S(M)
      LGTH = LGTH + S(M + 1)
      S(IPT + 1) = LGTH
      IF (LGL - LGTH) 251, 211, 211
  251 LGL = LGTH
      GO TO 211
```

```
207 IF (LINK - (M + 1)) 206, 208, 206
206 IF (LGL - LGTH) 210, 209, 209
210 LGL = LGTH
209 IPT = LINK
    GO TO 211
208 U = H(1)
    K1 = 0
223 IF (U) 221, 206, 221
221 IF (U - M) 222, 224, 222
222 K1 = U
    U = S(U)
    GO TO 223
224 LGTH = LGTH + 1
    S(IPT + 1) = LGTH
    IF (K1) 226, 225, 226
225 H(1) = S(U)
    GO TO 204
226 S(K1) = S(U)
    GO TO 204
    END
```

DISCUSSION

Garwick:

The system which you have used there does not seem to be fool-proof and it is not secure. You can get your records scattered all over the place, in such a way that you cannot compact them, and you still need space. Have you considered a much simpler scheme, which I will describe? You start out with one continuous store which has been set to zero. Now each time you want a new record you just take it from the lowest area of this store. Then, of course, to get a record is extremely fast. Finally, you run out of free space. At that time many of the records you have created earlier are no longer pointed to by anything. You now are able to find out where the pointers are, because you know the types of records you have created. You can compact the storage - move it all into one end of the store. Zero out what is left and continue in the same way. This compacting - the time taken is mostly dependent upon the amount of data you have to move. The time taken to recognise the pointers is extremely short - I am talking from experience - and on a reasonably fast computer, e.g. CDC 3600 - the complete garbage collection of about 20 thousand words is of the order of 50 milliseconds.

Parente:

You are correct in saying that there is no security built into this system. It does assume that the user has a great deal of responsibility and as I said, I think that security can be built in at a much broader or higher level than down at this basic mechanism level.

Garwick:

I am sorry - I did not mean security in that sense. What I meant was that you can get into a situation when you have enough core store but you have nowhere in the store a big enough gap to put your records.

Parente:

Yes - I agree that that is the problem. I do not know the solution. The reason we did not do as you suggest is because we have the situation where the user is allowed to move pointers around and store them as variables or as attributes of his records and it is not in general possible for us, through the systems mechanism, to update all of these pointers.

Laski:

How does this system compare with the other systems that are well established for dealing with this problem? For example, Doug Ross's AED system and the Burroughs B8500 system. Do you think that there is not required some communication from the user to advise the storage allocater as to what kind of special records there should be and has anybody simulated this?

Parente:

I agree that this is very similar to the AED approach. I do not know the B8500 system.

Dahl:

I want to know whether you have had any practical experience with this and how does it behave in different situations?

Parente:

Very little - mainly because the system for which it is being implemented is not complete. This is a working program but only very minor tests have been made.

Ross:

The system described in Parente's paper is almost without change a sub-set of the free storage system that we have had in use for some time now in the AED system. The specific points which I would like to make are that I prefer to use the word "allocation" for the strategy aspect of using storage and keep that separate from the mechanism of storage allocation. So in particular, Parente described not a part of the allocation but a part of the free storage machinery. Our experience has shown that the allocation strategy is something which is very much problem dependent. We separate out this strategy in what we call 'Help procedures' - these are places where the system free storage machinery calls for help from the particular user of the storage, concerning what type of strategy is appropriate.

This is less important if you have only a single domain of storage. We break storage into zone structure which is hierarchical, and then you can have separate block sizes - we call then chunks - in each zone. So you can have separate strategies and separate types of records in each zone.

Now, with respect to Garwick's comment on the very simple method of treating storage - this is one of the many versions of strategy which we can have, and is appropriate in some cases. It is not appropriate in all cases - especially where you have many different record types and complex uses of pointers. We do, however, have it in use in various places - especially in some of our storage structures that go with our graphical display system in which the user of the graphical display has no idea at all how the structure is being physically represented in the computer. Finally, Dahl asked about experience on this storage mechanism: we have had lots of it and it works fine, providing that you do have the richness of many different forms of allocation and that you tune the form you use to the particular job. This I think is supremely important: the business of how you physically use storage and how you dynamically allocate it is an integral part of the problem solving process.

GENERAL DISCUSSION - SESSION 3

Krasnow:

I think that several major subject areas have been opened up this morning and I would characterise them as follows. First, the notion of extendibility of language, which is in one form or another something like motherhood: - most people seem to want it but the questions seem to be "How ? - by whom ? - in what form ?" and so on. Dahl raised the question of security on how far we could go in this direction, at what cost. We have the questions concerning distinction between the data structuring aspects of simulation languages and simulation control and finally the subject area of data structuring and its effect on storage allocation.

Ross:

I think that Garwick's operator definition system is a case of augmenting in the sense that we used it yesterday. I am coming to the conclusion myself that the only way that you can truly extend a language is by modifying the language processing scheme itself. Notice that if you do bring in parallel and quasi-parallel routines, these are true modifications of the underlying mechanisms of an ALGOL 60 type of system, so that a simulation language is a real extension of ALGOL 60.

Nygaard:

There is at least one conclusion which seems to come out of this conference on a rather controversial subject. This is that programmers can be divided into two groups - one which may be called the high priests or the 1% group, and the 99% group which have quite a large range of names and classifications.

It is the common belief here that this Conference consists of people belonging to the 1% group - this is not true, since I am a representative of the 99% group and I think since we are so many and we are going to use these tools, we should have the right to say something here. We are simple-minded men but we have complex problems and we are forced to face these complex problems. Just as Dahl said in his presentation, we may have no previous experience with programming but we are forced to solve these complex problems, for example, by simulation. When Garwick talked about

his language, he said this was a super language which solved all
problems. Of course, even if it looked a little frightening still I
was relieved.

But then - what happened? He said that this is just for the 1%
group - but for the 99% we are going to provide a number of different languages which are defined in the general language so, therefore, we are forced to learn all these languages instead. This is
not what we want. What we want is to be given concepts so that we
can handle complex problems in a manner which we are able to
grasp.

We also have a number of other problems. We want security.
We want to be able to learn this language and not afterwards have
to learn machine language. We want to be able to debug in this
language. Here is another point; it is that we may work on a variety of levels. Some of us have quite definite problem areas and
if some person would create a dialect for us which will provide us
with highly aggregated concepts, for our areas, this is sufficient.
However we know that sooner or later we have to extend this dialect.... Therefore, it should be possible to create dialects in a
way which makes it possible for us to structure out the concepts of
the dialect.

Strachey:

It seems to me that you will never achieve simplicity without
understanding. The way in which you achieve simplicity in a language is by understanding its concepts and the problems that underly them. If you are not prepared to put in the effort to understand
the concepts of computing or writing programs, then you will never
get a simple language - you will get a language which is a weak language and which requires a great many atoms of very short instructions. A simple language is one which corresponds to the important
ideas.

With regard to the extension or augmentation of a language: it
seems to me that there are two sorts of modifications to a language.
There is the sort that the designers of the language have thought of
to start with. That is to say, for example, in **ALGOL** by using the
syntactic form of a procedure and writing a new procedure. Now
that is not really extending the language at all - that is just using it.
It extends its power because by using sub-routines or by procedures,
you obviously increase the power of the language. You encapsulate
a new idea into a small easily used package.

The other thing that people seem to ask for is the ability to
change the syntax of the language - to change the meaning of operators or their binding power or something like this. Now that I think

is extremely dangerous because, as Ross said, this almost certainly means getting inside the processor and changing that.

I have got a hypothesis to put forward about modification - I
think a programming language should be easy to modify if and only
if it is a bad programming language. Now one part of this is obviously true.... if it is a bad programming language, it should be
easy to modify it to get it right. The other part I suggest is open
to experimental verification.

Now one last point, if I may, about something quite different.
This is about storage allocation. I think there is another point which
we need to bear in mind and that is that the efficiencies of our strategies of storage allocation depend very much on the hardware we
have. If there are one or two spare bits in a word which are not
concerned with the information used in processing, then it is much
easier to write storage allocation routines. In particular, one would
like to have some marker bits in the word to say whether or not you
have got a pointer here. Now it seems to me that this is the sort of
thing that language designers should be making a fuss about. This is
the sort of thing we should tell the engineers that we want - two or
three extra bits on every word.

They refuse because they never have to write storage algorithms
themselves.

Knuth :

I would just like to say that I believe there is another axiom or
theorem which says: "All programming languages are bad". I think,
in connection with Strachey's remark, this is quite significant.

Petrone :

Regarding Parente's paper, I would like to mention that the solution of maintaining lists of records of the same size was also
used by McNeley in his implementation of SOL. This system is
well-suited for use in systems which are well balanced, in which
nearly as many records die as others come to life. In addition this
system may be combined with compacting which will move all active
records to one end of the storage, only when the first way fails.

Dahl :

Regarding storage allocation mechanisms and strategies, I
would just like to recall the experience we have had with SIMULA
for $2\frac{1}{2}$ years. The storage allocation strategy is roughly of the type
that was presented to us by Parente: a little more uniform but a
little more time consuming perhaps. We have found that it behaves

rather well for the type of jobs that we have had and they have been all sorts of simulation problems.

We have not felt the need for different strategies - perhaps because we have had only that one. Now, very recently, we have started out to try to compare this method that we have been using with the compacting method that Garwick recalled. We are not quite sure yet but it does seem as if compacting behaves at least as well for typical simulation problems. Is that something Ross could correct?

Ross:

I think the only expensive part about compacting, as Garwick pointed out, is the actual manipulation of pointers in the records being moved. This is quite an inefficient job even with present day hardware, so that the trick is in the recognition of which pointers need to be moved. My own feeling is that the business of controlling the way in which storage is used, pays still better. We make the analogy between the use of storage and constructing a building: when you construct a building, you also construct scaffolding which is used only during the building process. This scaffolding is returned to free storage on completion and you are left with the building which has been constructed. Now it is very easy to know the difference between scaffolding and part of the actual building, during the building process. Then you actually get new records of these two types from two different places. When you are done with the building process, instead of having to return or compact or do anything to each record individually, we can free an entire zone, which is feasible if you have made sure that you only put the scaffolding type of records in that zone. This I believe is the best of all strategies - to make the use of storage a part of the problem solving process. Know the difference between scaffolding and non-scaffolding and when you are through with scaffolding, get rid of it all at once. You are then doing things on a wholesale basis rather than retail and I think that is where the real pay-off lies. It does require that you have the richer free-storage machinery.

Garwick:

I shall just answer some of the people who have talked about GPL here. Ross asked the question whether something is an augmentation or extension: this is obviously a question of definition. But he said that it was an extension if you introduce quasi-parallel programming. Well, that is very easy to do in GPL - you can even operate co-routines. You can already do that without changing the compiler, so really I do not understand the difference between aug-

mentation and extension. Nygaard claims that he is simple-minded
but obviously if he was, he would not be qualified to define a new
language. So we cannot take him at face value. Furthermore, a restricted language is a subset of the full language i.e. you do not
have to learn something new in order to use a restricted language.

Then, all the concepts in SIMULA which are different from
ALGOL - they are all translatable into GPL, contrary to Laski's
opinion. Finally, Strachey mentioned the dangers of re-defining
operators. In GPL you can change the meaning of an operator but
you cannot change its priority. This has one advantage - that you
are able to simulate the arithmetic of one computer on another
when re-defining the meaning of, say, multiplication of two real
numbers.

Laski:

I have four criticisms of SIMULA. Three of them are unimportant; they are about the lack of quantified expressions, which is a
matter of taste and of how much spice you want in your syntax. Also, I do not like their hierarchical objects but I think one can model
with them. I think that they are moving towards external data as
they find great need for it.

On a serious point as opposed to a matter of opinion, I do not
feel that the sequencing mechanisms are adequate in the case of
simultaneity, e.g. in the case of conflicts between processes which
require scarce resources and in the case where there is more than
one processor and you want security of data used by one process
against being fouled up by other genuinely parallel, as opposed to
quasi-parallel, processes.

Dahl:

First of all, I agree entirely with Laski that we have not in
SIMULA as yet any basic concepts relating to physical parallel
processors and if you are going to deal with such things you have
to add more concepts. That is a very interesting area in which to
do research just now. With regard to the missing quantifiers, I
should like to state that the language which Laski was moving towards in his paper does not seem to be applicable to computers as
they exist today.

Now, I also want to say that it is of course a very worthwhile
activity to envisage such languages, also in the hope that this activity might influence the builders of machines. But the SIMULA
language has been thought of as a bridge between problem areas
and existing machines. I suggest that the execution times of programs are proportional to the size of your problems measured

roughly in number of components, raised to some power. If you encourage the use of facilities that will make that power greater than
it ought to be, such as abstract set mechanisms, then you are, in
effect, often preventing yourself from being able to analyse life-
size systems on computers as they are today.

Nygaard:

I completely agree with Laski in his serious criticism on
SIMULA. We are moving into new problem areas - therefore, we
need more flexible sequencing. In SIMULA 67, it will be possible
to build up alternative sequencing schemes. We have one made already by us using the philosophy which we adopted in SIMULA. But
you can create others.

Ross:

This is not really so much a reply to Garwick as a clarification
of the distinction between augmenting and extending.

First of all, the mere fact that one has co-routines in a language,
does not do violence to the concept. We have things that are even
more complex than co-routines. I think the key thing is that for any
given processor, there must exist some other things which cannot
be processed by that language processor and those are the things
which would come into the extension domain. I think really that what
Garwick was pointing out was that GPL is rich enough so that it will
already encompass most of what others talk of as extension and
thereby will not seem to need extension. But I certainly hope that
we are not at the last possible step and that there will still exist
things which do require modification of the basic method of operating. These would then require true extensions.

PANEL DISCUSSION ON DATA STRUCTURING

Introductory note by Hoare

The problem of including data structures in a high-level language involves the reconciliation of a number of conflicting objectives. These objectives may be summarised under three headings:

(1) Security: a good programming language must remove, as far as possible, the opportunities of coding errors. No incorrect program submitted to a computer should produce results which are unpredictable, or which are unintelligible to the programmer in terms of the language itself. Notations should be clear, precise, and readable, and their static structure should correspond to the dynamic structure of the algorithm, and should facilitate proof of program validity. It should be easy to submit programs for inspection and verification by others, either privately or by publication. It is only by achieving security that we can solve the central problem of computer programming, which is the construction of *correct* programs.

(2) Efficiency: many interesting problems are of a size to absorb nearly all the computing power and storage capacity available for their solution. If the use of a programming language involves significant penalties in time or space, it will be quite impossible to use the language on such problems. With data structuring, the problem of efficiency centres around the garbage collection technique, and the use of backing stores. The choice of efficient methods will have an influence on the design of the language features.

(3) Flexibility: in principle, a programming language should be capable of solving any problem which could be programmed in the machine code of the computer. Flexibility may be sought by one of two approaches:

a. By abstracting the basic concepts of algorithmic procedures, and providing a minimal framework of facilities which may be used to program any desired new feature.

b. By inclusion in the language of a large number of features and facilities, which will cover the major part of the known requirements of problem programs. This second approach is probably suited only to fairly special-purpose languages.

It is obviously easy to design languages which satisfy any single one of these criteria; and it is not difficult to design languages which satisfy any two. But it seems quite impossible to design a data structuring feature which is entirely satisfactory according to all criteria. A successful language must therefore be something of a compromise between all three objectives.

The proposed objective of the panel discussion is:

(1) to illustrate the manner in which the requirements conflict, by considering the choices made by various language designers;

(2) to explore technical solutions which will minimise the conflict of objectives;

(3) to evaluate the relative importance of the three objectives in the establishment of a satisfactory compromise.

* * * * *

Hoare:

I have made available a brief note which I have circulated to my panelists, in which I have tried to set the scene within which we can have a fruitful discussion.

I think that there is a tendency in the design of software and the design of languages for the designers to work in an atmosphere of complete freedom. This is a field in which the imagination is free to invent anything of which the mind can conceive. In some ways, this area is very similar to subjects such as philosophy, metaphysics or theology. Perhaps this explains why it is so difficult to conduct a calm and rational discussion on these topics.

I think the solution must lie in the recognition that in designing languages or any form of software, we are really only designing a tool to be used by other people, and that there are certain fairly objective criteria by which the user is able to judge the tool that we are putting into his hands. We are like the designers of any piece of equipment - any piece of hardware - a car or an aeroplane. We have to recognise as clearly as possible before we start, exactly what it is we are trying to do, and what the service is that we wish to give to the customer.

I have given in my note a summary of a large number of different aims under three major headings - security, efficiency and flexibility. I have tried in the summary to give a fairly broad interpretation to each of these words. I think it would be instructive to see how, in fact, language designers are influenced by these three major objectives or major classes of objectives. To illustrate this theme, I have invited the panelists to comment on the ways in which these objectives are reflected in their designs, the ways in which they have devised technical solutions to minimise the conflicts between the objectives and, where technical solutions have not been discovered, the ways in which their judgement of the user's requirements has led them to produce a compromise solution in order to resolve the conflict.

Nicholls:

First of all, I would like to say that I speak as a representative on behalf of a general language, rather than with any special knowledge of simulation problems. One of the themes of this conference has been that these in fact are very closely related and it seems that, from the work of Petrone and Greenburger and Jones at this conference, PL/1 has some of the qualities that one might need of a general simulation language.

I would like to give my own feeling of what particular items and features of PL/1 are relevant here. I do not think these can be considered completely in isolation - one of the difficulties and interesting features of language design is the way these features interact with each other. I would suggest that the relevant features in PL/1 are in the program structure and in the idea of the block structure in its handling of data; the ability to dynamically create data structures, the interrupt handling, the handling of sequencing and the facilities for parallel or quasi-parallel operation.

These seem, from the comments at the conference, to be relevant to the simulation problem. Two of the features needed, known as tasking and list processing, have not yet been scheduled for delivery but - to clarify a point that was raised yesterday - it is intended to implement them.

This particular panel is concerned mainly with data structures and, therefore, I would like to spend most of the time on the data structure aspect and especially the pointer mechanism and similar topics.

Let us look at the total ability in PL/1 for data structures - there are three facets to it. Firstly, arrays, secondly what PL/1 calls structures and thirdly the facility for dynamic references. There is not much need to talk about arrays; they are fairly conventional and the only slightly unusual facilities offered are the ability to check subscript bounds, which is an aspect of security, and the ability to allocate arrays dynamically during the course of a program, not just on block entry.

The second type of data structure is what is called 'a structure'. This is a hierarchical data structure whose elements may be of any type. These structures have to be completely known at compile time and, therefore, they have very good efficiency and security but are not quite so flexible. There is some flexibility because the elements of structures may be dimensioned and the stream lengths in them may be variable; and again they have the property that they can be allocated dynamically during the course of the program quite irrespectively of the block structure of the program.

The referencing mechanism is a completely compile time deducible system and uses the familiar "qualified name" concept.

And finally, we have dynamic data structures in which the structuring is not known at compile time and this sort of facility is useful in creating lists, rings and trees and so on. The general facilities for the dynamic creation of these structures are as follows.

Firstly there are pointer variables - a pointer in this sense is taken as a means of accessing data. Together with that goes a based storage class - an attribute of data saying that it will always be referenced by pointers. These two concepts together seem to be a primitive in data processing. They give great flexibility and with them you can define various other familiar mechanisms in a language - like the array mechanism and parameter mechanisms. Although one can think of a pointer as an address, I think it is preferable to think of an address as a pointer. In fact, the address as conventionally used in a machine is an illustration of a means of accessing data in a particular machine structure.

We have three main ways of setting pointers. Firstly, for the creation of data structures we have a statement (ALLOCATE); when you create the data structure you set a pointer to point at it.

Another way is by input/output in which you have buffered transmission. The programmer, I should explain, is not responsible for the allocation and control of buffers in PL/1. All he has to say is whether his I/O is buffered or not. And finally, it is possible to set pointers by assignment.

There is also a facility for local storage management - the general principle is that the main storage management of structures is left to an operating system but there is a way of doing local storage management in what is called an "area". This is a means of suballocating based variables. Areas themselves may belong to a program: they may be allocated, assigned, passed as parameters and so on.

From all this there comes the idea of a generalised reference which is of the form of a pointer expression associated with a based variable. A pointer expression may be any expression which returns a value of data type "pointer" and the based variable is the description of the data. This generalised reference is the construct which gives you the ability to create these dynamic structures.

Now in this area of the language, the efficiency and flexibility of the system are emphasised and security is not imposed by any

checks required by the language in the run time system. I think
this is a point of view that we have adopted in one or two areas -
that of providing optional ways of checking and obtaining security
but, in some cases, allowing the programmer to access this mechanism in whatever way he chooses.

Laski:

As a designer of programming languages, I do not regard myself as an applied metaphysician but I do regard myself as an applied meta-mathematician. Though I am all for the objectives like
motherhood and security and efficiency and flexibility, that are put
forth in Hoare's note, I feel that they are based on a misconception
of an enormous magnitude of the logical status of the problem with
which we are concerned. If we are concerned with things that may
be named, i.e. data objects, we are in no way - until we come to
implement them - concerned with their representation within the
machine. We must manage in a representation- and interpretation-
independent way to specify these data objects by describing the
characteristics of the operations, selections, modifications and
predicates that may be applied to them. We must define quite independently of the implementation the way in which they may have different values through time and the way in which they work.

We then have a second problem - the problem of interpreting
these data objects and the way they behave in terms of some physical medium, like for instance, a computer of today's generation.
We have then entirely separate problems of seeing what part of our
ideas can actually be realised. In order to achieve security, efficiency, flexibility and clarity, we must divorce ourselves, in my
opinion, from the petty details of bits and attend to the intended
meanings and intended use of our constructed objects.

We must, I say, keep our implementation and engineers' hats off
while doing this in order not to allow questions of the particular
local state of machine availability and present interpretation to
corrupt the clarity of what we wish to do. Then we must change
our hats - and interpret or represent these data objects by fixed
patterns within the machine, interpret the operations that we wish
to perform on these objects by little bits of code in terms of the
basic operations of the machine and choose to implement, not the
conceptual objects with which we are dealing, but an interpretation
of them.

Now this has one very important implication. We have to verify that this interpretation - that this realisation in fact, works the
way we said it should. We must eschew the conveniences that may
come by having two different kinds of conceptual data objects inter-

preted, say, by lists, because then we confuse ourselves that the conceptual objects we are dealing with are (because they have the same interpretation) the same kind of objects.

It seems to me that unless we keep clear in our mind the distinction between what we are trying to do and how we may best actually do it, we will find the compromises, that every engineer must inevitably make when he produces a local working system, persisting in our understanding and corrupting the later working systems that do not require the compromises of the original interpretation. Given the concept, for example that some people call a set and I call a "prex", I can see a number of ways of representing it by different kinds of lists or perhaps by different kinds of table look-up mechanisms and I can see many ways in which, for considerations of efficiency, in particular environments, one or other interpretation is to be preferred. Nevertheless, the conceptual data object - that which we are dealing with for clarity and in order to know what we are talking about - is independent of the particular local representation on a particular local machine. If we do not keep these ideas separate we are going to get into more of a muddle than we are in at the moment.

Parente:

I think before I say anything, I should like to try to put some of the things that we are talking about here into some context. I think that one of the difficulties - at least that I have had - in discussing things with Dahl and Nygaard and some others arises because we think on different levels. For example, a machine is made available to us by the hardware designers and certainly the people who are operating it at the bit level with assembly code are thinking differently and doing things differently than the people who are just feeding in data to applications programs. I think some of the difficulties that we are having at this conference in seeing eye-to-eye perhaps or understanding each other, has to do with this question of levels.

Hoare mentioned in his opening remarks that when you design a simulation language, as when you design any language, you have to decide just what facilities you want to provide. To do this you have to decide who it is you are trying to provide them for.

My feeling is that if simulation is ever going to be widely used in industry, it has to be at the call of either managers or staff people to managers. In order for them to be able to use simulation, I do not think that they are going to be operating at the level of the language that we are talking about here at this Conference. I think that they want fairly specialised simulation programs that can be used within a particular business and they probably need more than one of these available. The only way this can come about, I think - is if we provide good tools for some programmer who can be told what this manager or staff analyst wants and can provide it for him on a reasonably short time scale.

I would add a fourth item to Hoare's list - responsibility; I think you can match flexibility with responsibility in that when you are designing a system, you can make it as flexible as you wish but the more flexible you make it the more responsibility for using it correctly you give to the user of the system. The more rigid you make it the more responsibility you take as a systems designer.

Now, in the NSS language the approach we have taken is to say that there are certain structures which are built into the system. These structures are manipulated by the system and it is responsible for any references that it builds or creates. If a reference is no longer meaningful, then it is up to the system that implements NSS to take care of it, so that an incorrect reference cannot be made. On the other hand - if the user is allowed to build data structures, dynamically or otherwise, then he should be responsible for maintaining references to this type of structure and he is really the only one who knows when a reference is incorrect.

I think there is no clear cut line here as to when the system should do it and when the user should be doing it and I have no objection to the Dahl and Nygaard implementation of SIMULA. All I can say is that they have picked a particular implementation which works for their particular context but any time you do this, you are establishing some kind of context - security only has meaning really when in context.

In closing, I will just say that I think security and efficiency and all these things are a matter of systems design and it is a matter of who has the responsibility for doing it - the systems designer or the user of the language.

Peck:

Editors note: Professor Peck gave a short description of some recent developments in ALGOL X at this point, at the Chairman's request. The Editor has not included this section in the Proceedings; though of interest to those attending, he thinks that publication here of a partial description of ALGOL X could be prejudicial before its complete formal publication elsewhere.

Ross:

What I would like to do as a participant in this panel is not to talk about data structuring as the title says - if the Chairman will allow - and if not, I am through already, I guess.... but rather

about the purpose of data structuring. I will try to give a little of
my view of where the major unsolved problems lie. They lie just
ahead of us - whether we recognise them or not! That is what I
would like to try to bring out.

First of all, I believe that data structuring is only a part of what
we really are always talking about, and this is what, quite a few
years ago, I coined the word "plex" for. I would like to try to bring
out what I mean by the term and then to tie it into some current research where I believe a major set of problems lie and where we
need a lot of new ideas.

So, what is a plex? A plex is not a data structure only. A plex is
data and structure and algorithms. It is a trinity in the proper sense
that if you take any part away, the whole thing disappears.

Let me give a condensed summary of my classic example of the
fact that this really is what we do talk about - all of us. In our
parsing of language in our system, we have a structure for the
parsed version of an expression in which each vocabulary word is
represented by a node or record which has pointers for giving left
and right context and also other pointers which show what we call
the semantic parse - the sequence in which you should evaluate that
expression. Now if we represent that structure in the computer, in
the terms of records, then the chain of pointers running through what
we call the precedence stream, which shows the sequence to evaluate, takes 15 binary digits per pointer and two pointers per record.
We have a completely equivalent version of the same structure
which we call the octal stream. In this form, this information which
used to take 30 bits now takes 0 bits. We have not violated information theory at all. What we have done is that at the same time that
we have mapped the data structure, from the tree form with the
string of pointers running through it into the linearised form which
is the octal stream form, we also at the same time have made corresponding modification to the algorithms that work with the data.

You are all perfectly aware that you can store information in an
algorithm just as well as in a data structure, by which branch did
you take in a flow diagram or some such feature. Well, this effect
is happening here. The total data + structure + algorithm information in both forms is the same and represents the same thing. They
are part of an equivalence class in some real sense.

So I claim that we can find many, many instances of this fact
that when we model or represent something, we are using data,
structure and algorithm and that we really give our attention to all
of these.

Let me now just leap right ahead into this major problem area
on which we are trying to do some useful research. I would like to
have more people aware of the problem: it concerns the fact that as

soon as you start to model anything with records - as soon as you
get beyond the most trivial or atomic level, you start to make whole
structures. Now, the problem is not only in making sure that the
records that you are referencing are still around, which is the way
we have been using the term "security" so far today, but also in
knowing whether the interconnection of those records still represents what you intended it to represent. A record, if you will, is
only a condensed version of something to which you could give more
elaborate detail. This again gets you into playing around with the
mappings of the algorithms into more and more detailed forms. So,
even when we have a single record, you can think of it as representing a very complex data structure with algorithm in a different domain. Now the converse is true that any time that you have a single concept and you represent it as a whole inter-connected structure, how do you make sure that as you manipulate the whole structure, it still has integrity and represents what you intend.

The approach that we are taking to this is as follows. We have
a nice simple starting example which is concerned merely with representing objects which are composed of polygonal faces joined
along their edges. We call this the polyphase package problem. We
are using this as an exercise ground to start to get a handle on the
implementation techniques. We prefer to work with implementations
of real things and see how they work in the laboratory rather than
how we think they might work if everything worked out well. So what
we do in this case is, we assume that the system is equipped already with a generic triangle which is represented by records
standing for the corner points and the edges and the faces.

The only way that you can create new objects in this system is
to copy something which already exists or do a local operation
which will preserve the integrity of the modelling represented by
this inter-connection set of records. To do this, it seems to be
that the key step is to include, along with the data structure, an
algorithm which we call a 'Mouse' algorithm because it runs around
like a mouse solving a maze. The key thing about this algorithm,
which is an integral part of the total plex, is that it will visit each
pointer in this structure exactly once as you follow it through. Furthermore, it gives a code at each step giving the local context so
that you can tell whether it is the first time that it has come to a
record that represents an edge or the last time that you are going
to reach an edge, and so forth. This algorithm ties together the
entire plex structure - this entire data structure into one unit. It
provides a backbone on which you can then compose operators to
operate on the entire structure rather than on just a single record.
The ideas are the same as we have used in processing language and
are described in the 1963 SJCC proceedings [122].

I think that if we are going to really succeed with the high-blown things that we all want to have in languages we must recognise the fact that it is not sufficient just to focus on records and field decla-ration for records and existence spaces for records, zone struc-ture, free storage and so forth, but we must study what are they used for. They represent big objects, complex objects and we must make sure that our languages and our implementations are able to work with those whole objects at once.

Dahl:

I agree that one should not really talk about data structure with-out taking everything else into account. On the other hand, we are in - I believe - a rather difficult situation here because the compu-ter is limited in space and time; and for large problems, which I guess all of us are concerned with, we have to adjust our structur-ing so that we do not hit one of these limits.

So, therefore, I heartily disagree, in a sense at least, with using the compound closed objects that Ross talked about. In an abstract sense of course, they may be equivalent, but in the real practical world where we are using computers to do work, they are most certainly not.

One of the points I should like to mention right now - it has been mentioned before by Garwick, is that core store is getting cheap - at least you can buy it if you have money. There is essentially no limit to the physical size of your machine, but there is a definite limit to the obtainable speed. Now, I have found it a useful working hypothesis that the solution time of a problem will probably depend on some power of the data volume. Efficiency, at least when it comes to execution time, is measured by K and by P; i.e. execution time is of the form

$$E = KN^P,$$

where K and P are constants, and N is a measure of the "volume" of the model, such as the "number of components". The point that I want to make is that whatever you do, it does not matter so much if K is a bit larger than it could have been but it does matter very much indeed if P is one higher than necessary. And that is the main concern, I think, in deciding how to structure your data.

Chairman:

I would like to remind you of some of the points of view which have been expressed by the various panel members.

Nicholls describes the facilities provided in the PL/1 language, which certainly seem to me to give the programmer very good control over efficiency and a very strong flexibility in his use of pointers and data structures, similar to what he has in machine code. The objective of securing security has not been considered to be of prime importance in the design of the language itself.

Laski has made a very valid counter claim to my idea that the design of a programming language is rather a matter of engineering than of abstract thought and correct conceptualisation. I think that his point is valid but I myself find that, perhaps through deficiency in my ability to abstract and conceptualise, I prefer to make many passes through the two states that he mentioned. I prefer to look both at the implementation aspects of the design and the conceptual aspects, back and forth many times. I feel that the disciplines of implementation ideas can help to channel our conceptual approach so I do not make such a firm division as was made by Laski between these two.

Parente made a very forceful plea for the idea that security should not figure in too over-riding a fashion in our design. He thinks that a basic language should provide a tool whereby responsible and skilful systems designers can construct packages which can be used successfully, efficiently and securely by the great 99% that we know so much about... and that one needs to design languages and software on several levels, oriented towards different percentiles of each "ability and expertise" class of programmer.

I have no ready comments on Peck's address except to thank him for his clear exposition of some of the basic ideas of a very interesting language.

Ross promised me that he would surprise me by what he said and he has! I have many times experienced that when Ross says that there is a problem - a problem shall we say that he has not already solved - then it is a very serious one and when we have thought about it for perhaps a year, we will begin to understand what the problem is. By that time he will have solved it himself.

Dahl I think was very modest in his claims and I would like to rectify the situation. We heard this morning of a scheme for the design of data structures in a language which seemed to me a most successful technical solution to the problem of reconciling three basic objectives that I set out at the beginning. The class and subclass proposal seems to go further than anything I have seen before in maintaining complete security, very high efficiency and most extraordinarily little loss of flexibility.

Ross:

I refer to the remarks of Laski, Dahl and myself, on the need for abstract correctness independent of mechanisation on the computer. The term that I like to use for this is "ideal" and "idealised": we have an idealised conception and then we talk about many different ways to mechanize that single idea. You will recall that Dahl said that he disagreed with me and that there was a big difference between two different mechanisations. I agree 100%: the way this happens without getting into a contradiction is that the "ideal" is the thing that stays the same. The different mechanical forms of the same ideal in my example have very different properties. In fact, that is why we use the two: the tree-structure form is very useful and flexible when making changes and so forth, whereas the other form where the data structure is linearized is much better for other purposes: it is more compact, it is also relocatable and it has many other nice features. We do want our things to be ideally or abstractly right and correct but we also want them to be efficient. This then reflects back on how we build our systems. Most of the features in our own family of AED systems come from the attempt to put into the language processors the right features, so that the user of a language can easily map from one mechanisation to another to achieve the best utility of his actual hardware but still while not losing track of what is his problem really all about.

Dahl:

I will just tack on a little appendix to this. There is one point that might not be remembered here. You might be able to think of nice concepts to have, which are nice for you to think with and then you may try to implement them and then you use the implementation of these concepts together with a program in your language to solve your problem. My point is that if you start out with drawing concepts out of your hat without thinking of the machine, you may very well end up with a solution time to your problem which, referring to my equation, has a value of P several degrees too high. I feel it is essential, even at the initial stage while you are selecting concepts, to know whether they will be efficient.

Strachey:

At this point Strachey gave a presentation on the compound data structures intended for incorporation in CPL. This is not included here, as with Peck's presentation on ALGOL X, for similar reasons.

Ross:

I would like especially in view of what Strachey has just presented, to re-raise this question of whether the reference concept is the thing which we should have in our basic language. The question is whether you allow the user to manipulate objects without having at his disposal the concept of a pointer. An implementation will no doubt contain pointers galore, but should we hide them from the average user? Also, type checking at run time should be, I think, eliminated as far as possible by the compiler. All type comparisons should be done at compile time, but on the other hand in order to have all possibilities, we feel quite sure that you must have the idea of a "typed pointer".

Strachey:

In fact, there are more compound data structures in CPL than I mentioned; in particular there are pointers and there are a lot of other sorts of structures as well.

Garwick:

I would like to make a few remarks on data structure in general. I shall end up with discussing references. First of all you may have observed there has been quite a conflict between Nygaard and myself and I think that it is possible to explain this. Neither he nor I are absolute fools so when a conflict appears it probably has a reason. I think, and I think Nygaard will agree with me, that we have rather different styles of programming. To some people, including Ross, it seems that data is strongly connected with the algorithm which does something to it. Therefore they represent a data block as continuing those procedures which operate upon it. For me, data has a certain abstract value per se. I would therefore like to collect my data in one place and have several programs operating on it. Now this difference in programming style is I believe the main cause of differences in the way SIMULA and GPL have been constructed as to their record structures. Finally I will get to the point of our references. There is no word "reference" in GPL but there are pointers. If I have a pointer to a variable this is exactly the same as a reference. For people who write implementations, a reference is an address and not much else. A pointer, again when people are writing implementations, is the same as a "pard" as Dijkstra called it: i.e. a parameter descriptor or a mechanism for producing the address of the entity it points to. This can be simply the address of a variable, but it can also be the address of the result of a long calculation and so represent the "call by name" feature.

Laski:

I would like to distinguish between a mess of bits and understandable meaningful data. A mess of bits thrown into a store is without value unless you are able to interpret it in terms of its intended content. I think that the fundamental difference between various people around this table is; which comes first, the bits or the understanding? A second issue that I would like to comment on is Strachey's use of the term "manifest" and the binding at compile time of type information. I think that if data is external, in other words not necessarily known at compile time, it may be necessary to interpret at run time. I regard what one can bind at compile time as a nice little improvement in efficiency rather than as any particular change in the generality of achieving what one intends as interpretation. Of course it is important and valuable but I believe that the effect one wants in certain cases can only be got by allowing run time interpretation. I suspect it is this notion of external data, data whose type is not known at the time of compilation, that is necessary in simulation languages and is necessary more particularly in data base management languages. It is not necessary in languages in which there is an enclosing block within the scope of which all data exists.

Nicholls:

Laski asks, which comes first, the bits or the understanding. Well of course they must be present at the same time but they are not always physically present in the same record and sometimes you do have to process just the bits. And the understanding is separate.

Strachey:

Just one thing about Laski's comment about external data; if you do not know what it's type is I do not see how you can write a program to operate on it. It seems to me that it may be necessary to check dynamically that the information coming in from the outside world is the type you expect; but in that case the purpose of using types is to give you some security that you are performing meaningful operations. Surely if you are going to write a program on data coming from the outside world, you must know what it is.

Laski:

This comes from an idea I have, probably not yet well expressed, of semantic type, that is quite close to what Hoare calls "record class"; something which is interpreted in terms of another record, so that the type in a certain sense is a parameter which has to be filled in to get the selectors or constructors by reference to other describing information.

Ross:

I would like to reply to Garwick's point. He said that he prefers to have the data not associated with the program block i.e. that it is a separate kind of thing from the block structure in the ALGOL sense. I concur entirely. This idea of zone structure of free storage is the mechanism whereby you can get efficient control over the existence space of objects as they are referred to from different algorithms and different blocks of program. I feel strongly that we should have our high-level languages written and designed cohesively enough and according to the best choices that we can make, such that the average user can in fact work with complex objects, things which require records and whole structures of records, and still not have to get into the troubles that come along with pointers.

Strachey:

I think a lot of the confusion about references and pointers is a confusion between the two values which are associated with an object. One of these in CPL we like to call the "L-value", which ALGOL X calls the "name" in I think a rather unfortunate way. The other we like to call the "R-value". I think of the L-value as being the address or part of the machine in which the object needs to be stored, and the content of that address is the R-value. It is very important to recognize that there are, for any variable or any expression, potentially two values associated with it. You can evaluate an expression and get an L-value or you can evaluate the expression and get an R-value. The question is, when you are talking about compound structures, what is the L-value and what is the R-value? We have to settle what these mean before we can decide what we mean when we are talking about them. I interpret the R-value of a compound structure to be, in an implementation sense, a small area of store, which contains enough information to get at all the rest of the information associated with it. So it is like the code word system for dealing with arrays. When you assign one of these things, you merely copy the code word. You do not copy the elements of the structure. As Ross says, we need a system function at this stage called "Copy" which produces a fresh copy of the complete structure. When you deal with compound data structures you are faced with a whole new series of problems about structures which share components and share parts of the information. This problem simply does not arise until you have more complex structures than ALGOL 60 will allow. When it does happen, it is extremely important that you should get quite clear in your mind which bits you are sharing and what you are doing with them. I think a great deal of the difficulty with references, pointers and values is due to confusion about whether we are talking about the area of the store of the content of the area of the store.

Peck:

In ALGOL X we felt that the reference was really what was being used in the computer and that if you can show this explicitly in the language and allow the programmer to handle it, then you will be able to express things very clearly. I am delighted to hear that ALGOL X has many of the features of CPL. This just shows that it is going in the right direction. And this was recently confirmed by some remarks of Strachey concerning the devices which are used to handle LISP in CPL. I can assure him that the same devices are in ALGOL X but of course in a different form. Just another point; Garwick referred to pointers, saying that pointers could handle the call by name. I just wanted to remark that in ALGOL X what used to be the call by name in ALGOL 60 is now handled by two devices. There are really two calls by name - one is the simple type where you wish to present an identifier as the parameter. The other is the type where you wish to present an expression as the parameter. If you are going to present the identifier as the parameter, then you handle this call by name using the reference.

If the parameter is going to be an expression then this is handled by declaring the parameter as a procedure. I am sorry that Strachey is distressed by the way in which we use "name". Name in ALGOL X refers to an internal object: the external object is the identifier. If that nice word surprises him, then there are a lot more surprises awaiting him when he reads the report.

Strachey:

Can I make a comment about the misuse of words in ALGOL It started in ALGOL 60 when they used the gramatically incorrect form "if... then... else" which gives everybody who has any feeling for the English language, the willies. They are now using the word "name" to mean what most people would call "address" or "generalised address" and what CPL would call an *L*-value. What everybody else in the world would call "name" they call "identifier". So we get things like "a rose by any other identifier smells just as sweet". Or "give me your identifier and name" meaning "give me your name and address".

I entirely deplore this. When you look in the telephone directory it has a whole page full of the same identifiers, they are all called John Smith. I deplore the use of words which have a common use which is not very well understood and is often perhaps misunderstood but even more I deplore using them in an entirely new sense. Many of the L-values which arise inside a computer are in fact indescribable. You cannot write them down. They are strictly anonymous, so what they are doing is calling the anonymous value of a lefthand quantity, a name. I do not think this is going to lead to very much clarity of thought.

Knuth:

Regarding lefthand values and righthand values, I was glad to see that Garwick this morning in GPL switched them around and put the variable to receive the value on the righthand side of the assignment statement, where it was in the first 10 programming languages until FORTRAN came along. This is a much more logical place for it; but of course L-value and R-value would now mean. . . . .

Strachey:

That does not matter in the least. I personally would like to call them "A-value" and B-value". I do not mind what they are called. The thing is, nobody would know what an L-value is unless you told them, whereas everybody thinks they know what a name is. One other comment about Garwick's arrow going the wrong way; I cannot resist telling this story. There was during the war a type of military shell which had a notice on the outside saying "This shell has to be stored upside down. In order to avoid confusion the bottom of the case has been marked 'top' ". That is why the arrow goes the wrong way in Garwick's language: in order to avoid confusion!

Laski:

May I remind you of an English quotation - "words mean what I want them to mean", and a name is of course a word.

Hoare:

I think that underlying the confusion that has been so amply illustrated if not actually cleared up in the last few minutes, there is in fact a matter of substance. Whatever you mean by your words, they should be kept distinct. Or one should at least reserve some words for keeping these things distinct.

Dahl:

Of course the meat of the problem is the assignment statement. We write "X becomes $X + 1$" and mean something entirely different with the two X's. In order to get a clean programming language, we should really state more clearly what we mean and introduce some difference in notation between those two. It is nearly impossible I think to get a secure understanding of this, especially when we bring in pointers and references because there is, at least to my mind, no distinction between an L-value and a reference.

Hoare:

I see that the sun is shining outside, if not within! We are now talking about matters of notation which I think are even more profound than the problems of metaphysics and theology that I set out to try and avoid going too deeply into, and so the time has come to draw the panel to a close.

ON SIMULATION METHODS
AND ON SOME CHARACTERISTICS
OF SIMULATION LANGUAGES

K. ČULÍK
Czechoslovakian Academy of Science, Prague

1. SIMULATION

The study of a real system by *simulation* consists in replacing the simulated system by another simulating one which is *similar* (from a certain point of view) to the first and which is more convenient for the study than the first. If the degree and the type of similarity are sufficient then some of the required results obtained for the simulating system can be transferred to the original simulated one. If one is authorized to transfer the results then the simulating system is said to be a *model* of the simulated one.

It is in general hardly possible to determine when a simulating system is a model of the simulated one, i.e. what degree and what type of similarity are sufficient to authorize the transferring of the required results. On the other hand, there are good experiences with simulation in many particular cases. Very often the question whether or not a simulating system is a model of the simulated one must be answered empirically and by inductive reasoning. But in fact any inductive reasoning is based on a general methodological principle by which it is assumed that "similar systems have similar properties". Thus the concepts of similarity, simulation and of model are the most fundamental indeed.

2. DIFFERENT SIMULATION METHODS

There are important differences as to the types of similarity required for the simulating systems.

On one hand the similarity between a simulated system and its simulating one concerns near all the *physical, chemical* etc. properties and simultaneously all the *space* and *time* relations too. E.g., little dams or bridges being models of the real big dams or bridges belong to this category. The only difference between an in-

234

vestigated system and its model very often lies in the size all the
physical properties being not only similar but even identical here.
Therefore, the simulating systems must be investigated in the
same manner as the real ones, i.e. empirically by measuring and
experimenting.

With this category of models all different sorts of analog computers are connected very closely, because here again a certain
similarity (but never identity; i.e. the degree of similarity is lower
than in the previous case) of physical properties is required and
the measuring is the essential manner how to investigate the model.
None of these just mentioned and extremely important simulation
methods and models will be dealt with here.

On the other hand, the similarity between a simulated system
and a simulating one concerns neither physical, chemical or other
property nor any space relations but only the *distinguishability* of
the particular situations in the simulated system by the corresponding "situations" in the simulating one and - when time is relevant at all - the time relations too. The models of this category
are very often said to be *abstract* or *symbolic* or *mathematical*
which should express that the nature of the model is unessential at
all. In all cases these distinguishing models consist in certain expressions of a language (the corresponding "situations" are nothing
else than particular propositions expressing the real situations) although obviously each expression has its physical background too.

Here exactly, the distinguishing models will be dealt with only,
i.e. on the level of mathematics and logics or more generally on
the level of language theory on the whole.

Time relations are simulated in a well known and the same way
as all other quantity relations at all. But in the theory of probability
and in statistics there is an essentially different type of simulation
which must be distinguished from the previous one. Let us consider
an example introduced and discussed in all details but in a slightly
different form in [26]. The question is an automatic car wash installation giving service to cars, one at a time. The problem consists
in prediction of average and maximum queue length and the waiting
time spent in the system by individual cars, if a second similar
wash machine were installed.

Example 1.

There is a set of *cars* $C = \{c_1, c_2, \ldots, c_n\}$ where $n \geq 1$ is an integer. Each car c_i arrives to the wash machine at the *arrival time*
$a(c_i) = a_i$, where $0 \leq a_1 < a_2 < \ldots < a_n \leq s + d$ and $s + d$ determines
the *duration* of the service within one day. The *washing time* $d > 0$
is equal for each car. If a car c_i $(1 < i \leq n)$ arrives and the machine
is engaged, then the car c_i enters a waiting line till the previous

car c_{i-1} is washed on a first come first served basis, and the first car c_1 starts being washed at once. Thus the *beginning time* $b(c_i)$ when the washing of the car c_i begins is determined as follows

$$b(c_i) = \max(b(c_{i-1})+d, a_1) \text{ for } 1 < i \leqq n \tag{1}$$

and

$$b(c_1) = a_1.$$

Further the *waiting time* of a car c_i is determined as a difference $w(c_i) = b(c_i) - a(c_i)$ for each i.

Now it is clear that "to be in the queue" is not a property of the cars c_i themselves but always only together with respect to some instants t. Thus the object c_i is something else than the object c_i in the instant $t \geqq 0$. The first can be called a *historical object* (because it can change in time) and the second can be called an *instantaneous object* (it cannot change at all) and will be denoted by the following couple $[c_i;t]$. Thus the name c_i of a historical object serves to identify this object independently on its properties (which can completely change in course of time). This fact is very well illustrated on a historical object queue q and its instantaneous object $[q,t]$ because for some t it can happen that really there is no queue at all but later the queue consists of one single car etc.

Now the situation (or the state) when a car c_i is in queue q in an instant t can be expressed by putting $[q, c_i, t] = 1$ and otherwise by $= 0$. One can use a well known discretization of time scale by dividing it into disjoint intervals of the type $\langle x, y \rangle$, i.e. closed from left and open from right, where x is so called *critical time* (the instant x represents the whole interval $\langle x, y \rangle$ if y is the next critical time, because all the instantaneous objects $[c_i, t]$ or $[q, t]$, where $x \leqq t < y$ have the same properties as $[c_i, x]$ or $[q, x]$, and therefore they need not be considered with respect to distinguishability at all). Obviously here the critical times consist of the arrival times $a(c_i)$ and of the beginning times $b(c_i)$ for all $i = 1, 2, \ldots, n$, together with 0 and $s + d$ which are the first and the last one. Let $0 = t_0 < t_1 < \ldots < t_m < t_{m+1} = s + d$ be an ordered set of all the critical times, thus $m \leqq 2n$.

Now it is clear that $[q, c_i, t] = 1$ if and only if $a(c_i) \leqq t < b(c_i)$ for each i. Further the *length of the queue in a critical time* t_k $l[q, t_k]$ is determined as follows:

$$l[q, t_0] = l[q, t_1] = 0 \tag{2}$$

and for $k > 1$

$$l[q, t_k] = l[q, t_{k-1}] + 1$$

if there is i such that $a(c_i) = t_k$ but there is not j such that $b(c_j) = t_k$,

$$l[q, t_k] = l[q, t_{k-1}]$$

if there is i such that $a(c_i) = t_k$ and there is also j such that $b(c_j) = t_k$ and

$$l[q, t_k] = \max(l[q, t_{k-1}] - 1, 0)$$

if there is not i such that $a(c_i) = t_k$ but there is j such that $b(c_j) = t_k$. Finally the *average* and *maximum queue lengths* aver $l(q)$ and max $il(q)$ resp. are determined in a simple usual way

$$\text{aver } l(q) = \frac{1}{s+d} \sum_{k=0}^{m} (l(q, t_k) \cdot (t_{k+1} - t_k)) \qquad (3)$$

$$\max il(q) = \max_{0 \leqslant k \leqslant m} \; il[q, t_k]. \qquad (4)$$

All definitions and equalities introduced in the previous Example 1 generate an usual distinguishing model which depends on the parameters $a_1, a_2, \ldots, a_n$ and s and d. As a matter of fact, the question is a finite discrete problem, which is moreover sufficiently simple.

It is clear that the values of s and d are determined by the investigated wash installation and by the working day, but is not clear what are the values $a_1, a_2, \ldots, a_n$.

Either they are results of an empirical measuring, i.e. $a_1, a_2, \ldots, a_n$ are the observed arrival times during a working day. One day is probably an unsufficient sample for a prediction of the arrival of cars, but there are some empirical reasons when a sample is sufficient.

Or further observations are not available for some reasons and then it may be appropriate to use a *statistical model* to represent the arrival of cars. Here the statistical model simulates the random-values $a_1, a_2, \ldots, a_n$, which are the input values for the distinguishing model described in Example 1. Thus really the statistical model is different from the distinguishing one.

Finally, it can happen e.g. when the time intervals between consecutive arrivals do not follow the Poisson distribution, that the computation of the required average queue length from the given distribution is very complicated. One speaks again about a *simulation method (in contradiction to the computation)* if the average queue length is obtained from a rich statistical material directly (it does not matter whether the material has been generated artificially by a random or pseudo-random generator or the material consists in real empirical observations).

The different simulation methods and corresponding models are distinguished in order to show by which of them the features of simulation languages are influenced and by which not. By the Example 1 it was shown sufficiently that the most influencing models are the distinguishing ones and not the statistical ones. That is the reason why in the next sections only the distinguishing models are dealt with.

Further a real system simulated by the distinguishing model in Example 1 is called *dynamic* in [26] and the fact that time and changes in time are taken into account seems to be the most important and influencing with respect to the simulation languages. The dynamicity causes that the categories as an event, process, system time etc., are introduced in [26]. But in some further simulation languages also such categories as a set, an ordered set, a special manipulating with ordered sets and sometimes generally many further categories of predicate calculus are introduced.

In the following sections we shall try to show in more details what the distinguishing models are and how it can be verified that they are models (in the sense of mathematical logics) of some mathematical theories. The verification being essentially different from the usual mathematical proving, is nothing else than a special simulation method consisting in testing all the possibilities but not in the real system itself but on its distinguishing symbolic model only.

3. REAL SYSTEM AND ITS DISTINCTIVE MODELS

It is assumed that in the investigated *real system* the particular objects are distinguished and that some of the particular properties of the objects and their mutual relations are chosen. A meaning (i.e. an intension) of a property (or of a relation) is the corresponding empirical decision procedure according which one can decide whether an object has or has not corresponding property (or whether among the ordered objects the corresponding relation exists or does not). The considered properties and relations are very often quantitative ones, i.e. the corresponding procedures are some measuring ones assigning a quantity to the considered objects. Finally, if necessary, any space and time determination of the real system and its objects can be added.

It is necessary to stress that it depends on the aim of our investigations which objects, properties and relations should be chosen and which not, i.e. in the same part of the reality many different real systems can be distinguished, because many different properties and relations can be chosen.

In fact what is taken into account and what not in the considered real system is uniquely determined by the corresponding *distinctive model* being nothing else that an enumeration of names of all considered objects (called *individual constants*), an enumeration of names of all considered properties and relations called *predicate constants* and finally an enumeration of all *primitive propositions* which express all the simplest situations in the real system in such a manner that each two different real situations, objects, properties and relations are unambiguously distinguishable from each other by the corresponding expressions in the chosen language.

If P is a chosen 2-place predicate and a, b, c are the chosen individuals then instead of enumerating all the primitive propositions containing P, e.g. there are three $P(a,b)$, $P(a,c)$, $P(c,c)$, one can introduce the following set $\{(a,b),(a,c),(c,c)\}$ denoted by the same symbol P, because it is essentially an extension of the relation expressed by P but expressed by the individuals instead of the objects themselves. Similarly, if P is a k-place predicate and I denotes the set of all considered individuals then P must be a subset of I^k. Finally, if P is a quantitative k-place predicate then P must be a subset of $I^k \times U$, where U is a set of numbers (or even of numerals), e.g. P contains a $(k+1)$-tuple $(x_1, x_2, \ldots, x_{k+1})$ such that $(x_1, x_2, \ldots, x_k) \in I^k$ and $x_{k+1} \in U$.

Thus each distinctive model consists of several sets the elements of which are either the individuals or the sequences of the individuals or the sequences of the individuals the last element of which is a number. All these sets are determined by an enumeration of their elements and exactly one is distinguished as the set of individuals.

Obviously the whole distinctive model is a language expression over a fixed alphabet A having only a finite number of basis symbols.

The above mentioned requirement of distinguishability which determines a special type of similarity between the real system and its distinctive model can be briefly formulated as follows: if one imagines the objects, properties and relations and the situations in the real system on the one hand and the individuals, predicates and primitive propositions in the distinctive model on the other hand, then the real system must be a homomorphic image of the model (the required homomorphism is determined by an assignment of the meanings to the expressions in the considered language).

If the meanings of the individual constants and predicate constants are not considered the distinguishing model is a special mathematical structure which will be called a *distinctive system*. Thus a *distinctive system* becomes a distinctive model of a real system if the above mentioned homomorphism can be established (i.e. if there are mappings of the set I onto the set of all objects and of the set of all predicate constants onto the set of all properties and relations such that there is an induced mapping of all primitive propositions onto all situations, etc.).

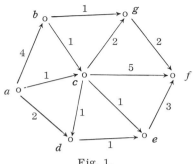

Fig. 1.

In fig. 1 there is a diagram of a real system (this diagram is not considered as a distinctive model here) consisting of seven places and of twelve oneway highways connecting some of them with the determined lengths in miles. The distinctive system S consists of two sets I and C, where $I = \{a, b, c, d, e, f, g\}$ and $C = \{(a, b, 4), (a, c, 1), (a, d, 2), (b, g, 1), (b, c, 1), (c, g, 2), (c, f, 5), (c, e, 1), (c, d, 1), (d, e, 1), (e, f, 3), (g, f, 2)\}$, i.e. C is a quantitative two-place predicate.

The distinctive system $S = \langle I, C \rangle$ becomes a distinctive model of the investigated real system after determining which places are denoted by the particular individuals and after determining which quantitative binary relation is denoted by C (obviously if by these assignments of meaning or in other words by these interpretations a homomorphism is determinated). A decision and measuring procedure corresponding to C consists in finding a highway starting in the first place and ending in the second with the measuring of its length.

It is clear that a distinctive system is essentially nothing else than a mathematical structure which allows in contradistinction to a pure logical conception - to use numbers whenever it is necessary. But all the basic categories are very well known and clear because of belonging to the set theory together with a part of arithmetics. Therefore the whole framework of set theory or of predicate logic can be used here and this is a very important advantage of the distinctive systems.

If time determinations are required too, then it is always necessary to discretizate the time in the intervals being short enough and then to introduce the critical times. Besides the objects two further types of objects are distinguished: instantaneous and historical ones. If x is an individual expressing an object, then $[t;x]$ is an *instantaneous individual* expressing the object in the instant t and a set of instantaneous individuals $\{(t;x];l_i \leqslant l < l_j\}$ is said to be *historical individual* during the interval $\langle t_i, t_j \rangle$. This *historical individual* is denoted as $[t_i, l_j;x]$ and expresses the history of the considered object during the time interval $\langle l_j, l_j \rangle$. An analogy with the notions of a differential and an integral of calculus are obvious. Furthermore *instantaneous* and *historical predicates* and *instantaneous* and *historical propositions* are distinguished with respect to the instantaneous and historical objects concerned.

E.g. in Example 1 there are distinguished the individuals $c_1, c_2, \ldots, c_n$ (cars) and an individual q (queue). The usual one place quantitative predicate a is determined by enumeration i.e. $a = \{(c_1, a_1), (c_2, a_2), \ldots, (c_n, a_n)\}$ but another predicate b of the same type is determined recursively by (1) etc. An instantaneous two place qualitative predicate $[Q, t]$ (not explicitly denoted in Example 1) expressing that a car c_i is in queue q in an instant t would be determined as a set of the triples $[t, c_i, q]$ for some i, $1 \leqslant i \leqslant n$, i.e. $[Q, t] = \{(t;c_i, q);a(c_i) \leqslant t < b(c_i), 1 = i = n\}$. Furthermore the instantaneous one place quantitative predicate l is determined by (2). Finally the average and maximum queue lengths are both historical quantitative one place predicates determined by (3) and (4) because really the historical objects queue i.e. the set of all instantaneous objects queues are taken into account.

It is clear by this example that the historical distinctive systems are composed not only of a set of the instantaneous distinctive systems (which are the particular stages of historical one) in which only the instantaneous individuals, predicates and propositions occur, but also of the historical individuals, predicates and propositions concerning many instantaneous distinctive systems.

Here the greatest advantage is the fact that again essentially only the well-known framework of set theory or predicate calculus is used, which means that all changes are eliminated and not denoted at all. It is the most important difference to the mentioned categories in the simulation languages as event, process, transaction etc., by which some changes should be denoted. This is avoided here.

4. HOW CAN A MATHEMATICAL THEORY BE APPLIED?

If one tries to investigate a concrete particular real system then (because of sufficiently developed sciences and their theories) one is looking for a theory the results of which could be applied to the real system. Therefore, let us consider a mathematical theory $T^{(1)}$ determined by a finite set of axioms $A_1^{(1)}, A_2^{(1)}, \ldots, A_k^{(1)}$ and further let us assume that a distinctive model S of the real system has been constructed.

An application of a theory to a distinctive system (which is in fact a mathematical structure) is allowed subject to the considered system satisfying all the axioms of the theory, i.e. in other words if the system is a model of the theory, where the term model is used in usual sense of mathematical logic (in [24] the model of theories and the models of reality were distinguished). If so, all the theorems of the theory are valid in the system, thus any application is immediate.

Thus, first of all one must verify whether or not the considered system is a model of the theory. But how one can verify that a system satisfies a condition especially here the conjunction of axioms? One can distinguish two possibilities with respect to his knowledge concerning the investigated system.

A) If one knows, that the given system S is a model of another mathematical theory $T^{(2)}$ which is stronger than $T^{(1)}$, i.e. all the axioms $A_i^{(1)}$ (and therefore all its theorems too) follow by the axioms $A_1^{(2)}, A_2^{(2)}, \ldots, A_j^{(2)}$ of the theory $T^{(2)}$, then it is really sufficient to prove $A_i^{(1)}$ by $A_1^{(2)}, A_2^{(2)}, \ldots, A_j^{(2)}$ for each $i = 1, 2, \ldots, k$. Thus the method of verifying that S is a model of $T^{(1)}$ consists in well known mathematical or logical proving that $T^{(1)}$ follows by $T^{(2)}$. The deductive method of proving is obviously sufficient only under the essential assumption that one knows that S is a model of $T^{(2)}$. Thus here only the original problem of verifying that S is a model of $T^{(1)}$ is reduced to a similar problem of verifying that S is a model of $T^{(2)}$. Therefore, the single deductive method is always an indirect method of verifying that a system satisfies a condition. In fact, the assumption that S is a model of $T^{(2)}$ is stronger than the original problem whether S is a model of $T^{(1)}$. That is a very important fact with respect to the efficiency of the mathematical methods used for problem solving.

B) If one does not know anything about the given system S and if quite generally S is determined by enumeration of all of its sets then exists only one direct way how to verify that S is a model of $T^{(1)}$. This way will be shown in the following.

Example 2

Let S be the distinctive system being a model of the real system described in fig. 1, i.e. $S = \langle I, C \rangle$. Then only for simplicity a new qualitative two place predicate C^* can be introduced as follows: $C^* = \{(x, y),$ there exists $v \in U$ such that $(x, y, v) \in C\}$.

Further let $T^{(1)}$ be a theory of acyclic graphs the single axiom of which (in fact there are infinitely many axioms for $n = 1, 2, \ldots$) looks as follows (P is the unique basic binary predicate of $T^{(1)}$)

(5) (acy) $\qquad \forall x_0 \forall x_1 \ldots \forall x_n [(P(x_0,x_1) \ \& \ P(x_1,x_2) \ \& \ldots$

$$\& \ P(x_{n-1},x_n)) \rightarrow \sim P(x_n,x_0)].$$

How one can decide whether S satisfies (acy) or not? First of all one must interpret the basic predicates of the theory. There is only one possibility here that C^* corresponds to P. Further it is necessary to choose all possible sequences $(y_0, y_1, \ldots, y_n)$ of individuals of I (for $n = 1, 2, \ldots$) such that $(y_{i-1}, y_i) \in C^*$ for each $i = 1, 2, \ldots, n$, to construct a pair (y_n, y_0) consisting of the last element and the first one of the sequence and then to decide whether $(y_n, y_0) \in C^*$ or not. In the first case the sequence $(y_0, y_1, \ldots, y_n)$ satisfies the condition (5) and in the second case it does not. If all possible sequences $(y_0, y_1, \ldots, y_n)$ satisfy (5) then one says that S satisfies (5) and vice versa.

If one looks at fig. 1 and tries to verify whether or not the considered graph is acyclic then one proceeds exactly in the way described above but one does not choose all possible sequences of individuals $(y_0, y_1, \ldots, y_n)$ but all possible sequences of pairs

$$((y\binom{1}{1}, y\binom{1}{2}), (y\binom{2}{1}, y\binom{2}{2}), \ldots, (y\binom{n}{1}, y\binom{n}{2})) \text{ such that } y_1^{(i)} = y_2^{(i-1)} \text{ for each}$$

$i = 2, 3, \ldots, n$ and further one stops if $n \geq 8$.

The method of verifying (just described in the Example 2) that a system S is a model of a theory T is very clear but a fundamental one. At the same time it is a *simulation method* because it consists in simulating the empirical verifications which are used in a real system by the similar verifications which are used in distinctive model of the real system. Really, in a real system one can empirically verify by driving along highways consecutively from the place denoted by y_0 to one place denoted by y_1, etc. to the place denoted by y_n and finally to the place denoted by y_0 again. If one succeeds in doing so then there is a "real" cyclus in the real system. This decision procedure was simulated in Example 2 in the distinctive model by taking the pairs (y_{i-1}, y_i) instead of the highways (in the same order) and finally by taking the pair (y_n, y_0). Obviously the similarity concerns only the distinguishability and no physical or technological properties.

In fact, one deals with the individuals, the sequences of them and with sets in the same way as with the objects. Thus it is a metamathematical point of view usual for the mathematical theories and used here for the distinctive models, i.e. the meanings are not taken into account.

In general, instead of (5) a more complicated formula of predicate logic can occur. In this case the verifying will consist in many repetitions of basic operations on sequences of sequences of individuals and numerals the result of which is again a sequence of the same type. These operations can be expressed by schemes using the variables. A scheme corresponding to (5) is O_1 determined as follows:

$$O_1((x_0, x_1), (x_1, x_2), \ldots, (x_{n-1}, x_n)) = (x_n, x_0). \tag{5}$$

Further (2) is an operation of omitting the last member of a sequence used by constructing C^* from C in Example 2

$$O_2(x, y, v) = (x, y). \tag{6}$$

One can imagine a much more complicated operations of that type e.g.

$$O_3((x, y, z), (x, y, w), (y, x)) = (w, x, z, y). \tag{7}$$

All these operations are basic ones showing what the computer must be able to do and what must be possible to express in the corresponding programming language.

In (8) and (9) are some other simple operations

$$O_4((x_0, x_1), (x_1, x_2)) = (x_0, x_2) \tag{8}$$

$$O_5(x, y) = (y, x) \tag{9}$$

corresponding to e.g. an axiom of transitivity (or atransitivity) and to the axiom of symmetry (or asymmetry) resp. of a binary relation. These axioms can be formulated as follows:

(tra) $\forall x_0 \forall x_1 \forall x_2[(P(x_0, x_1) \ \& \ P(x_1, x_2)) \rightarrow P(x_0, x_2)]$

(atra) $\forall x_0 \forall x_1 \forall x_2[(P(x_0, x_1) \ \& \ P(x_1, x_2)) \rightarrow \sim P(x_0, x_2)]$

(sym) $\forall x \forall y (P(x, y) \rightarrow P(y, x)$

(asym) $\forall x \forall y (P(x, y) \rightarrow \sim P(y, x)).$

Continuation of Example 2

If one chooses as a second theory $T^{(2)}$ the theory of partially ordered sets the only two axioms of which are (tra) and (asym) and if one has verified that S is a model of $T^{(2)}$ (i.e. by simulating method one used both operations O_4 and O_5) then it remains to try to prove that (acy) follows by (tra) and (asym). It seems to be easier to verify (tra) and (asym) and to prove (acy) by (tra) and (asym) than to verify directly (acy). Thus in this case it seems to be useful to use the theory $T^{(2)}$ but it seems to be also probable that in some other cases to verify a stronger theory $T^{(2)}$ will be more difficult than the simpler theory $T^{(1)}$.

There is a possibility to measure the complexity or difficulty of particular mathematical problems.

5. SOME CHARACTERISTICS OF SIMULATION LANGUAGES

According to [26] a simulation language should aid the systems analyst in building a model by presenting a conceptual framework for precise thinking and furthermore it should serve as a programming language for digital computers. Here the term model is used in a broad and not specified sense.

If one restricts oneself on the distinctive models, then the required conceptual framework for precise thinking is the well known set theory or even the predicate logic (both a little modified) and no other fundamental categories need be introduced. In fact, it is necessary to deal with distinctive systems, especially to construct some new systems of the original one because very many important problems are e.g. the extremal ones requiring to construct (or to find) a new system satisfying a special condition. Thus the problems of proving theorems are not the most important with respect e.g. to different economic complex problems.

In any case the necessary conceptual framework for simulation problem depends on the determination which problems are considered as those of simulation. Similarly all the basic features and categories of a language depend on the type and sort of problems which should be solved by this language, i.e. the syntax of a language is very seriously influenced by its semantics. But it was shown in section 2 that the determination of simulation problems is not simple. Thus it is not clear enough today to state how broad problem area should be solved by the simulation languages.

In [26] as well as in many other simulation languages the most important fact is that time and change are taken into account. But in fact the system time is a real (eventually discrete) variable as any other variable used in all programming languages. Here only the interpretation of this variable is important. It seems to us - if we are thinking of a very broad class of problems concerning constructions of distinctive systems satisfying different conditions - that this fact is included in the framework of distinctive systems, i.e. in the framework of finite set theory together with arithmetic. And this fact must influence the simulation language in a decisive manner.

DISCUSSION

Laski:

I believe it to be true that the only possible model of a formal system is another formal system and I want to suggest that those people who are attempting to say that a formal description of a program can be proved to be really true to reality, are wasting their time. It is philosophically impossible. The beautiful clarity of the equivalence between two formal systems described in this paper reveals that though this solves an important theoretical problem it does not solve the practical problem that concerns us; whether we want to prove the correctness of computer programs for algorithms or for simulation experiments. I would like Dr. Čulík to comment.

Čulík:

It is rather difficult for me to comment because I am no expert in this area. I wanted to work from some concrete examples which are solved by simulation methods, to be able to understand the general problem of simulation. I wanted only to find the characteristic features and after all I came to the conclusion that there is nothing specially characteristic. My talk was in the level of mathematics, but mathematics is also a language, therefore it seems to me not so difficult to transcribe simulations into it. I try to find the mathematically equivalent terms to simulation terms. Mathematicians or logicians believe that the framework of mathematics and logic are sufficient for describing everything; it is an article of faith for them. I try to answer the question whether it is possible to express the terms used in simulation languages like process, activity, model and state of model, and so on, in the categories very well known to me as a mathematician. If I succeed sufficiently - that means it is possible to define in the normal mathematical way these categories - then I will be happy and I can have an exact idea of the scope of problems which are treatable by simulation methods. If not, I will be much more happy because it is necessary to introduce some new essential categories in logic or mathematics. It seems to me for example the category of time may be an example because in logic time is not considered at all. We are forced to make a distinction between this instantaneous object and a historical object. This is a fruitful idea that should be developed in the frame of logic.

Laski:

I agree you have succeeded in your own terms: I am only concerned about the misunderstandings that may arise. Programmers who are insecure in their description of reality may believe it possible to prove in some mystic way that a description of reality is in accord with reality. In fact, one empirically obtains sufficient evidence to have a reasonable degree of faith.

Steel:

I have two comments to make, one relating to Laski's last remark. It seems to me the direct inference from what you say is that mathematicians ought to quit doing business because somebody might get confused.

I think there is an important point to remember in considering this paper. The approach that Čulík is describing is an analytic approach. He presents a set of equations, and the order in which these equations are presented is unimportant. You can change them around and they still describe the same thing. This is quite different from a programming description, an algorithmic description of the thing where there is an implied order and therefore another piece of structure that does not appear in the words.

SELF OPTIMIZING SIMULATION

G. MOLNAR

Centro Studi Calcolatrici Elettroniche del C.N.R., Pisa, Italy

1. INTRODUCTION

In many cases the aim of simulation is not restricted to the gathering of experimental information about the behaviour of a model of a given system. Rather it is performed in order to find an optimal structure for the system. A currently used technique for this purpose is that of making many different models, and comparing the data obtained from their simulation in order to choose an optimal one according to some given performance criteria.

The aim of this paper is to present a general strategy which makes it possible to change automatically the system during the simulation in order to optimize a given set of criteria defined by the programmer.

2. FREEDOM AND OPTIMIZATION CRITERIA

For speaking of the optimization of a system, two essential concepts are required:

a) the structure of the system must be defined with a certain *freedom*;

b) there must be one or more *criteria* of optimality according to which an optimal structure is to be selected.

In computer simulation of discrete event systems this freedom can be reduced to the values of some appropriate variables. Though we may have a variety of variable types, e.g. integer, real, element, etc., we may distinguish between two classes of variables: a class of *numerical* variables and a class of "finite valued" or *discrete* variables. A numerical variable (real, integer, complex, etc.) is characterized by the fact that generally speaking small changes of their values have little influence on the behaviour of the system, while larger changes have a greater influence.

For a discrete variable, on the other hand, two different values, however close they are, have in general nothing in common. For example, the integer values 3 and 4 may be by no means closer to one another than for instance 3 and 15, when they are used as subscripts either in a *go to* statement or for an array variable. In any practical case the number of possible values of a discrete variable must be finite.

A criterion is a measure for estimating the performance of the system, and specifying what properties or characteristics of a system are to be optimized. Therefore a criterion must be capable to assume an ordered set of values. Finding an optimum means to find a state of the system which yields a minimum or a maximum for the criterion, or it makes the value of the criterion as near as possible to a predetermined value. In simulation of probabilistic systems, in most cases, a criterion is a statistical average of an observable quantity.

In many cases we can be interested in considering more than one criterion. Sometimes it is reasonable to consider a single criterion which is a combination of others, but there might be cases for which it is more natural to consider a number of distinct criteria especially when it seems hard to discover their logical relationships.

For example in the case of a traffic simulation a criterion may be the time needed to cross a district, another one the number of accidents happening in it, etc. Since they are presumably in conflict and difficult to combine in a single figure one could decide to optimize the system at the critical points where accidents are most frequent, only with respect to the number of accidents and to optimize the crossing-time in the areas when the number of accidents is practically zero, Therefore, in these cases it is natural to permit an optimization with respect to different criteria at different points of the simulated system.

3. AN OPTIMIZATION STRATEGY

Let us consider the following case: there is a basket full of small objects with different shapes and let us consider as optimum an arrangement of the objects for which the level of the basket is a minimum.

To reach this aim we may use different techniques. One of them is the following: we empty the basket and we replace the objects in all possible ways noting, in each case, the level and selecting the minimal one. This would be a very long process. We could devise some better procedure by making use of an appropriate strategy of reducing the number of tests; however, the work involved remains in any case too hard.

A different approach for obtaining the requested result might be to shake the basket and let the objects arrange themselves. This

method may not lead to the best solution but most probably it offers
a solution better than the original state. It is essentially this second idea that we have adopted for a definition of self-optimizing simulation system.

Let us examine what happens in this case. The freedom of the
system is given by the possibility of any object to move in the three-
dimensional space. The main criterion is the level of the basket
which is to be minimized. However, for each object, there is another local criterion, its potential energy, which is in correlation
with the main criterion. Each object tries to occupy a position with
the lowest possible potential energy. There is another remarkable
aspect of this method. The displacement of an object is not determined by the actual level of the basket, but it is an effect of the
shaking of the basket, and of a large number of actions depending
on the geometrical and mechanical properties of the system.

This can be considered as random process, where for each configuration a test is made whether for every object the new position
is more convenient or not. We consider this process as a model of
a self-organizing system, where all objects are considered as active and moving simultaneously.

4. A SIMPLE OPTIMIZATION PROCEDURE

In the following we shall describe a method for changing the
value of both numerical and discrete variables in order to optimize
some criteria. Usually we deal with probabilistic systems but this
is not a necessary condition since in any case we introduce probability into the system by random changes of the value of the free
variables. Changing the value of a free variable is a discrete event
whose effect on the criterion usually is not immediate.

We have therefore to distinguish between the present values of
both the free variable and the criterion and their values at the moment of the last change of the free variable.

Let us call them V, C and Vprec, Cprec respectively and let us
consider separately the two cases of a numerical and a discrete variable.

4.1. For optimizing a system by a change of the value of a numerical variable, we use the following method: First of all we distinguish for any such variable a "current value", and a "nominal
value".

Whenever a change for a numerical variable is requested, its
current value is drawn from a symmetric (normal) distribution
which has the nominal value for mean. This is the active feature of

such a variable. There is a continuous examination whether there exists a correlation between the numerical variable and the criterion. If such a correlation does not exist (i.e. it is zero) a change of the value of this variable does not influence the criterion and therefore it cannot be used for optimizing it. Thus in this case the mean value of the normal distribution from which the current value of the numerical variable is drawn must not be changed. Otherwise, as we shall say below, it may change. Before drawing the new current value, the program examines whether the last change of the current variable caused a variation of the criterion and in which sense. If there has been no variation, the nominal value is not changed. If the value of the criterion has become nearer to the optimum, the nominal value is displaced in the same direction of the last change of the current value, in the other case in the opposite direction. A single displacement of the nominal value may not be significant or may not occur in the right direction; however, the global displacement, which results from a large number of such displacements and which is the sum of the single ones, causes an optimization of the criterion. If the observed correlation between the free variable and the criterion is zero, this may be due to different reasons.

One of them - the banal case - is when the variable has nothing to do with the criterion; we omit this case. It may, however, happen that it is only for the actual state of the systems that it does not exist a correlation. In this case the optimization due to this variable is automatically suspended until a positive correlation shows up.

Another possibility is that a certain time is needed in order that a change of the value of the free variable might cause a change in the criterion and the interval between two changes of the variable is shorter than this time. This fact may cause not only a zero correlation but also a false correlation. Therefore, the change of a variable must be explicitly programmed by appropriate "changing statement".

Let us see more precisely what happens when such a changing statement for a numerical variable is executed.

First of all the value of the correlation between the variable and criterion (Rvc) is evaluated. Then one computes the change DC of the criterion in a normalized form with respect to the time of the last change of the value of the free variable.

In ALGOL notations we can write

$$DC := \text{abs}(Rvc) \times (C - Cprec)/dC ;$$

where dC is the standard deviation of the criterion.

In order to optimize the criterion, we displace the nominal value of the free variable, according to the formula

$$Vnom := Vnom \pm (V - Vprec) \times DC \; ;$$

where the + sign is used for maximization and the - sign for minimization.

The case of "approximation" will be considered either as a maximization or as a minimization according to the sign of the difference between the actual value of the criterion and the value to be approached. After that we store the present values both of the free variable and the criterion as the precedent values for the next change:

$$Vprec := V \; ; \qquad\qquad Cprec := C \; ;$$

Finally we drew the new current value for the free variable V by the formula

$$V := normal(Vnom, dV) \; ;$$

where dV (the standard deviation of V) must be specified explicitly by the programmer.

4.2. For optimizing the system by a change of the value of a discrete variable the technique used is somewhat different. First of of all we compute the change DC of the criterion as:

$$DC := (C - Cprec)/dC \; ;$$

not taken into account, for simplicity sake, a possible correlation between the free variable and the criterion. A new value for a discrete variable is choosen in a random way according to an appropriate probability distribution P associated to the variable.

When a change statement for such a variable is executed this probability distribution is changed according to the following rules:

i) indicating with k the actual value of a discrete variable, its probability is first changed as follows

$$P[k] := P[k] \times (1 \pm c \times DC)$$

where c is a factor which may be constant or variable and the + or - sign is selected as explained before for the case of numerical variables;

ii) all values are then changed proportionally in order to renormalize their sum to one.

Moreover these values are adjusted so that they can never become less than a prefixed small positive quantity, in order to avoid the loss of a possibility in case its probability becomes zero.

A new draw is taken for the value of the discrete variable as follows:

```
a := random; b := 0;
for i := 1 step 1 until n do
begin
    b := b + P[i];
    of b > a then go to OUT;
end
OUT : V := T[i]; k := i; Cprec := C;
```

where T is the array of the possible values of the discrete variable V. The value obtained in this way is then assumed as the actual
value of the criterion. Of course this method of optimization, based
on correlations, requires the evaluation of mean values and standard deviations.

The system must, therefore, have a certain "past" from which
these data can be obtained. Therefore, until a certain minimum
time no change in the structure of the system will be allowed.

Now we have to remark that as the structure of the system is
changed during the system time, we have to evaluate continuously
the mean values, the correlations, etc.

In these calculations, however, we are usually not interested in
what happened at the beginning of the simulation, because it may
well happen that the initial values are no more significant for the
system.

It seems, therefore, more suitable to use a limited record. Let
us call this interval *recall length*. For the computation of the time
mean values, which are the base for the calculation of the various
statistical quantities, we are using the following procedure, which
was proved to be a good approximation of a limited memory of the
past:

```
procedure mean (newvalue, meanvalue, last changing time);
real newvalue, meanvalue, last changing time;
begin
    real z;
    z := time - last changing time;
    meanvalue := if z > recalllength then newvalue else
    if time < recalllength then (lastchanging time × meanvalue
    + newvalue × z)/time else ((recalllength - z) × meanvalue
    + newvalue × z)/recalllength;
    last changing time := time;
end;
```

The initial value of a free variable can be explicitly defined; if there
is not such a definition the initial value for a numerical variable is
zero, whereas for a discrete variable all the possible values can
be choosen with the same probability.

5. A REFINEMENT OF THE OPTIMIZATION PROCEDURE

If we have a system with more than one degree of freedom, i.e. more than one free variable, the above described optimization strategy may result too slow or it may happen that the state of the system does not tend toward an optimal one. We have therefore looked for a way of accelerating the optimization.

First of all let us remark that for any real system we can usually consider besides one or more criteria to be optimized, a number of other characteristics of the system, which we shall call index-quantities.

Thus, for instance, in the case of a firm management, besides the profit, which is the criterion to be optimized, there may be a lot of other index-quantities - as prices, costs, stock levels, occupation levels, salaries, etc. - which may be correlated not only among themselves but with the criterion - profit - as well as with the free variables of the system. Of course, these correlations are functions of the state of the system; however, in the neighbourhood of a determined time they may be characteristics. Therefore, when examining whether an arbitrary choosen new value of a free variable yields a better result than its previous value, we may examine also these index-quantities and take into account both the correlation between the free variable and the index-quantities, on the one hand, and the correlation between the index-quantities and main criterion, on the other hand.

Moreover, such index-quantities may be more directly influenced by the change of a parameter, than the criterion itself. This seems a very natural way of thinking. If I am a clerk and I wish to convince the director of the firm on some point and I have little influence over him, I have to look for some intermediate person - medium level chiefs of the firm - in order to influence them first and let them influence the director. But to this effect I have to take into consideration the relation between myself and the chiefs, as well as the relation between the chiefs and the director so to avoid that my activity, though efficient for convincing the chiefs should not turn out to be dangerous for me with respect to the director, if there is a bad relation between him and the chiefs. If I know that these relations are "negative" I could try to direct my activity in the opposite side, thus hoping to obtain anyhow the wanted effect on the director.

Thus, in calculating the change of the criterion in a change statement for both a numerical or a discrete variable we may take into account also the changes of these index-quantities. Therefore, besides the principal criterion - which is the only criterion that must be optimized by this statement - we may have a list of asso-

ciated index-quantities, let us call them IQ, to be considered for
evaluating the change of the criterion.

In particular for the numerical case we proceed as follows:

$DC := 0$;
for $i := 1$ step 1 until m do
$DC := DC + \text{abs}(Rviq[i]) \times Riqc[i] \times (IQ[i] - IQprec[i])/dIQ[i]$;
$DC := DC/m + \text{abs}(Rvc) \times (C - Cprec)/dC$;

where

$Rviq$ = correlation between the continuous variable and the
         index-quantity
$Riqc$ = correlation between the index-quantity and the criteri-
         on
$IQprec$ = precedent value of the index-quantity
dIQ = standard deviation of the index-quantity

For the discrete case we use the same form except for the omission of the correlation between the variable and the other quantities

$DC := 0$;
for $i := 1$ step 1 until m do
$DC := DC + (Riqc[i] \times (IQ[i] - IQprec[i])/dIQ[i]$;
$DC := DC/m + (C - Cprec)/dC$;

6. A COMPLEX OF OPTIMIZATION STRATEGY

As we saw, the optimization process considered up to now and
consisting in changing the value of a free variable, takes into account the values of a list of other system variables through a linear expression of the changes of such values weighted by appropriate correlations. This linear expression is very useful in many
cases, in particular when its value (i.e. the average change of the
index-quantities) yields a good indication for the change of the criterion.

It may happen, however, that the relation between these variables is not a linear one but follows a more general pattern.

In order to discuss further this point, let us consider a single
changing statement for numerical variable as an "input-output
block". The changes of the criterion and of the index-quantities
are the inputs and the value of the numerical variable is the output.

Let us imagine the whole simulation system as a set of variables interconnected by the simulation rules. By the introduction of

optimizing statements within the system we have realized a certain
feed-back connecting the already interdependent variables to themselves by means of these input-output blocks.

The important feature of these blocks is that they become effectively operative only if the optimization is possible, i.e. when non
zero correlations show up. Thus, from the point of view of the system optimization generally we are not making any error if we connect the variables of the system by these input-output blocks in an
arbitrary way, because usually a formal connection which does not
correspond to a real one is practically nullified by a zero correlation.

It follows that a numerical variable whose value is the output of
an optimizing block may well be an input for another block so that
a numerical free variable can appear itself as an index-quantity or
a criterion in other blocks. In this way, we can construct a whole
network of optimizing input-output blocks, superimposed to the to-
pology of the simulated system, with its own loops and feedbacks.
We are not in a position to make any rigorous statement but it
seems reasonable to admit that appropriate networks of optimizing
blocks may accelerate the optimization in a very sensible manner
in simulation time. On the other hand the gathering of correlations
is a very time-consuming process, so that the research of an optimal structure for the optimizing network is a programmer task,
and he has to make a skilful guess upon which variables depend on
which others.

7. AN EXAMPLE OF SELF-OPTIMIZING SIMULATION

For illustrating self-optimizing simulation we shall present the
following example of a cross-road.

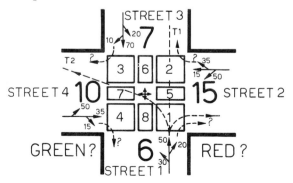

Fig. 1. Problem of an intersection.

We have considered two narrow streets (fig. 1). Cars coming from any direction may proceed in any other direction. However, the width of the street permits to the cars to precede only on a single line without distinguishing whether a car has to turn right or left or to go ahead. A street light controls the traffic. The green light permits a car to go ahead or to turn in both cross directions. Red lights do not permit to a car to enter the intersection so that it has to wait until the light changes to green. Yellow lights do not permit to a car to enter the intersection but if a car is already there it allows it to exit. Yellow lights follow both the red lights and the green ones. We have simplified the crossing procedure by dividing the intersection in discrete fields which must be occupied by the cars crossing the intersection. Occupying a field was considered as a discrete event. Priority rules were taken into consideration. The structure of the intersection is symmetric with respect to each street; however, as it is shown in fig. 1, the arrival pattern, which is generally a negative exponential distribution, and the probability to turn or to go ahead is different for the different streets. The long size figures indicate the average time in seconds elapsing between the arrival of two cars; the small figures represent the probability (in percent) that a car in that street has to turn to the left or to the right or to go ahead.

The aim of the simulation (criterion) was to reduce the number of cars in the system, i.e. the number of the cars which are crossing the intersection or are waiting that the light changes to the green.

The free variables were the length for both the green light and the red light (represented by numerical variables) and a set of four two-state discrete variables for deciding, for each street, whether to permit to a car to turn right during the red light, provided it is the first in the waiting queue. The length of the yellow light was taken as constant. Thus the system was defined with six degrees of freedom.

For accelerating the optimization we have taken into consideration as index-quantities the average times required to cross the intersection in eight different combinations (see fig. 1). These times were calculated as the average crossing times of the last 30 cars in these paths. The whole diagram of the optimization is shown in fig. 2, the arrows indicate information lines.

8. EXPERIENCE WITH SELF-ORGANIZING SIMULATION

Making reference to our previous example we began our examination with the initial values of 15-15 seconds for each light

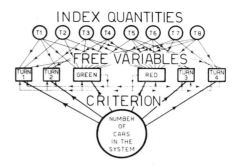

Fig. 2. Optimization block diagram of the intersection.

(green and red) and with the decision of not permitting to the cars
to turn to the right during the red light. In order to obtain reference
data, we made a simple simulation of the intersection with these
initial values. We have noted a very large oscillation of the number
of cars being simultaneously in the system, due to the negative exponential distribution of car arrivals; a relatively constant average
number of these cars was obtained after two hours of simulation
times and this number was found as 18.

The optimizing simulation was five times slower than the simulation without optimization, with respect to the same simulation
time. This difference is due to the necessity of gathering correlations. After a run of 5 hours of system time the following values
were found for the free variables: green 41 seconds, red 18 seconds and cars were permitted to turn in red light in the streets
Nos. 1 and 3. We performed another single simulation with these
data and we have obtained 9 as average number of cars in the system.

Let us add some remarks on the "velocity of convergence" of
our optimization process. Although we cannot make yet any definite statement about it, we shall summarize our experience on the
preceding example and a few others as follows. We have found that
the velocity of "convergence" of a system toward the optimal shows
very large variations.

The complexity of optimization, as follows from our previous
discussions, increases linearly the running time of the simulation.
In our cases the rate of increase was between 2 and 10.

The recall length has an interesting influence on the velocity of
optimization. If it is too short the oscillation of the system is
very high and therefore, the optimization may be very slow. This
oscillation may be due to two different causes. First, the natural
oscillation of the system in consequence of its own randomness,

second, the randomness introduced by the random change of the values of the free variables. If the *recall length* is too long the effect of the change of a free variable may be very small, so that optimization is slow. There exists an "optimum" *recall length* which permits the greatest velocity of optimization (fig. 3).

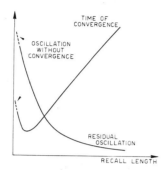

Fig. 3.

When the system reaches an optimal state, it has a remaining oscillation which seems to be propertional, in inverse ratio, to the *recall length* (fig. 3). The standard deviation of a numerical variable in a change statement has an important role. It must be small enough for allowing one to consider the change of the behaviour of the system as linear, but it must be large enough to permit to compare the "natural" oscillation of the system with the change of the state of the system due to the change of the numerical variable. Moreover it seems that the number of the degrees of freedom of the system has a little influence on the velocity of optimization, in contrast with the number and the appropriate selection of the index-quantities.

9. LINGUISTIC ASPECT OF SELF-OPTIMIZING SIMULATION

The self-optimizing simulation technique previously described is not bounded to any simulation language and is realizable, more or less easily, in any computer language. Rather it is a general technique - or strategy - for optimizing probabilistic dynamic systems. However, it is possible to introduce in a simulation language appropriate declarations and statements especially suitable for dealing with self-optimizing problems.

In order to start experimenting the proposed optimization technique we have introduced a few special phrases of this sort in our simulation language SL/1 [102], which is a reduced SOL with a few features of SIMULA.

Since we consider this language essentially as an experimental one we omit here its description. Rather we shall present a suggestion of how to insert self-optimization facilities in a highly organized and well known simulation language as SIMULA.

With reference to the SIMULA manual [28] and the ALGOL defining report [106], we shall consider the following extensions of the language:

⟨declaration⟩ := ⟨as in the manual⟩|⟨numerical type⟩⟨numerical declaration⟩|⟨discrete declaration⟩
⟨numerical type⟩ := integer |real
⟨numerical declaration⟩ := numerical⟨numerical list⟩
⟨numerical list⟩ := ⟨numerical segment⟩|⟨numerical list⟩, ⟨numerical segment⟩
⟨numerical segment⟩ := ⟨numerical identifier⟩|⟨numerical identifier⟩⟨bound pair⟩
⟨numerical identifier⟩ := ⟨identifier⟩

A numerical variable, outside a "change statement", is used as an ordinary arithmetical variable of type integer or real. If the range of the values of a numerical variable is bounded it must be declared by means of a bound pair.

⟨discrete declaration⟩ := discrete⟨discrete list⟩
⟨discrete list⟩ := ⟨discrete segment⟩|⟨discrete list⟩, ⟨discrete segment⟩
⟨discrete segment⟩ := ⟨discrete identifier⟩⟨bound pair⟩
⟨discrete identifier⟩ := ⟨identifier⟩

A discrete variable, if used outside a change statement is considered of integer type. The possible values of a discrete variable must always be bounded.

⟨SIMULA statement⟩ := ⟨as in the manual⟩|⟨change statement⟩
⟨change statement⟩ := change⟨free parameter definition⟩⟨optimum condition⟩⟨criterion⟩⟨index-quantity list⟩
⟨free parameter definition⟩ := ⟨discrete identifier⟩|⟨numerical identifier⟩, ⟨standard deviation⟩
⟨standard deviation⟩ := ⟨arithmetic expression⟩
⟨optimum condition⟩ := min|max|appr.(⟨arithmetic expression⟩)

The optimum condition specifies the requirement that the value of the criterion must tend to a minimum, a maximum or to the value of the arithmetic expression, respectively.

⟨criterion⟩ := ⟨numerical identifier⟩
⟨index-quantity list⟩ := ⟨empty⟩|⟨index-quantity list⟩⟨index-quantity⟩
⟨index-quantity⟩ := ⟨numerical identifier⟩

At this stage we shall not suggest considering numerical or discrete arrays because besides compilation difficulties, it would permit either an inconsistent use or it would be extraordinary memory and time consuming for gathering all relevant correlations.

⟨variable⟩ := ⟨as in the report⟩|⟨discrete identifier⟩|max
(⟨discrete identifier⟩)|⟨numerical identifier⟩| nominal(⟨numerical identifier⟩)|recall length|prob(⟨discrete identifier⟩,
⟨arithmetic expression⟩)

respectively indicating: the current value of the discrete variable; the value of a discrete variable in which has the maximum probability to be chosen; the current value of a numerical variable; the nominal value of a numerical variable; the recall length as previously defined; the probability of a value to be chosen for a discrete variable.

10. SOME INDICATION ON FURTHER RESEARCHES

Very little has been said up to now about how to gather correlations. This is in fact an open problem requiring further consideration.

The correlation between two variables X and Y is defined, as it is well known, as:

$$R = \frac{M(X \times Y) - M(X) \times M(Y)}{D(X) \times D(Y)}$$

where M and D indicate mean value and standard deviation.

We have already described the method for computing these functions which is automatically applied at any effective change of the system time. This is a linear correlation computed on simultaneous values. It may happen, however, that a variable is not instantaneously correlated with another variable but only with a certain delay.

To avoid gathering false correlations we have generally used time weighted mean value for the criteria and the index-quantities and we observed the correlations between them. If the length of the recall interval is great enough in most cases the problem of delayed correlation can be considered as automatically solved. However, this is not always the case and at any rate it makes the opti-

mization slower than it would be by directly gathering the delayed
correlation.

Another problem is the *recall length* itself. In our system we
presumed a commom *recall length* for the whole system. This may
be satisfactory in most cases, but we can presume that in general
dynamic systems some variables change more quickly with respect
to others so that is would be more realistic to introduce different
recall lengths. However this poses many problems requiring further study not only from a linguistic point of view but also for the
calculation of the correlations between variables having different
recall length.

DISCUSSION

Dahl:

I think that this contribution is a very interesting one, because
one always feels when one has made a large model that one does
not quite know what to do with. To really explore the whole multidimensional space is just impractical. Any way of simplifying or
making it more easy for the programmer at least to include optimization features in a model will be of very great value indeed.
The aim of a simulation study is very often exactly that.

Nygaard:

I also would like to compliment the author on his paper; we need
very much more work in this area and we need to take more pains
to organize the experience which accumulates on using simulation
and have all kinds of critical analysis of the ways we are using it.

Jones:

I just have a question about the time scale on your diagram. How
long approximately both in simulated time and in actual computer
time does it take to reach those state levels?

Molnar:

Well, that is really a practical and interesting question. The
time scale was a system time of course, and gathering correlations
is a very time consuming operation. The only data concerning this
question we can give is that comparing the running time with and
without optimization, we found very different ratios from one prob-

lem to another. In the cases we tried this range was between two and ten but they are not absolute limits.

Baukneckt:

I would like to know if you have experience with optimization and simulation of road networks. Here you have one intersection only and I suppose you could do your optimization with mathematical programming rather than by simulation.

Molnar:

This was done as a simple experiment and the only one which was done with road networks. I am not a specialist on that problem.

Caracciolo:

I believe that what has been proposed here is an essential strategy for mixing optimization procedures and simulation. In Pisa we have begun some experiments on these ideas quite recently and we still have to collect more data and results. One difficulty is that we are in a University centre and we do not have, or at least we have not had up till now, actual access to real problems. We have to try to think up simulation problems. The situation will be changed in the near future. Another remark I wanted to make is this; that the strategy is obviously independent of the simulation language used, though in fact some special instructions have been included in the experimental simulation language which has been designed by Molnar in Pisa in order to facilitate the use of this strategy.

Krasnow:

I think there is a possibility of converging on an apparent solution which is very far removed from a true optimum and I was wondering if Molnar might like to comment on possible ways of avoiding this occurrence or whether or not there is any assurance in his technique that this kind of a situation can be avoided automatically.

Molnar:

As I said there is not any assurance. It may happen that there is not a convergence in the system. However as a method it is not less satisfactory than an ordinary simulation. It is built round a simulation, therefore we may all have the outputs of the simulation. If we have no convergence then we may change something in the system or we may give up this method.

Caracciolo:

I would like to add some remarks connected with the fact that in Molnar's strategy there is a possibility to consider more than one optimization criteria which might even in some sense be conflicting. Molnar has made very few experiments on that so far. I think that the question has been very well posed. It is a subject on which it is extremely difficult to give an answer. What we feel generally is that we should do experiments on this subject in order to get farther inside the problem.

Petrone:

I did not understand Molnar's answer. If there is no convergence you say that you may well keep your simulation and use its results as for normal cases. I am asking whether, when you make parameter changes in your simulation looking for optimization, you lose the validity of the normal results of the simulation? The simulation run gives you an estimate of some parameters; queue length, mean averages and values of this sort. If you move around changing your parameters and in the end you come to no convergence, you simply lose your time and invalidate your normal results.

Molnar:

If you wish you can stop optimization if that is your special requirement. However, you may change the randomness of the system by changing parameters less than the natural randomness of the system and so you could still avoid false results.

Parslowe:

It appears that you have a very sensitive method for changing this optimization. It seems to me that this is a reasonable method of operating if you have a fairly homogeneous group but it might not work so well for a group of small population or an inhomogeneous group. Say, for instance you put in your simulation a large truck which arrived once a day; this is going to throw the whole of your simulation out at one particular step in the optimization. Have you got any method in the system of de-sensitizing to avoid the problem?

Molnar:

We have a probabilistic system to optimize, of course, and a single event must not have a very great influence on the results. For a criterion, we use a statistical average and we observe the change of the statistical average and you can define the length of time on which the average is based.

SIMULATION LANGUAGE STANDARDIZATION *

T. B. STEEL Jr.

*System Development Corp., Commercial Systems Div.,
Santa Monica, California 90406, USA*

The problem of standardization is to many people's mind a very dull and uninteresting one. It is, nevertheless, important, and of course has a very long and somewhat tortuous history. In order to put the subject into context I would like to make some remarks about the historical background of standardization.

Standardization is really as old as mankind. Once we learn to use a language, we have standardized something, having agreed upon conventions.

The first bit of standardization which came into the world, standardization in the formal sense where there was a conscious agreement on something, had to do with weights and measures. The job of standardization that the ancients did was really rather poor; e.g. in the course of the Roman Empire their standard for lengths changed by a factor of one part in 150, and their standard for weight changed by one part in 30. This clearly would be intolerable now.

Some people have claimed that the first real committee on standardization was the council at Nicea. Industrial standardization, however, began in the Middle Ages for a very practical reason. There was a problem in ensuring that merchants did not adulterate their merchandize and the 15th century guilds began to develop the rudiments of what we now see in industrial standardization.

The first serious scientific attempt to generate standards can be traced to the French during the revolutionary period when they were reorganizing the entire world. Of course I speak of the metric system. There is an interesting and illustrative story about development of the metric system. It characterizes standardization efforts even today. A committee was established to generate standards for weights, measures, time etc. in the year 1790. Its first report was made five years later, in 1795 - that is the first typical aspect. The second: the report in 1795 produced a standard for

---

* Editors note: This section is a transcript of an unprepared talk, not a
pre-written formal paper.

mass (the gramme) which was based on the standard for length (the meter). The standard for length was not itself defined until the report of 1799, four years later.

With the industrialization of the world expanding rapidly in the 19th century, there was a growing need for normal procedures of standardization going far beyond the question of weights and measures and other scientific matters; such problems as making sure that the cars would run on the railroad track, for example. With the development of electricity we had the problem of making sure that a plug would fit into the hole in the wall. These things sound trivial, but they come into everything we do.

At about the time of the first World War it became clear that, rather than each industry or each country separately and independently developing its own standards and thereby creating a series of conflicting standards, larger, more comprehensive organizations were necessary, first on a national level and later on an international level.

The problem of describing the organizations that conduct standardization activities is almost hopeless. If you will recall, the other day we were discussing the problem of displaying a graph of a complex system where all the boxes were so small that we could not identify them. That is the kind of problem one has in describing standards organizations; committees on top of committees on top of further committees.

I am not going to attempt here to describe in any sort of generality either any national standard organizations or the ISO. However, I think that in order to discuss this topic properly it is necessary to give a little indication of how these organizations work. I am going to concentrate on the international level; since this is an IFIP conference that seems appropriate.

The international organization is made up of representatives of various national standards organizations - almost every country has one. In most, I believe in fact in all cases except the USA, the official industrial standards organization is connected with the Government. In the USA the situation is a little bit different. The organization now called USASI, United States of America Standards Institute, is a reorganization of what used to be called American Standards Association. Most of you have probably heard of that; it is a private corporation, it has a number of members which include departments of the US Government, but also includes various industrial organizations and even private individuals when they want to pay the entry fee.

Each of these organizations in the various countries has the responsibility for conducting standards activities across a broad

spectrum of fields. Usually the one exception, the one field that is
not contained directly in this organization is that of the electrical
and electronics standards. One of the reasons for this is that very
early in the game the electrical engineers felt the requirement for
standardization and they developed their own organizations before
the general industrial standards organizations were born.

This in fact carries us over into the international situation. It
is important for information processing because there is clearly
a serious problem of standardizing electrical characteristics of
data processing machines and there is also a problem of standardizing other aspects such as programming languages, character
sets, the electro-mechanical parts of the machines, etc. Two separate organizations exist all the way up to the international level,
to deal with these problems, and the interaction between them, and
the cooperation between them is a difficult thing with which to deal.

On the international level, the International Standards Organization is the body that establishes international standards. I might
point out that in spite of the long history of efforts there is no such
thing yet as an international standard. The reason for this is quite
simple. An international standard requires unanimous approval of
all members and that has so far been impossible to come by. However, there is something called an international recommendation
which is something that has been approved by a majority of the
members.

There a number of international recommendations and they have
the de facto effect of a standard. Even in nations that have voted
against a particular proposal, if it is approved as an international
recommendation it is often adopted locally. The international recommendation is the equivalent of a standard.

In the case of the computers and information processing field
there is a technical committee, Technical Committee 97 of ISO,
whose concern is all of the non-electrical problems of standardization in information processing. Technical Committee 97 is divided into a number of sub-committees concerned with different
aspects of the problem. I will not turn through them all; there are
three that are, perhaps, significant for the congress here; Sub-
committee 1 concerned with vocabulary and standardization of terminology, Sub-committee 2 concerned with codes and character
sets and Sub-committee 5 concerned with programming languages.

The procedures for developing a standard or a recommendation
are extremely elaborate and on the average it takes four years
from the initiation of the activity to the establishment of the recommendation. One of the reasons for this is the way these committees do business; the best analogy that I can think of to describe the
atmosphere and the behaviour of these committees is to ask you to

imagine Johnson, Wilson, Kosygin, de Gaulle, Madame Ghandi and Mao Tse Tung sitting at a table trying to decide what wine to chose for dinner.

A number of tactics are employed by the committees to smooth proceedings. For example, about three years ago in Berlin was a meeting of Sub-committee 5 where the two major problems were standardization of ALGOL and standardization of FORTRAN. Two ad hoc working groups were established at the meeting, one to consider ALGOL and one to consider FORTRAN. The chairman of the ad hoc group on FORTRAN was Professor van der Poel from the ALGOL group and the chairman of the ad hoc working group on ALGOL was Mr. Heising from IBM.

Since our business here is languages I am going to devote the rest of my time to the question of languages. There are five languages that have been seriously considered at the international level with respect to standardization. ALGOL and FORTRAN are parallel examples; the procedures in both cases has been the same. The ISO Sub-committee 5 requested an outside group to do the development work, to provide a document that would contain the proposed standard. In the case of ALGOL it was IFIP, and this responsibility was delegated to Working Group 2.1. In the case of FORTRAN it was the then-called American Standards Association and they established a Sub-committee for this purpose. The status of these two languages in ISO is that everything has been done except the final bits and pieces of the required French translation of the document. I mention this status as of a couple of months ago and it is possible that the translation has been completed by now. From here on it really is a matter of formality. It will take another year to get all the formalities over but once something goes beyond the official Sub-committee concerned, it almost never gets overruled.

Two other languages are being considered now and will be discussed at the next Sub-committee 5 meeting which will be in Paris in November. One is COBOL, where the work of the United States of America Standards Institute and the CODASYL Committee will be the development agency. The other is APT, the language for numerical control and there is an international development group, a private group, concerned with that. Finally, there is some interest in PL/I at the international level, largely sponsored by ECMA, the European Computer Manufacturers Association.

These five languages are really the only ones that have, as yet, been given serious consideration at the international level. There are a number of others at various national levels.

I would like to turn now to discuss the questions of what can be standardized, why should we standardize, or whether we should

not, and indicate a few implications for the languages that are of
concern at this conference. There are several things that one
should think about when considering topics for standardization and
they are not all concerned with language in the sense of programming language. An important one is the question of vocabulary. We
have discovered already here that there are some vocabulary problems, that different people mean different things by the same word
and a group like this can make a contribution if it would agree on
recommended definitions for words. I submit two that are not yet
included in the proposed glossaries: "simulation" and "quasi-
parallel processing".

A second thing that has some impact on our work is the question
of character sets and their representations. I think not so much of
the ordinary alphanumeric sets but more of the next step in that
kind of thing. I recall your attention to the discussion of Lackner's
paper and the graphic symbols. This is something that has not yet
been given consideration in standardization and as we heard on Mon-
day it is something that well might profit from it.

Third, there is, of course, the question of specific languages.
There are certain existing programming languages, as I have indicated, that have been considered. We have talked about other languages here; one might speculate on the desirability or lack of desirability of proposing standardization of any of these.

And finally, something that is perhaps in too preliminary a stage
of development to enter standardization yet but is something that
should be kept in the back of our minds; the question of standardizing, not so much on languages, but on techniques for describing
languages.

Now let us consider the question "why should one standardize?"
Some of the rationale is apparent. There is the clear desirability
of exchanging things so that you can use what I have got and I can
use what you have got. Without standards this kind of exchange is,
as is well known, difficult.

Second, going beyond the question of physical exchange of, say,
programs, there is simply the question of person to person communication. If we have a standard language, then one can publish
in it and presumably everyone can understand it.

The third, and sometimes overlooked, reason for standardizing
in such an area as this is the whole problem of education. The universities are busy teaching programming languages, teaching people
to use computers, with a certain amount of standardization. There
is a great deal of improvement in the ability to teach concepts and
techniques that can be used wherever one can standardize.

Why should we not standardize? What are the arguments against
it? There are two principal ones, one of them valid and the other

one, I believe, invalid. One should be very careful of the point in time when you standardize something because if there is insufficient understanding of what it is you are proposing to standardize, the result is liable to be disastrous. I submit that ALGOL as it stood in 1960 was a case in point. Now the fact that it has taken 7 years to develop an understanding of what is really intended and to develop a description mechanism that was adequate is a safe-guard against premature standardization: that is one of the virtues of this often apparently clumsy and elaborate mechanism that is employed to generate standards. But this is a point that must be considered in each case.

The second argument against standardization is one that has a certain superficial apparent validity but if carefully explored, particularly in light of the first point, disappears. That is the point that standardization may stifle research and advancement. If you standardize on something and everybody uses that then we have no progress. Well, in practice one finds that this is not the case. First of all, the human animal is sufficiently curious and sufficiently stubborn that he is going to go ahead and develop things anyway even if there are standards. Furthermore, carefully drawn standards can permit advancement on top of the standard; the question of extension and augmentation that we have talked about.

So there are several considerations to weigh when deciding whether or not it is the appropriate time to standardize on something and we might look at them in terms of the simulation language question. From one point of view one might say that simulation languages in some sense are today in the same state vis-a-vis the standardization question as general purpose languages were in about 1958 or 1959. But there is another way of viewing it; we have this debate that crops up in almost every discussion session on whether a general purpose language is really all we need for a simulation language anyway. Many of the existing simulation languages are built on top of other languages that are already in the standardization process; SIMULA with its basis in ALGOL, SIMSCRIPT with its basis in FORTRAN, the SPL Petrone described with its basis in PL/I, and so on. As yet I have seen no simulation language, certainly none was reported at this conference, that has its basis in COBOL.

I do not want to make, myself, any specific recommendations other than the point that I made about vocabulary. I think that this is important and somehow the kind of knowledge and experience represented in this room ought to be able to get an input to the vocabulary people. I do not have any specific recommendation as to how this is to be accomplished. It is perhaps something we could discuss.

I would, however, like to encourage some discussion on whether or not standardization of existing or proposed simulation languages is a desirable thing.

In closing, I would like to point out that by 1970, depending on whose estimate you take, we may have anywhere from forty thousand to a hundred thousand machines of a sufficient size that simulation of the type we are discussing can be done sensibly. Again, depending on who you talk to, you will have anywhere from one half to two million programmers. Ninety-nine percent of two million is a sizeable number, even if only a small fraction of them are engaged in simulation activities, their number will be substantial*. More and more universities are becoming concerned with this problem and are teaching aspects of it. If we are to bring rationality into this business, something has to be done.

It does not mean necessarily standardizing on one simulation language. I call attention to the existing situation with respect to general programming languages. There are a number of different languages being standardized upon. Now this officially runs contrary to established principles of ISO and the various national organizations which say there should be no conflicting standards and one can easily argue that ALGOL and FORTRAN, for example, are conflicting standards. There is obviously, however, sufficient dispute in the computing community to preclude selecting a language and saying this is to be the standard language and all others should be thrown away. I believe that same situation exists now in respect to simulation languages and I predict that it will remain so for a long time to come. Nevertheless, I think we ought to at least reflect on some of these questions.

---

* Note added in proof: I did, in fact, say "ninety-nine"; please read as "one", TBS.

DISCUSSION

Strachey:

I want to say something about the standardization of vocabulary as opposed to the standardization of programming languages in particular. The way in which we think is very much assisted by our words. We think in symbols and we use words to describe symbols. It is very important if we are going to standardize on the words or on the meanings of words that they should actually correspond to the significant concepts in the field we are talking about.

If we standardize on the meanings of words before we have

sorted these out we make two rather serious errors. We may either define one word to mean two things without realizing that they are different, or we may define two words to mean the same thing. Both these errors can lead us into very considerable confusion. The example that I would like to give you from the history of mathematics is the first, and I think more dangerous error. It is in the field of mechanics. In the early days of mechanics, there was a long and impassioned argument about whether the effectiveness of a moving body was proportional to its velocity or the square of its velocity. Some people produced examples where the effectiveness was clearly proportional to the velocity, meaning of course the momentum, and in other cases it was clearly proportional to the square of the velocity, meaning the kinetic energy. And until the two concepts of kinetic energy and momentum had been sorted out, the single word "effectiveness" caused a great deal of confusion.

Now, I think it is quite easy to standardize prematurely on the meanings of words in this way, and I think we have to be very careful not to do this.

Laski:

I would like to support with all the vigour at my command Strachey's plea for a clear awareness of the distinction between words and ideas. In this connection I would also like to recommend to standardization people the logical techniques of explication introduced by Carnap which enabled the notion of probability to be explored into its constituent parts. I feel we need a mechanism to permit temporary assignment of words to meanings - to be standard locally in time.

Steel:

I would like to address comments to both of the last speakers. I, of course, endorse the principle behind Strachey's comments, but one has to be careful that one does not get additional confusion by having no words that mean anything, so that there is clearly a balance here between agreeing on meanings and premature agreement on concepts.

With respect to Laski's comments, he obviously did not hear a word which I repeated many times in my talk when I said "industrial standardization". The problem here is not one of pure science, it is one of practical reality. Ideally, of course, we should fully and completely understand all the concepts involved in language and concepts of definition, etc. As several people mutter in the background: "impossible". At the moment there is need for bringing some kind of order into the chaos that exists in the whole information processing field, and the industrial standardization efforts are an attempt to bring a balance between the needs of the moment and the needs of the long range scientific ideal.

Laski:

I entirely agree with Steel that as an ad hoc engineer's convenience something must be done. Though these words may possibly sound derogatory, they are not intended to do so. From time to time I think it is proper for scientists to take off their pure hats and put on constructive engineer's hats. But what bothers me is the belief, that underlies so much informed engineering standardization, that there is some platonic ideal reality that may at some stage be approached. I do not believe in the second coming.

Brennan:

I should like to offer just a few words of information regarding the activities in the continuous simulation world on standardization. Simulation Councils Incorporated formed some two years ago a committee for developing a recommended next-generation language. That committee is composed of approximately two dozen people. They have worked on manuscripts from their sub-committee of about half a dozen people. There has been a surprising agreement - I would not call it unanimity - but surprising agreement as to the general characteristics of the kind of continuous system simulation language that the members would like to see. There is a general disagreement as to the form and format of the recommendation document, but nevertheless this activity has made very surprising and admirable progress. We have achieved a fair agreement as to the language characteristics. We are, I think, in this aspect somewhat ahead of the discrete field, if one thinks agreement is progress.

Caracciolo:

My impression is that there is obviously a distinction between the continuous simulation field and the discrete simulation field, and this is perhaps that the continuous simulation world has been in existence for a relatively long time. The discrete simulation system is quite a new concept. We do not yet really know how much is new and how it compares with other things.

There is, it seems to me, a clear indication that we feel that we have something new we do not entirely understand in quasi-parallel programming etc. And this might explain why there is, in a sense, a kind of negative reaction to Steel's very cautious words about what could become standardized.

Steel:

Two comments: I think there is a tendency in some of the remarks that have been made to be a bit disparaging about the "engineers" who are involved in the standardization effort. The fact that there are not many people who are sitting in this room that are interested in the subject does not imply any lack of competence in the individuals involved. I want to make that point quite clear.

Secondly, again apparently people did not quite hear when I pointed out the length of time that is involved in getting agreement. One of the reasons for this length of time is just to prevent the kind of difficulties that some people have pointed out; to allow a substantial period for argument and discussion and to make sure that everybody understands what they are proposing. There is a further length of time when the proposal is published as widely as possible, so that the entire community has a chance to look at it and to comment.

The whole system of formal standardization has been set up to take into account the kinds of difficulties that people are pointing out. It is not merely an affair of trying to get standards tomorrow, because it is an important kind of operation. I submit that, as Molnar has simulated Italian traffic, anything is possible.

Krasnow:

I would like to say with respect to languages in general and perhaps simulation languages in particular, it is not clear to me yet why one would want to standardize at a language level. I can see a fairly wide range of reasons that would give rise to a need for standardization of FORTRAN or ALGOL. But can you suggest any specific criteria which would help to clarify at what stage in the development of an emerging field standardization becomes an issue that is worth looking at seriously?

Steel:

I can certainly indicate the kind of criteria that have been used in the past with respect to general purpose programming languages. They are really quite simple. The problems are three. First, one looks for a language that is of a broad utility. Roughly speaking, that means a lot of people at a number of different places are using it on a number of different machines. A second criterion is that if people have a desire to publish examples, algorithms and programs for communication purposes, then it becomes desirable to agree on what this communication language is. Finally one begins to see pressure developing from various universities, so that they can teach the same thing, or so that when a graduate student appears from another university he already understands the language that they are using.

The extent to which these conditions apply to simulation languages at the moment I am not prepared to answer.

Strachey:

I would like to force Steel to comment further about the competence of the people who are in fact doing the standardization. I think standardization in certain circumstances is extremely useful and furthermore I have been much impressed with the caution and the care and the skill with which this is being carried out. I had myself some contact with the early stages of standardizing, when people first started to say, "we must standardize on a programming language". There was for quite a long time a general sort of feeling that what was wanted was a standard programming language. After some time it gradually percolated that what was wanted was not a standard programming language, but standards for existing programming languages. We did not want one standard programming language; we wanted a standard FORTRAN and a standard ALGOL. This is a very good example of how proceeding fairly slowly helps you to do something sensible and not something which is obviously silly.

There is one point where I disagree with standardization; I do not think that it is necessary to standardize completely on languages for publication. We do not standardize on natural languages and the attempts to do so have not been very successful. Human beings are much more flexible than machines; we are able to deal with divergencies from standards which are locally convenient. The purpose of standardizing, I think, in programming languages is to provide a standard for machine use, so that compilers can be written which will accept the language. Standardization seems to me to be a thing not for human beings but for machinery. And this I think is the important thing; if we cannot standardize on ideas we cannot standardize on their representations.

Beltran:

I remember that Leibnitz at the end of the 18th century was involved in two big fights; one was the unification of the Christian churches and the other was a fight for multiplication and addition tables to be taught, at least in the universities. There were a lot of people who thought 99% of the population were not able to learn addition and multiplication tables. Fortunately they were standardized and happen to be historically proven useful standards.

The other remark is that I do not know why people tend to think that standards are static phenomena in the universe. Fortunately there is nothing static and I think that Strachey put it very well in his last remark. Standards are frames of reference and they allow always all the necessary changes for local conditions.

Steel:

A piece of information that I neglected to mention in the course of my discussion is that in both national procedures and international procedures for standardization you find mandatory view points where a previous standard or recommendation is automatically brought up for review and consideration. There is a built-in process of review and evolution that is essentially statutory in origin.

Lackner:

I want to go back to Krasnow's comment a little earlier on the question of the utility of standardization in the simulation field at this moment. About six years ago Jack Little at the Rand Corporation called together several people that he had heard of, who were working in simulation. A committee was formed which eventually became part of SHARE and is still there in the System Simulation Project.

The first two activities of this committee were the production of a glossary and the production of a bibliography. It was a very good educational process to attempt to construct this glossary. It led, I think, to a fairly good understanding among Americans at that time of the ideas in GPSS, SIMSCRIPT, SIMPAC and DYNAMO and one or two other systems, many of which are obsolete now. The terms "transaction", "event" and "activity" were seen to have differences and similarities. Just as the point has been made earlier in the conference that the production of a simulation model is often the most useful part of the simulation effort, so the experience acquired in the attempt to construct a glossary is often one of the most valuable results of a standardization effort.

Gaskill:

I would like to say a little more about the Simulation Software Committee of Simulation Councils Incorporated in the USA. We have been attempting to develop a standard language for continuous systems simulation and our approach has been quite different from what has been described by Steel. Instead we are attempting to construct a new language which would pool together the common features of probably 20 or 30 existing languages.

I fear that perhaps this standard language will never become an active language, but the mere process of attempting to synchronize the 20 or 30 existing languages I feel is going to contribute to work in this area.

One of the motives for attempting to establish a standard is that we were afraid if we did not propose some standard which met the requirements of diverse users, some large manufacturers such as IBM would arbitrarily suggest their language and because of the size of the organization would almost automatically establish a standard.

We have felt that we were a little bit late; there was a fairly standard language for discrete systems simulation in GPSS, and I believe SIMSCRIPT was also widely accepted. We had nothing approaching this in the continuous simulation field.

We have been successful - I hope - in influencing IBM to produce a language which follows, at least in generalities, the wishes of our Simulation Software Committee. I hope that, if this language (which will be available in about one month, I understand, from IBM) does become a de facto standard, it will be more useful than if our committee had not taken any action.

Krasnow:

The comment was made earlier concerning the fact that one can standardize on a representation of concepts or ideas rather than standardize on the ideas themselves. I think this explains the prime distinction between the continuous simulation problems as they relate to standardization and the problems that we are confronted with here. In the continuous case there exists a well defined body of concepts which people have been working at for some time to develop good representations. Therefore the notion of a standardization committee there seems extremely appropriate.

In our case it is very clear from what has been taking place this week that we still have the problems of conceptualizing what we wish to do. We may identify some of the areas where concepts have been accepted broadly enough to consider some preliminary agreement on terminology. But it certainly seems clear to me that we do not have the body of knowledge yet available to accomplish the kind of thing that you describe in the continuous simulation case.

Laski:

I wish to distinguish between two explications of the term "standard", which I will call "standard I" and "standard II". The explication of standard I is convention, working convention, and this explication of standard by convention gives its range of relevance and applicability, which is enormous. The explication of standard II is the Mosaic law, *mutatus mutandus*.

Unfortunately, manufacturers and those concerned with imposing standards on others, think that standards work is standard II rather than standard I, i.e. Mosaic law, rather than working convention. I would welcome as much effort as possible by those doing the work of standardization to explain to managers that what they are doing is standardization I, not standardization II.

Steel:

The distinction that Gaskill made between the type of standardization that the organization solely concerned with standards do and the kind of work his simulation council is doing is a very clear distinction between the functions of technical committees and those of standardization organizations. It is not in the charter of any of the formal standardization bodies, either national or international, to develop languages or magnetic tapes or what have you. Their job is to standardize, to go through a formal procedure of adopting as standard something that has been proposed by, and developed by, somebody else. The development work that the simulation councils are doing is exactly parallel to the work that Working Group 2.1 did in the ALGOL area, that a FORTRAN committee did in the FORTRAN area and so on. The process of standardization in the formal sense is to take something that has been designed and developed elsewhere and adapt it, modify it and cast it into appropriate form that can be distributed to everybody concerned for formal agreement. Now this sort of thing is really standardization by convention.

I would like to point out that if one goes too far in trying to debate what ought to be an appropriate standard, and one does not simply be conventional and agree on something less than ideal, one never gets anywhere. Consider the possibility of the railroads debating endlessly the ideal track width: you would never get any railroads built. It is precisely this point that the existing standards organizations are trying to overcome by adopting evolvable but convenient standards that will, so to speak, do for the moment. As time goes on, and whatever science we are concerned with develops, we can modify the standards, change them, scrap standards that turn out to be bad and adopt new ones that are better.

GENERAL DISCUSSION - SESSION 5

Lackner:

Čulík point out that the notion of "process" is very difficult to deal with at present. I think this is so because "change" itself is not studied formally very much. I think mathematicians might spend some time attempting to develop better expression of change, instead of leaving it entirely to developers of languages like ALGOL.

We did a little bit of work on this at SDC while I was there and produced a calculus of change which was not very powerful but was capable of expressing some systems which yield change. I would much prefer to see mathematicians and formal logicians who are quite adept at these things make some attempts to deal formally with the notions of change.

Čulík:

It seems to me a rather philosophical question. The notion of change so far as I know was by mathematicians through all the history of mathematics eliminated from consideration. Any changes were described by two things - descriptions of the state before starting to change and afterwards. The concept of change as far as I understand the matter, in mathematics and logic too, is replaced by the concept of function. I do not believe that anybody from the Greek philosophers onwards has devised a very good way to introduce as a basic notion, the notion of change - that is my opinion.

Strachey:

I think that it is basically important that programming languages in general require the concept of change in a way that is quite foreign to mathematics. This is one of the reasons why programming languages are difficult and one of the reasons why mathematicians do not like them. The really difficult and awkward component is the assignment statement and the trouble about the assignment statement is that something changes and after the assignment statement, things are no longer the same. We can no longer say that "$x = x$" and this breaks down one of the most fundamental mathematical concepts - that if you write down the symbol "x" and then the symbol "$=$" and the symbol "x" on the other side, you have something which is true. But it is not true, even in ALGOL. "$x = x$"

may be a boolean expression whose value is false. Just replace x
by a parameterless procedure generating random numbers.

Caracciolo:

I support what Strachey has said. In programming languages we
have something different from what we have in ordinary mathematics and it is exactly the elimination of change in mathematics
which makes it so difficult to understand what programming languages are from a mathematical point of view.

Čulík:

I refer to a remark of Strachey's on expressing the assignment
statement. Considering left and right sides it is clear that an assignment statement is a couple. Therefore, your change is expressed in ALGOL or in other languages by a set of couples; nothing else than a function. I believe it is no contradiction.

It seems to be that there is no other way if you want to describe
a history of a complex situation than to make "movies" of the old
history.

Nygaard:

I think that to regard programming languages as being for the
expression of changes is perhaps a little misleading. I would rather
say that programming languages are languages for describing sequences of action. There are a very large number of things which
it is necessary to have in programming languages which are actions completely different from those we encounter in arithmetic.
The thing is, of course, that they are important actions, but since
the use of computers started with numerical applications perhaps
a little too much emphasis is placed upon them. I think that we
should regard a language as describing sequences of actions. This
is a mode of describing a system which is different from the mode
which we have in mathematics, where we describe permanent relationships which exist between certain conditions.

Strachey:

I absolutely agree that the semantic description of programming
languages in mathematical terms at the moment has to be done
without reference to change. It seems to me that the ideal description of the semantics of a programming language is to describe it
in mathematical terms which do not involve sequences of events,
but the trouble about using sequences of events as a method of ex-
plaining programming languages is that we do not know how to com-

bine them. All we can do with events is to sequence them one after the other and we do not have a calculus of combinations. All you can do is look at a program and follow it through and see what happens. With partial transformations in the ordinary mathematical methods of doing things, however we have by now developed various techniques for combining and compounding and abstracting, all of which are operations which you can perform on function expressions but which you cannot perform on programming languages at the moment.

One of the difficulties about programming languages is that there is no way in which you can take different instances of the same symbol dotted over the page and say they mean the same thing - they do not - or at least, you have to be very careful about what they mean.

I think the whole business of semantics in programming languages is concerned with the fact that the assignment statement means that we have several values attached to one thing - not one.

Lackner:

In programming languages we do expect a sequence of actions to take place as a result of making some formal expressions , which I think Nygaard agrees with - but I disagree with Nygaard's statement that we want to express a sequence of actions, in simulation in particular. We want to express rules which will be combined and will operate simultaneously and whose effect will be a sequence of actions. But that sequence of actions is one that we do not originally express. We express a number of simultaneously operative rules which will later yield a sequence of actions.

Nicholls:

I do not think that it is just the assignment statement that is a problem. As we get into more advanced languages, there are other aspects of programming languages which raise even larger problems than that of assignment. I think assignment is reasonably well understood. In the work on the formalisation of PL/1 that is going on in Zemanek's group in Vienna, the attempt has been made to describe a system which is the minimal system - the minimal set of objects which represent a PL/1 program. The conventional parts of the language are reasonably well understood. The part to do with simultaneity and similar aspects are still not well enough understood because, I think, of the lack of the study of this aspect of complex systems by mathematicians, in the past. We are still groping for a better understanding of this sort of system as we try to describe it in the precision we want.

SIMULATION PROGRAMMING LANGUAGES - NORTH-HOLLAND (1968)

IMPLICIT INTERACTION IN PROCESS MODELS

G. P. BLUNDEN
IBM Data Centre, London W.1, England

1. INTRODUCTION

Models of dynamic system behaviour are most flexibly biult up from component types of system state-change. To facilitate model building, the components should themselves be flexible in scope and self-contained (except where direct communication has a real-world counterpart).

The "process" approach to the description of state-change encompasses, within a single framework, the features of duration, parallelism, and interaction which characterise component actions in dynamic systems.

This paper emphasizes, briefly, the importance of *implicit* interaction between processes in simplifying the formulation of simulation models, in both logically simple and highly interactive situations.

2. PROCESSES

In process-based modelling languages such as SOL [76], SIMULA [28], and NSS [112] each component of system state-change is specified as a behaviour-pattern consisting of a series of instantaneous actions (i.e. events).

A process is an individual performance of some behaviour-pattern. A process is thus an (operational) entity, which exists over a period of time in the system and modifies the system-state as events in its behaviour-pattern (qualified by attribute or parameter values) occur; these event may be time-dependent or conditional on the existing system state. Overall system behaviour is thecombined effect of processes operating in parallel over simulated time.

Through its attributes and actions an individual process may represent, for example, a "transaction" flowing through a service network - (the basic view in SOL, which derives from GPSS); or a "machine" performing its work-cycle; or a pure operation whose attributes identify any physical resources involved.

A process performing a null behaviour corresponds to a simple (non-operational) entity with attributes - (thus in SIMULA all entities are treated as processes). A behaviour-pattern consisting of a single event specification is an "event-routine", and associated processes correspond to "event-notice" entities.

The process approach thus offers wide flexibility in identifying and modelling the physical and operational components of dynamic systems. Its utility rests largely on the ease and generality with which behaviour-patterns can be specified in the modelling language.

3. BEHAVIOUR PATTERNS

Behaviour-patterns are the basic units from which a description of system operation is constructed. To aid model development, and to simplify the mapping of operational components commonly identified in real-world systems, it is important that these behaviour units may be self-contained - a complete and concentrated specification of a given behaviour can be separately revised, and processes performing such a behaviour, once initiated, proceed quite independently. Direct communication between behaviour-patterns must exist, however, when management or control functions are to be modelled.

To permit specification of behaviour-patterns, the modelling language must then include facilities for event-to-event control within a given process behaviour, and for direct control between processes. Direct control facilities include initiation of new processes, termination, and immediate and time-scheduled reactivation of other processes. Event-to-event control includes the suspension of activity in the current process either for a scheduled period or indefinitely - requiring direct reactivation by some other process.

These facilities admit a self-contained behaviour-pattern only when all its events are time-dependent. Conditional events demand cooperative behaviour-patterns through which a process which established some new system state (and is aware of the implications) explicitly reactivates some other process which is waiting (indefinitely) for this condition.

Independent processes can be established for time-dependent (including cyclic) sequences such as data input, system-phase setting, and report output. But in a multi-server queueing system (for example) a process which introduces a "new arrival" into the queue must check if some idle server process is to be reactivated, while a server process must examine the queue after one service

operation to determine whether a new service operation or indefinite suspension should follow.

The server behaviour is not self-contained, and conditions governing the "start-of-service" event are partially contained and
duplicated in the arrival behaviour.

In a previous paper [7], a capability for implicit interaction between processes was proposed, permitting the specification of
conditional events within behaviour-patterns. The NSS language
incorporates this independent observation of the system state
through a facility for conditional wait - i.e. suspension of activity
in the current process until specified quantitative state-changes
occur; as with time-scheduled events, an underlying Control Program is responsible for automatically reactivating the process.

4. IMPLICIT INTERACTION

Implicit interaction occurs between a process which changes
some item of the system state and a suspended process which has
requested observation of that item. Automatic process reactivation
may be implemented with reasonable efficiency for state-change
due to (non-specific) assignment to system variables and entity-
attributes, and for population changes of entities and in sets.

Conditional events may now be included within behaviour-
patterns, allowing a more complete and logically simple treatment of many operational components.

In a queueing system in which operational server entities have
been identified, the server behaviour may check for an empty
queue, and specify a conditional wait for change in queue population, before the start-of-service event (which selects a queue
member); the arrival behaviour independently adds members to the
queue - which is under observation by any waiting servers. There
is no explicit cross-reference between arrival and server, and no
duplication of condition analysis.

In general, a behaviour may specify conditional wait for change
in any of a number of items which might permit its next, conditional, events to occur. Behaviours which produce one or more of these
state-changes are not directly concerned with consequent effects.
The absence of explicit cross-reference between behaviour-
patterns greatly simplifies the specification of systems in which
resources may become available in a number of different ways or
may take part in a number of different activities.

If the queueing system were described in terms of transaction
flow and facility (server) entities, the transaction behaviour-
pattern might include a conditional wait for a change in some attri-

bute value (e.g. availability) of a facility, or for a change in the setting of some system switch variable.

It may be seen that implicit interaction between processes involves a generalisation of the conditional wait capability already provided, for a restricted (largely predefined) system state description, in SOL and GPSS.

Two further extensions in modelling capability are provided through generalized process interaction. Firstly, independent observation for change in entity population permits a conditional wait for the termination of some process - thus allowing the performance of a sub-process (by initiating the process and then waiting for its completion) and thus the modular construction of a behaviour-pattern in terms of subsidiary patterns. In addition, if reference arguments may be passed when a process is initiated, a library of pre-defined (and self-contained) behaviour-patterns can be provided - this has particular application in behaviours which monitor changes to an argument quantity and develop time-weighted statistics. Once initiated, such processes would independently accumulate observations over the simulated period.

5. SIMULTANEOUS EVENTS

Parallel process operation may give rise to events simultaneous in simulated time. When events are conditional on the system state, and made feasible by some state-change, the order in which processes are reactivated determines which of the feasible events in fact occur at this time.

Priority must be incorporated as a fundamental attribute of processes, with the priority value at any time indicating to the Control Program the relative importance of the next event in each process. Events which release resources may be given higher priority than events which require resources, while these may be ordered according to the importance of different possible uses of the resources. The use of priority and conditional wait allows processes to proceed in parallel, independently and correctly, for logically simple systems - where the priority of conditional events is not itself dependent on the current system state.

This case does arise in multi-resource situations, where the managed allocation of available resources to competing operations (possibly processes of the same type) must be modelled. An example is the choice of "best" combinations of simultaneously available machines (differing in capacity) with queued jobs (of varied sizes). In this situation, competing machine processes cannot operate independently - the parameters and reactivation of the "start of work" event (or the initiation of some equivalent pure operation involving job and machine entities) must logically be under direct control of a single "management" process.

This controlling process can itself interact implicitly with the rest of the system; it monitors the availability of relevant resources (including waiting processes) and, on the basis of appropriate decision rules reactivates (or initiates) one or more chosen processes with suitably assigned parameters. The behaviour of the control function is cyclic - waiting conditionally, when no further action can be achieved, for any of the various state-changes which might permit successful analysis of system conditions.

A number of different event types may be supervised by one control process, with event priorities governed by the sequence of decision logic. When the number of factors affecting decisions is large, comprehensive monitoring of system state is achieved by waiting only for change to the simulation clock. The control process is then automatically active at every system time state, examining the system-state and activating events according to system conditions. This closely resembles the activity-scan technique which has proved particularly suitable in modelling complex conditional (highly interactive) situations.

6. CONCLUSION

The process concept provides a flexible framework of modelling facilities, which can accommodate many different views of the structure of discrete dynamic systems.

Facilities for conditional event specification permit implicit interaction between processes operating in parallel over simulated time. This simplifies model structure, formulation and development, by reducing explicit cross-reference between behaviour components. In addition, general capabilities are introduced for sub-process structure, predefined statistical observation processes, and scan control of complex conditional activity.

The effect on absolute execution efficiency of requirements for implicit interaction must be considered in the light of its contribution to overall modelling capability.

DISCUSSION

Lackner:

I would like Blunden to elaborate a little on the notion of sub-process; in particular, what parts of a process would he break apart or, if he is not inclined to do this in a general case, in some specific instance what parts of a process would he break apart?

Blunden:

I would like to answer that by saying that I would not really view the sub-process as a technique for breaking apart. I would view it as a technique for building up. The sub-process should, in fact, be a process which has been invoked as a sub-process of some wider process. If we envisage as an example something in say a job shop manufacturing situation, the particular piece of work may need several operations on it. We would like to construct an operation which is the work on this particular job and you build it out of the separate complete processes through which it has to go. It is really a technique of building up rather than breaking down.

Lackner:

I did not mean to say that you could only break down or only build up. I think the two are part of the same thing. If you can build something up to form a whole then the whole, if you can con-ceptualize it as a whole prior to building it up, might have been broken down in the conceptualization, if you follow me. I suggested earlier that parts of a process that are usually separated either prior to building them up or antecedent to breaking them down, are the beginning, the ending, the duration and the interruption. I would like to hear your comments.

Blunden:

I think that is more of a formalism. I think some of those are almost non-processes. One of the great problems in discrete si-mulation is that duration, which the rest of the world views as ac-tivity, we in fact represent by no activity at all. You could break any process down into these steps you describe but I am not sure whether I personally would. I certainly was saying that a sub-pro-cess was in correspondence to physical components or physical behaviour components rather than as components of the notion that we have a process. My notion of a process is that it is simply a sequence of related events, which may be a naive view of it.

Laski:

Should processes be reactivated explicitly or implicitly? There is a genuine and serious conflict here between those who are concerned with convenience of modelling and those who are concerned primarily with efficiency of operation. With a philosopher's hat on I would go to the first, with an engineer's hat I would go to the second. It seems to me that if one has the kind of implicit interaction that Blunden wants, and I entirely support this, then one may, as is suggested in Knuth's paper, over-ride this on certain changes that the analyst knows very well will make another process critical.

Let me just give a specific example. Supposing one has a process which is an emergency process when a certain store gets full. It is reasonable to attempt this process when the level of the store increases and not when the level of the store decreases. So one wants, I feel, to be able to mix implicit and explicit interaction according to the cocktail that is best suited to the needs of the moment.

In this connection I would like to make a fairly specific proposal and that is for a language in which the norm is implicit interaction, during program development and early running, with a report on where interaction has been explicit. When running this system to get results or running this system for management, and I am not quite sure whether these are the same activity, you can specifically insist that implicit interaction only takes place where you have made it explicit. In this way I think that a moving compromise between generality for conceptualization and program development, and specificity for efficiency and program running may perhaps, with a great deal of complication for the 1%, be achieved for the 99%.

Caracciolo:

I think that this problem of the explicit versus implicit interaction is a serious and important one although I did not find this paper really enlightening on this point. Rather I would add another point here and this is on what is said about simultaneous events. It is written in the paper that "priority must be incorporated as a fundamental attribute of processes with the priority value at any time indicating to the control program the relative importance of the next event in each process". Then it also says "the use of priority and conditional weight allows processes to proceed in parallel, independently and correctly for logically simple systems where the priority of conditional events is not itself dependent on the current system state". I have read this because I wanted to point out that priority can be incorporated only if it corresponds to actual features of the system which is being simulated. This I believe is the most important point. It has also something to do with explicit and implicit interaction because in making a simulation one must be very careful about what are the actual properties of a system. We cannot force or impose certain properties on the system simply because we like to have a clearer model. We ought to be very careful on what I would call an adequacy condition between the model and the simulating system.

Blunden:

I would like to say something on the question of simultaneous events. The notion of priority between simultaneous events seems to me something which one does have to consider. The simulation is not only going to be a reproduction of the real world; one of the implicit aims in discrete simulation is in fact to develop simultaneous events when maybe they were not there before. That is, a discrete time scale leads probably to more simultaneity in the simulated system than there was in the real one and this has been an aspect which the analyst certainly has had to consider in past systems or has been in error when he did not. I think that if there is priority in the real system, then the order of simultaneous events is significant in the system that one is modeling.

Nygaard:

I am going to start with a comment on Lackner's remarks. I thoroughly agree with Blunden and his approach: the problem is not to be able to devise a method for splitting up into some kind of basic constituents in the process of life. The important thing is instead the opposite - we must be able to organize the things which naturally belong together into constituent components of the system. I do not think it is interesting to be able to observe, and give names to certain transient stages between actual phases of progress unless you view the system as a whole. What we would prefer is to take objects which belong together and split the system up in partial activities. This is the basic philosophy of the process concept.

Another thing there is the question of priority and the question of sequencing. I am very much in agreement with Krasnow when he says that priority should only be introduced if it is an important part of the system itself. We have been looking into the question of priority. Should we provide some associated priority with event notices? We found that if you have priority associated to event notices, then you must build your own sequencing scheme for that purpose. This is also our approach to this sequencing situation where you want to use the "wait until" statement. I would say that in these situations there are such large demands for variations of the scheme that to believe that you are able to devise a combined scheme which will solve everything correctly for you, is a little too optimistic.

Blunden:

I would like to indicate this was a definite approach to really complex systems, particularly the ones where you are involved in scanning predicates over lists and so on. If you choose to implement any sort of "wait until" form in these systems you should be honest about it and wait for particular changes to data and what you cannot reference as a particular data change you are unable to incorporate as an implicit "wait".

COMPOUND DECLARATIONS

John L. McNELEY

Judson Branch Research Center, Allstate Insurance Companies

1. INTRODUCTION

Declarations within a programming language serve to define properties of the quantities used within a program and associate these quantities with their identifiers. This property association with a variable, for example, is "cast in concrete". When any deviation from the defined rules is desired, the user must, with varying degrees of difficulty, program the desired changes into each procedural situation involving the quantity. The programming is usually straightforward if the deviation is to further restrict the range of values the variable may assume. However, if it modifies how an operator behaves, the programming usually becomes complex.

It would, therefore, seem desirable to have a language which allows quantities to be given arbitrary properties at the time they are declared. One way in which this can be accomplished effectively is to allow, within a single declaration, the association of a procedure or a "process" with a list of variables, as well as the conditions under which the specified actions are invoked.

The concept of procedures associated with variables is a familiar one, in special circumstances. For example, several languages provide a declaration such as TRACE, which causes an output when a variable appearing in a TRACE list is changed. This is usually accomplished by calling a systems procedure, TRACE, prior to storing the new value in the variable. The purpose of this paper is to show how generalizations of this idea, called *compound declarations*, introduce a good deal of useful flexibility into programming languages.

2. FORMAL STATEMENT OF CONCEPT

The following syntax and semantics of compound declarations are described here in relation to the language description of SIMULA [29]. The idea of compound declarations facilitates

efficient implementation of useful features not currently in the
SIMULA language. It also allows flexibility in the detailed definition of new features. The notation used throughout the illustrations
and examples of this paper is:

capital letters ::= user defined identifiers or routines

small letters not underlined ::= system variables or routines

small letters underlined ::= reserved symbols

2.1. *Syntax*

⟨fetch association⟩::= <u>fetch</u> ⟨procedure statement⟩|
      <u>fetch</u> ⟨process designator⟩

⟨store association⟩::= <u>store</u> ⟨procedure statement⟩|
      <u>instead</u> ⟨procedure statement⟩|
      <u>store</u> ⟨process designator⟩|
      <u>instead</u> ⟨process designator⟩

⟨action association⟩::= ⟨fetch association⟩|⟨store association⟩|
      ⟨fetch association⟩ ⟨action association⟩|
      ⟨store association⟩ ⟨action association⟩

⟨action associated variable declaration⟩::= ⟨action associa-
tion⟩ ⟨type declaration⟩|⟨action association⟩ ⟨array decla-
ration⟩

⟨specifier⟩::= <u>string</u>|⟨action association⟩ ⟨type⟩|⟨action asso-
ciation⟩
    array1⟨action association⟩ ⟨type⟩<u>array</u>|<u>label</u>|
    <u>switch</u>|
    <u>procedure</u>|⟨type⟩<u>procedure</u>|⟨type⟩|<u>array</u>|⟨type⟩
    <u>array</u>

2.2. *Semantics*

Variables declared with a process designator or procedure
statement association allow either the direct scheduling of a process or the invoking of a procedure statement according to a fetch
or store action on the associated variable. The fetch association
implies that after the value of the variable has been obtained, the
associated process or procedure statement is activated prior to
continuing further evaluation of the statement in which the variable
appears. The store association implies one of two actions:

If the symbol <u>store</u> is used, prior to altering the current value
of the variable, the associated process or procedure statement is
activated.

If the symbol <u>instead</u> is used, the process or procedure statement is activated in place of storing the value.

There can be more than one fetch association or store association with any variable. The order in which these actions are invoked is as declared, that is, left to right. However, all store associated actions with a variable must be either all <u>store</u> or all <u>instead</u> specifications, not both.

The processes associated with a variable are created by the process designators at the time the block head in which the declaration appears is entered. The elements created with each such process are then associated with the variable. For example, the nth association with the variable X is addressable by the system function elmt (N, X). The value <u>none</u> will be returned if a nonexistent association is addressed. For the purpose of clarity, it should be noted that when a process designator is associated with an array declaration, a process is created and associated with each element of each declared array.

The invoking of the procedures or direct scheduling of the processes associated with a variable by declaration can be overridden by replacing the syntactic unit ⟨variable⟩ with

$$⟨variable⟩.[⟨procedure \ statement⟩]$$

within a statement. This replacement is valid on either side of the replacement symbol. If the variable did not already have an association, the fetch association is assumed provided the value of the variable is not being changed and the store association is assumed otherwise. Of course, if there were many associations, all would be replaced by the single procedure. This procedure can invoke any of those suppressed, since it can address all the associated processes and can call any of the associated procedures. In case either the direct scheduling of the associated processes or the invoking of the associated procedures is to be suppressed for a particular instance, the symbol <u>inhibit</u> is substituted for the procedure statement in the specific statement. Thus

$$X.[inhibit] := Y$$

would inhibit all store associated actions on X.

Formal parameters of activity or procedure declarations which do not appear in the value specification may not specify associations in their type specification. However, those formal parameters which appear in the value specification may have action associations in their type specification. This new association is valid, of course, only within the scope of the formal parameter. In the case where the actual parameter has a fetch association, $A1$, and the formal parameter has a store association, $A2$, then $A1$ will be activated prior to storing the value into the formal parameter during the replacement of the actual for the formal parameter.

In SIMULA, a set is a type of variable. It can only be operated upon by basic system procedures and it does not have a value in the conventional sense. A fetch associated action will be activated when the set is referenced by one of the basic system procedures only to examine an element of the set, but not change its membership. This means that the set name must be an actual parameter to the basic system procedures which recognize the association. A store associated action will be activated immediately prior to the change in membership of the specified element by one of the basic system procedures. In this case the basic system procedures require both the set name and specific element as parameters in order to recognize any association. In other words, a procedure which removed an element without mentioning the set name as an actual parameter would not invoke a store associated action.

The symbol <u>declared</u> may be used as an actual parameter in the process designator or procedure statement in an association declaration to mean that the particular variable with which it is associated is to be substituted. The symbol may also be marked as a string, '<u>declared</u>', indicating that a string representing the variable name is to be the actual parameter. For example, if $A(X, Y)$ is an activity declaration with X defined as a real variable and Y a string, then the declaration

<u>store</u> A(<u>declared</u>, '<u>declared</u>') <u>real</u> <u>array</u> $B[1{:}5]$;

would create a process for every element in B. For example, the process designator used for $B[3]$ would be

$$A(B[3], 'B[3]')$$

and this process would be activated prior to changing the value of $B[3]$.

2.3. *Additions to SIMULA*

In SIMULA, the formal parameters of an activity declaration are less general than those of a procedure declaration. Labels, switches, and procedures are not allowed and all other parameters, except arrays, are called by value. This means that the value specification is not needed. This paper will also exclude labels, switches, and procedures, but will assume the other parameters need not be call by value. With an activity declaration, "call by name" will mean that the actual parameter is a variable, and the formal parameter becomes a local name on the data specified by the actual parameter. As for procedures, they retain the same meaning, that is, the actual parameter is substituted for every occurrence of the formal parameter in the procedure body.

A set used as a parameter will be considered call by name

where the current SIMULA considers it call by value. A set used
as a parameter which this paper considers "call by value", will
mean that the formal parameter becomes the set head of a new set,
and new elements are created and placed in this new set for each
element in the set specified as the actual parameter.

A new addressable value for every process can be obtained by
writing

$$result(X)$$

where X is some element. At the beginning of a statement this
value is undefined. At the time a store associated action is activated, the value in result(X) is that value which has been computed
to be stored. At the time a fetch associated action is activated, the
value in result(X) is the value which was fetched. It also denotes
the value which will subsequently be used to continue evaluation of
the expression containing the fetched value. Thus, a fetch action
might change result(X) if a nonstandard value is to be used.

In the case of a set, result(X) will contain the element which is
being examined in a fetch association and the element whose membership is about to change in a store association.

2.4.

Several usable language features which exhibit some of the flexibility of compound declarations are given in the following examples.

Consider the compound declaration which associates a process
of class MONITOR with the variables X and Y.

1.1 store MONITOR(declared, 'declared') real X, Y;

When control enters the block head of which this declaration is a
part, a process for each of the variables X and Y will be created.
For X, the process designator MONITOR(X, 'X') will create a process and the element created will be stored in a place retrievable
by the system function elmt($1, X$). This process will be scheduled
immediately prior to the time when X assumes a new value.

Thus, the activity declaration, MONITOR, provides, for any
real variable with which one of its processes is associated, an
output list showing the times at which variables changed value during a simulation. It would appear in the SIMULA block head as:

```
activity MONITOR(V1, V2); real V1; string V2;
   begin integer COUNT;
      COUNT := 1; V1·[inhibit] := 0.0;
START: write (time, COUNT, V2, V1·[inhibit], result(nextev
   (current))); cancel(current);
```

```
        COUNT := COUNT + 1
        go to START
  end;
```

Assume that process $P1$ is the current active process, which contains the declaration of the variable X and is currently executing the statement

$$X := 7;$$

After fetching the value 7 but prior to the assignment, 7 is placed in result (current) and the associated process given by elmt$(1, X)$ is directly scheduled.

If this is the first time that X has been assigned a value, COUNT is set to 1 and a zero is stored into $V1$. Note that the $V1$ store association is inhibited. This was necessary since ALGOL does not allow a variable to be used prior to its being assigned a value. Then a statement is executed which outputs the current simulated time; the number of times this variable has been changed; the identifier X; the current value of X; and the new value of X. Note that in obtaining the current value, any fetch association is inhibited and that the value 7 is obtained from the set of procedures result(nextev(current)). The process then becomes passive. Subsequent assignments to X again directly schedule the associated process. It will increment the COUNT variable and branch to the statement which produces the output.

Another example of store association is given by the declaration

1.2 <u>store</u> TIMEINTEGRAL(<u>declared</u>) <u>real</u> X, Y;

The activity declaration, TIMEINTEGRAL, provides for every variable for which one of its processes is associated, the quantity

$$\int_0^{time} \text{value } (t) \mathrm{d}t.$$

It would appear in the SIMULA block head as:

```
    activity TIMEINTEGRAL(V1); real V1;
        begin real LTIME, TINT;
            LTIME := time;
            TINT := 0.0;
    START: cancel(current);
        TINT := TINT + V1.[inhibit]X(time - LTIME);
            LTIME := time;
        go to START
    end;
```

The first time a value is assigned to the variable X, for example, its associated process will store zero into TINT, the updated sum of the product of the current value of X and the length of time it has had that value, and the current simulated time into LTIME, the time the last interval computation occurred. The process then goes passive, returning control to the process making the assignment. Succeeding assignments to this variable will compute TINT and assign to LTIME the current systems time.

The associations of 1.1 and 1.2 can be combined by using a declaration like

> 1.3 store MONITOR(declared, 'declared') store TIMEINTE-GRAL(declared) real X, Y;

In this case, two processes would be associated with each variable. The first of X, for example, would be addressable by elmt$(1,X)$ and the second by elmt$(2,X)$. In the execution of the assignment statement

$$X := 7;$$

in process $P1$, MONITOR would be activated, and when it goes passive, TIMEINTEGRAL would be activated. When it goes passive, control would be returned to $P1$. The value held in result(current), 7, would then be stored into X.

Many applications of simulation languages are enhanced by the use of variables which act like registers in a computer. At some clock time t_0 assume a register has a certain value. Between t_0 and the next "clock time", t_1, several actions may use that register including one to assign it a new value. Since these actions are going on in parallel, all of them can use the value of the register at t_0 time and the new value is not assumed until t_1 time. However, in the simulation of this situation on a computer, the actions would be carried out in a sequential order and with normal variables an assignment statement assigns the new value immediately. Therefore, the simulation would probably yield a different result. Of course, a programmer could program around this every place he could predict that it would happen, but it can be handled more conveniently by declarations.

Consider the declaration

> 2.1 instead SYNCHRONOUS (declared) real array $A[1:N]$;

which associates a process of class SYNCHRONOUS with each member of the array A. Such a declaration will, for each real variable with which it is associated, delay the assignment of a new value for the variable until all processes scheduled for the current system time have been executed. Control will be given to the user if a conflict is detected during the assignment of a new value, and, in the case where more than one assignment is permitted, an arbitrary choice from among the assigned values will be made when the assignment takes place.

One way to accomplish the desired actions is to specify the following activities. A process designator for the data-carrying activity HOLDR will yield a process to hold the value to be assigned. A process designator for the activity SYNCHRONOUS will yield an associated process to schedule the assignment of the new value, if it is not already scheduled, to detect conflicts, and, to place the new values, TEMPR of HOLDR, into a set. A process designator for the activity SYNC will yield a process which chooses the value from the one or many assigned to the specific variable.

These activities would appear in the SIMULA block head as follows:

```
activity SYNCHRONOUS (X); real X;
    begin set S, Boolean B; element S1;
        B := false;
        S1 := SYNC(current);
    START: if ¬ B then begin activate S1 at time; B := true; go to
        L1
    end;
    CONFLICT;
    L1: include (HOLDR(result(nextev(current))),S);
        cancel(current);
        go to START
    end;

activity HOLDR(TEMPR); value TEMPR; real TEMPR;

activity SYNC(E); value E; element E;
    begin integer I;
        inspect E when SYNCHRONOUS do
            begin if cardinal(S) = 1 then inspect first (S) when
                HOLDR do
                    X := TEMPR else begin
            I := randint(1, cardinal(S), U);
                inspect number(I, S) when HOLDR do X := TEMPR
                end;
        clear(S);
        B := false
        end
    end;
```

Suppose at time t_1 processes P1, P2, and P3 are scheduled for execution, that they all have access to the variable $A[3]$ which appeared in a declaration 2.1, and the current value of $A[3]$ is 7. If

$P1$ executes an assignment statement

$$A[3] := 5;$$

then the process given by elmt(1, $A[3]$), is directly scheduled.

Assuming this was the first time in the simulation that this process was activated, it will create an associated process $S1$ of the activity SYNC. In any case, the assignment statement $A[3] := 5$ will schedule the associated process $S1$ to follow the activation of $P3$ for this period in systems time. It then creates a process from the activity HOLDR, and by the parameter mechanism the value 5 is placed in TEMPR of HOLDR and included in the set S of SYNCHRONOUS. The process goes passive, thus returning to $P1$.

Since this was an instead association, that completes the action of the assignment statement. Any reference to $A[3]$ by processes $P1$, $P2$ or $P3$ will yield the old value, 7. When processes $P1$, $P2$ and $P3$ have been executed for the current systems time, the SYNC scheduled by the SYNCHRONOUS of $A[3]$ becomes active. Provided $P1$ was the only process which assigned a value to $A[3]$, the new value, 5, is stored into $A[3]$. If $A[3]$ had been assigned more than one value, a random draw from those values in the set S would have selected the new value to be assigned. In either case, the set is emptied.

A "stack" of values may be associated with a single identifier using a declaration such as

3.1 fetch STACKF instead STACKS(declared) real X, Y;

In this example the fetch associated process produced by the process designator STACKF and the store associated procedure statement work together to handle the stack mechanism defined in the following manner. When the associated variable is assigned a value, this new value is placed at the top of the "stack". When the variable is fetched, the value used is removed from the stack. In other words, it works in the conventional manner, "push-down" on store and "pop-up" on fetch.

The procedure declaration, STACKS $(V1)$, must have been declared in the same block or a block global to the one containing the declaration given in 3.1. It would appear as follows

```
procedure STACKS(V1); real V1;
    inspect elmt(1, V1) when STACKF do
    prcd(first(S), HOLDR(result(current)));
```

Assume that process $P1$ is executing the assignment statement

$$X := 7;$$

where X is specified by 3.1. Since the action association is instead, X itself will never be assigned a value. When STACKS(X) is in-

voked, the process designator HOLDR(7) creates the process which
is then placed in the set S defined by the process of class STACKF
associated with X in 3.1. Using the system procedure prcd($E1, E2$)
where $E1$ and $E2$ are "elements", the new process of class HOLDR
is placed as the first element of set S.

The activity declaration STACKF would appear in the SIMULA
block head as

```
activity STACKF;
    begin set S;
START: extract first (S) when HOLDR do
        result(nextev(current)) := TEMPR;
        cancel(current);
        go to START
    end;
```

The extract statement in using the specific element removes
that element from the stack. In order to modify the "result" field
of a process, result(X) must be allowed to appear on the left side
of an assignment statement, as it does here or be a parameter to a
code body procedure which would alter it. Consider the statement

3.2 $$X := X + X;$$

where X is specified in 3.1.

Assume that the set S, in the associated process of class
STACKF, has the "stack values", through the processes of class
HOLDR which are members of S, 7, 5, and 4. The top value of
the stack is 7 and the bottom is 4. The statement given by 3.2
would yield a stack with the values 12 and 4 after its execution. If
S were empty or had only one value when the statement 3.2 is executed, an error condition would arise since at least one of the values to be used for X would be an undefined value. This is, of
course, a desirable action and consistent with ALGOL in that a variable which has not been assigned a value can not be used.

The final example is one which facilitates the handling of one of
the most common situations in modeling. That is where one or
more processes are waiting to become active, when a particular
variable assumes a specific value or a specific relationship between two variables is established. A rather effective solution to
this can be accomplished in the following manner.

The variables would appear in a declaration such as

4.1 store WAITPAUSE(declared) real X;

where the process designator WAITPAUSE(X) would appear in
SIMULA block head as

```
activity WAITPAUSE(V1); real V1;
    begin set S; element E;
        START: if empty(S) then go to L2;
        E := last(S);
    L1: activate E after current
        E := pred(E);
        if E ≠ head(S) then go to L1;
    L2: cancel(current);
        go to START
    end;
```

This activity declares a set which will hold the processes which are waiting for X to change its value. When X does change value, all the processes in the set are activated. Note that the elements in the set are taken from the bottom, since the processes are scheduled to be placed following the current process.

The procedure declaration

```
procedure WAITUNTIL(B, E1); Boolean B; real E1;
    if B then go to L2;
    inspect elmt(1, E1) when WAITPAUSE do
        include(current, S);
    L1: cancel(current);
    if ¬ (B) then go to L1;
        remove(current);
    L2: end;
```

Consider the following statement in process $P1$ which involves the variable X described in 4.1.

$$\text{WAITUNTIL}(X = 14, X);$$

The procedure would examine to see if $X = 14$; if it is, the condition is satisfied and control passes to the next statement. If it was not 14, the current process, $P1$, would be placed in set S of the process given by $\text{elmt}(1, X)$. $P1$ becomes passive. When some other process changes X, then $P1$ is scheduled to occur immediately following the execution of the process which changed X. If the condition is not met, $P1$ again becomes passive. If it is met, $P1$ is removed from the set S and $P1$ begins execution of the statement which immediately followed the WAITUNTIL statement.

3. CONCLUSION

Compound declarations allow the declaration of quantities with arbitrary properties. Several examples have been given and have shown the flexibility of this concept by showing that the user can decide the desired properties and actions to associate with named quantities. The more commonly used procedure and activity declarations can be collected and placed into the systems library and many valuable associations can be made as if they were available declarations in the language. The concept of compound declarations is one of the important steps in allowing the development of natural languages for different classes of problems. The other, the association of non-standard algorithms with the standard operator symbols, will be the subject for another paper.

ACKNOWLEDGEMENT

The author wished to express his appreciation to Don Knuth for his presentation of this paper and his suggestions for its improvement. The author would also like to express his appreciation to R. V. Bock and J. Merner of General Electric for their helpful suggestions.

DISCUSSION

Ross:

It is my pleasure to be the first to say that this is an excellent contribution to the conference. This seems to me an excellent example of both extension and augmentation of an underlying processer. You will notice that these facilities such as "current" and "cancel (current)" are things which would require an actual augmentation of the processor because they relate to the actual state variables of the processor itself. The syntax does bring up into the user domain the ability to augment the behaviour of the language and associate these processes with the various actions being taken on variables of the program. I think that this kind of behaviour is indeed very important and something that should be greatly exploited, and it is very nice seeing it being proposed as an actual extension and augmentation of the system.

Knuth:

I want just to make a slight correction: "cancel(current)" and "remove(current)" are SIMULA features and not part of McNeley's proposal.

Ross:

I meant that if you did not have a SIMULA processor but an ALGOL 60 type of processor, then they would be an extension.

Caracciolo:

I also want to stress that I think that this is one of the most prominent contributions to this conference and to the idea of including self-defining features in a language. In fact in Pisa, when Molnar developed a simulation language for experimental purposes, we tried to combine certain features of SOL and SIMULA. Also, in the second attempt to do self optimizing, we considered the possibility of defining inside the program what one actually wanted instead of doing fixed things. We felt obliged to provide fixed facilities because we did not have such a powerful and flexible system.

Editors Note:

Further discussion of McNeley's paper was postponed until the general discussion in this session.

SOME PROBLEMS IN THE SIMULATION
OF MULTIPROCESSOR COMPUTER SYSTEMS

G. K. HUTCHINSON
Texas Technological College, Lubbock, Texas, USA

Abstract. In this paper, several problems encountered in simulation multiprocessor systems will be discussed. An attempt has been made to share the experiences of one investigator, to the benefit, hopefully, of others. As in many other situations, there appear to be no optimal solutions to many of these problems; only feasible ones which may be improved upon as time and experience indicate new approaches.

1. INTRODUCTION

There are few sectors today in which as much money is being spent, yet in which there is as little basic understanding, as in the field of multiprocessing systems. These are defined as systems possessing one or more sets of resources, with one or more identical members in each set, operating under central, stored program control, and capable of processing one or more programs at any given point in time. This lack of knowledge exists, not at the level of hardware design of single components, but at that of systems design in the cases of both hardware and software (especially systems monitors). Experience, which has provided such a wealth of information for systems design in the past, may now be less useful, since much of this backlog of experience is not applicable to multiprocessor systems. The question arises: Why cannot existing systems be used for design experimentation? The reasons are two: 1) long lead times are involved in obtaining and integrating the hardware and software components to be tested; 2) this method tends to be very expensive. Additionally, it is becoming increasingly apparent that systems cannot be thought of individually as "the hardware system" or "the software system"; on the contrary, the two must be considered a unified whole, each complementing and interacting with the other. A further complication arises in determining the amount of actual work performed by a computing system. Systems designers frequently use an illdefined term, "throughput", but this writer knows of no user-oriented, operational means of measuring the amount of work performed by a computing system. Without an operational means of work measurement, it is impossible to compare alternatives objectively.

The high cost and long lead times typical of these systems, coupled with lack of quantitative measures of work accomplished, have predisposed systems designers more and more toward the employment of simulation as a design and evaluation tool. Multiprocessor simulations present to the analyst some intensified problems which are not, however, unique. Before going into these problems in detail, a conceptual framework within which to view a multiprocessor must be established.

2. BACKGROUND

Analysts have frequently found it convenient [2,49] to consider multitask, multicomponent processors as extensions of the basic job shop. In the basic job shop, interchangeable machines are grouped, and jobs are defined by linear listings (routings) of the machine groups, together with appropriate work times, through which the job must pass to achieve completion. Restrictions often associated with the basic job shop have included uninterrupted, continuous processing; completion of a job on a single machine (no parallelism and no interruptions); and independence of processing times, regardless of processing order. Early extensions of the basic job shop included PERT-like job routines [95,152] and shared machines [95].

The early job shop simulators and their extensions were capable of investigations of information processing systems at the macro level, i.e., as relating to the total system, and probing such typical questions as, "Should another computer be added?" and "If so, which computer?". By means of artful input manipulation, they could often provide the data necessary to decisions at a more detailed level [66], such as, "How much secondary storage is required?". When it came to the detailed examination of multiprocessor systems, a few of which are described below.

The purpose of both job shop and multiprocessor simulations usually is to investigate resource management. This frequently requires simulation of each incidence of conflict for resources, and the manner in which this conflict was resolved. In the job shop, the demands for resources were *jobs*, often broken down into *tasks*, which competed for the *machines* in the machine groups. In the multiprocessor these entities will be designated correspondingly as *programs*, *routines* and *resources*. In the job shop, a job competed for a machine, but having captured it, controlled it to com-

.pletion and then continued. Frequently in the multiprocessor a program's routines require resources of several different types simultaneously, and, having once captured them, must continuingly compete with all other current routines to maintain possession of them. This is the essence, in fact, of multiprocessing: the continual sharing of the components of the system so that each user will have the total power of the system at his disposal without the corresponding financial commitment. Interesting questions of both operating system and simulation thereof, are raised. Suppose, for example, that a routine requiring three types of resources for processing has captured them, and a routine of higher priority requires one of these. Must the first routine vacate this resource? Can possession of the other resources be maintained by the first? Should the first routine be given a higher priority for its subsequent competition for the resource of which it was deprived? Must the first routine start from the beginning when it is able to resume processing, or from the point at which it was deprived of its needed resource?

In another vein, the jobs in a job shop were described as a linear list, typically with few entries, say 15. In the multiprocessor simulator, with each incidence of conflict being considered, it is necessary to describe each routine of each program in detail, the degree of detail being determined by the analyst's objective. Often the result is hundreds or thousands of repetitions of a series of routines, such as, "read a card", "compute", "output". It soon became apparent that for practical purposes it would be impossible to describe the logical structure and interactions between routines in the multiprocessor as they had been handled in the job shop.

Typically, the job shop has a manager whose decisions determine the manner in which it operates. Simulation of job shop management is frequently accomplished by routines for major functions, such as assignment of jobs to machines. In the multiprocessor, the management functions are present, but are performed by software, usually an operating system, which is itself a program requiring resources. The management process thus competes for and consumes resources which might otherwise be assigned to the workload programs. In addition, the time required for the management functions can be highly significant in the multiprocessor. Because of difficulties such as those described above, a multiprocessor which would overcome them became an interesting project to designers. The necessity of handling both minute detail and higher level activities, in addition to more conventional requirements, resulted in some problems which, although not unique to multiprocessor systems, are emphasized. Three of these problems: degradation of the ability to differentiate between times of event occurrences; simulation of simultaneously occurring events on a sequential machine; and development of a language for describing jobs with great detail and many repetitions of event cycles, will be discussed.

3. ABILITY TO DIFFERENTIATE

In most even-oriented simulation languages (e.g., SIMSCRIPT [10]), a monotonically increasing master clock is kept for the entire system under study. Event times are calculated during the course of the simulation and added to the master clock time (t_m), to schedule the time of the occurrence of that event (t_e). The master clock time is stored in a finite number of bits, typically, one computer word and floating point notation. Given the foregoing, at any t_m greater than zero (and greater than t_e), there will be a t_e which is so small that the result of adding t_m and t_e will be t_m. This t_e is defined as:

$$t_e^* = t_m/b^n,$$

where t_e^* is the largest t_e, which can be added to t_m without increasing t_m; b is the number base of the computer; n is the number of bits used for the mantissa of the floating point number. For example, in a 36 bit, binary machine with floating point having a 27 bit mantissa

$$t_e^* = t_m/2^{27} \approx 7.45 \times 10^{-9} t_m.$$

The first and perhaps most apparent problem resulting from the above is that if a t_e less than, or equal to, t_e^* is calculated for the time of the scheduling of a recurring event, the simulation may go into an endless loop, with simulated time remaining unchanged. A further and more insidious problem is that as time increases, the ability to distinguish between the times of event occurrences decreases; thus, events which could be differentiated on the basis of time of occurrence at low values of t_m, will not be distinguishable at a later point in the simulation, when t_m has increased sufficiently. The accuracy of the measurement system has changed as the simulation has progressed, much as if the length of a scale were to vary in measuring the different rooms in a house. Many problems can arise from such a situation, contributing in varying degrees to degeneration of simulated results. For instance, imagine two boys working, with a piece of cake the prize for the one finishing his task more rapidly; in the event of a tie, the prize to go to the better student. Suppose, further, that this contest is repeated frequently. If the tasks are the same, started at the same time, and the poorer student is very slightly the better worker, throughout the repetitions of the contest he will receive the cake. In a simulation, analogously, when t_m is sufficiently large, the better student may grow fat as the result of ties. A comparable situation develops in the simulation of multiprocessors as a result of the inability to differentiate between the completion times of routines vying for a single resource, such as a disk. In such a case, results may be disastrous insofar as value of the simulation is concerned. If a high priority job were inadvertently to capture some scarce resource as the result of this degradation of ability to differentiate, the entire course of the simulation might well be changed, and the results made worthless from the viewpoint of realism.

With computing speeds measured in nanoseconds, it is not necessary to run through many seconds of simulated time before this degradation problem becomes apparent. In the machine previously discussed, t_e^* was approximately $7.45 \times 10^{-9} t_m$. In such a case, when the master clock reads one second, the simulation fails to differentiate between events occurring 7 nanoseconds apart, while at one minute, events taking place 325 nanoseconds apart are indistinguishable. It is clear, therefore, that consideration must be given to the degradation problem as a function of both the object time computer, and the particular simulation. It should be noted, also, that the magnitude of the problem decreases as the word length of the object time computer increases. A decrease in the degradation effects is achieved, also, by use of double precision for storage of the master clock time. Another method of fulfilling the same purpose, is that of using cascading accumulators for storage of the master clock time. The price exacted by these methods is that of increased execution time.

4. SIMULTANEOUS EVENTS

Degradation of the ability to differentiate can increase frequency of simultaneous events in a simulation, a serious problem in itself on a sequential machine. All too frequently this problem is either disregarded, or "resolved" by an arbitrary rule such as: the first event placed in the set of events occurring at *this* time shall be simulated first. The only logic applied to the ordering of simultaneous events, thus, is that relating to the simulation system itself, and *not* that of the system under study. Under these conditions, very different results could easily be obtained by running the identical model and data on different computers. Naturally, the amount of this difference would be a function of the number of simultaneous events, and the consequences resulting from the different orderings at each.

These differences, furthermore, can have widely varying effects upon the value of the results obtained in the simulation. A rough rule of thumb which is intuitively appealing, at least, is that the more detailed the level of simulation, the greater the effect of these differences. To the degree to which this holds true, the simulation of multiprocessors becomes a candidate for the category of "worst case", particularly when algorithms for resource allocation are being investigated.

It might be hoped that designers of multiprocessor computer systems will soon develop better methods and algorithms for the allocation of system components, thus improving system performance. Several potential algorithms come immediately to mind: shortest job first; highest priority job first; job with the most eminent time out first; job requiring the smallest amount of memory first; etc. In fact, choice of the algorithm for incorporation in the actual system would be likely to be one of the factors motivating the experimentation. With this as an objective, it becomes very important to base *all* decisions on the particular algorithm under study, and not to confound the effects of the simulation language or its implementation with other factors under study. Suspense sets often can be used to alleviate problems raised by the sequential handling of simultaneous events. When they are to be used, the calendar of events is searched at each decision-making time for all events scheduled to occur at that time. These events are placed in a suspense set. The algorithm under study is then applied to each of these events in turn, to order them before any changes are made in system variables (i.e., before the event is "executed"). If there are potential conflicts for particular resources, they are resolved by the ordering determined by the algorithm. Once the proper ordering is completed, the events can be either inserted into the calendar and the simulation allowed to proceed normally, or removed from the suspense set and executed individually in the process. In either case, a major problem occurs if the execution of one event routine schedules another event at the time of execution of the first; or, as previously, at a time which is indistinguishable from that time.

It is easiest simply to avoid this problem by not allowing an event to schedule another without advancing time. A similar technique is to accept the situation as a fact of life, and plan the simulation around it (i.e., effect the independence of the results obtained by this simulation from the situation's occurrence or nonoccurrence). Both of the above evade, rather than solve, the problem.

There may be no "right" way of guaranteeing the proper handling of simultaneous events when the scheduling of another is allowed, with, to all practical purposes, no increase in master clock time. Several possibilities seem most promising. One is to move, as suggested, all events scheduled for the present time into a suspense set; order them; and execute them out of the suspense set, subsequent events scheduled to occur at that time being placed in the calendar of events. All original events having been executed, the entire cycle may be repeated. This process still has a major defect: that not *all* of the events occurring at the same time are given equal treatment. Another technique is to give each event an attribute which would indicate whether or not it could create subsequent events at the same time. This attribute could be a major factor in determining priority for those events which can generate other, simultaneous, events. By executing these high priority events first, the subsequently generated events scheduled for current execution could be handled currently with the ones remaining in the suspense set. Again, the problem is that the ordering of the suspense set by this artificial attribute of the events may prevent its ordering by the criteria dictated by the logic of the system under study.

A third approach is to examine each event in the suspense set and form a subset of those which can schedule other events simultaneously. Each of the events in this subset could then be examined (not executed), and, if it should prove necessary to schedule a new event for current time, a surrogate event could be created, using the logic of the event under consideration. This surrogate event, properly identified with its causing event, would then be placed in the suspense set. Problems, even at this point, are obviously not over. This surrogate event itself could cause other events at the same time, and ad infinitum. Another hurdle appears, in that if system logic dictates that a surrogate event occur before its causing event, an inconsistent situation, from the simulation viewpoint, has arisen. Even if this latter condition does not eventuate, great care must be exercised in keeping track of system variables and relationships between events in pursuance of the logic associated with the original creation of the surrogate events, and their subsequent transformation into actual events. This list of problems is not meant to be either exhaustive, or discouraging. It is intended, merely, to give an indication of the problems associated with simulating simultaneous events on a sequential machine. There are other techniques which could be developed, at least one of which, hopefully, will overcome all of the shortcomings of the preceding.

5. PROGRAM DESCRIPTION LANGUAGE

In simulating multiprocessor systems, one of the major difficulties is that of determining a method for adequately describing the programs which the system is to process. These programs are composed of routines which are defined as being uniform in resource requirements and without parallelism. The routines may be constrained by either lack of resources (resource constraint) or the processing of their immediate predecessor routines (technical constraint). A language, Program Description Language (PDL), which was designed to describe these routines adequately for simulation purposes, is elucidated.

As previously mentioned, routines are defined as being uniform in resource requirements and without parallelism. In PDL, parallelism within a program is simulated by execution of routines si-

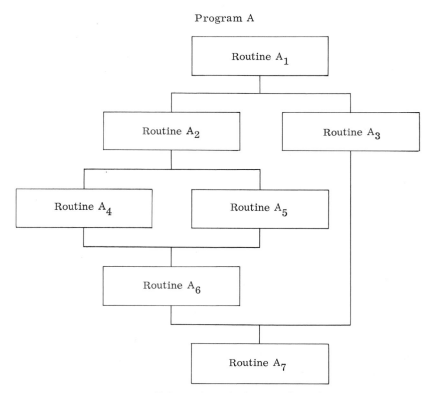

Fig. 1. Parallelism through the use of routines.

multaneously, as shown in fig. 1, for **Program A**. Each routine is technically constrained until all of its immediate predecessors have been processed, e.g., Routine A6 is constrained until Routines A4 and A5 have been processed. A routine is resource constrained until all of its required resources are available and assigned to it by the operating system. When more than one routine is eligible for processing on a given resource, the operating system must determine which of these routines is to be processed, and which are to be delayed. Since the operating system itself is a competitor for the resource, both occupying storage and consuming time at each of these allocation points, the operating system must first obtain the resources which it, itself, needs; then allocate available resources to the user programs. The above series of events occurs frequently during actual multiprocessor operation, hence during the simulation of multiprocessors. Since **PDL** was designed to describe the logical relationships between a program's routines and each routine's resource requirements, it is often convenient to describe portions (or all) of the operating system in **PDL**. In appearance, **PDL** is very similar to a procedural language such as **MAP** or **FORTRAN**, having a tag, operator and one or more operands. Many of the operators, such as the arithmetic and fetch-up pairs, are typical of most procedural languages; others, such as **GENERATE** a request, and **ISSUE TYPE A** request,

GNR	– Generate a request	SRR	– Store resource
RQA	– Issue type A request	INI	– Interrogate integer
RQB	– Issue type B request	INF	– Interrogate floating point
RLQ	– Relinquish resource	TFR	– Transfer
WAT	– Wait	DRN	– Draw random number
OCC	– Occupy	SRE	– Store data
VAC	– Vacate	RVE	– Retrieve data
CNL	– Cancel	GRD	– Get routine data
PFM	– Perform	PRD	– Put routine data
SET	– Set data	GID	– Get request identification
ADI	– Add integer	DSE	– Destroy suspense entity
ADF	– Add floating point	CON	– Constant
SBI	– Subtract integer	CRF	– Create file
SBF	– Subtract floating point	DEF	– Destroy file
MUI	– Multiply integer	RTS	– Reserve temporary storage
MUF	– Multiply floating point	SIP	– Store in profile
DVI	– Divide integer	STP	– Store type in profile
DVF	– Divide floating point	END	– End of routine
CLL	– Call subroutine		
GMT	– Get merit		

Fig. 2. Program description language (PDL) repertoire.

314 G. K. HUTCHINSON

are unique to PDL. The repertoire of PDL operators is given in fig. 2.

In fig. 3, the PDL is given for Program A (previously shown in fig. 1). In the series of instructions shown, no simulated time would elapse from their execution. The function of most PDL operators is to describe the relationships of the program's routines, and to control the logical flow of the program. The only operator consuming simulated time is the PERFORM verb, which causes the elapse of the amount of time indicated on each of the containing routine's resources. An in-core matrix inversion subroutine, thus, might be simulated by a single PERFORM verb. Naturally, many other verbs might be required to describe when and under what conditions the matrix inversion should take place.

In fig. 3, the sequence of instructions for the execution of each

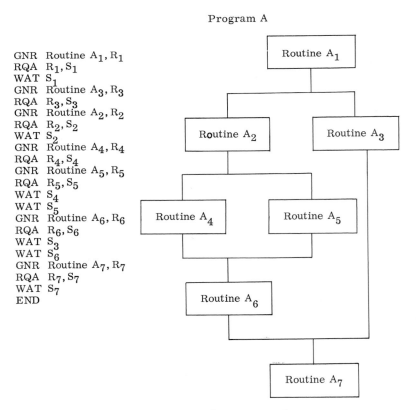

Fig. 3. PDL for program A.

routine is: 1) *Generate* a request for the routine, e.g., routine X, and designate this request by the letters RX(GNR X, RX); 2) Issue the request, RX, and generate a suspense entity, SX(RQA RX, SX); and 3) Wait for the release of the suspense entity, SX, indicating the completion of routine X(WAT SX). The generation of a request for a routine and its issuance are separate and distinct events. Thus the analyst is able to generate a request in one routine, and issue it in some other routine, either at the same, or at a later simulated time. The ability to do this is particularly important in the light of the requirement that each routine be uniform in resource requirements. For instance, suppose that placing a telephone call is desired, but it is necessary first to look up the number. The first activity requires a directory; the second, a number and telephone. Different routines would be required in PDL. The first would generate a request for the telephone call routine. The second would issue the previously generated request when the telephone became available. The separation of the request and issue events is a convenient device, also, for specifying alternative resources for fulfilling requirements. Suppose a man with two cars wished to go to the store as quickly as possible, but his wife has one car, his daughter the other. In PDL, the request for the trip could be generated in one routine and the request issued at a later point, triggered by whichever occurs first, the return of, symbolically, the wife or the daughter.

Parallelism in PDL is obtained by generating and issuing requests for more than one routine without intervening WAT or PFM instructions, such as the sequence for Routines A_2 and A_3 in fig. 3. Since PFM is the only instruction in PDL the execution of which results in a change in simulated time, such a sequence may be executed simultaneously, for the purpose of simulation, if the resources required by the respective routines are available and assigned. Unlimited parallelism can be obtained in this manner; for instance, Routines A_3, A_4, and A_5 may be performed simultaneously.

When a request for a routine is issued, an associated suspense entity is created. When the requested routine has been completed, i.e., the END instruction executed, all routines which are waiting for the suspense entity are released. A suspense entity consists of two sets: the set of constraining routines, and the set of constrained routines. The completion of any routine in the constraining set will release all of the routines in the constrained set. Thus OR conditions, in addition to AND conditions may be included in programs, i.e., the completion of Routine B_1 or Routine B_2 will allow Routine B_3 to proceed, as illustrated in fig. 4. This can be a convenient method of handling such things as simultaneous events

PDL for program B

GNR Routine B_1, R_1
RQA R_1, S_1
GNR Routine B_2, R_2
RQA R_2, S_1
WAT S_1
GNR Routine B_3, R_3
RQA R_3, S_2
WAT S_2

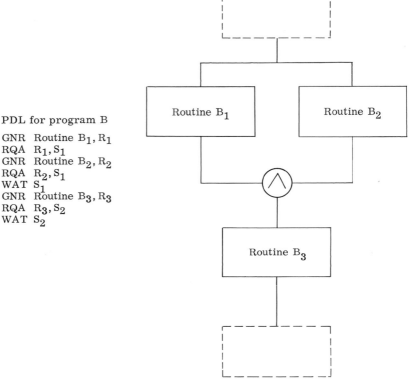

Fig. 4. Logical OR.

when uncertainty exists as to their completion times, and events
which can be triggered by the completion of any of an unknown number of prior events. Analogously, the winning of a horse race may
depend upon the first horse crossing the finish line, but horses
may be added to or withdrawn from the race and their speeds may
depend upon events which take place during its course, such as a
sudden shower. It can be very advantageous to issue a request for
the completion of each, figuratively, horse's race, using the same
suspense entity, so that the first of these events taking place would
initiate the event, the winning of the race.

The above method of handling the logical relationships between
routines provides the analyst with great flexibility in describing
programs. A routine can be delayed to coordinate with another
routine which has not yet started. For instance, it is possible to

wait for the end of a telephone conversation that was expected, but which had not yet begun; or for all or any of a series of such calls. It is possible, also, to indicate alternative equipments to process a routine, as in the previous situation involving the return of motor cars for a trip to the store. As an alternative method of solution, two routines could be requested, one with, figuratively, the wife's car as a resource; the other with the daughter's. The first car to become available would allow execution of its respective routine, which would cancel the other.

Two instructions, OCCUPY (OCC) and VACATE (VAC) in PDL, are used to control resources which are dedicated beyond the confinement of a single routine. The OCCUPY instruction reserves the specified resources, either discrete or continuous, until a corresponding VACATE instruction is executed. The operating system can reclaim, in the interim, any or all of these resources, but they must be restored before the routine can continue. Each use of OCCUPY creates an entity which stores its necessary characteristics. The identification of this entity can be passed from routine to routine. The VACATE instruction, thus, can be executed by a routine other than the occupying one. Analogously, a seat in a plane may be reserved while a drink is obtained, and reclaimed upon return, figurative activities which may be simulated by different routines.

Another interesting aspect of PDL is that each execution of a routine is an individual entity, requiring a separate set of the temporary data used by the routine. As in actual multiprocessors, a single routine using identical, separate units of its required resources may be simultaneously in-process as requested by several different programs, as shown logically in fig. 5. This property of multiprocessor routines is often referred to as reentrant, or transparent, code. The simulation of this aspect of routines presents, at least, all of the problems of the real situation and possibly more.

As multiprocessor operating systems become more comprehensive, users will undoubtedly have to become more sophisticated, in order to use multiprocessors efficiently. An aspect of this sophistication may well be the detailed specification of the logical relationships and resource requirements of the various routines in their programs. It is not unlikely that command languages will be developed to serve this purpose, and that many of their features and functions will be similar to those of PDL.

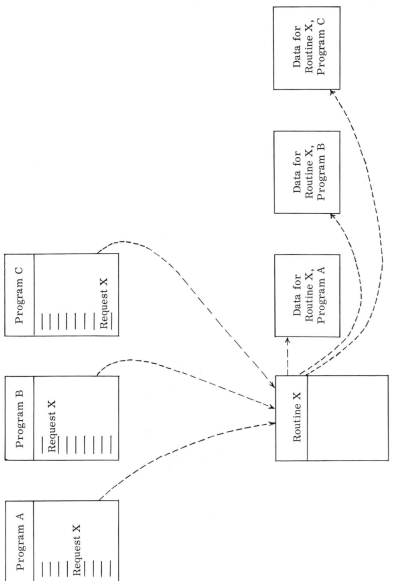

Fig. 5. Multiple simultaneous executions of a single routine.

ACKNOWLEDGEMENT

The author is indebted to Mrs. Maxine Daly for the technical editing of this paper.

DISCUSSION

Laski:

It seems to me a great pity that a great deal of analysts time was wasted by the acceptance of an unsatisfactory language to handle simultaneous event. It seems in the engineering sense important to see which is the scarce resource, engineer's time or machine time, when we are considering what kind of language, with what kind of facilities, is required for practical use. It seems dangerous because we are inhibited from thinking outside the language we have to express ourselves in, if the basic simulation language available does not take account of simultaneity and despatching. These are extremely difficult problems and in this connection I am sorry that there have not been invited to this meeting those people who have been concerned in real time with this problem that we touch in simulated time. In particular I would refer you to a Project MAC paper by Saltzer on "traffic control in multi-process systems" which raises, discusses and clarifies a large number of these issues.

Conway:

I would like to comment on the initial remarks that Hutchinson made on the simulation of multi-processor systems. I think that we as a field have to recognize that we have missed an opportunity and had a significant failure over the last couple of years with the introduction of the 3rd generation machines, particularly with some of the more sophisticated systems such as the GE 645 and IBM 360/67. Even the conventional large configurations of machines have either not been simulated or have been simulated inaccurately or very inadequately. I do not know whether this is because the people who have been specifying these configurations are unaware of simulation or whether they find it too awkward to use or whether they do not trust the results once they have been used. I think the configurations are being planned in an amazingly ad hoc manner by people doing so intuitively or with wishful thinking.

In particular I have been an interested party in and victim of
the IBM 360/67 situation, and it is interesting to observe that the
most accurate simulation of the machine was conducted in a language which has been rather rejected here; that is, FORTRAN.
This was done at Stanford and all other available languages were
rejected for one reason or another. I do not wish to comment on
whether this was wise. The fact is that the best simulation of that
machine was done in FORTRAN and that turned out itself to be not
too accurate. A computer manufacturer in West Chester County is
now facing the problem of predicting performances of some of
their larger system configurations, the things that we would all
claim ought to be done with a nicely parameterized simulation model
They do it simply by setting up a laboratory that has a 360/75 with
all possible devices on it and they simulate in situ by actually systems generating every configuration you would like to have and
running test cases against them. In other words, when it really
comes down to predicting performance for user configurations,
they are taking no chances, they are going actually to try each one
in practice. Simulation has just had a signal failure in predicting
the performance or even being used for 3rd generation computers.
We ought really to ask ourselves why. Are our languages inapprop-
riate, are their predictions unreliable or are we inadequately in-
forming the community of the existence of the procedures?

Hutchinson:

I could not agree with you more that we, as a field, had a failure
there. At the time, it was not my intention to generate a new language. None of the ones available were particularly appropriate
for the problem. I agree with your comment of the other day, made
in private, that one of the things that is needed is order of magnitude improvements in simulation languages, in particular in the
question of the way that we decide to name something, whether we
are going to identify it or name it.

I think there is a kind of a basic question here that I raised in a
previous session as to who was doing simulations and why: Whose
understanding are we trying to improve? I have for a long time been
of the opinion that the typical systems programmer feels that the
sole reason for the existence of user programs is so that his system
will have something to monitor. I am afraid that for a while I saw
a similar phenomenon here; the sole reason for doing simulations
was so that the language developers would have something to write
a language for. It still seems to me that you have to ask the question first with regard to simulation languages - "who is going to be
the user of this language; am I trying to design something of beauty

or something of use?" I think this may be one of the reasons we have had for our failures. People that are actually going to make these decisions, as to what a configuration is going to be, are frequently faced with time schedules and they have not got time to work with new and complicated languages. We have to be able to do these things faster and be able to communicate with the people who have the problem and not with ourselves.

Nygaard:

In reply to Conway - You said that people had failed to use simulation in developing the 3rd generation computer. I think you are generally right and I think we should do more to remedy that. Of course, the present paper is a contribution in this direction. But I must say that I know of a manufacturer in St. Paul who has been using simulation quite a lot to develop software. Their most advanced monitor system has been thoroughly analyzed by simulation.

Hills:

I would like to come back to this question of time degradation which seems to me is maybe one of the biggest problems in simulating computer systems. Did you consider one method of solution which is to split in the simulation up into a macro-simulation in order to determine the likelihood of different sorts of conflict situations occurring, so that you could tell when the different conflicting requirements on the hardware were going to occur, then secondly to simulate these on the micro level to see just what would happen?

Hutchinson:

We did consider this but decided against the technique, because it complicates the problems of analysis, programming and experimental design.

Knuth:

First with respect to time degradation I think the method Hills suggested is perhaps exactly what I wanted to say in another way; it was mentioned in the paper as the method of cascading accumulators. It can be reformulated in this case perhaps by saying that the times that are kept in the master counter within the simulator are kept relative to something: at periodic times in the simulation this relative base is set back to zero again but whenever the actual value of the master clock has to be computed the base is added on.

Caracciolo:

I would like to come back to the remark of Conway. I remember
that I took up this problem with Iverson who had given in his language a description of a 360 system. He has in fact used that language with some parallelism which was not very clearly specified.
So I raised the question whether he would consider trying to define
parallelism in his language by taking into account what has been
done in simulation languages. I was not absolutely able to make
him understand the problem. My impression is that the problem
has been realized but there are many people who do not understand
it.

Lackner:

Referring also to Conway's point about simulating computer systems and configurations, I seem to recall that the manufacturer
based in Poughkeepsie was doing quite a bit of simulation of the
360 while the machine hardware was under development and also
while the software operating systems were under development. I
think aside from the difficulties of dealing with salesmen and managers who are not too technically competent, one problem with
that effort and with others by other manufacturers was that these
models were never very well published. Now why they were not is
a question that needs investigation of course. There are many reasons why a manufacturer would not want to publisize his simulation,
but I think that an intelligent manufacturer would call on what help
he could get from people such as are in this room in the construction, evaluation and the study of the results of simulations like
these. I think all of us would be spared many grievances if this
took place.

Brennan:

There have been several comments addressed to the fact, I
think one could call it, that the 1% have been remissed towards
the 99% as far as public relations are concerned. I should like to
suggest one possible avenue of improving that situation. You may
not all be aware that Simulation Journal now covers not only analogue simulation but discrete and continuous digital simulation,
with Kiviat as associate editor. He is actively looking for application articles on the discrete simulation field: this is one way in
which you people might do something to improve your public relations.

Laski:

The failure in this generation of machines is due not only to the fact that the machines were not simulated before but after they were built, but also to the fact that the designers of the operating systems were unable to make use of the insights into parallel processing that simulation languages had produced. In my opinion writing a simulation of a computing machine with an operating system is not different from designing an operating system for a physical computing machine to run in real, as opposed to simulated time. In this connection I am aware of a manufacturer that is intending to use SIMULA to write its operating system and I think there is an order of magnitude greater probability as a result that it will achieve an operating system that does what is intended, as compared with those who lose themselves in the forest of machine code.

Hutchinson:

Simulating an operating system can be as difficult a task as writing one.

Laski:

Calling these languages "simulation languages" has done us much damage in this area, and hindered their use.

Caracciolo:

I would like to comment on what was said by Laski and I think I should agree but I have still some doubt whether in the simulation languages field, we have really entirely clarified the subject. I believe that we have done something but I am not entirely sure that we have clarified it, and I would add a remark to what he said previously that it is a pity that we do not have here people who have been dealing with real parallel systems. It seems to me that this is somewhat contradictory: in the sense that in order to clarify the ideas we have to hear what people having had to deal with actual parallel system have done, and on the other hand we should apply to them simulation concepts as already basically clarified.

Laski:

I entirely agree with Caracciolo.

Ross:

Far be it from me to say anything against SIMULA and I do not intend this remark to go that way at all. However it does seem to me that there is a legitimate question as to whether a system such as SIMULA, which has a built-in way of scheduling these quasi-parallel processes, whether or not this exactly matches the requirements with respect to these operating systems.

I am not quite sure but it does seem to me that the crucial matter is to get down to the finest level of, if you will, open macros which are needed for the detailed steps of the simulation or operating system and then to ensure that we have a higher level language than is shown in Mr. Hutchinson's paper to finally close this loop and provide a tool which will satisfy these needs.

Nygaard:

First I wish to comment on Laski's plea for another name than "simulation": I think that the name "simulation language" has done us quite a lot of good. For one thing it has succeeded in attracting this audience. The second thing is that the rapidly increasing need for simulation has contributed to more rapid spreading of languages which have these new features. However if you look into the future I think it is quite correct as Laski says that we are going to use these languages for other purposes as well. Then we should of course not be tied down with a sequencing scheme which is created just because we want to simulate systems where simulated time is the basic concept. Therefore in the new SIMULA 67 the sequencing scheme will be modifiable and there is a clear separation between modelling and sequencing.

GENERAL DISCUSSION - SESSION 6

Petrone:

On McNeley's paper - I would like to mention here that there is a feature in PL/1 which is very close to the "store" concept of Mc-Neley and this is the ON CHECK feature. This may be declared attached to any variable and the effect is to execute a procedure, and this procedure may be called with a task option which may be something equivalent to an activity execution.

Strachey:

My remarks refer to Blunden's paper - It seems to me that the design of a simulation language is very similar to the logical design of the structure of a computing machine. The question that sparked this off in my mind was the question of whether you have implicit control or explicit control. This is the difference between doing an ordinary transfer of command and having a machine trap which happens automatically on a certain condition. It seems to me that many of the problems which have been faced by people who have been designing simulation languages, have also been faced by the logical system designers of machines. I do not know how many of you here have ever designed a machine but it seems to me that the problems are very similar and I think it is rather an interesting parallel. Secondly, I want to come back to McNeley's paper. It seems to me that there are a number of new ideas in this paper, or at least apparently new ideas, which need separation. Most of these ideas come under, I think, three headings. There was the question of being able to define rather more complicated ways of accessing and storing associated with variables. There was the question of the "inhibit" function which is I think mostly tied up with the problem of initialising arrays in ALGOL and then there was the incorporation of these two concepts in a co-routine structure in a simulation language which enabled co-routines and activities to be going on simultaneously.

I am sorry to have to talk about CPL again at this stage. The first two concepts have been incorporated in CPL in a way which is syntactically more elegantly sugared than the paper we have this morning but the activity or co-routine business has not so far been put into CPL. The essential concept I think about having more control over what happens when you fetch or store is derived from the concept, which we developed in CPL, of allowing functions on the left hand side of assignment statements. If you have a function on the left hand side of an assignment statement then it becomes necessary to generalize your idea of the "address". Normally speaking, when you think of an assignment statement, you say that when we evaluate what is on the left, we find an address. This is something which I think ALGOL X calls a name and I call a left hand value.

On the other side, you get a value and then we store the value into the address, roughly speaking. Now if you have a function on the left hand side it becomes necessary to decide what sort of thing it is that it produces as a value. From this, we develop the concept of a generalised left hand value; that is, something which is not necessarily just a single address or location in the store but the generalisation of the properties which are associated with that. The fundamental properties associated with a location in the store are that you can get something out of it or fetch the contents of it for which we use the word "load", and you can "update" the contents of it. You can take something out and put something in and these are the two fundamental concepts which together make up the basic properties of a left hand value. We call a general left hand value like that a "LUP": a "Load Update Pair". Some functions are allowed to produce left hand values - that is to say they are allowed to produce results which are load up-date pairs and McNeleys "monitor" can be written in CPL as such a function. It is written as follows:

$$\underline{\text{let}} \text{ Monitor}[\underline{\text{ref}} \ x, \ \underline{\text{val}} \ \underline{\text{string}} \ X] \ \underline{\text{be}}$$
$$\underline{\text{fix}} \ n = 1$$
$$\underline{\text{load}} \ \underline{\text{result is}} \ x$$
$$\underline{\text{update}} \ \S \ \text{Write}['*n', \ \text{Time}, \ n, \ X, \ x, \ \underline{\text{rhs}}]$$
$$n, \ x: = n{+}1, \ \underline{\text{rhs}} \ \S$$

The parameters are x, the left hand value of a <u>real</u> variable, and X, the string which is its print name. The result is a general left hand value also known as a Load-Update Pair (LUP) consisting of a load function which gives the right hand value, and an update routine which updates x by the quantity <u>rhs</u>. The word <u>fix</u> indicates an <u>own</u> variable which is only accessible to this particular LUP and which is initialised when the LUP is created by the application of the function Monitor.

The use of Monitor would be as follows. Suppose we have a program which includes a <u>real</u> variable p which we wish to trap in one particular block only. We preface this block by the new definition

$$\underline{\text{let}} \ p \simeq \text{Monitor}[p, \ 'p'].$$

The effect of which is to introduce a fresh variable (whose name is also p) for this block only. The left hand value of this new p is the LUP produced by applying Monitor to the old p. A statement such as

$$p := p+2$$

in the body of this block will now refer to the new p, defined by this LUP - which therefore produces the R-value of the old p.

When the assignment is done to the new p on the left, the <u>update</u> part of the LUP is used with <u>rhs</u> having as its value the value of $p+2$. This will first print out the monitor information (i. e. New-Line, Time, Countnumber, Printname, OldValue, NewValue) and then increase the count by one and assign the new value ($p+2$), to the old p. This, I think, is exactly what McNeley wanted to achieve and it can easily be done within the existing framework of CPL.

Caracciolo:

I refer to Hill's remark on cascaded time intervals. I have considered this technique as a possible solution to the problem of time degradation. However, I believe that even there one should carefully discuss the adequacy of taking this attitude. What I mean is that certainly one can take this approach, but the problem is to see whether this approach reflects actual properties of the simulated system. In order to solve certain logical probabilities one must not take up a possible logical solution which does not reflect the actual features of the system.

Another point was regarding the question of engineering design and its connection with the problem of simultaneity and incompatibilities. I have tried to discuss this problem with a group of engineers we have in Pisa and there again I found it extremely difficult to get in touch with them. I tried to discuss with them the similarity of the equations which arise in simulation languages and in designing systems. My impression was that they refused to consider what is the actual situation, just because they wanted to have a given situation which was satisfacory for them, forgetting that we have to do with real systems and for which we obviously have to try to have adequate models and not simply to try to superimpose on reality what we would like it to be.

Ross:

Coming back to the McNeley paper, the subject of this additional comment is the broadness or conciseness of context within which these behavourial procedures or actions are to apply. I would like to try to state my view of this kind of thing. I would like to call, for the purpose of this discussion, the objects of the simulation or the

real world that we are simulating, the variables whereby we hold
and manipulate these things and the operators we use, basic or a-
tomic operations. I would then describe the basic "fetch" and
"store" which were being discussed in the McNeley paper as manipulators, or sub-atomic operations. It seems to me that the objective of this whole area is to associate some sort of bahaviour,
described in one of these action algorithms, with specific objects
or with whatever objects are currently the values or variables.
The behaviour then is to be invoked whenever the object is in some
specified context.

The context may be expressed in terms of the sub-atomic manipulators, i.e. the fetch and store. Let me try and clarify why I am
calling them manipulators or sub-atomic. Before doing an operation such as add, subtract, multiply, divide I must fetch the values
and then when I am through with the addition, subtraction, multiplication or division, I must store or put away the result. It seems
to me that we should be able to separate into this class of manipulating actions, the sub-atomic manipulations that underly the framework for the actual semantics of the various operators proper.
Thereby, if we express our context in terms of these sub-atomic
things, then the action will be invoked every time we do any operation which invokes a fetch or a store; that is, in a very broad context.

A more precise or localised context would be to associate the
behaviour with a particular operator or set of operators. For example I might specify a action to occur whenever X is associated
with a plus or a minus but not if the X is associated with a comparison operator or a divide operator. This would then be a more restricted context. Similarly, the context may also be attached to the
bodies of certain blocks of the program in the ALGOL sense, or
only with respect to certain functions or procedures being executed.

It seems to me that the important thing is to get a good context
expressing language so that we can have a full control over just
exactly when these actions are to apply.

Knuth:

I think the fetching could also be considered atomic. Since we
did not write fetch and store operators, we just failed to realise
that it was atomic. Your second point, with reference to the generalisation of the idea that you want this to occur in particular
contexts and so on, is discussed in the Dahl/Nygaard paper on
Class and Subclass declarations. If you study the examples in that
paper you will find that as part of the structure of a various element, of a class, you define a procedure for that structure. Now

this goes part way towards solving the problem, though you would have to use procedures for operators. I feel in my own mind that the syntax sweetening provided by the Dahl/Nygaard paper looks like the most promising way to express these concepts in languages that I have seen so far.

Ross:

Yes, I agree with your remark on the subatomic versus atomic distinction. This whole terminology is of course heirarchical and so they would come into the same context when we have an adequate solution to the thing. On the other hand you mention that even with the Dahl/Nygaard language proposal you would have to use procedures to have these actions if they were not associated with the objects or entities themselves. It is precisely my point that we should like to have this still further extended so that it does in fact apply to the operators of the language as well as the entities being manipulated by the language.

Knuth:

It is in my experience that this type of augmentation usually occurs with new types of symbols which are not the classical traditional mathematical operators but are things which are less traditional, such as set inclusion and so on. In other words it certainly does not give us all the generality but it perhaps matches the needed generality.

Dahl:

I should like to tack on to this interesting discussion with an actual example. I have defined here a class sreal, "special real" if you like:

```
class sreal; virtual: procedure side effect;
begin real V;
        procedure becomes (X); real X;
        begin side effect; V := X end;
end sreal;
```

There is a procedure associated with the class, which I call "side effect". Since I do not care to define what it does here, I make it a virtual procedure. The variable V corresponds to the value part of a pointer-value pair in ALGOL 67. The pointer part would be a reference to an sreal object.

I have in this example declared a procedure "becomes", which calls for the side effect and then performs an assignment to V.

There could be procedures for other operations as well, such as
plus, minus and so forth.

Now I can declare a qualified reference variable Q, and initialize it to point to an object of class sreal.

$\underline{ref}$ (sreal) Q;...;Q:=sreal ;

It might be a convenient syntactic sugaring to permit underlined
sreal as a declarator, and to define

$\underline{sreal}$ Q ;

as equivalent to the above declaration and initialization.

If you now call the "becomes" procedure which is declared local
to the object referenced by Q,

Q. becomes (3.14) ;

you achieve what you want: a side effect followed by an assignment
of a real value. By the way, the side effect would in this case be a
run time error message, because there is no actual counterpart of
the virtual procedure for this particular object. However, you could
define any side effect you wish for objects belonging to subclasses
of sreal.

Two further remarks are of interest here. Firstly one could envisage a preprocessor transforming any assignment statement such
as

Q: 3.14 into Q. becomes (3.14)

Secondly the language would force you to distinguish by notation between left and right hand values in Strachey's sense. Here Q is a
left hand value, and $Q.V$ is the corresponding right hand value.

Strachey:

I want to take up with Doug Ross the questions of subatomic and
atomic processes and when one wants to be able to interfere with
them or have other processes going on at the same time. I think
there is a fundamental difference both in programming languages
as we have them at the moment and, I suspect, also in concept between the sub-atomic things and the atomic things. The "fetch" and
the "store" correspond to the right and left hand values associated
with variables or with names or with objects or expressions or what
have you. In my own view these are fundamental semantic concepts
and have a different nature from the operators "plus" and "minus"
and the other functions which you may wish to perform. If you
change your language in such a way as to make the meanings of the
symbols depend on the context, then you have to be very careful in-

deed or you lose some of the most important properties of mathematical notation.

There are two terms I want to use: the "applicative structure"
of the language and its "referential transparency". The latter is a
very unfortunate term; it means roughly speaking that you may replace any expression or any suitably indicated area of the text by
another expression which has in some sense the same value. We
may replace "2 plus 3" by "5" without in any way changing the overall meaning of the expression. If you have applicative expressions,
that is to say, expressions in which there are some parts which represent operators and some which represent operands (most programming languages and nearly all mathematics fall into this class),
then it is very useful to have the additional property of referential
transparency. It allows the expressions to be manipulated and it
makes it possible to have some hope of proving that a given two expressions have the same result.

Now the introduction of more context dependence may be a convenient device for when you are considering one thing happening after another. When you are considering a long complicated expression, context dependence, like side-effects, is just a nuisance. It
makes it difficult to see what is happening, difficult to understand
the expression and impossible very often to transform it into anything else. There is, I think, a very important distinction here. I
think we have to be very clear about whether we are going to preserve referential transparency and therefore the possibility of
transforming one expression of the programming language into another, or whether we are going to deal with a sequence of commands to the machine in which case I think we give up the hope of
transformation.

Laski:

I first want to comment on Stracheys remark and suggest that
this is entirely involved in the problem of whether one compiles or
interprets and when one binds the meaning of expressions or strings.
This seems to me over the past year or two in programming languages to be getting more and more flexible and moving further and
further towards interpretation. This has dangers and advantages
and I do not know whether I agree or not. But an extremely interesting case has been produced by the difference in technique of handling
the McNeley ideas, by Strachey and Dahl. Dahl, as far as I can see,
handles the "store" in a preprocessor and binds it before the compilation of the program. It is not clear to me whether he can also
handle the "fetch" in this way and I would like further explanation.

Strachey on the other hand can handle both the "fetch" and the
"store" within the program itself.

Hutchinson:

Laski brought up the essential idea that I was going to put forward, that we are getting more and more toward interpretation rather than execution of these languages. I would like to have these people comment on the price that is paid in the execution of programs with these features.

Knuth:

First of all, on this last point, the aim which McNeley has in mind is of finding a way of expressing it so that you are not paying any more penalty than you would have to in order to get this type of a facility any other way. The question of suitability for implementation should always be in the back of the mind in any discussions. In my opinion I think the suggestion made by Dahl looks as though it is easier to implement than Strachey's CPL but that is possibly just because CPL involves so many concepts that I do not know how to implement.

I want to bring up again McNeley's example of having the two associations with the same variable. It did not seem that in either one of the approaches given by Strachey or Dahl we had a simple way of concatenating more than one association with a particular variable. I believe this is an important thing since I am hoping that the things that are associated are, by and large, standardised things which a person wants to take out of a library of associations so that he does not have to write them himself in most cases. In his example, Dahl pointed out that he gave a system error since no side-effect was achieved. But actually what we would like is something which, when there are no side-effects specified, does nothing, but when there are two side-effects specified it does both.

Ross:

I apologise to Dahl for not having studied SIMULA, especially SIMULA 67, recently enough to be sure of what your example was indicating but from my cloudy understanding of what you were presenting, it seemed to me that you were associating the side-effect with the procedure. Your "becomes" procedure is a procedure which can be called for many different types of objects. This seems quite similar to the way that we now do the same sort of thing by ad hoc techniques. If indeed it is possible for a pre-processor to turn your "$Q = 3.14$" into the form that says "becomes" then I think this is fine. That would indicate that the things we are talking about, if you have a SIMULA as your underlying processor, can be done by augmentation rather than extension and that would make me very happy.

With respect to Strachey's remarks, I fully agree that these effects that we are talking about must truly be side-effects, because if they are not truly side-effects then we do violence to the mathematics of our operators. So as with all powerful devices they must be treated with care. Side-effects can always be abused to obscure clarity and that again is something which we just do not know how to control. You can say "leave them out", but I think they add power.

Finally with respect to Hutchinson's remark on Laski's remark, about whether we are tending towards interpreters, I believe that there is a sufficiently powerful growing body of knowledge of how to do compiling such that we need not degenerate into making interpretive languages. You can in fact have these powerful effects which do, if they are properly applied, add clarity and apparent power to the language. You can get these effects without a heavy overhead of interpretive burden.

Strachey:

One of the difficulties, I think, in Dahl's method of doing it by effectively introducing the side-effects with the pre-processor is that it seems to me that you have to know before you write your program which operations you wish to effect the side-effects on, rather than which entities you wish to associate the side-effects with. That is to say, the pre-processor has to replace the assignment statement by "becomes" rather than doing something to the arguments. As I understand the problem, it is not to alter the operations, unless you make a systematic meaning all the way through permanently in all programs of what the assignment statement means, but to be able to change the values or the meanings associated with the variables so that in some circumstances their values were printed.

To answer Knuth's question about whether it is possible in CPL to have several side-effects, the answer is that it is perfectly possible to do so - you compound the functions like taking $\sin (\cos(x))$.

Nygaard:

This pre-processor which will make it possible to use these usual symbols like + and -; it is just a mere matter of convenience. I must say that I am not at all sure that I would want to use this facility. I think we should stress the fact that we have a different operation by writing it not with the ordinary symbol.

Strachey:

If you do that why not write in the "monitor" straight away?

Knuth:

Well I think the answer Nygaard would give, if he understood Strachey's question the way I do - is that he would say that indeed it is possible to think of the assignment operator as consistently being replaced by "becomes" for every possible type and through-out the language, and that the pre-processor he was talking about was merely implied as one way of bringing this about. But it is really just a convenient way of describing the language; the pre-processor does not in fact need to exist. I want to emphasize what I think is a fairly new concept and not completely understood yet, but potentially very powerful, which appears in ALGOL X and the Dahl sub-class declarations and probably in CPL. In our data struc-tures we not only have real, integer, boolean types of quantities as part of the nodes or elements or entities or whatever you want to call them, but we also have procedures. Dahl's example showed a procedure that was essentially part of an object. I think that this fairly new idea deserves a lot of thought as to exactly what it means and how it can be exploited to best advantage. It certainly was a re-velation to me when I first realised this.

Laski:

God made the integers - the rest is the work of man. I under-stand what "plus" means when applied to the integers but usually I am modelling something which only for convenience I map onto the integers and therefore the meaning of a "plus" is purely con-ventional. It seems to me the value of changing the meaning of the operators would be in interpreting the operators according to the type of objects they operate upon. We could then avoid forcing the analyst to "gödelise" everything into the integers as was the habit in the days of ALGOL 60.

Dahl:

I just wanted to add one remark about the pre-processor. Knuth is right that in my mind it was sort of an abstract thing. I did not commit myself to the pre-processor, but it would be quite feasible to do it.

Ross:

I just want to say that some people may have doubts concerning the utility of these concepts; sometimes these extended discussions

get to seeming rather abstract to those who have not already played
with the ideas and fail to see what it is really all about. I would just
like to state my view that the exploitation of these mechanisms is
an extremely powerful way to get at extremely powerful systems.
We have not actually changed the language in the AED system since
some time in 1964 but have continued at a great pace the increase
in techniques that we use. We have done almost all of this by means
of introducing new integrated packages of procedures which inter-
lock together and represent some powerful extension of the language. Almost always we find that the best implementation of a new
feature is to exploit these techniques of embedding procedures in
data structures and having the data structures themselves actually
constitute the control mechanism. It is by these techniques that you
need not reduce to interpretation. You remember that I said in our
terms "plex" is data, structure and algorithm; you can get a very
nice powerful interlocking of these things if you exploit the very
type of techniques that we have discussed this morning.

PANEL DISCUSSION
ON QUASI PARALLEL PROGRAMMING

Steel:

The official subject of this panel is "Quasi Parallel Programming"; the actual subject is "Are General Purpose Languages identical with simulation languages". The essential point here is to discuss the question of whether there are linguistic elements that are not present in general purpose languages that are essential or at least important for discrete simulation.

It should be pointed out that simulation languages by and large are not used by professional programmers but rather by people with problems with which they are concerned. Their object is to solve a problem, not to get elegant with the language. As evidence for that statement I would like to cite two reports done by people somewhat outside the orbit of the people in this room. These were done about the same time and by rather different groups. The Share Systems Simulation project in March 1966 published some statistics on the users of simulation. It was rather surprising to see that the set of people who go to the U.S. for ACM conferences and participate actively in the professional activity, were not those by and large using simulation. Secondly, at the University of Pennsylvania in the same month there was a work-shop on simulation languages and at that work-shop the survey taken showed that the majority of users were not experts in programming languages.

I would like very briefly to survey the sequence of events that have led to multiplicity of simulation languages. In 1963 and early 1964 we can see what is really the first generation of simulation languages; a whole string of attempts to take existing programming languages or build new ones that were aimed at solving some of the fundamental problems that come up in attempting to write digital computer programs for simulation processes. The list is almost endless; GPSS, CSL, SIMSCRIPT, SIMPAC, etc. One could go on and on.

Some time later on, in 1964 and after, say, there began to be attempts to synthesizethe basic ideas that were found in these various first generation attempts. This led to such languages as SOL, SIMULA and NSS. Such things as the "process concept" were identified and explicated. One can talk perhaps about a third generation of simulation languages where the on-line aspect was brought in.

However, the question still remains with us as to whether general purpose languages are sufficient in their basic concepts to express the kind of notions that are involved in discrete simulation. And that I want to bring to the attention of the panel this afternoon.

I would like to ask each of the panelists to state their views on this question. Then there are one or two questions that I propose to put to the panel, and after that we will have general discussion.

Garwick:

A general purpose language is sufficient for any purpose: this is a definition. It is of course doubtful if any language in existence today, even CPL, can be said to satisfy this definition. Some languages approach this target more than others, but because they are general purpose, simulation is only one of the areas they try to cover and they should not make any more specific efforts in order to cover this field than to cover any other field.

A general purpose language is not sufficiently efficient in any field, such as simulation, but it should not be replaced, in my opinion, by a language which specializes exclusively in this direction.

The design of a general purpose language which is also reasonably simple and efficient is a very difficult task indeed. I know this, because I have tried to do it, but I believe that under the present state of the art or at least within the very near future, it should be possible.

On the other hand, the design of a special purpose language, even in a difficult field like simulation, is comparatively easy. The designers of a general purpose language have learned from the efforts in the simulation area as well as from efforts in many other areas, but even if they have not yet succeeded, their efforts should not be discarded and replaced by the present multiplicity of special purpose languages. We should put more effort into finding out what are really the basic concepts of programming, so that these basic concepts can be included in a general purpose language.

I find the present confusion of languages absolutely catastrophic and if it continues in this way it will not help programmers at all. You will not, on any given computer, be in possession of compilers for all these languages.

The only salvation for the programming world is the really general purpose language. Even if it does not exist yet, it is clear that that is the only thing we must strive for if we are going to give all programmers access to the necessary tools. We can not just produce new special purpose languages the whole time, because they will not be widely implemented.

Therefore I conclude by saying that the general purpose language, even if it does not exist today, is the only thing we must work for in order that it may eventually exist. And, it is better to use a slightly imperfect general purpose language than to use 500 special purpose languages.

Steel:

I would now like to call on members of the loyal opposition to consider the possibility that Garwick is totally wrong. I suspect that is what you are going to talk about anyway.

Lackner:

I do not know how directly in opposition I will appear to be. I agree that general purpose languages are hard to design; I think that situation is apparent to all of us. The relative ease of designing special purpose languages I am not so sure of. I think in talking about simulation languages it is necessary to distinguish between two kinds of languages; a language for implementing a simulation scheme, and a language for constructing models given that a simulation scheme exists. These are two quite different aims. I think you want to implement a simulation scheme, using a general purpose language. For constructing models, on the other hand I think you want a correspondence between the things you say in building a model and the elements of the system. Almost any general purpose language can be used to build simulation schemes. In the new version of SIMULA, for example, you could implement a different simulation scheme than the one normally supplied.

The language designers however tend to try to make their language one that appeals to everybody and in doing so I think the difference between the simulation scheme and the model building language itself gets lost.

In the general language one wants for forming a simulation scheme I think the problems of unpredictable task allocation need to be faced up to. List processing is a virtual necessity if the kind of scheme which most of us have come to prefer, is going to be used.

I will not talk about the other kind of language, i.e. the language for modelling, because I am neither very interested, nor very qualified to talk about them. I never worked with one. The persons that Steel was referring to, who want to build models, are typically not programmers; they are people who are thinking about an object system, very often one that does not exist yet. They want to put together a model. They want to observe its behaviour, and they want to be able to interpret the behaviour in terms of the object system.

Starting with that picture, which I think is unquestionable, this person wants a way of conceptualizing the object system. This is where I find some people who agree with me and some who have other preferences. Some would like the modeller to be able to conceptualize the system in any way that he pleases. Others want to provide much more structure to the person building a model. However one is going to conceptualize an object system, one wants reasonable confidence that the important characteristics of any object system can be captured and expressed in any suggested general way of conceptualizing systems.

A basic way of conceptualizing is to use the idea of archetypes. One uses archetypes in building a model and these archetypes will basically allow one to contemplate separable components of the whole object system. The archetypes are to be of few enough kinds that one can learn them and remember them. On the other hand they need to be sufficiently different to allow a great variety of forms to be expressed and a great variety of different structures to be put together.

To find examples of archetypes, let us talk about the difference between behaviour exhibition and behaviour determination. Most of us, I think, find it quite convenient to represent the behaviour exhibiting parts of the system in terms of classes, entities and attributes. They allow one to distinguish different parts of an object system in a fairly natural way.

Now, there are vast differences in the way people try to conceptualize the area of behaviour determination. Personally, I prefer processes, but of course I have my own interpretation, as all others do, of what processes are. Basically, I think we agree that we want to think of processes as operating in parallel. It seems a natural way to think about processes, and it does not require a fundamental understanding of a digital computer.

Some might want to break apart processes or to give subcomponents to them; I like to, others do not. Some would like to have great freedom in expressing a process and to have almost anything happen with the process. I think it is useful and aids the modeller to insist that processes have parts. The parts, in my opinion, are the beginning, the interruption, the duration and the completion.

What I wish to suggest is that this particular way of thinking about processes allows one to differentiate and to imagine both discrete and continuous effects of the process.

With these archetypes, we return to simulation languages, and what they should be able to do. I would say that it is a very simple thing they are to do. Given these archetypes, the task of the language is to provide a facility for individualizing various instances of the archetypes.

Strachey:

I would like to say something about the distinction between general and special purpose programming languages, not only for simulation purposes but for any other special purposes.

In the first instance we should appreciate that in any survey of the use of any form of programming language, general or special, we find, unless it is very peculiar language like CPL, that almost all the users are not programming language experts. That after all is the main purpose in designing a programming language. CPL is in a particular situation in this respect, because it has not yet been published. The publication of CPL is one of the activities well described by the instruction "just wait until..."

Special languages, as I think I said the other day, almost always need in one form or another most of the facilities that exist in general purpose languages. It is necessary always to do things like control loops and jumps on conditions. It is nearly always convenient or useful to be able to define and call procedures and functions. Nearly all the apparatus which is the basis of a general programming language is necessary in a special programming language. And nearly all the traps that you can fall into in designing a general purpose programming language, such as getting confused between addresses and names and values, await the designer of a special language.

The particular way in which special purpose programming languages differ from general purpose languages is that there are or should be some special syntactic features built into them to make it particularly convenient to deal with the particular area which the language is designed for.

The difference is mostly in providing more functions, more special built-in operators and more special syntactic devices.

It is not true, I think, that languages are made simpler by leaving out some of the powerful features of general purpose languages. I think it is a great mistake to think that a language is made simple by merely containing a few ideas; it may be quick to learn, but it will be of little use. It is not true that a computing machine which has no floating point arithmetic is simpler to use than one which has floating point arithmetic. It has fewer operations, there is less to learn, but on the other hand the addition of floating point arithmetic generally speaking makes the use of the machine easier.

Now to come to the particular question of simulation; do simulation languages have a difference in some essential way from existing general purpose languages? The crucial point here is whether it is something essential; in other words, do they contain or require some concepts which have not yet been incorporated in any general purpose language? And if this is the case, then the sooner they are incorporated in general purpose languages, the better. If there are any necessary concepts in simulation languages which are not in general purpose languages, it is a very interesting defect in general purpose languages.

I think it may be that this is the case.

It seems to me that the essential concepts which are necessary in a language which would be able to deal with simulation problems are the following: firstly, data structures of a rather complicated sort, of the sort that cannot be handled in say ALGOL 60. These are extensions which most general purpose languages have not yet got or are only just incorporating. To talk about my own work, CPL compound data structures are even less published than the rest of the language. They are of course actually developing right now...

However, compound data structures are very useful in all the general purpose languages and I think that simulation languages have been very useful in emphasizing the need. It is unfortunate that mathematicians on the whole have ignored commercial data processing which would, if they had been aware of it, have given them an indication that more complicated data structures were interesting and not merely commercial.

Secondly it seems to me that what simulation languages require is the ability to do parallel or quasi-parallel processing. I have not been able to comprehend perfectly what conceptual novelty this involves. I think it involves something new; I have not yet been able to integrate it with the rest of my understanding of programming languages and I feel very uneasy about it. I am hoping to get myself sorted out one of these days!

I think the new concept is connected with the problem of the extent or existence of an object being different from its lexicographical scope but I do not think this is quite all. I think there is also a fundamental conflict between the block structure of ALGOL 60 and the requirements of parallel processing. SIMULA makes a big step in the direction of doing something about this.

The third basic property that simulation requires is, quite simply, everything else in general-purpose programming. Useful but trivial extras are features like statistics collection devices and random number generators. Also, a scheduling mechanism of some kind seems to be needed for processing through the various activities. I do not know if this is vital, but I think it would be a "bady" instead of a "goody" if it is not accessible to the programmer when he needs to change it.

Laski:

On this problem of the real nature of parallel programming, I would like to mention some work by Caracciolo which he quoted to me at lunch today. If I interpret him correctly, he claims to have shown that the resolution of access conflicts between a number of processes operating on a common data base was probabilistically rather than categorically determined, and that the functions computable by automata of this sort were a wider class than the general recursive functions.

When we express models of the real world by means of parallel processes that are quasi-independent, we want to be sure that, where they are in danger of fouling one another up, they behave properly. Now, effectively what we must do is to have a means of putting into the probabilistic automation (which consists of the several independent processes) sufficient sequencing to cause the significant results of the computation to be the same rather than different every time we run it.

The essential quality of quasi-parallel programming is that it is convenient to express ourselves in parallel processes in such a way that the system can map it into a single process. Genuinely parallel processes are all the structure we need to provide, when describing what we want to happen. Because I am a lazy fellow, I do not like to do anything unnecessary. I do not like asking the user to put ad hoc structure in, that is only dependent upon the implementation and not dependent upon his meaning and understanding of what is going on. We have genuine parallel processes in the real world; the processes are not merely cooperative but competing. As a result of this theoretical result, we require a means of bringing order into chaos and this, I think, is the second contribution that simulation languages, or languages to manage parallel processes with a common data base, give to general purpose languages. The first was the need for an awareness of data structure.

Steel:

I would like to begin the recursive discussion by making an observation - the point came to me this week in reflecting on the people who insist that general purpose languages are the highest achievement in computing. I tried to carry their point of view to its ultimate conclusion and I have designed a language which I call CGPPL; "completely general purpose programming language", which it turns out requires only three lines of syntactic description and one paragraph of sematic description. It consists of the single instruction: "Subtract and replace". It has been proven (by Van der Poel) that this is sufficient to solve all problems.

It seems to me that there is a pertinent point here in that one can take any programming language and strip the inessentials away with the result that you have left something very simple to describe and completely general purpose; it will solve all the problems and why do we not use it? I would like the advocates of the general purpose language to carry on that point.

Garwick:

Special facilities cannot be coded by 99% of the users. But the conclusion that special facilities are not needed is in my opinion completely erroneous. In the same way as we today publish algorithms, we can also publish special systems. In fact the coding of features, as distinct from concepts, has to be done by specialists in the same way as the extension of the language is not something to be coded by general users. They should use a set design done by somebody who knows his business.

But what I still maintain is that all these special features are founded upon a very small number of basic concepts, not as small of course as Van der Poel's "replace and subtract" - this would reduce it, as Van der Poel himself pointed out, to the ridiculous.

We will need a system with which we will reasonably efficiently be able to express what we want. And "efficiently" is a very important point here. General purpose programming languages should be able with efficiency to express the special purposes which we need, and that is one of the really great difficulties in designing a general purpose language. But if we succeed in this, all the special features required, be it in simulation languages or be it in the writing of a compiler, should be expressible inside this hopefully successful general purpose language.

Lackner:

I think that the need for different kinds of syntactical forms and devices in languages is based on the psychology of people. There is certainly a limit to the number of interactions or the complexity, if you will, of a given situation that one can contemplate all at one time. The problem in simulation and other special purpose languages is one of trying to minimize the number of expressions one has to write in a language or draw in graphics that do not have anything directly to do with the object system.

Strachey:

I suggest an alternative to Steel's proposal of CGPPL - it is called PPL, the Perfect Programming Language. It has one instruction only: "Solve"; that solves all problems.

As an awful warning about a simple programming language which
has very little in the way of concepts in it and very little in the way
of a compiler either, I offer you the General Purpose Macro Generator, which can be regarded as a programming language. Its implementation takes about 200 machine instructions and the programs
that you write in it are almost totally incomprehensible. If you care
to look at some examples, you will see that it is not a very nice language. It is exactly the sort of language which we do not want; it is
not a simple language for the user but it is a simple language for
the compiler to interpret.

Steel:

I draw one conclusion from this. It is difficult to express, but it
appears to me that the difference between those who want to see a
language specifically designed for simulation with names and concepts in it that are pertinent to the problem at hand, and those who
argue that the general purpose programming language is the appropriate thing, is really a matter of semantics. If one follows up
Garwick's comments we can imagine a language, a general purpose programming language, in which the basic computing concept
is expressed. Attached to it is a large library of procedures which
express concepts that are pertinent to a particular subject. The
design of that library is really the design of the simulation language or whatever other kind of language you want to talk about.

I sense that there is really not all that much difference between
the points of view that are expressed here, but rather it is a difference in what you look upon as the fundamental language.

Ross:

I want to express a view in opposition to this one, that all we do
when we make a special purpose language is to add a suitable library to a general purpose language. It seems to me that the key
point is that both general purpose languages and simulation languages are special purpose languages, if we consider that the one
thing that is universal is language processing.

I have noted that this view-point does hold water, in that some
systems described here use the complete translation of a language
by the preprocesser into another language. Every single phase is
employed, so it is not a vacuous concept by any means, and I really
think that it is quite essential to have this view.

Now I would like to come back to Garwick's first point. He was
saying that it was no good to have a multiplicity of languages because the user would not have access to all these different languages. Here again, if we have a common processer which we do

try to make available for all the different computing machines and if our languages are published like algorithms and are able to be input to the single processer on any particular sort of hardware, then we can in fact have these languages in a multiplicity available to the user. The users are not going to be programmers, not even members of the 99% that we have been talking about. They are going to be completely unscrubbed, much less unwashed, and they could not care less about machines, or our problems in designing languages.

Nygaard:

Dahl and I started out to make a simulation language, but of course we have spent so much time with all these people working on general purpose languages, that I must admit we have to some extent fallen in love with the concept of general purpose languages. So we have now our language, based on ALGOL 60 which I believe was a general purpose language. We have added to it list processing, the concept of a "process" which makes it possible to operate a collection of mutually interrupting programs, the class and subclass declarations and a number of other things.

Now my question is, what should we remove from SIMULA in order to make it a general purpose language?

Lackner:

It is not a question of removing something and making it a general purpose language, it is a question of removing something and making it a simulation language.

Dahl:

I have a comment on the concept of sequencing algorithms. The thing that distinguishes a programming language from mathematics is that the language has an underlying sequencing algorithm. I should like to stress the importance of having in a language a sequencing algorithm which is simple. If it is so difficult to comprehend that you cannot actually follow the sequencing algorithm, then you will replace a clear understanding by a feeling of understanding, which is false.

I am very concerned about languages which tend to induce such a feeling, because when you express yourself in such a language, you will not be expressing yourself accurately. A particularly dangerous statement to allow in a language is the "wait" statement; so long as we talk of sequencial programming, i.e. quasi-parallel programming, the "wait" statement probably needs a sequencing algorithm which may in some cases turn out to be quite desperately complicated.

Garwick:

I agree with Dahl. The sequencing algorithm should be simple and if you use a general purpose language as I propose, and which is supported by Ross, there are really only two sequencing algorithms; one is to take the next instruction or statement and the other is to go somewhere else. All other possible and necessary sequencing algorithms are expressed in terms of this.

Strachey:

I think it very dangerous for anyone to think that the basic sequencing algorithm behind programming languages is simple; I recommend him to look again at the example I wrote up the first day, of the ALGOL program not describable by a flow diagram.

Laski:

I entirely agree that a simple sequencing algorithm is needed, though I would suggest that Garwick does not understand what this is, in the case of parallel processes. However, if we have complex situations, encoding them in terms of this simple sequencing algorithm is incredibly difficult. I feel it necessary to augment a language, which has the required sequencing concepts in it for the kinds of processors on which it will work, by a published, well understood library of augmenting facilities to make it easier to use by applications people. I want very strongly to support Ross's view that simple, easy to use application-oriented packaged subsystems are required for people who want to make use of computing and information systems.

But it is our job, it seems to me, to provide the infixed structure which will underpin the work that people can do in writing and using such packages.

Lackner:

I will make it unanimous. I agree with the underlying sequencing algorithm being clearly understood; whether it is simple or not, is not the question. The reason it needs to be understood goes back to the fact that in modelling you want people to think in a natural way of parallel operations, when of course nothing will really happen in parallel, as Garwick said. In the expressions in the language you want people to feel that there is a "whenever" or "always" qualifier attached to some of the expressions that they write.

Laski:

I must take issue with Lackner when he says nothing will ever happen in parallel. If there are two asynchronous processors in an information system, there is parallelism, not quasi-parallelism, and this is a different and difficult situation to comprehend. It is assumed both processors have read and write access to some data in common, and that they are not simply two independent unconnected processors.

Petrone:

I have the impression that people at this conference are using some terms with a different meaning. Therefore I feel it necessary to clear the ground by attempting to define some fundamental terms. In doing so, I will not stick to a pretended inherent meaning of the English words, but rather to their established use in a technical context.

I am specifically referring here to the three notions of
(i) "genuine parallel processing"
(ii) "parallel programming"
(iii) "quasi-parallel programming".

The notion of "genuine parallel processing", I contend, is of very little relevance to our discussion here. Here we are concerned with objects known as discrete state automata provided with a finite tape. So let us get rid once for all of the real continuous world and suppose that someone else did for us the job of building a discretized model of reality (even if only a mental model); and of being worried by "adequacy" problems. It is only at this point that we will get involved in the specific task of translating this (perhaps mental) discretized model into procedures, data structures or tasks.

On parallel programming (PP) versus quasi-parallel programming (QPP): it has been usual to make a distinction between processes in the sense of PP and processes in the sense of QPP. Specifically, the former have been called *tasks* or *jobs* and the latter *processes* (or transactions).

It is my intention here to clarify their mutual relations.

To eliminate another difficulty, let me say that the term "parallel programming" is somewhat misleading. One is always tempted to think that the actions of two parallel programs (or processes) have to be, in some way or another, related in time. *This is not so.* There does not exist a time relation between two parallel processes (tasks, jobs). It is not even known whether they are really concurrently progressing or being executed one after the other. And in the first case their relative speed ratio is unknown.

If a specific order relation is wanted, one, at least, of two processes is to be stopped (for synchronization purposes) and *no parallel processing exists any longer.*

Therefore, in my framework, a parallel programming scheme is characterized by the fact that a certain set P_i of processes, a subset of the set A_i of the activated (or "alive") processes is progressing, but their rate of progressing is undefined (and this for the successive discrete steps, $S_i, S_2, \ldots$ of the computation).

It is the responsibility of a concealed "god", perhaps an operating system, to switch off from any of the processes belonging to set P_i to any other of the same set P_i, according to his own criteria or the availability or resources.

It is the responsibility of the user to define, for any i, the sets P_i; that is to switch from a set P_i to the successive P_{i+1}.

In the primitive multiprocessing environment built up this freedom was very limited and was usually expressed through peripheral units by putting into execution a new job; a task situation is more flexible since this freedom may also be expressed by program.

The user may, in a parallel programming environment, set up conditions that can possibly reduce the set P_i *to only one element. Then we have quasi-parallel programming.* In this context, QPP is a particular case of PP.

After having analyzed the dynamic aspects of QPP and PP, let us now consider the problem of exchanging of information.

Jobs do not communicate in any way, tasks and processes do. Tasks have been devised in PL/1 within a binary relation framework: "attaching", "attached" (= father, son). This rather complicated the job we performed, in the paper presented to this conference, of imbedding QPP into PL/1, that is, into an instance of PP.

However, it is my opinion that if a PP language were to be newly designed it should be done with the objective in mind of using it as a QPP language. This requires access to the queues concealed behind the PL/1 event variables, or references to tasks, as also pointed out by Dahl in the 1966 ALGOL Bulletin [25].

This opinion is motivated by conceptual and money economy. It is a hard job to build up a software system which, besides all else, has to take care of an indefinite number of stacks, as is necessary for a PP or a QPP language. Thus let us build only one, if it is possible. And it is!

Garwick:

It seems to me that many of us somehow underrate the power of general purpose programming languages and that the problems of parallel processes, whether they be quasi-parallel or really parallel, are easily handled in a general purpose programming language. You need only to design one procedure which, borrowing a name from PL/1, would be called "task". This procedure admittedly cannot be expressed in GPL. It has to be a special purpose one, and the effect of it can only be described in natural language.

This procedure has two parameters, one is a Boolean and the other is, to use ALGOL 60 terminology, a statement. What it does is this. If the Boolean variable is false, then it delivers to the operating system or single processor or our multiple processors this statement for execution. And when this statement has been executed, the Boolean variable will be set to *true.*

You can now have any sort of join-up of branches by testing whether these various Boolean variables are *true* or *false.* And furthermore it is absolutely without any interest whether you really have two processors or this was really done by one processor at different times.

We have had long discussions here on the conflict problem when we have real parallel processors and they are operating on each other's data. If you as a programmer permit this to happen, you presumably have a meaning for it; if you do not have a meaning for it, you should stop writing programs. I think it is as simple as that. If you let two parallel processors change and use the same data, and you have no way of finding out whether one processor is using this data before or after the other has changed it, either this was your intention, or else you did not know what you were talking about.

Laski:

I would like to congratulate Petrone on a very clear exposition. But there seems to be a danger that one could reduce the set of processes P_i from one to zero by presenting incompatible blocking conditions among the processes and this is a problem I do not understand. The second point I want to make with reference to his remarks is on distinguishing quasi-parallel from parallel. Even with a single processor system, where your own concurrent processes exist within a framework of an operating supervisor that has been written by somebody else and therefore you do not understand, it seems to me necessary to treat the problem as a problem of parallel programming, even though it operates as quasi-parallel programming.

I therefore question whether the simplification he proposes is acceptable for those who are concerned with working under operating systems.

Petrone:

If we choose a single processor operating environment then the set P_i is the responsibility of the operating system. Within this set, the operating system behaves as a user, and the same criteria that the careful user will use in order to avoid conflict between processes the operating system will have to follow. There are possible conflicts in the situation in which one process wants something, and another wants it too. I think there are people who have resolved partially those problems; may-be there are operating systems builders who have been concerned with them.

Conway:

I have spent a good part of the last couple of years arguing for simplicity of programming. As a teacher, I usually defend this argument on behalf of the students who are just learning the process but I really believe that it is more important than that. There is some very large fraction of our 99% who can use a more simplified programming language than the ones which have been offered.

The characteristic of this fraction of programmers is not their lack of intelligence but their lack of experience. Perhaps what is most important is the fact that they are intermittent programmers; they are primarily engineers or scientists or mathematicians. They pick up a task and do a bit of programming, do none for another couple of months and then come back to it, during which time they have forgotten all the niceties of punctuation and rules of the language and have to study it all over again. So a simple language stands them in very good stead. I would like to turn Strachey's example round on him - he gives me a very good vehicle by citing the floating point problem and saying that it would not be a step in the right direction or toward simplicity to omit the floating point capability from a language. I agree that the floating point facility is important and I suggest that what you can do is to omit the fixed point features. For a large part of these programmers, the only reasons for having a fixed point capability in the language are efficiency, which is irrelevant, or the ability to do integer arithmetic which can be provided for satisfactorily by an appropriate compiler routine, or something to do with input/output and that also can be provided for by the compiler itself.

The additions beyond the minimum number of statements that are required to perform the obvious functions in a language are often justified by things other than increases in power. Some of them provide ease of writing. This has to be looked at rather carefully.

Many of the additions to programming languages, I think, are in the interests of taste or elegance or compactness of expression. The type of programmer I am referring to, has neither the experience nor the knowledge to have good taste: The elegance is unappreciated and compactness not necessarily a virtue.

The choice that we offer to these programmers I think often leads to confusion rather than anything desirable. I am reminded of the instance in 1958 or 1959 when a number of the Universities first had access to the Burroughs implementation of ALGOL 58, which was, to my knowledge, the first of the free form programming systems. We did not have to have a fixed programming sheet and at first we thought this was wonderful. It was only a matter of a month or two before all of the Universities discovered that this was not a blessing at all and had gone back to printing programming forms. The flexibility and freedom of layout that the professionals were very fond of, caused to the intermittent and neophyte programmer, nothing but confusion and we discarded it very quickly.

Strachey:

I would like to say something on this point. I suggest that you transfer some of the remarks and thoughts you have made to the simplicity of the notation of matrix algebra, which is now generally accepted even by engineers.

This involves quite an effort in learning but when you have learnt it, it becomes very well worthwhile. I think the occasional user who just wants to solve one or two simultaneous equations would not be very happy at having to learn matrix algebra to do it. It is generally now accepted, in some parts of engineering anyhow, that an ability to deal with matrix algebra is a useful one.

It seems to me that some of the constructions in programming languages are of this nature. They are difficult to learn and difficult to remember unless you have understood the basic concepts that lie beneath them. When you have, they become as natural as an integral sign, which after all is quite difficult to understand until you have spent a few months learning it.

My view is that in the long run, the use of computing machines and programming languages offers a mathematical tool which is probably of much greater power than the invention of calculus. In the long run, and again it may be rather a long run, people who are going to use computers, will have to spend some months or years learning about the techniques of computers and programming languages. When they have done this the subject will become an extremely powerful branch of mathematics. Until that time, of course, people who are prepared to learn will of course find it much easier to learn smaller sets - it is much easier to tell people to add all those numbers together than to take an integral.

As for the business of teaching, it seems to me that when you are teaching beginners how to program, or people who are not going to do a great deal of programming, the important thing to do is to be careful how you teach them. I think if you get into difficulties with teaching general purpose programming languages, it is because you are teaching them badly. There is no need to teach all the facilities of a programming language at all. On the whole, you should teach the simpler ones first and the more recondite ones later. Nobody in their senses would teach the use of left-hand functions in CPL on the first day - it is a dotty thing to do!

Steel:

There are those who believe that it is a dotty thing to do to teach that any day! I would like to make a comment of my own here - taking the chairman's prerogative - simply to point out that today we teach in our secondary schools concepts that were considered rather radical when Newton invented them and that perhaps the same principle applies to the concepts of programming languages. Now is there anyone on the panel apart from Laski who wishes to pursue this subject before I let Conway back?

Garwick:

I am extremely happy to hear these remarks by Conway because they are exactly the ones I made during my speech here at the beginning of this week. I was highly criticized then when I proposed to teach people a sub-set of my GPL because the full language is far too complicated for the normal user. I will say, about Strachey's left-hand functions, that they are far too restricted. You should be able to do much more general things than he can do with his left-hand functions - as you can, in fact, in GPL and I am not even certain that GPL is general enough. You should definitely gloss over that sort of thing for people who only occasionally use the programming language. I think a proper programming language is made, as Conway says, in such a way that you only need tell people a little bit about it for them to start using it. If they want to do something more general, then please tell them a little more.

Steel:

It has been suggested that one of the things we ought to do at these working conferences, is to follow the precedent that has been established for large meetings where we charge exhibition space for those who have products to advertise!

Laski:

I value Conway's contributions to emphasize the need for designing powerful languages that are capable of being sub-setted, as was
proposed for PL/1. Like many things in PL/1, between the desire
and the reality falls the shadow - but this produces one further order of difficulty in the job of designing high-level program languages. I would like to quote, however, John McCarthy who expressed the view that programming was more difficult than driving
a car, and easier than driving an aeroplane - and it should be a facility thoroughly spread in the whole of our society at whatever
level is appropriate for the needs of the user.

Conway:

I think in general introductory programming is rather badly
handled. The books I have seen and the people I have talked to,
emphasize things which are largely irrelevant to what you are trying to accomplish. I think few of us have spent adequate time trying
to define what is the really essential principle that you are trying
to convey during a first exposure to computing. I am sure that it
has little to do with number representation or the format propensi-
ties of a particular language. If you identify perhaps the ideas of
value, assignment and sequence control, which I think are the essence of a language, you can put these across in a matter of an
hour or two and put the students to work doing rather interesting
problems that exercise this. This is what I think we are really
trying to accomplish.

Again Strachey gives me a good example by raising matrix algebra, which I propose turning around on him by saying that the computing fraternity have long been remiss in this area. The engineering mathematics faculties in our colleges have long recognized
matrix algebra as being a basic tool. They teach people to think in
terms of matrices. Somewhere in the second year they are then
exposed to programming and all this is undone because they have
to write **FORTRAN** programs with three levels of nested loops in
order to multiply two matrices together.

Programming languages which will deal with arrays and have
the appropriate operations, subject only to the normal rules of
conformability, are long overdue. PL/1 was an enormous step
backward in this respect by defining completely absurd element by
element operations upon matrices. As a result, it is quite inap-
propriate for use by undergraduates in engineering and science.

Peck:

What I have to say does not concern the virtual name of this panel which appears to be "The teaching of programming" - it is perhaps closer to the actual name and may have something to do with the formal name - sorry, official name, as well.

I have been trying to discover what is the particular fundamental element which distinguishes a general programming language from one which perhaps can be a simulation language as well. I hope some time to find the answer to this.

In order to set the scene for the answer, I would like to draw your attention to the first steps which have been taken in ALGOL X. They are as follows (I hope I will not be presented with a bill for this!). I was glad to hear that Strachey regarded the first fundamental as the ability to have structured values, and this, of course, is in ALGOL X. But something much more to the point perhaps is the question of parallelism.

We did use the word "parallel" in the ALGOL report and the working group last week threw that word out as being too much used already and the fashionable word now is "collateral". So what we have then are phrases or expressions which are collateral. The phrases are expressions of elementary actions and the collateral elaboration of phrases means an unspecified merging of the elementary actions.

There are perhaps two reasons for putting this into ALGOL X. One is to be able to say that operands are elaborated collaterally an unspecified merging, and the other reason is to allow the programmer to say specifically in his program that something does not have to be elaborated in serial in which case he can write it as a collateral expression.

There is one other fundamental addition and this is the one upon which I invite some comments. The report does not state which of the actions described are, in fact, elementary. It does, however, give the programmer the opportunity to specify that certain actions are elementary and this is done by writing the word "elementary" preceding a closed expression. Thus, if you have the expression "$x := x + 1$" and if you write in front of that "elementary" this means that $(x := x + 1)$ is one of the things which is merged as a whole and nothing is merged in between its members.

Laski:

The first facility, if I may precede the gentleman on my right, (editor's note; i.e. Strachey), has to my knowledge been in CPL for a long time. It is good to see that ALGOL X is coming along.

Secondly, however, "elementary", I think would be interpreted

in most machines we have today by something like "inhibit interrupt" and "enable interrupt" orders - is that so?

Peck:

I think your understanding is about right.

Laski:

Then I assert from my knowledge and understanding of the problem that the solution is inadequate.

Steel:

Perhaps what we need is a dissertation on perpendicular programming!

Caracciolo:

Well, there are a number of things which should and could be
s aid. First I would begin by saying that of we take the title of this
panel "Are General Purpose Languages equal to Simulation Languages", I think three points should be discussed. One I would say
has been more or less entirely discussed and that is complex data
structure.

The second point is parallelism and quasi-parallelism - much
has been said but I think that more should be said. This relates to
the work cited by Laski at the beginning of this session. I will do
that in a moment.

I would like to consider another point which seems to me lacking in general purpose languages. This is the distinction between
active and passive, which seems to me quite important in describing interacting dynamical systems. In general programming languages, we usually take the attitude of someone who describes sequences of actions to be performed. Instead, if we consider a complex dynamical system which interacts in many ways, there is a
concept which seems to me quite primitive and this is the concept
of being active, becoming passive, being re-activated and so on.
I do not think that this concept exists in the general programming
languages.

Now, I would like to take five minutes just to say a few words
about the work which has been quoted by Laski.

The papers in question concern what I have called a constructive unified theory of probabilistic and parallel concurrent processes, as well as a discussion of the resolution of incompatibilities.

The first topic concerns an extension of the theory of Markov

Normal Algorithms (which are equivalent to Turing Machines) developed as a basic *universal* constructive model for processes in the sense of modern logic. It includes (besides single deterministic sequential processes) an elementary model for probabilistic elementary processes as well as sets of parallel concurrent processes. The main results are described in [17] and in a paper submitted for publication to the Journal of the ACM and can be summarized as follows. Elementary probabilistic processes are obviously an extension of deterministic processes, since the latter can be simply regarded as particular probabilistic processes in which every step has a single alternative to be taken with probability 1 instead of a finite number of alternatives. The most important results are:

(i) the possibility to build a *universal* simulator for such processes (in the sense of a universal Turing Machine) provided one simply admits the capability of selecting with probability $\frac{1}{2}$ between two distinct alternatives;

(ii) the probability distribution functions of obtaining a particular result starting from a given initial state are usually non-computable in the sense of recursive function theory. This means so to speak that we can simulate more than we can theoretically analyze. However interesting these results may be the motivation was not a study of probabilistic processes *per se*, but rather that of studying parallel concurrent processes. The reason is that a set of parallel concurrent processes may give rise to conflicts, which prevent one from following up all of them separately. One must find some way of getting out of the trouble arising from the fact it is quite possible to *request* the performance of incompatible actions but not *actually to perform* them. Now two things are to be essentially considered in this aspect: first - that there is no unique logical solution for incompatibilities, but one has to give additional rules for solving them; second - that even if the concurrent processes are 'per se' deterministic processes, it is possible to get an overall probabilistic process, if one admits a random selection rule for solving incompatibilities.

In the quoted papers it has in fact been shown that, vice versa, every probabilistic process can be reduced to a set of deterministic conflicting processes, with a random solution rule for incompatibilities.

The basic motivation for these studies was to get some deeper insight into the basic problem posed by simulation languages as a description of parallel concurrent (and therefore possibly conflicting) processes. This problem has been more directly considered in a third paper presented at a "Round Table on Simulation Languages" held in Pisa in May 1966 [168], which includes a discussion

of the problem posed by the sequentialization of parallel processes
i.e. their reduction to quasi-parallel processes.

The basic observation made in this work is that if we take a set
of parallel processes and we apply them in all possible different
orders two things might happen: i.e. we get different results or we
obtain the same result. Now I think that we can say that only those
processes which, if sequentialized in any order, do not give different results, also give rise to no conflicts and can be done in parallel. If instead, conflict arises then these processes cannot be done
in parallel. What happens then?

We have more or less the same situation as discussed for the
elementary models quoted before. There are, in fact, many possible solutions all of which are equally feasible from a logical
point of view. We can introduce priority rules. We can introduce
random selection rules. The basic problem is that one cannot
choose a solution only by logical reasons; one must have additional
information on the actual system behaviour. For instance we cannot impose as a general rule a deterministic solution looking for
priority rules. Certainly this could logically be done, but when simulating a real system, one is not free to introduce priority rules
which are not actually present in the system. On the other hand,
one can consider also the probabilistic case in which case however one should investigate what are the actual probabilities between the various choices.

As a consequence of this, in our experimental simulation language SL/1 developed in Pisa by Molnar, what we have done is that
when we had any set of events scheduled for the same time, we
made random selection. We considered this somewhat more reasonable than assuming any specified fixed priority rule, on the
basis that if there are priorities, they have to be explicitly programmed. I believe that there is a danger in transforming a set of
parallel concurrent processes into a set of quasi-parallel processes
without being very careful that the priorities which have been introduced really reflect actual properties of the system. Otherwise it
is better to know that the result is a probabilistic one. However,
I think that in general, the only safe thing that one can say is that
the result is undefined and that more information is to be given.

As a consequence, I think that in simulation languages one
should pose a problem of security, not only with respect to the
data structure and referencing but also a problem of security in
trying to be sure that whenever a set of things are scheduled for
the same time, these are things which can be effectively done simultaneously, because if one simply sequentializes them, it is
quite possible that the sequentialization process makes disappear
what in the system were actual incompatibilities.

Steel:

I think that this has been a very worthwhile contribution. If nothing else, it shows us what general purpose programming languages are not!

Laski:

When Caracciolo says that the result of a computation in a parallel process system is probabilistic, of course, he is right. The result will be different each time it is performed. The job of the sequencing commands in a language is to ensure that the part of the result that we are concerned with is the same each time. It seems to me that this is the problem of designing traffic rules for parallel programming languages. I propose a set of rules in my paper. The first group of these is concerned with starting and stopping processes, and are reasonably familiar. But there is a second group - the blocking group which is just precisely that which Caracciolo introduces. These give one the facility to make demands on the integrity of data so that data that one wants to work on oneself cannot be fouled up by any other parallel process.

I now want to quote two lines from my paper - "These commands can easily jam solid all processes in the machine - the user is warned" and if anybody can tell me how to solve that problem, I will be extremely grateful and so perhaps will the users.

Caracciolo:

In my reply to Laski; I do not maintain that the solution is necessarily probabilistic, but this is a possibility which one must not rule out, and I believe that one has actually to have recourse to a probabilistic solution. In general, I say that a complete theory should consider both cases.

The point is that additional information must be given depending upon the particular system one is considering.

Laski:

I think this is the essential difference between quasi-parallel and parallel.

Ross:

I think that for the linguistic processing or model building aspect of these systems, I believe - the ordinary kind of sequencing is sufficient for the processing of the language itself and the construction of the model itself. Now when you turn over control to the model then you may need these unusual sequencing schemes.

Nygaard:

There is one thing which is much more basic and this is the process concept, where you have something which develops and you can leave it and you can transfer control to other objects or processes.

Ross:

Up to the point where you turn control over to the execution of the language being defined, in SIMULA, let us say, ordinary sequencing is adequate - is this correct?

Dahl:

If the question is "Can a SIMULA program be compiled by a compiler which is itself written in ALGOL" - the answer is yes. Of course, because you can do whatever you want in ALGOL and you can do whatever you want in machine language. Now another thing is that many compilers have been using the co-routine concept - very fruitfully. The concept of passes in a compiler is a very fruitful way of structuring for your own purpose in your mind the job that you are doing though it was originally devised as a means of utilizing a computer with a small core store. So then you are using the quasi-parallel sequencing mechanism at compile time but are you really concerned with that? Does it matter?

Ross:

I think of co-routines and passes as being differently sugared - maybe it is not syntactic sugar - but differently sugared forms of natural processing. Not in the sense of Caracciolo's discussion of truly parallel or truly quasi-parallel or whatever processing.

Dahl:

Let me state again that quasi-parallel programming is a concept that has been defined just for the purpose of the programmer. It has nothing to do with the machine. The machine cannot do anything more or less whether you choose to think in terms of quasi-parellel programming.

Garwick:

My remark was occasioned by Nygaard's question "What should be taken out of SIMULA on order to turn it into a general purpose language". I did not answer this at first because I thought it required quite a little thinking. I believe that I have now done this and

of course my remarks apply to SIMULA and to any language. The
essential thing is not what is going to be taken away but what are
you going to add. You must add the ability to generate new features.
You must add accessibility to the elements of your language. When
you have done that you remove from your language everything which
now can be created within the language and then you have approached
a general purpose language.

Strachey:

I just wanted to say something about languages which have actual
and not virtual parallel operations built into them. There are some
languages, of which I am afraid CPL is one, in which there are parallel assignments - where you can say "$x,y := y,x$" for example
and this means that the assignment is considered as being genuinely
simultaneous. Now, I do not know whether this is a new concept or
not but clearly you can translate it into sequences of operation so
long as you sort out very clearly what you mean to do.

Krasnow:

It is very clear that the sequencing mechanism taking place here
leaves a good deal to be desired. First of all, I was motivated initially to respond to a comment that Dahl made - quite a while ago -
concerning his desire not to include a "wait" statement in a language. Now, I feel that this is intimately related to the discussion
which is currently taking place and I would like to try to discuss it
briefly in that concept.

First there is a consideration in line with the comment that
Ross made - is it necessary to have quasi-parellel concepts in a
general purpose language? I think the answer would have to be
- when the question is phrased that way - obviously not. The questions that we have to ask are not, whether given features are necessary, but whether they are useful and how generally useful are
they? It is certainly my opinion that when we get to the essence of
this question of quasi-parallel programming, that this is a very
generally useful capability and that it does distinguish what we
have referred to as simulation languages from what we have generally referred to in the past as general purpose languages, simply as a feature that has been included in the one which has not yet
been included in the other. As far as an explication of what do we
mean by quasi-parallel, I think it has been explained very well by
many people here including Laski, Petrone and Caracciolo. In that
context, I would like to address myself to the "wait" statement.
One of the notions that characterizes quasi-parallelism is the existence in real time of processes. They are no longer simply exe-

cutions of sub-routines or procedures from which we immediately
return in a standard way but they continue to have existence while
we do other things. The question then that is forced on us is the
question of sequencing. Now, specific sequencing algorithms are
a separate consideration. We could invent sequencing algorithms
from now until a decade from now and they will be of greater or
less futility in particular instances. However, I think what characterizes the sequencing algorithm is somehow or other the ability
to synchronize processes on the state of the system. In the case of
the particular sequencing algorithm present in SIMULA, one is
constrained to a particular state variable, namely the simulated
clock and one maps all of ones sequencing of these quasi-parallel
processes in terms of a single variable.

Now, this is a practical way to proceed and one can proceed
quite freely and quite far in that direction. However, in modelling,
it is frequently helpful to say what process is waiting for what condition. There may be many processes waiting for many conditions
in certain complex situations and, in effect, a network of relationships is built up in a dynamic way.

I feel that to implement this network, some form of a "conditional wait" is necessary. This raises questions of efficiency of
implementation as a subsidiary question which must be addressed.
It also raises questions of protection or security. In this sense,
that the user can get into a lot of trouble using these features, particularly if he does not know what happens in certain circumstances.

But this is true of many useful features. In programming languages, they make it possible for users to get into trouble if they
do not know what happens, and I feel that both of these objections
can be overcome and must be overcome in order to make an effective use of quasi-parallel programming. This is one of the problems that we are confronted with.

Petrone:

I would like to mention here a very similar situation which occurred in the theory of automata. There, in order to prove theorems,
some people introduced the notion of a non-deterministic automaton and a non-deterministic automaton has nothing to do with a probabilistic automaton. If it is an automaton in which the next state
is not definite but is one out of a certain set, then this notion of
"non-deterministic automaton" has something to do with parallel
processing. Those mathematicians also demonstrated that a non-
deterministic automaton is no more powerful than a deterministic
one. They introduced it only for the purpose of more easily demonstrated theorems.

So, why should we not do the same? There is also another concept connected here and it is that of non-deterministic algorithms
which could be introduced in the same way as non-deterministic
automatons. We could introduce those non-deterministic algorithms
in order to define in a shortened way a combinational problem. One
simple example is that of an algorithm which could be very easily
defined in terms of a non-deterministic algorithm and then, after
the definition, you could let a standardized sequentialism algorithm
do the work for you of reducing the non-deterministic algorithm into a deterministic one. In fact, in my opinion the non-deterministic
algorithms can be set in motion as quasi-parallel processing.

Caracciolo:

I am concerned about the ALGOL X definition of parallel processes. Well, as far as I could understand, I believe that the actual
position which has been taken in ALGOL 67 is quite correct because
parallel processes are then defined as "sequentialisable" in any
order; they use another word which is "merging" in any order. I
think it is more or less the same concept and I think that this position is correct in as much as if one defines a set of parallel processes to run together - if they terminate the result is undefined
and this is what I mean by indeterministic. Indeterministic is what
in the ALGOL report is considered something really undefined.
This is quite different concept from the concept of indeterministic
automaton as used in automaton theory.

Dahl:

I should like to return to the "wait until" statement. There are
several difficult aspects about this. I am surprised that Krasnow
mentions the word "security" as he did because I feel that there is
indeed an element of security in this and in fact, I feel that if properly implemented, the "wait until" statements might provide security.

I am speaking now out of experience: I have been in trouble with
debugging one model that I can recall which contained much interaction between processes. The difficult thing that happened was that
the model just stopped working - one process after another just
died down. Now, this is not exactly the same of course but it is a
kind of situation which is quite difficult to handle. The trouble is
you cannot easily put your finger on the original cause. So this is
one of the rather nasty aspects. Whereas a "wait until" which is
fully implemented would enable me to be secure in the respect
that the process would indeed continue when it should. Of course,
what had happened in my model was that I had forgotten to include

one essential "activate" statement. The other nasty thing is already mentioned: the necessity of having a transparent and easy to understand sequencing algorithm. A third problem is that of efficiency. I am concerned with efficiency; that rather special kind of efficiency which concerns the exponent P in my working hypothesis of the execution time of a model.

It seems to be the case that practical simulation models will fill the available space. The more space you have, the more interesting models you can make, the more phenomena you can put into your computer and the more valid results you can get.

Now I think we can see a trend that computers become larger and larger but they cannot become, to the same extent, faster and faster.

And now if you have a model whose execution time is proportional to say n^4 - then there is a certain limit which you cannot exceed, possibly because of the time limit. Suppose, I say; well, I will just have to buy a better computer - a faster computer. Perhaps you buy a computer which is twice as fast, but also it will be twice as big and so you can solve a problem which is twice as big, which means that it will take eight times as long to execute on the better computer.

Now the sad thing about the "wait until" as I see it is that it involves a number of operations which are, or may be, proportional to the size of the model. Each instance of the statement will take an amount of time which is proportional to n and this I think tends to raise the power in my execution time formula. I have a very strong feeling that programs or models based on "wait until" statements will tend perhaps to run very much slower.

Steel:

I think Krasnow should be allowed to defend himself.

Krasnow:

I would just like to establish one point. As I interpret your remarks, you are not objecting to the "wait until" statement on the grounds of its utility - you are objecting to it solely on the grounds that you do not at this point see an effective implementation of it, which means I would assume that you do not consider the implementations that were suggested this morning by McNeley or Blunden as adequately potentially efficient.

McNealey's methods of monitoring store and fetch operations is effectively a mechanism for implementing a "wait until" capability. Blunden expressed the idea that one does not necessarily have a completely general "wait until" any arbitrary complex condition,

but perhaps a specialized implementation which waits on a changed
state situation, which can perhaps be controlled in implementation.

Dahl:

I can see no objection to these suggestions of course. What I
am very afraid of is a mechanism that would, whenever you have
made an assignment to some variable, go through a list of n processes, testing one condition for each of them, which is probably
false.

Krasnow:

But this is an implementation - not a conception.

Garwick:

I think that this discussion on the complexities of sequencing is
a very strong argument in favour of not having simulation languages
but general purpose languages. It proves that the two names for
this panel are well chosen. It is clear that the only way to gain experience with sequencing rules and to change them at will is to describe the sequencing rule in a program and not have it as a built
in feature in your language.
A short remark to Dahl's other remark about increasing the
size of computers ... I agree absolutely - it is a well known theorem that on any computer the biggest problem fills the store and
runs for 20 hours.

Laski:

In my paper I have shown how the "wait until" can in general be
interpreted in terms of the "wait" even if it includes further complications which I believe to be relevant to dispatching. This extra
facility is not a necessity - it is a convenience but as a convenience,
it is far better programmed by the experts than by the inexperienced. It is wanted by the users and we must not only give it to the
users in a way they can make use of, but in a way that will be as efficient as possible in terms of what their actual needs are and we
must express thoroughly clearly how we are doing it for them.
That is - the "wait until" is convenient - it is an augmentation, not
an extension, providing you have the necessary basic set of instructions.

Ross:

I owe the chairman an apology for not stating my question in the first place clearly enough so that it did not trigger as much confusion. The remark of Strachey's on parallel assignments, also Caracciolo's reference to the ALGOL 67 forms are things which I would include along with the co-routines as so called normal sequencing. To me there is a difference between sequence, independence and parallel. If something is parallel, then I believe it means that the components do in fact go side by side with respect to real time and I think of all these other sequence independent devices as highly suitable for putting into the processor. In 1958 or 59 or 60, or whenever it was that McCarthey first started working on list systems, I heard in passing that they were working on list processing and being naive enough to think that that meant they were actually processing lists, we started working on a thing, which never even got documented within the project properly. This was, in fact, a list processor that processed lists simultaneously in parallel, and we could not possibly have had that language, which even required a two-dimensional notation in order to write it down, in any form of implementation without this true parallel, i.e. side by sideness included in the actual implementation of the language, so I think there is a distinction.

Hutchinson:

On the sequencing business, I submit again the fact that the suspense mechanism seems to work - I am not sure how efficient it is in comparison with anything else because I have nothing else to compare it with. It does work as near as we can tell. As for blocking of systems, I have some experience with two different simulators in which we are sharing resources. The method that we finally arrived at was just making darn sure that we never put in jobs with requirements such that they could require more than the system could deliver.

Secondly, I think that if your allocation scheme is such that you can block, then I think you had better reorganize and reprogram it or rethink your process through because you have got a real problem on your hands. Finally, as far as data goes, I think there are many circumstances under which your data is based as another resource which you can handle just as you handled the other resources in the system.

Nygaard:

Well now, Garwick wishes to resort to the sequencing rules in order to find the simulation languages. However, with his definition of the general purpose language - it is a rather drastic thing he proposes. If we follow his definition in his previous remark we

are left with something extremely basic which puts a great burden
on the programmer, whereas we want to provide something which
is useful for people who are wanting to model complex systems.
Between Krasnow and us there is no disagreement that we need a
sequencing scheme available in which events are ranked according
to time. We need, therefore, a sequencing set. We agree on the
usefulness of having a process concept. We agree on the necessity
and desirability on having the ability to create flexibility in this
scheme and our disagreement is now about this "wait until" statement and the consequences. I must say that I am not afraid of the
statement "wait until something" where this "something" is not
something defined as a special feature. Another reason why I have
a tendency to approve of this is because of the situation where you
want to work on this system and gradually transform it into something interacting with the real world. Then, the "wait until something"
very often will become "wait until interrupt", and you should have
the same mode of expression in the two modes of operation.

Garwick:

It seems that you all insist upon misunderstanding me; packages
are to be provided by expert programmers to be used by the inexperienced.

Gaskill:

I wanted to comment on the general question of General Purpose Languages versus Special Purpose Languages with specific
regard to industrial users.

We have some peculiar problems with regard first of all to education. I just want to say that industrial users are faced with an
education problem. No matter how good a job is done in Universities, the people who learn programming in Universities cannot immediately put this programming to use because they do not have
sufficient engineering experience. Those with engineering experience do not know the latest programming techniques. Also those
with engineering experience generally are somewhat set in their
ways and we cannot use the same teaching methods as are used in
Universities. We have to use a sort of sub-liminal brainwashing
technique.

As of a few years ago the engineers did have some understanding of analogue techniques so we provided a continuous simulation
language for them which made the computer look like an analogue
computer. This was a highly restrictive language with a standard
input and output format. There was no dimensioning, no subscript-
ing capability. The engineers delighted in this and found that with

some ingenuity they could use the language for general purpose use and even in some cases for discrete system simulation. This was of course very awkward in some cases, but it was deemed less awkward than having to face the problem of dimensioning and formating. Of course, as the engineers became more familiar with the use of digital computers, and desired to simulate larger and more complex systems, they found that perhaps they could put up with some of the difficulties of FORTRAN and in effect they then graduated into FORTRAN.

My other remarks are with regard to conversion. During the past 2 years we have used IBM 7094, 7044, GE 625, CDC 3600 and CDC 6400. This has meant that our languages and programs have been in a continual state of conversion and I was interested to hear that one of our programs now running on the 6400 includes a simulation of the IBM 704 drums.

I would like to address a question simply to Garwick in order to cut down the discussion. I wonder whether this conversion problem is a strong argument in favour of a single language?

Garwick:

GPL was worked on while I was a temporary employee with CDC in Palo Alto and of course you cannot get a company like that to do that sort of work without some reason. You have always to produce a proposal for a project which will then be or not be accepted. One of the main points I brought forward as the reason for such a proposal would be that it would simplify these conversions. It is imaginable that you make pre-processors for the various languages which translate their syntax into GPL and then you only need one compiler for each computer. It was exactly the ease of breaking in new computers that was one of the main points in introducing really general purpose languages.

So I think the answer is definitely yes.

Strachey:

The answer is definitely no; I think that is pie in the sky. It would be very nice if this was the way things worked but it is not. A much more rational, much more achievable thing would be to standardize and say that we should only have one machine code. It is not in fact possible; the idea of UNCOL, the universal machine code or the universal language into which everything shall be and will be possible to be translated, assumes that we shall never think of any new ideas. It is not in fact practical. I think it is what everybody wants but we are not going to have it. It is a philosopher's stone.

Steel:

I feel I ought to have an opportunity to comment on this and
Strachey used a word that I had some responsibility for. UNCOL;
universal computer oriented language - I might point out that we
thought of it first before television got hold of it. The point behind
that was not the development of a programming language of the sort
that one can sensibly program in but rather as a device to be used
as an intermediate language. It turned out to be impractical and
Strachey is quite right. Nevertheless the attempt to try to develop
such a language turned out to be quite useful because we learned
a great deal about the process of translation and the basic concepts
involved.

Garwick:

The point here is that UNCOL being a computer oriented language has proved to be impossible. One must have a high enough
language to be accepted as common. I would still say there are definitely programming languages which cannot be translated into
GPL. For instance Wirth's "EULER" cannot be translated into it
but the majority of languages existing today can be.

Douglas:

I agree 100% with Strachey that there is no such thing as a universal language: There never will be and I hope that I shall be dead
anyway before it happens. I think, if we can go to the subjects we
are supposed to be discussing for a change, Strachey said earlier
that it was essential to have all the facilities of a general purpose
language in a special purpose language. This is a questionable remark so I ask myself - is this true? Thinking about it, if it is a
free standing language, that is to say it is independent of all other
aids, I think the answer must be unhesitatingly - yes it is true. For
the simple reason that somebody has to maintain and extend the language at some later stage, and if the language is to be maintained
and extended in itself, as it has to be, under those circumstances,
you have no choice but to write what is really a general purpose
language. If I can reply to something that was said earlier, my definition of a general purpose language as against a special purpose
is whether or not you can maintain and extend it in itself and indeed this seems to me to be the only difference. I find it almost
impossible to define any other that is meaningful.

Let us then go on to consider what remedies have been put forward for this. One seems to me to be that we accept it and we
write lots of special purpose languages. O.K.; this is a task which

is for a great many programmers for the next 25 years on a great many machines and good luck to you all. If, on the other hand, one looks at it from another point of view, the remedy which Garwick is offering us as I see it is a language which basically does the maintenance extension but has a certain number of facilities which allows one to do problem-oriented subsets. Strachey classed this as being near an impossibility and I think if I want to get around to a question to the panel, it is really this - what do they rate the probability of success of producing such a language, and when, because from a commercial point of view, these are the only two questions I am interested in?

And what sort of problem description language do we get to? I detect that there is no real unanimity in the panel on this. Lackner has spoken of a problem description language but we have heard no definition of exactly how deep this is supposed to go. Need it be a Turing Machine, and is it a Turing Machine? Can it in fact be a very simple set of parameters asked for from the analyst or does it in fact have to go much deeper than that? I have not heard any discussion of this and it bothers me because what interests me is saving the analysts time. Am I going to do it this way or do I have to go deep, and teach the analysts more?

And if we are going to teach them languages, I do not think language learning depends only on the difficulties of concepts. In fact I am not very frightened of teaching people difficult concepts. What I am frightened of is the appalling number of exceptions that arise and the complexities of error analysis and correction. This usually arises from lousy analysis of what the language is about, which is then built into the language. If FORTRAN has a fault, it is simply that it has such a frightful number of exceptions and so many difficulties in error analysis, and what is more we seem to be propagating it on a huge scale. What I would like to ask the panel is can this be stopped?

Steel:

In the interest of time, I will answer for two of the panellists an earlier question you asked, that is - what is the probability of success and when? Garwick would say that "I am one and I have already done it". I believe Strachey would say "the probability is zero and therefore the time is eternity".

Lackner:

I just want to say something very briefly about going into the languages a little bit, that would be used with the simulation scheme that I referred to. I say that it would be in the direction that you

mention of supplying suitable parameters; always the same parameters for the same things or archetypes. The underlying language
would be some general purpose language. Which one, I really do
not care much. Some people would rather use JOVIAL, others
would rather use FORTRAN, others would rather use GPL or CPL
or whatever it might be. In other cases they might prefer to use
machine language.

Laski:

Man never is but always to be blessed. More precisely - in
answer to a very real question raised by Douglas, I think that
given any well-defined area, and it is his job in the commercial
world to define these problem areas within a finite time, depending upon the complexity and generality of the problem area, there
will come to be a language for which the concepts are well understood and the syntax is clean and possibly even that somebody has
implemented. For complete generality I can only make another li-
terary quotation and remind him of the Foster short story - "The
machine stops".

I must introduce a new question, just to put it on the record.
We have spoken about sequencing actions of parallel programming.
It seems to me that there is a further question and that is the definition of retained data and the management of retained data which
is not handled in the so-called general purpose languages such as
ALGOL X or CPL. These are needed for a truly general purpose
language and these are needed in simulation languages and data
base management languages.

CONTINUOUS SYSTEM MODELING PROGRAMS
STATE-OF-THE-ART AND PROSPECTUS
FOR DEVELOPMENT

ROBERT D. BRENNAN
IBM Corporation, Los Gatos, California, USA

1. INTRODUCTION

The well-established position of simulation in 1967 might shock
the scientist of a hundred years ago who considered the use of models to be "an aberration of minds too feeble to think about abstractions without visual aids... a substitute for the available alternative
of taking the scientific theory 'straight', and who regarded models
as "disreputable understudies for mathematical formulas" [4]. Such
comparisons are still with us from time to time. There are those
who think of mechanisms as "disreputable understudies" for formulas, preferring to work with the laws of mass and force in their
pure form, and those who resort to theory only in desperation. And
then there are those working with discrete system simulation and
those with continuous system simulation. From our vantage point
in 1967, it seems clear that this last pair of opposites - and the
other pair of apparent rivals - are in fact partners in a common
effort, as we shall see.

Simulation as we know it is a widely used tool for investigating
phenomena ranging from information flow in business organizations
to the dynamic behavior of complex mechanical systems. The former have often been simulated as discrete processes on digital
computers through the use of such discrete system simulation programs as GPSS and SIMSCRIPT. By contrast, those continuous dynamic systems that are the usual concern of engineers and scientists have traditionally been modeled on analog computers.

The analog computer, the veteran of innumerable such studies,
has proved a convenient and flexible tool up to a point. But the analog user faces some irksome problems. He must always scale
his variables into reasonable voltage levels, and must tolerate the
operational difficulties inherent in analog circuitry. These limitations become more serious as the size, complexity, and accuracy
requirements of the problem increase. It is not surprising, there-

fore, that recent years have seen the development of special digital languages for the simulation of continuous systems.

The programs identified as "digital-analog simulators" account for much of this activity, with more than thirty separate programs being reported during the past ten years. Each has provided a complement of functional elements similar to those of the analog computer and a block-oriented language to specify their interconnection. These digital-analog simulators model the elements and organization of analog computers, and provide numerical routines that are equivalent to such standard analog elements as integrators, summers, multipliers, and function generators. They also provide the special-purpose devices commonly assembled from several analog elements, e.g., absolute value, square root, limiting, dead space, and time delay units. Just as the analog computer patchboard electrically links analog computing elements, the simulation language interconnects the numerical routines. Each successive program has sought to put increased digital computing power within the reach of the engineer and scientist. While the programs differ in details, there is a common approach - a block-oriented input language.

In early 1965, several programs appeared which initiated a distinct step beyond digital-analog simulators. This new class of programs, termed "continuous system simulators", retain the block modeling capability but add the power and convenience of algebraic and logical statements. The FORTRAN-like language they provide is designed for either parallel (non-procedural) or procedural programming.

This paper reviews these developments briefly, and then examines the present state of the art as exemplified in two of the most recent simulation languages, 1130 CSMP - a digital-analog simulator, and S/360 CSMP - a continuous system simulator. Selected examples in engineering illustrate the power, flexibility, and relative advantages of these two classes of simulation programs. Finally, we consider future possibilities in continuous system modeling, including the possibility of amalgamation with discrete system simulators, perhaps on the basis of a common language.

2. BRIEF HISTORICAL SURVEY

Recent advances in computer technology are making digital simulation an increasingly effective and economical technique for the study of dynamic continuous phenomena. As the digital-analog simulator programs are refined and the more powerful continuous system simulator programs emerge, simulation is being employed more extensively and more incisively as an engineering art. This section will attempt to present these developments within the over-all context of simulation to facilitate comparison with other techni-cal approaches. To that purpose, some definitions are appropriate. In its general sense, *simulation* means representing some aspects of the real world by numbers or symbols which may be more easily manipulated to facilitate their study. The three phases involved might be called *visualization, modeling,* and *solution.* The first phase involves the abstract decomposition of relevant aspects of the phenomenon under investigation into an interconnected set of unidirectional cause-effect or functional relationships. This means deciding specifically which aspects are relevant and selecting the major lines of cause and effect from the many possible lines of in-fluence. The modeling phase requires the development of an inter-connected assemblage of computer system functional operators in a model or representation of the abstract visualization. In the solu-tion phase, we implement the model on an appropriate computer system and manipulate the simulation to investigate the particular phenomenon of interest.

The dichotomy between discrete and continuous system simula-tion is first realized at the visualization phase. Some phenomena are more readily conceived as discrete rather than continuous sys-tems. Purchase orders, for example, are processed one by one, whereas the vibration of an aero-dynamic surface is more readily understood as continuous. This distinction is far from absolute, since the nature or purpose of the investigation is always to some extent the determining factor. We ask "What is it for?" or "What do you want it to do?" before we can decide how to simulate it. Where system statistics are of chief interest, the problem is most commonly solved with discrete models; for the study of transient response, continuous system models are most common. The model of a continuous system may be represented either *functionally* or *mathematically,* i.e., by interconnected functional block elements or by a set of equations and logical statements. Simulations formu-lated for analog computers require functional representation, as do the similarly structured digital-analog simulators. When a mathe-matical representation is already available, as is often the case, reformulating the model in functional terms is at best an extra step requiring considerable time and effort. If that step could be elimi-nated, the problem could be solved more economically by working directly from the mathematical representation. This was the chal-lenge accepted by the designers whose programs were the progeni-tors of the continuous system simulators.

When an analog computer is manipulated by an experienced user, it is highly versatile, and this responsiveness at the solution stage accounts largely for its early popularity. Although the modeling phase was burdened by the necessity to scale problem variables, and the solution phase complicated by operational difficulties with the electronic circuitry, the analog computer could, and often did, simulate continuous systems quite effectively. Encouraged by this degree of success, engineers began to pose more complex problems and expect more of simulations - more accuracy, flexibility, reliability, and repeatability.

The digital computer first became a serious contender in the simulation field in the early 1960's, with some decisive advances in computer equipment technology and in corresponding software. Faster arithmetic units and a growing assortment of input/output devices made digital computers more practical tools for an engineer, and digital simulation programs and languages were developed to facilitate communication between the engineer and the computer. The digital-analog simulator programs provide: (1) a complement of functional elements similar to, but usually more extensive than that of the conventional analog computer, and (2) a language to facilitate their interconnection. The details vary widely, of course, from the first reported program developed by Selfridge in 1955 to the latest, 1130 CSMP, developed by IBM in 1966. All, however, draw their inspiration and motivation from the popularity of the analog block diagram as a simple and convenient means for describing continuous systems. The practical advantages of modeling by means of the functional representation are not always apparent to those whose training is restricted to formal mathematics. For the engineer dealing with highly nonlinear, intercoupled systems, the block diagram technique - far from being a "disreputable" understudy - is an excellent means for visualizing system complexities.

Reading the evolution of digital simulation from some of the survey articles available [10,11,18], we see the pattern that, as might be expected, a small number of the programs introduced real innovations. These were recognized and adapted by the more astute designers of subsequent programs. Most programs did little more than adapt previous developments for special purposes. The following list includes those few programs notable for their wide-spread acceptance and use, or for their historic significance as milestones.

1955	SELFRIDGE (program unnamed)
1957	DEPI
1958	ASTRAL
1961	DYNASAR
1962	PARTNER
1963	DAS, MIDAS
1964	PACTOLUS, DES-1
1966	1130 CSMP

Details of many of these programs are available in the references listed in the bibliography (Appendix to this paper).

The early digital-analog simulator programs were modeled very closely on the elements available in the then-current analog computers, with both good and bad features included for the sake of compatibility. In some programs, the digital simulation language incorporated the amplifier gains and sign reversals, and the scale factors associated with servo resolvers. This feature provided a simple means for obtaining a "check solution" to initially verify a simulation; the simulation could then be varied extensively with the assurance of valid results. In some cases, a single simulation diagram sufficed for both approaches, analog and digital. For example, the ASTRAL program (developed in 1958) provided functional elements corresponding to the potentiometers, summers, integrators, servo and electronic multipliers, dividers, limiters, resolvers, function generators, and switches of the PACE analog computer.

The next substantial trend in program development was to eliminate those aspects peculiar to analog computer simulation. Digital floating-point hardware meant an end to the tedium of scaling, long accepted as an inescapable adjunct of simulation studies. The positive advantages of digital computation finally began to be incorporated within digital simulation programs. By 1964, programs routinely included sorting algorithms to automatically achieve parallelism, algorithms for implicit loops, and advanced integration formulas. Computer consoles and remote terminals permitted on-line interaction with the simulation; graphic output devices helped interpret the results.

One pivotal program was MIDAS, intended initially to check solutions to support an analog computer facility, but soon accepted as an alternative to analog simulation. Its block-oriented language was convenient and simple to use, and within a few months (in 1963) MIDAS was in use wherever an IBM 7090 was available. PACTOLUS, the next year, played a similar transition role, substituting digital simulation on the smaller IBM 1620 for conventional analog methods.

The cumulative effect of all these developments can be seen in the newest addition to the family of digital-analog simulators, the IBM 1130 Continuous System Modeling Program. In a subsequent section, this application program will be described "in action" to illustrate the way such programs work.

In mid-1964, it became evident to a number of digital simulation developers that a rapprochement between analog block modeling and conventional digital programming was both desirable and feasible. As a result of their labors, the new class of "continuous sys-

tem simulators" emerged in early 1965. The first of these, and
perhaps the most advanced conceptually, was DSL/90, based on
FORTRAN and developed within IBM for its own engineering laboratories. A second program, EASL, began at the level of assembly language operation codes. Uninhibited correspondence between
several groups of program developers provided a first forum on
the features desirable in the continuous system simulator. Surprisingly, a consensus was quickly reached and within months several programs then under development began to bear marked resemblances. MIMIC, which began as a second-generation version
of MIDAS, finally emerged as a continuous system simulator after
an informal series of debuts - each marking a new stage in its rapid transition. Additional stimulus was provided by the formation of
a (SCi) Committee on Simulation Software. Simulation Councils,
Incorporated, an AFIPS member, is a technical society devoted
to the field of simulation. This committee, representing both simulation users and program developers, provided further opportunity
for refinement of the language features.

There is of course no absolute division between digital-analog
simulators and continuous system simulators, but subjectively we
recognize the basis for this distinction. Without intending offense
by omission, we would suggest that the following programs which
have all achieved practical significance, are clearly members of
the more recently developed family.

> 1965   DSL/90, MIMIC, EASL
> 1966   DSL/40, BHSL
> 1967   S/360 CSMP

Later we will describe the most powerful of these, the IBM S/360
Continuous System Modeling Program, to illustrate the versatility
and naturalness of expression possible with such simulators.

3. DISCUSSION OF TECHNIQUES

In addition to the historic relationship between analog and digital
simulation, and the newly-called-for distinction between the digital-
analog and the continuous system simulator, there is another pair
to be compared and distinguished one from the other. The problems
of continuous systems have been solved for many years by means
of conventional digital programming employing FORTRAN or AL-
GOL, for instance. Continuous system simulation differs from that
approach in some ways which should be noted. To take the points
of similarity first, digital simulation programs are closely related

to the "general differential equations solver" programs popular some years ago, in that both provide automatic integration and data output. The major distinction of the digital simulation programs is that their problem input languages are essentially parallel or non-procedural, thus "fitting the facts" in a unique way. Time itself is continuous rather than discrete, and most phenomena of interest to engineers and scientists involve continuous interaction of variables. Numerical integration is but the first approximation to the representation of phenomena in the time continuum, an approximation imposed by the discrete nature of the digital computer. There is, however, but one ethereal clock and all nature marks time in parallel. If the sequential or serial nature of the digital computer is ignored, the second approximation may be imposed upon the solution of a system of differential equations. The sequence of computations in evaluation of the derivative vector is a matter of importance. In terms of the digital-analog simulators, the output of a functional block ought not to be computed until updated values for the input variables to that block are available. The computations must thus be sorted into an appropriate sequence if "phase lag" is to be avoided.

All but the most primitive digital simulation programs provide some automatic algorithm for sorting. Although parallelism is the essential feature of these digital simulation programs, there exists little literature on either the philosophy or the techniques of sorting except for the 1960 paper of Stein and Rose [138]. The complexities of this problem, particularly in view of the sophistication of the most recent continuous system simulators, demand more serious investigation.

The sorting algorithm (as well as the numerical integration itself) is complicated by the existence of several distinct types of functional elements. These might be classified as follows:

Instantaneous Functional Element. An element whose output depends only upon the present value of the input; e.g., a multiplier or limiter element.
History Function Element. An element whose output depends on both the present value of the input, and the past values of the input and the output; e.g., the hysteresis element.
Memory Functional Element. An element whose output depends only on past values of the input and output; e.g., an integrator or dead-time (transport delay) elements.
Source element. An element whose output is either a constant or depends solely upon the independent variable, time; e.g., a signal generator.

Sorting procedures treat instantaneous and history functional elements identically. Since the outputs of source and memory elements are known or computable at any instant, such elements provide a starting point in the sorting algorithms. The algorithm used in the MIDAS program, for example, starts at the constant and integrator outputs and in effect looks forward along the signal flow paths and asks, "What might be computed next?" until all the functional elements are finally sequenced. Unless the simulation configuration involves a logical inconsistency, this procedure is guaranteed of success. Failure indicates the presence of an algebraic or implicit loop, i.e., there is a closed pathway on the simulation diagram (a signal flow path doubles back upon itself without an intervening memory element).

Stein and Rose proposed an alternative algorithm which started at the integrator inputs and proceeded backwards along the signal flow paths until each path was finally terminated by a source or memory element. A final sequencing was obtained by eliminating redundant entries and inverting the order of the list so obtained. This "backward looking" method is somewhat easier to implement than the "forward looking" method; the configuration statements associated with each functional element identifies the input variables and the signal flow paths may be easily traversed.

Further research is also needed in regard to the integration algorithms within the simulation language. Numerical analysts have commonly compared different integration algorithms on the basis of the number of required evaluations of the derivative vector. An additional factor which ought to be considered is that the "push-down" tables of past values associated with memory and history elements should only be modified after valid time advances. For algorithms incorporating automatic integration step-size adjustment, this implies an additional evaluation of the derivative vector when it is finally appropriate to push down the tables. If frequent tabular or plotted output is required, this too should affect the choice of integration algorithm for a particular problem. The abrupt discontinuities common in simulation problems may invalidate the basic assumption of nth order fit upon which the integration algorithm is based. Unfortunately, the neophyte finds little guidance available in the choice of integration methods. The simulation program designer must therefore be particularly conscientious to ensure against both calamitous results and computational inefficiencies.

4. THE DIGITAL-ANALOG SIMULATOR APPROACH

The 1130 Continuous System Modeling Program, an adaptation of PACTOLUS, is a new digital-analog simulator specially developed for online experimentation by the design engineer. It operates on the IBM 1130 - a small, fast computer. 1130 CSMP, in combination with the computing power of the IBM 1130, has demonstrated itself to be an effective and economical tool for simulation studies across the breadth of engineering practice and the physical and biological sciences. It provides a library of 25 standard elements plus five "Special" elements that the user himself may define. Interaction with the program is simple and convenient via the console keyboard and the console entry switches. From the keyboard, or via punched cards, the user enters 1130 CSMP language statements defining the configuration and associated parameters. During entry, automatically typed instructions and diagnostics guide the user through the procedures. These tell him how to initiate data entry, how to select the variables for printer and plotter output, and how to specify the integration interval, total run time, and output intervals. He may interrupt a simulation run at will to modify or extend the simulation, and need not follow a rigid schedule.

We can see the operational flexibility of 1130 CSMP in a simple but representative example. For the motor-driven cable reel shown in fig. 1, the engineer must devise a controller to maintain a constant linear velocity in the cable as the reel unwinds. The angular velocity, $\dot\theta$, of the reel must therefore increase as the effective radius of the reel decreases. A tachometer senses the cable speed and converts the measurement to a corresponding voltage level.

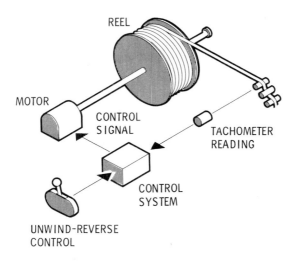

Fig. 1. Artist's Sketch of Cable Reel System.

The situation is further complicated by the fact that the moment of inertia of the reel is proportional to the fourth power of the effective radius and that both the torque motor and the tachometer have associated time lags. For this nonlinear phenomenon, ordinary analytic design techniques would be inadequate, and simulation is not only particularly appropriate, but perhaps the only workable method.

The system components may be described by a set of equations:

radius of reel
$$R_O = 4.0 \text{ ft (full reel)}$$
$$\dot{R} = -0.0008 \, \dot{\theta}$$
where θ is total rotation in radians
R (empty) = 2.0 ft

moment of inertia
$$I = 18.5 \, R^4 - 221.0$$

Tachometer Transfer Function

$$\frac{V_{measured}}{V_{actual}} = \frac{2.0}{s + 2.0}$$

Torque Motor Transfer Function

$$\frac{Torque}{Control\ Signal} = \frac{500.0}{s + 1.0}$$

Cable Speed

$$V_{actual} = R\dot{\theta}$$

Desired Cable Speed
50 ft/sec

Reel Acceleration
$$\ddot{\theta} = T/I$$

When all the pertinent data is assembled, the designer would proceed with 1130 CSMP by developing an appropriate simulation block diagram of a critical phase. In general, the user is guided by the complement of standard 1130 CSMP functional elements, minimizing insofar as is practical the programming of "Special" elements. The mechanics of the task should be subordinated to this question: Does this particular simulation implementation truly represent the phenomenon as the user visualizes it, keeping in mind the nature of the experiments he may wish to perform? For this cable reel design problem, the engineer would want to experiment with several control algorithms, observing the performance of each at cable start-up, braking, and reversal. In these respects, therefore, the simulation design should be as flexible as possible.

One possible simulation diagram for this problem is shown in fig. 2. Block numbers have been assigned in an arbitrary manner to emphasize that 1130 CSMP is a parallel or non-procedural language. Further, the corresponding configuration statements may appear in any order within the punched card deck, subject only to the restriction that the entire set of configuration statements must precede the set of parameter statements. Note that Block 43 is specified as "Special 3", an element specifically developed to provide convenient means for switching from cable unwind to braking or reversal. In the simple FORTRAN program which would be developed for such a purpose, two parameters would be associated with the new element - the first could be set to +50.0 (ft/sec) to signify that the reel should unwind, the second could be set to -50.0 to signify reversal. In such a situation, the output of the element can be switched from one value to the other by one of the console switches, the engineer can in effect "operate the controls" for the simulated system as he observes the plotted response during the runs.

Once the block diagram has been developed, the next step is to translate this description of the problem into the corresponding set of 1130 CSMP statements. A configuration statement must be prepared for each block on the diagram, with associated parameter and function generator statements as appropriate. Simple coding

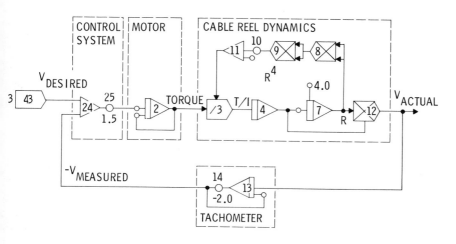

Fig. 2. 1130 CSMP Simulation Block Diagram for Cable Reel System.

forms can make this task relatively easy even for those unfamiliar with digital programming. For a simulation such as this cable reel problem, the designer could either prepare a deck of punched cards prior to using the program or could, with equal ease, enter the required statement directly via the console keyboard of the 1130. To do this, he would simply place blank cards in the Card Read Punch in lieu of a data deck, and enter the data from the keyboard, typing within the sets of parentheses provided for this purpose by the 1130 CSMP program.

Fig. 3 reproduces the first portion of the console printer record. Since a simple proportional control scheme should be sufficient for this cable reel system, the control signal is generated by a gain

```
                        CONFIGURATION SPECIFICATION

    OUTPUT NAME     BLOCK      TYPE     INPUT 1    INPUT 2    INPUT 3

    ERROR            24         +         43         14          0
    GAIN             25         G         24          0          0
    UNWIND - REWIND  43         3          0          0          0
                     13         I         12         14          0
    - V-MEASURED     14         G         13          0          0
    V-ACTUAL         12         X          4          7          0
    MOTOR TORQUE      2         I          0         25          2
    T / I             3         /          2         11          0
                      4         I          3          0          0
    RADIUS R          7         I          0          4          0
                      8         X          7          7          0
                      9         X          8          8          0
                     10         G          9          0          0
    MOMENT - INERTIA 11         0         10          0          0

                    INITIAL CONDITIONS AND PARAMETERS

    IC/PAR NAME     BLOCK     IC/PAR1        PAR2          PAR3

    UNWIND - REWIND  43       50.0000      -50.0000      0.0000
    MOTOR DYNAMICS    2        0.0000      500.0000     -1.0000
    REEL CONSTANTS    7        4.0000       -0.0008      0.0000
                     25        1.0000        0.0000      0.0000
    MOMENT - INERTIA 11     -221.0000        0.0000      0.0000
    TACHOMETER       13        0.0000        1.0000      0.0000
                     10       18.5000        0.0000      0.0000
                     14       -2.0000        0.0000      0.0000

    (     0.1) INTEGRATION INTERVAL

    (    30.0  ) TOTAL TIME

         5.0 ) PRINT INTERVAL
```

Fig. 3. Portion of Console Printer Output from 1130 CSMP Run.

element (Block 25) attached to the error signal from the summing junction (Block 24). If the resulting system performance proves to be too violent, the user might experiment with a more complex controller, perhaps inserting a limiter element to restrict the magnitude of the control signal applied to the motor. Fig. 4 shows the 1627 Plotter output from two runs in which the start-up transient was observed to get an initial "fix" on the gain setting of the controller. After reducing the gain, that is, the parameter associated with Block 25, the engineer proceeded with a longer series of runs in which he manipulated the appropriate console switch to test unwind and reversal of the cable throughout the operating range - first with the reel nearly full and then with it nearly empty.

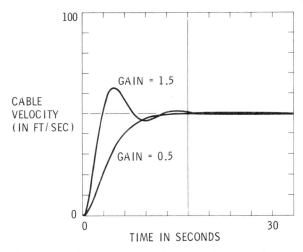

Fig. 4. 1627 Plotter Output for Cable Reel System Simulation
(Annotation Added).

5. THE CONTINUOUS SYSTEM SIMULATOR APPROACH

The S/360 Continuous System Modeling Program offers the best available illustration of what can now be done in continuous system simulation. This IBM program is an advanced version of DSL/90, the most powerful of previous efforts of this kind. S/360 CSMP incorporates a number of novel features: it can, for example, incorporate procedural coding within the definition of a macro element; it can conveniently calculate initial and terminal conditions (thus placing the entire simulation under programmed control). These new features provide the engineer a significantly more powerful and sophisticated tool for simulation. Working with a basic set of functional elements for modeling the components of continuous systems, the S/360 CSMP user specifies the interconnection of these functional elements by the (FORTRAN) equivalent of common mathematical notation for functional dependencies, namely, $Y = F(X)$. S/360 CSMP thus represents a rapprochement between analog block modeling and conventional digital programming. In addition to the block modeling capability shared with digital-analog simulators, this kind of program provides the power and convenience of algebraic and logical statements. Its FORTRAN-like language can be used as either a parallel (non-procedural) or as a procedural programming language.

We can see the possibilities of more sophisticated applications in a relatively simple example - the fin attached to a coolant tube to help dissipate heat by thermal radiation (see fig. 5). Such a device might be used to control the temperature of the power plant of a space station [67].

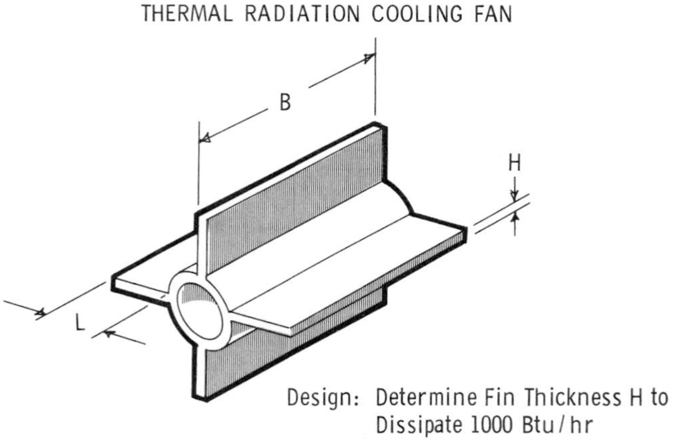

THERMAL RADIATION COOLING FAN

Design: Determine Fin Thickness H to
Dissipate 1000 Btu/hr

Fig. 5. Artist's Sketch of Cooling Fin.

The engineer might need to design the fin to dissipate 1000 Btu's per hour, for example, with constant temperature of 2000°R at the root end of the fin. If we assume a given metal and fixed surface roughness, the available design parameters are L, fin length, and H, the fin thickness. The steady-state heat flow within the fin at thermal equilibrium is described by the following equation:

$$d^2T/dX^2 = 2\sigma E(T^4 - T_s^4)/KH,$$

where

X = length from fin root
T = temperature in degrees R
T_S = temperature of surrounding space
σ = Stefan-Boltzmann constant
E = thermal emissivity
K = thermal conductivity
H = fin thickness

A basic design parameter is

$$H < 0.1 \text{ ft} ,$$

and these constants are involved:

$$T_S = 0^O\text{R}$$
$$E = 0.8$$
$$K = 25 \text{ Btu/hr/ft/}^O\text{R}$$
$$B = 0.5 \text{ ft}$$
$$L = 0.25 \text{ ft}$$

The boundary value conditions are as follows:

$$X = 0: \ T = 2000^O\text{R} , \qquad \frac{\mathrm{d}T}{\mathrm{d}X} = \frac{-1000 \text{ Btu/hr}}{\text{KBH}}$$

$$X = 0.25: \frac{\mathrm{d}T}{\mathrm{d}X} = 0$$

Note that the independent variable in these differential equations is X, the distance along the fin, rather than time, as when transient response is studied. Due to the RENAME feature of S/360 CSMP, the independent variable may be called X rather than time. This is no more than a convenience; it does not affect the computations.

Fig. 6 shows the set of input language statements which specify this simulation problem. Note that the data is separated into three segments by the control cards INIT, DYNAM, and TERMIN. The statements between INIT and DYNAM are performed at the beginning of each simulation run to compute initial conditions. The second segment (DYNAM to TERMIN) defines the dynamic portion of this simulation, corresponding to the differential equations. Computations between TERMIN and END are performed at the termination of each run.

Note that the simulation involves solving a two-point boundary

```
LABEL                    COOLING FIN DESIGN
 *
INIT
                     H    = 0.5* ( HIGH & LOW )
                     COEF = ( 2.*SIGMA*E ) / ( K*H )
                     DTDX0 = -Q0 / ( K*B*H )
       CONST          Q0   = 1000.,  T0 = 2000 ,  HIGH = 0.02,  LOW = 0., .
                     SIGMA = 0.173E-8, E = 0 8,       K = 25.0,     B = 0 5
 *
DYNAM
                     D2TDX2 = COEF * ( TEMP**4 )
                     DTDX   = INTGRL ( DTDX0, D2TDX2 )
                     T      = INTGRL ( T0, DTDX )
                     TEMP   = LIMIT ( 0.0, T0, T )
 *
TERMIN
                     RATIO = -( K*B*DTDX ) / Q0
         IF ( HIGH - LOW - 0.00001 ) 5, 5, 1
     1   IF ( RATIO ) 2, 5, 3
     2               HIGH = H
         GO TO 4
     3               LOW  = H
     4               KEEP = 2
     5   CONTINUE
TIMER               DELT = 0 0001,     FINTIM = 0.25
RENAME              TIME = X
END
  TIMER             OUTDEL = 0.01
  PRTPLT      TEMP (DTDX, D2TDX2)
END
STOP
```

Fig. 6. S/360 CSMP Statements for Cooling Fin Design Simulation.

value problem. The fin thickness must be so chosen that the rate of change of temperature at the end of the fin is effectively zero. The statements within the TERMIN segment affect a binary search algorithm which repeatedly adjusts fin thickness, H, until the constraint on the rate of change of temperature is finally satisfied. One additional simulation run is then performed to provide the printed and plotted output of the temperature distribution.

This simple example calls for only two types of S/360 CSMP functional elements, the integrator and the limiter. Typical problems would involve a larger assortment. S/360 CSMP labels facilitate entry of initial condition parameter values, and data associated with the integration, printing, and plotting. With but few ex-

ceptions, data input is entirely free format. Data and control statements may be entered in any order and may be intermixed with the
structure statements. Output options include printing of variables
in standard tabular format, print-plotting in graphic form, and preparation of a data set for user-prepared plotting programs. This
sampling of available features suggests the wide ranging usefulness
of this powerful new addition to the family of continuous system
simulators.

6. SUMMARY

The present status with respect to digital simulation of continuous systems might be summarized as follows:

Digital-Analog Simulators. This class of programs can be considered fully matured. The program design criteria appear to have
stabilized; reliable and effective programs are readily available
and supported by complete documentation and program maintenance. Whereas a "successful" early program might have had only
fifty users or so, the new programs will without doubt find acceptance with a much greater number, perhaps even several thousand
engineers and scientists.

Continuous System Simulators. The development phase of this
class of programs is now past and several polished programs are
available. These simulation languages, however, already embody
a number of sophisticated features for which application experience
has not yet accumulated. While such experience is building up, it
seems probable that there will be a moratorium on further developments in regard to language characteristics and features. Since the
differences between existing programs of this class are relatively
minor, the path for future work should be delineated quite clearly
as experience reinforces the strong points and exposes remaining
weaknesses in this approach.

In the opinion of the author, the next few years will see, in continuous system simulation, more extensive use of graphic devices
to facilitate data input during the modeling phase and data display
during the solution phase. Remote consoles operating within a time-
sharing environment will finally give the simulation user a tool
sophisticated enough to handle the highly complex problem, yet
flexible enough to be virtually a general purpose method. The im-
pending achievement of this objective will necessarily have a profound effect upon the day-to-day practice of engineering and many
of the allied sciences.

The possible conjunction of discrete and continuous system simulation within a single digital simulation language has been the topic of numerous informal discussions. Unfortunately these discus-

sions seldom go beyond the challenge of the theoretical possibility. Without doubt, the two types of simulation bear numerous resemblances, and within each type some programs are exclusively block-oriented and others are statement-oriented. With four possible combinations, we might design, for example, a continuous system simulator augmented by a subsidiary complement of discrete functional elements, or alternatively, a discrete system simulator augmented by functional elements common to the digital-analog simulator class. Indeed, such capabilities do exist in rudimentary form in some present simulation languages. The question then is not: Is the discrete/continuous combination possible? but rather: Would it be useful, practical, and economical? This can not be answered without extensive investigation to see how many application areas would actually be aided by the existence of such a composite simulation language. Are there significant simulation problems which cannot be adequately handled by existing languages?

For the individual user, learning a single simulation language would save time and expense though the apparent advantage would be lost if he had to learn twice as much material as he would for either of the two separate approaches.

Finally, one must consider the programming aspects of such a composite language. Are there indeed significant parallels, at the implementation level, between these two approaches? Or would such a merger simply result in programs requiring twice the amount of computer memory for storage? From the standpoint of program maintenance and documentation, would the composite program become unmanageable? Finally, could professionals in the two camps arrive at a meaningful consensus as regards language features? In the personal opinion of the author, it seems probable that the continuous and the discrete simulation approaches will develop side by side and amalgamation, if it occurs, is unlikely before the early 1970's. Within this expectation there is ample room for - and in fact need for - exploratory simulation programs of this sort, and continuing communication between users of discrete and continuous simulation programs. Such activities are fundamental to the continued development of simulation, promoting the professional maturity and objectivity which should be our primary goal. The question of amalgamation of simulation languages is only incidental to our understanding of the various techniques.

Recognizing the continuous as "the limit of the discrete" and the discrete as "a sampling of the continuous" [1], we can concentrate on devising solutions as ingenious as the problems are complex.

APPENDIX "A specialised bibliography of the continuous system
               field" (Editors note: these papers are also listed in the
               General Bibliography).

1955
Selfridge, R. G., "Coding a General-Purpose Digital Computer to
Operate as a Differential Analyzer", Proc. 1955 Western Joint
Computer~Conference (IRE).

1957
Kantorovich, L. V., "A Convenient Mathematical Symbolism for
Performing Computations with Computers", Doklady Akad. Nauk,
113:738-41, No. 4, April 1957.

Slayton, G. R., "DIDAS - A Digital Differential Analyzer Simulator",
Georgia Div., Lockheed Aircraft Corp., August 1957 (available in
SHARE library).

1958
Lesh, F., "Methods of Simulating a Differential Analyzer on a Digital Computer", J. of the ACM, Vol. 5, No. 3, 1958.

1959
Stein, M. L., Rose, J., and Parker, D. B., "A Compiler with an
Analog-Oriented Input Language", Proc. 1959 Western Joint Com-
puter Conference. Reprinted in SIMULATION, March 1965.

1960
Hurley, J. R., "DEPI 4 (Differential Equations Pseudo-Code Interpreter) - An Analog Computer Simulator for the IBM 704", internal
memorandum, Allis Chalmers Mfg. Co., 6 January 1960.

Paynter, H. M., "Computer Representations of Polyphase Alternating Current Systems for Dynamic Analysis and Control", Proceedings of First Internation Congress of I.F.A.C., Moscow, 1960.

Stein, M. L. and Rose, J., "Changing from Analog to Digital Programming by Digital Techniques", ACM Journal, Vol. 7, No. 1,
January 1960 pp. 10-23.

1961
Olaussen, Siving L. K., "Simulation of an Analogue Computer on the
Digital Computer 'FREDERIC', Programme Description", Norwegian Defense Research Establishment, Kjeller, Norway, November
1961.

Takata, Masaru, "The Programmed Digital Differential Analyzer", Information Processing in Japan, Vol. 1, 1961.

1962
Hurley, J. R., "Digital Simulation I: DYSAC, A Digitally Simulated Analog Computer", AIEE Summer General Meeting, Denver, Colorado, 17-22 June 1962.

Miyauchi, T., Takata, M., "Analysis of the Behavior of Salt-Metal Extraction Column for U-Bi Fuel", Chemical Engineering (Japan), Vol. 26, No. 9, 1962.

Stover, R. F., and Knudtson, H. A., "H-800 PARTNER - Proof of Analog Results Through a Numerical Equivalent Routine", Doc. No. U-ED 15002, Minneapolis-Honeywell Regulator Co., Aero. Divn., 30 April 1962.

1963
Byrne, E. R., "JANIS, A Program for a General-Purpose Digital Computer to Perform Analog Type Simulations", ACM Nat. Conf., Denver, Colorado, 27 August 1963.

Gaskill, R. A., Harris. J.W., and McKnight, A.L., "DAS - A Digital Analog Simulator", Proc. 1963 Spring Joint Computer Conference.

Hurley, J. R., and Skiles, J.J., "DYSAC - A Digitally Simulated Analog Computer", Proc. 1963 Spring Joint Computer Conference, AFIPS Conference Proc., Vol. 23, pp. 69.

Palevsky, M., and Howell, J. V., "DES-1", Fall 1963 Joint Computer Conference, Vol. 24, Spartan Books, Inc., Washington, D.C., 1963.

1964
Anonymous, "SDS DES-1", Scientific Data Systems Descriptive Brochure, No. 64-42-01C (1964).

Blechman, G.E., "An Enlarged Version of MIDAS", SIMULATION, October 1964.

Brennan, R.D., "PACTOLUS - A Simulation Language Which Makes a Digital Computer Feel Like an Analog Computer", SIMULATION, August 1964.

Brennan, R.D., and Linebarger, R.N., "A Survey of Digital Simulation: Digital Analog Simulator Programs", SIMULATION, December 1964, pp. 22-36.

Brennan, R. D., and Sano, H., "PACTOLUS - A Digital Analog Simulator Program for the IBM 1620", Proceedings, 1964 Fall Joint Computer Conference AFIPS, Vol. 26, pp. 299-312.

Cowley, Percy E. A., "An Active Filter for the Measurement of Process Dynamics", Proc. 19th Annual Conf. of ISA, New York, 12 October 1964.

Farris, G. J., and Burkhart, L. E., "DIAN - A System for Programming a Digital Computer in Terms of Analog Components", Dept. of Chemical Engineering, Iowa State Univ., Ames, Iowa, 1964.

Gaskill, R. A., "A Versatile Problem-Oriented Language for Engineers", IEEE Trans. on Electronic Computers, Vol. EC-13, No. 4, August 1964.

Harnett, R. T., Sansom, F. J., and Warshawsky, L. M., "MIDAS - An Analog Approach to Digital Computation, SIMULATION, September 1964.

Henry, J. W., "Some Numerical and Programming Techniques to Allow the Use of a Digital Computer in an Analogue Fashion", Fourth International Conference of AICA.

Hurley, J. R., Janoski, R. M., Rideout, V. C., Skiles, J. J., and Vebber, W. O., "Simulation of a Hybrid Computer on a Digital Computer", Fourth International Conference of AICA.

Linebarger, R. N., "Digital Simulation Techniques for Direct Digital Control Studies", Proc. 19th Annual Conf. of ISA, New York, 12 October 1964.

Peterson, Sansom, Harnett, and Warshawsky, "MIDAS - How It Works and How It is Worked", 1964 Fall Joint Computer Conference, AFIPS Conference Proc., Vol. 26, October 1964.

Strauss, J. C., and Gilbert, W. L., "SCADS, a Programming System for the Simulation of Combined Analog Digital Systems", 2nd Edition, Carnegie Institute of Technology (March 1964).

1965
Benyon, R. P., and Henry, W. J., "SIMTRAN in Australia", SIMULATION, September 1965.

Brennan, R. D., and Linebarger, R. N., "An Evaluation of Digital Analog Simulator Languages", Proceedings, IFIP Congress '65, Vol. 2, 14 May 1965, New York, New York.

Coleman, T. G., "A Time-Delay 'Special Element' for PACTOLUS", SIMULATION, November 1965.

Dahlin, E. B., and Linebarger, R. N., "Digital Simulation Applied to Paper Machine Dryer Studies, : Conference Paper, 6th ISA International Pulp and Paper Instrumentation Symposium, Green Bay, Wisconsin, 4-8 May 1965.

Durand, H. P., "DYNASAR Applications", Conference Paper, 1965 Joint Automatic Control Conference, Troy, New York.

Fahidy, T. Z., "Stability Analysis of the Numerical Solution of Partial Differential Equations via Digital Analog Simulation", SIMULATION, July 1965.

Fahidy, T. Z., "Regions of Asymptotic Stability of Dynamic Systems by the Combination of Lyapunov Techniques and Digital Simulation", SIMULATION, December 1965.

Gaskill, R.A., "Fact and Fallacy in Digital Simulation", SIMULATION, November 1965.

Kurek, N. B., "Use of the PACTOLUS Program for Simulation of Antenna Servos", SIMULATION, October 1965, pp. 365-368.

Lavi, A., and Reilley, G., "ANALOG ALGOL - A Programming Language for Hybrid Computation, 1965 JACC, Troy, New York.

Linebarger, R. N., and Brennan, R. D., "Digital Simulation for Control System Design", Instruments and Control System, Vol. 38, No. 10, October 1965.

Linebarger, R. N., and Brennan, R. D., "Digital Simulation for Bio-Medical System Studies", Proceedings, 18th Annual Conference on Engineering in Medicine and Biology, Philadelphia, Pennsylvania, 10-12 November 1965.

Lucke, V. H., "Analysis Methods Developed for the Dynamic Systems Analyzer", Conference Paper, 1965 Joint Automatic Control Conference, Troy, New York.

Matlock, J., "JANET, Digital Analog Simulation Program", IBM Program Information Department, PID #D320 and D3119.

Molinari, B. P., "SIMPLE - Simulation Problem Language for Engineers", The University of Western Australia, September 10, 1965.

Rideout, V. C., and Tavernini, L., "MADBLOC, A Program for Digital Simulation of a Hybrid Computer", SIMULATION, January 1965, pp. 21-24.

Sansom, F. J., and Petersen, H. E., "MIMIC - Digital Simulator Program", SESCA Internal Memo 65-12, Wright-Patterson Air Force Base, Ohio (May 1965).

Sashkin, L., and Schlesinger, S., "A Simulation Language and its Use with Analyst-Oriented Consoles", Aerospace Corp. Report, ATR-65 (59990)-5, San Bernardino, California (April 1965).

Watson, J. M., "DYNASAR Input/Output Concepts", Conference Paper, 1965 Joint Automatic Control Conference, Troy, New York.

1966
Brennan, R. D., and Fahidy, T. Z., "Digital Simulation", Instruments and Control Systems, Vol. 39, No. 3, March 1966.

Burgin, G. H., "MIDAS III - A Compiler Version of MIDAS", SIMULATION, March 1966.

Cowley, Percy E. A., "An Active Filter for the Measurement of Process Dynamics", ISA Trans., Vol. 5, issue 1, January 1966.

D'Hoop, H., Monterosso, R., "SAHYB - A Program for Simulation of Analog and Hybrid Computer", IEEE Transactions on Electronic Computer, June 1966.

Dineley, J. L., and Preece, C., "KALDAS, An Algorithmically Based Digital Simulation of Analogue Computation", The Computer Journal, Vol. 9, No. 2, August 1966.

Fahidy, T. Z., Perlmutter, D. D., "The Application of the MIDAS Digital Simulator of the Study of Kinetic Alternatives in a Chemical Reaction System", SIMULATION, March 1966.

Farris, G. J., and Burkhart, L. E., "The DIAN Digital Simulation Program", SIMULATION, May 1966.

Forbes, G. F., "An Engineering Simulator", Proceedings ACM 21st National Conference, August 1966.

Funk, J. E., and Miller, M. B., "SLASH-3" SRL-66-0007, Frank J. Seiler Research Lab., USAF Academy, Colorado, August 1966.

Hughes, F. M., and Brameller, A., "Digital Simulation of Analogue Methods", The Computer Journal, Vol. 9, No. 1, May 1966.

Linebarger, R. N., "DSL/90", SIMULATION, September 1966.

Malenge, J. P., "Calcul Analogique et Genie Chimique", Genie Chimique, Vol. 96, No. 1, July 1966.

Morris, S. M., and Schiesser, W. E., "Undergraduate Use of Digital Simulation", SIMULATION, August 1966.

Parkhill, S., "SIMTRAN II Programming Guide (Interim Version)", Tech Memo SAD, Weapons Research Establishment, Adelaide, South Australia, March 1966.

Schlesinger, S. I., and Sashkin, L., "EASL - A Digital Computer Language for 'Hands-On' Simulation", SIMULATION, February 1966.

Shah, M. J., James, C., and Duffin, J.M., "Simulation of an Ammonia Synthesis Reactor", 1966 Conference Proceedings, International Federation of Automatic Control, London.

Silberberg, Martin Y., "Using Digital Computers for Process Simulation", Chemical Engineering, 26 September 1966.

Smith, C. L., Jr., "All-Digital Simulation for Process Industries", ISA Journal, July 1966.

Smith, H. J., "Analysis of a Vibrating Heat Engine Using PACTO-LUS", SIMULATION, January 1966.

Strauss, J. C., "Basic Hytran Simulation Language - BHSL", Proceedings 1966 FJCC, Vol. 29, November 1966.

Syn, W. M., and Linebarger, R. N., "DSL/90 - A Digital Simulation Program for Continuous System Modeling", 1966 Spring Joint Computer Conference, April 26-28, 1966.

1967
Kurek, Nicholas B., "Digital Simulation of a Servo Tracking System", Electro-Technology, February 1967.

DISCUSSION

Lackner:

I think this a very interesting paper but a comment I would like to make is that I do not see the utility of the distinction between continuous simulation modeling and discrete simulation modeling. Harking back to GPSS, which was originated at Bell Laboratories by a group of engineers of whom Geoffrey Gordon was perhaps the most prominent; it was a block diagram language. It did not contemplate simply discrete or purely continuous systems and it attempted to grasp, and did so quite well, the notion of queues and stores. I think that GPSS had features of the sort that you are exemplifying in these several schemes presented today and I think that simulation languages of the future will have them as well. In other words I do not believe we ought to allow there to be two fields, one in continuous simulation modeling and the other discrete. I think that there are ideas in both that the others might well benefit from and thereby we might erase the distinction.

Brennan:

I think that thought was what motivated the organising committee in extending invitations to both schools. It has not been indicated in the past four days that the possibility is seriously considered, however. I think we have agreed to keep open minds on the subject but certainly the conversations of the last four days have indicated that the discrete people are going their separate way. We have made a sincere effort, first of all via the SIMULATION journal by broadening the scope to incorporate both continuous and discrete work. Our field has matured to the extent that we are no longer fighting so vehemently. The Simulation Council's Committee on Simulation Software have reached rather good agreement on the characteristics of the language they would like to see. If we were today to announce our willingness to marry up with the discrete field, I suspect there would be a great deal of blood-letting in this room when you people decided which one of your many languages to propose as the bride.

Steel pointed out yesterday that in two different studies, it has been found in both the digital and discrete simulation field that the users are typically not programmers. They are people who do not want to learn programming. They are the same kinds of people in both fields: they may simply have a slightly different class of problem.

Jones:

Why is there the distinction between the 1130 system and the 360 system? In the 1130 the user is oriented towards block notation and then he transcribes this into equations, whereas in the 360 he starts right out in the equations. Why not dispense with the block notation? On the other hand maybe this has certain meaning for the class of users that you are talking about. If so then why not have another 360 version?

Brennan:

The decision to make both of these programs was done simply on the basis of user needs and user demands. There are some people who want a block language and perhaps do not even want FORTRAN within it. It might confuse them. They do want the interactive capability; both PACTOLUS and DSL 90 had had singular success and so we made both programs in response to the clearly expressed desires of the users. I think we felt that when we were making a program for the 360 it should not merely be a block oriented language,

a digital analogue language. Conversely to try to put such sophistication into a small machine would have been very very difficult. It
takes a 360 with 128 K words of core and we worked very hard to fit
it into so small a machine.

Steel:

Listening to the presentation I was struck by the thought that
perhaps if one limited the designers of these languages to engineers
under the age of thirty, they might simply pick FORTRAN instead.
The tradition of engineering education is changing somewhat and
perhaps the orientation to the block diagram may change things as
time goes on.

Brennan:

I tried to indicate in the paper that I felt that the digital analogue
simulation field has reached its culmination. I would be surprised
if serious attempts are made to make further languages here. I see
them popping up in the literature from time to time, but generally
it is due to an immediate need; some chap has a computer of which
there are only a few and no available programs and he makes it for
his personal use, but I would doubt that that field goes much further.
The continuous systems modelling programs do in effect provide
FORTRAN in both the parallel and the procedural sense. The block
notation is really exactly equivalent to the FORTRAN function statement, and hence we are going very close to FORTRAN. One of the
most interesting statements to come from the Simulation Council
committee was a hope that we would not simply be reinventing
FORTRAN; we feel we have not reinvented it but augmented it, in
a way that is meaningful to this particular field. But the parallels
are quite obvious.

DYNAMO II

Alexander L. PUGH III

School of Industrial Management, Massachusetts Institute of Technology,
Cambridge, Massachusetts, USA

1. INTRODUCTION

DYNAMO is a programming system to translate and run continuous models. It is in the compile and go format, checking and translating the model into machine language, running the model, tabulating and plotting the results, and running the model with parameter changes should that be desired. The machine code is never saved; the user works exclusively in the source language and does not need to know anything about any other language. While failure to save the compiled code may appear to be a waste of computer time, the high speed of the DYNAMO compiler plus the saving of the time normally spent by a relocatable loader completely justifies this mode of operation.

2. NOTATIONAL SCHEME

DYNAMO was developed by the industrial dynamics group at the Massachusetts Institute of Technology * to simulate models of industrial, economic and sociological systems. As many users are unfamiliar with analogue computers and have limited experience with differential equations, the notational scheme is patterned after the actual computational method that is used to calculate the results. Thus, a user who lacks confidence in what the computer is doing with his model is able to check his output by hand calculating several time steps without reference either to manuals or to unfamiliar mathematics. Once having gained confidence that DYNAMO does exactly what it says it will do, the user is able to proceed with DYNAMO acting as a tool rather than a mysterious black box.

Consequently, the notational scheme reflects a difference equation approximation to a set of differential equations. Variables are followed by a time subscript reflecting the time for which they are

---

* The development of DYNAMO I was supported by a Ford Foundation grant and the M.I.T. Computation Center. DYNAMO II's development has been supported in part by Project MAC at M.I.T.

being calculated or were calculated. The current time is considered time K and the previous time step is time J. An equation which is an integral has the form

$$L.K = L.J + (DT)(\text{IN}.J - \text{OUT}.J).$$

Such equations (and the variables they determine) are called levels. As can be seen levels are computed for time K from variables at time J. One other type of equation is needed - the auxiliary which relates a variable at time K to other variables at time K. Obviously, auxiliaries must be carefully ordered so that all the variables on the right of the equal sign are computed prior to the computation of the present auxiliary. If such reordering is impossible the model is rejected; simultaneous equations are not permitted. A typical auxiliary equation is

$$A1.K = A2.K / L.K$$

When reordering is possible it is done automatically. In fact, there are no requirements on the order of the equations. The user organizes the model in whichever manner is best for him. For additional details on DYNAMO I, see [119].

Implicit in the above notational scheme is a very simple integration formula - rectangular integration. This was chosen for two reasons. (1) It is simpler to understand for the individual who is unfamiliar with the various problems of integration formulae, and (2) if one is not seeking high accuracy there is little if anything to be gained by the use of the more sophisticated formulae. In much of the work for which DYNAMO has been used the coefficients are not known within a factor of 2, let alone to 1 or 2 percent.

A complete model consists of levels and auxiliary equations, constants, initial values for the levels, and print and plot requests. One of the unique features of DYNAMO is that the initial values may be stated in terms of auxiliaries for which no initial value has been given. In such cases DYNAMO uses the auxiliary equation as an initial value equation. This in turn may cause DYNAMO to use still other auxiliary equations as initial value equations. The process continues until either an initial value can be computed or a set of simultaneous equations is detected. As the former condition is generally the case, this feature greatly simplifies initializing a model.

DYNAMO has been in use for eight years, during which time users have found it very easy to learn and to use. In fact, it is unnecessary to spend any classroom time teaching the use of DYNAMO even to individuals with no computer experience. One of the reasons for the ease of use is the fact that the checking is thorough and the error messages are in terms the user can understand.

The only errors that are totally undetected by the compiler are of the type of the wrong sign before a variable or a wrong variable used in an equation. Thus, while the output may not be what the user is hoping for, he can easily relate the output to the input. Consequently, the user does not have to become familiar with sophisticated debugging aids.

3. DYNAMO II

Following a major revision in 1959, DYNAMO I has existed with very few changes from that time to now. It was modified for the 7090 and several years ago it was made available on the time sharing system at M.I.T. It has also been modified for the 7040 but none of these changes have been major. With the latest generation of computers it was no longer possible to make minor changes in the machine language source for DYNAMO and have it continue to operate. Consequently, a major rewrite was started about one year ago. As these circumstances are ideal for reconsidering the whole method of compilation, two major changes were considered advisable. (1) Permit any valid algebraic statement rather than restrict the user to a limited set of algebraic expressions as he was in DYNAMO I. DYNAMO I permitted any algebraic expression, but if it did not conform to one of the subsets the expression had to be subdivided into ones that were available by defining intermediate variables. While most of the frequently used expressions were available the principal shortcoming of the rigid structure was that users made more errors than they would if any algebraic expressions were permissible. (2) A wholly different philosophy towards errors was decided upon. In DYNAMI I if an error was detected there was almost no effort made to recover and continue. The first error within any equation stopped the scan of that equation. Thus, the users were occasionally forced to submit a model two or three times before all errors were detected and corrected. In DYNAMO II some sort of recovery is made from every error and at least checking continues. In most instances the model is actually run. Thus the user is able to get a working model with much less elapsed time. While this feature is less important in a time sharing environment, those of us who must continue to use batch processing will be very pleased with this new feature.

Another feature of new DYNAMO is permitting the user to define his own functions. The functions will be defined in the DYNAMO language, thus precluding any features not already built into DYNAMO, but this does permit the user to devise a functional shorthand for any frequently used expression.

DYNAMO II is being written in AED-O, a dialect of ALGOL that is being developed at M.I.T. AED had been designed with compiler writing in mind. In fact, AED itself is written in AED. Thus, most of the shortcomings of other languages as compiler writing languages have been overcome. Early evidence is that the new compiler is almost as fast as the old one and the creation of the compiler has been vastly simplified by writing it in a higher language. At the time of writing the new DYNAMO is actually in operation on the 7094. As AED will be implemented on a number of the new generation of computers, the conversion of DYNAMO to these machines should be relatively simple. Conversion to the IBM S/360 and the GE 645 are a minimum.

The preceding has been a brief description of the DYNAMO simulation program. It described the ease of learning and using DYNAMO I and how DYNAMO II will be even easier to comprehend and to employ.

DISCUSSION

Krasnow:

DYNAMO was developed initially in the late 1950's at which time none of the continuous simulation systems that Brennan discussed were in existence or were widely known. The motivation in creating DYNAMO at that time was twofold. First, there was simply the desire to orient towards, as Jones noted, the business community as opposed to the engineering community. This meant converting some straightforward engineering and mathematical concepts into a simplified form. The second motivation is the motivation which I think underlies much of the work that Brennan described, and that was simply that analogue computers were felt to be inadequate for the type of problems which were being addressed, or which Forrester wanted to address. So he felt the need to do essentially the sort of work that he would have liked to have done on an analogue computer, on a digital machine. And this lead to the creation of DYNAMO.

With the intervening history and with the widespread acceptance which the continuous system simulators seem to be enjoying, there seems in my mind to be some question now as to whether or not DYNAMO represents a really useful contribution, other than the fact that it is directed at a different community of users.

Jones:

I think that last phrase is the key, and I think that is what the DYNAMO people would say. Indeed this is a special case of a continuous system modelling program, and it is especially tailored for one type of user. The notation is very simple and the writing of the models in DYNAMO is really quite straightforward.

Gaskill:

I have a question regarding the graphical output. I judge from what you said that the graphical output would normally require about ten times as long as the execution time. This makes me wonder whether you are essentially restricted to off-line output.

Jones:

In the time-sharing system the standard complete print file is developed on the disk and then is printed off about two or three hours later. The user has the ability to use special commands in the time-sharing version of DYNAMO to inspect portions of this file; to look at every 10th line, for example.

I have not used this, I really do not know how well it works but I gather that it is suitable, at least in the early stages when you just want to find out if your output is going completely off scale. That is normally the way you find out that there is an error in your program.

Caracciolo:

It seems to me that DYNAMO has a somewhat different approach from other continuous simulation languages, in that it is based on differential equations in some form. The other systems, which are described before, make the transformation to the integral representation of the equations. This is perhaps something which justifies its easier use for certain unexperienced people.

COSMO

COMPARTMENTAL SYSTEM MODELLING
DESCRIPTION OF A PROGRAMMING SYSTEM

EVZEN KINDLER

*Biophysical Institue of the Faculty of General Medicine,
Charles University, Prague, Czechoslovakia*

1. INTRODUCTION

The system COSMO (Compartmental System Modelling) has been developed at the Biophysical Institute of the Faculty of General Medicine, Charles University, Prague (Czechoslovakia). Its original purpose was to model transport of substance in living organisms, completed by tracer's flow. Some specialists have expressed their opinion that it could be applicable also in other branches, e.g. in the sociology and even in the branches which do not investigate the transport of substance (see the examples in the last chapter).

In the biophysics, the compartmental systems are commonly used as abstract systems where the substantial properties of real systems are mapped and studied by the exact methods. The compartmental system consists of a finite number of compartments. For every compartment the following information is necessary and sufficient:

1. the volume of contained substance,
2. the measure of the entering substance, from other compartments,
3. measure of leaving substance.

All the values can depend on the time and moreover on the other values concerning any compartment (it maps the case of control in the system - in biophysics e. g. nervous, hormonal).

All compartments are considered as homogeneous, i.e. the substance which enters into a compartment is supposed to be immediately mixed with the substance which has remained in the compartment.

We can model the flow of a tracer; this word has been used accordingly to its original semantics in the place of its developing. Originally, the "tracer" has meant a substance which flows with the other substance but which can be detected and measured by

proper methods (e.g. radioactive substance). After having neglected
its original destination, we can consider the tracer as any valuation
of the transported substance. The only demand is that the own decrease or increase of this valuation (not caused by the transport and
mixing) must be proportional to the size of this valuation (this demand has been satisfied by the fission of radioactive substance but
also by some expressions used in the calculus of interest etc: in the
last case, the semantics of the "tracer" has nothing in common
with tracing methods).

As far as the programs and the expressions are concerned, we
have decided to permit only very simple programming means: an
expression can have at most two variables (or constants) joined by
an arithmetic operator; a program is a sequence of statements similarly simple: at the most three-address assignments, standard
procedures, input, branching. We have decided on this simplification in order to make the system COSMO acceptable for any center
while we can assume that the mentioned features are built into programming systems of any center. In practical use, the mentioned
features seem to be sufficient.

The numerical method used in the compiled programs is very
simple: the terms of the modelled system are interpreted as addresses the contents of which are modified in every step due to the
declarations of the compartments. Naturally, this method is not a
fine one regarding to the differential equations which can describe
the modelled system: but it is suitable for the investigation of objects of the physical and biological universe where no compartmental systems exist: compartmental systems are abstractions influenced by classical mathematics and, if we use them, we cause inaccuracy against the nature (this inaccuracy has been admitted because before the use of computers there has been no other means
for solving the given problems). Using COSMO, one can reduce
some errors of this type, because the inexactness caused by the
numerical method can correspond to the "imperfectness" of the
natural substance (e.g. delaying the mixing and in control). Thus
the programming system or a programming language offers to be a
means used not only for studying but also for expressing the quantitative properties of a system; this means can be more precise
than differential equations. Moreover, there can be expressed even
a system which is consciously not compartmental, as is demonstrated in section 15.

2. USED SYMBOLS

A compartmental system (see e.g. [120] or [132] is composed of

n compartments $(n = 1)$, m inputs of the system $(m = 0)$ and r outputs of the system $(r = 0)$. We shall identify the compartments $C1$,
$C2, \ldots, Cn$, generally Ci, where i is called the order number.

The volume of a compartment Ci is identified Vi. The input Gi
into this compartment called more exactly partial input, is measured in the same physical units; the meaning of their number indicates the volume of accepted substance in the considered time interval (see section 4). The partial input is generally a sum of components which come from compartments and from inputs of the system. Special symbols are not used for them in COSMO, as it is explained in section 9. The output from the component Ci, called
more exactly the partial output, is identified Ki; it can be branched
into different compartments, but we do not declare a formalism for
its describing in COSMO: as every branch of Ki is an input component into some compartment or some output of the system, it is
sufficient to declare there the corresponding information.

The words input and output have two different meanings, unfortunately both habitual ones: for example input means an input into
compartmental system or a partial input into a compartment. In
order to eliminate possible confusions, we shall use the words input and output only for partial inputs and outputs of compartments
while the inputs and outputs of a system will be considered as compartments with special properties. An input of a system is its special compartment (called in-compartment), for which only the volume of substance which flows through it is substantial. Theoretically, the in-compartment is considered as a compartment without
its partial input and volume. An output of a system is its special
compartment (called out-compartment) for which only the volume
of substance which flows through it, is a substantial one. This substance can be mixed from other compartments. Thus, the out-compartment behaves as a compartment without its partial output and
its volume.

Therefore, we make the following new rule in COSMO: the compartments, the inputs and the outputs of a compartmental system
are considered as compartments, they need to have all different
order numbers and their common identifying is $C1, C2, \ldots Cs$ where
$s = m + n + r$ (see the beginning of this section).

The other symbols used in COSMO are T for the time, D for the
time step.

The letter C followed by an order number is the identification for
a part of a compartmental system. It has no numerical interpretation. The letters T, D, K, V, G (the last three followed by order
numbers) correspond to real numbers which express the quantities
measured in certain physical units. In the whole description of a
model in COSMO we must use the same measure for T, D and the

same measure for V, G and K. The name of the measure is not expressed in COSMO (e.g. $T = 3$, 5 means that the value of time is 3, 5 units). Measure of tracer contained in a part (a point) of a compartmental system is identified by HV, HG and HK followed by order numbers; for example $HV1$ means the measure of tracer leaving the compartment $C3$ etc. The tracer is measured by appropriate units independently on the units used for volume of general transported matter.

The expressions T, D, V, G, K, HV, HG and HK followed eventually by order numbers are called terms. They can occur in any arithmetic expression or program in COSMO (see section 3). If the hypothesis is interpreted in the model, that the tracer has no influence upon the run of the experiment, terms HV, HG, and HK do not occur in the declarations of compartments.

In the declaration of a part of a modelled system certain terms can occur which concern other parts not directly connected with the previously mentioned part. The transport of the matter may not exist between all these parts. This feature, admitted in COSMO, expresses the relation of controlling among parts of the compartmental system; it interprets communication without transport in the system (e.g. hormonal, nervous).

3. PROGRAMS, EXPRESSIONS, SYNTACTICAL DEFINITIONS

The usual form of a declaration of any term is e.g.

    ITS VOLUME = 37
    or
    ITS VOLUME: READ X

The meaning of the first example is, that the volume of a compartment has 37 units, the second example declares that the numerical value of the volume of a compartment is to be read from the computer input.

We generalize the first sort so, that after the sign of equality not only a special number can occur, but an arithmetic expression as well. Let us define this conception: an identifier is any term or any general number, identified by a letter (followed eventually by a natural number or by another letter identifying a natural number). An unary expression is a special number or an identifier, a binary expression is composed from two unary expressions connected by an arithmetic operation + - * / (the last two signs identify the multiplication and division respectively). Finally let us define a common conception of arithmetic expression: it is a unary or binary expression, or a name of a "standard function" followed by a unary expression. The names of the standard functions are SIN, COS, TAN, ARCSIN, ARCTAN, LN, AXP, SQRT and ABS. The examples of the arithmetic expressions:

3.245	M+S7	Note: in the compiled programs
T	2-V5	(see chapter 13) the operation
V3	G3+T	of the type $a = b/c$ means a
X	V1/D	macroinstruction: if $c = 0$ then
P	2.75-1.24	$a = 0$ else $a = b/c$. This inter-
ZR	43.27	pretation corresponds to the
A+4	SIN X	semantics of COSMO.
EXP 2.25	LN T	

Similarly, we generalize the second sort of the declaration. A program can occur after the colon; the program is a sequence of statements where the statement is any expressing unit which satisfies one of the following rules:

1. Identifier is followed by the sign of equality and by an arithmetic expression.

2. The words GO TO are followed by a natural number (called reference number).

3. The words GO TO are followed by three reference numbers, then by the word IF, then by an unary expression, then by the sign of equality and finally by an unary expression.

4. The word READ is followed by an identifier; the word PRINT or PRINTLINE is followed by an unary expression.

5. The word STOP.

6. A natural number greater than 4 (a reference number) is followed by the colon and then by any statement satisfying one of the preceding rules.

The meaning of the described types of the statements is similar as in usual algorithmic languages. The third rule is valid for the conditional jumps: if the relation mentioned in the statement is satisfied, the jump to the central reference number is realized to the first one or to the second one if the relation of "or" respectively is satisfied instead of the equality. We complete the described matter by a definition that the reference number 0 is also admitted: it identifies the following statement in the program; thus also an empty statement GO TO 0 can be simply written.

In the declarations of properties of a compartmental system, the use of program is illustrated by the following example:

```
ITS VOLUME: GO TO 0 11 11 IF T = 10
X = 275
GO TO 12
11: A=T-10
A = EXP A
X = 274+A
12: GO TO 0
```

It declares that the volume (of some compartment) is constant ($=275$), but after the time $T = 10$ it increases exponentially. The identifier X notes the declared object. Thus we present the following rule for COSMO: there are two sorts of programs: the declarative programs can form the parts of declarations: there, the declared value is identified by X while the corresponding term identifying the declared object expresses the last value of this object computed before (it is of some use in recursive definitions); the additional programs can be joined to the declarations but they do not form part of them. Every object is noted there by corresponding identifier. The additional programs are important in defining the initial conditions, but they can be joined elsewhere too (see below).

Limitation: The identifiers used in the programs and in the arithmetic expressions can be the terms, X and other letters except $I, H, B, C, F, L,$ followed eventually by a natural number or another letter identifying a natural number. The first and the second cases need no other notes in COSMO. In the case of using an other letter we must declare it in the headings (see section 13).

Although it might be suitable to realize an exchange of models, the author would not like to specify the properties concerning spaces and lines in COSMO. The only rule is that the newline signals of COSMO texts, as they are presented in this paper, correspond to any other equivalent physical signal (e.g. new punched card, semicolon). In the hardware representation at the Biophysical Institute in Prague, we must separate all the declarations and the additional programs by empty lines. Simple arrangements of COSMO texts, received in future eventually from a college center can be done manually or by simple translators: they can solve not only the differences between the format of COSMO texts but also arrange the modifications (dialects) of COSMO implied by special needs of centers (e.g. other forms of expressing of conditional jumps in programs). The author has made this decision after analogical experiences of unifying other programming languages.

The programs and expressions admitted in COSMO are of the most simple kind, in order to satisfy maximum of the conditions for the exchange between computing centers and for the easy realisation of COSMO compilers even in the centers possessing only small autocode systems (see section 14). Moreover, the author considers the described features as sufficient ones for the practical use.

In the following syntactical definitions of the parts of COSMO, the texts written in small letters belong to the metalanguage of COSMO, i.e. to the language which describes COSMO, while the texts written in capital letters are the texts of COSMO.

Examples:

ITS VOLUME = arithmetic expression
From Cj: declarative program

The first example means that the considered parts of texts in COSMO ought to start by the words ITS VOLUME, then the sign of equality follows and then an arithmetic expression must occur. In the second example, after FROM a letter C follow, subsequently an order number, a colon and any program (it can follow in the next lines). The letters i and j are used in this report as "metasymbols" for natural numbers.

The word comment, used often in the following syntactical definitions, means an empty text or any sequence of the symbols which contain no new-line signal (or equivalent). Thus, a possibility of explications in COSMO text is established. For example:

COMPARTMENT 1: ERYTHROCYTES

The comment begins by the colon and goes on by ERYTHRO-CYTES; it tells the reader that $C1$ models the set of erythrocytes.

4. THE REALISATION OF MODELLING; FORMAT DECLARATION

If a real system is investigated the most suitable way is to measure the values in certain points of this system. This measuring can be made discretely, in given time intervals (they need not to be equal during the whole measuring).

The use of COSMO on an automatic computer models the same situation but instead of a real system there is a mathematically modelled system. This system is to be described by declarations (see below). The time moments in which we need to obtain the "measured" values is to be declared, as well. In a so called format declaration we describe the parts of the modelled system the values of which are interesting for us, the form in which they are to be printed and the accuracy. The format declaration has the following form:

in the first line there is the word FORMAT;

in the second line there is the heading of the printed record, i.e. a list of identifiers;

in the third line there is an information how the numerical values noted in the heading are to be printed: this information is expressed by the "typical form": an asterisk means a digit and the point means the decimal point; the spaces between these expressions are reproduced in the printed form. Zeros after the first significant digit are to be omitted even if they are in the place' corresponding to an asterisk. An example:

FORMAT

```
    T    V1   HV1    V2   HV2
   **   ***.*   ***  **.**   **
```

It means that under the heading the values of T, $V1$, $HV1$, $V2$, $HV2$, are printed, the value of T having two digits, the value of $V1$ having three digits before the decimal point and one digit after it etc. The sign of minus, if it is needed, is automatically joined before the first significant digit of the corresponding number. Each line corresponds to the moment in which the "measuring" is made, each column corresponds to a measured point in the system.

5. GENERAL PROPERTIES OF COSMO TEXTS

The COSMO text describes a model in 4 phases:
1. Heading - it describes the number of all compartments.
2. Initial conditions.
3. Body - it describes the time division, the parts of modelled system, the characteristics of an eventual tracer, the format and the duration of modelling.
4. Appendix - actions at the end of the modelling.

The first and the third phases are usually of the form of tables, but the programs can be put into them. The second and the fourth phases are of the form of programs: the second phase is usually a sequence of simple assignments eventually readings from a computer input unit, the fourth phase contents usually the only stop statement.

6. TIME DECLARATION

It has one of the following forms:

```
TIME = arithmetic expression
TIME:  declarative program
STEP = arithmetic expression
STEP:  declarative program
TIME IS NORMAL
```

By the first form the value of time is determined by the arithmetic expression on the right side. If the identifiers T, D occur there they mean their values in the preceding step. Example:

$$\text{TIME} = T + 23 .$$

It means that the time rises 23 units in a step. The same information can be expressed by STEP = 23 using the third form. By the
second form the value of the time is determined by the last value
of the identifier X, which must occur in the program. The meaning
of T and D is similar as in the first form. Example:

>TIME: GO TO 11 10 10 if $T = 25$
>11: $X = T + 1$
>GO TO 12
>10: $X = T + 5$
>12: GO TO 0

It means that the time increases 1 unit in a step until 25 and then it
increases 5 units in a step. The same information can be expressed
by the fourth form:

>STEP: GO TO 11 10 10 if $T = 25$
>11: $D = 1$
>GO TO 12
>10: $D = 5$
>12: GO TO 0

Another example: TIME: READ X
The last form is an abbreviation for one of the following four equivalent declarations:

>STEP $= 1$
>STEP: $X = 1$
>TIME $= T + 1$
>TIME: $X = T + 1$

7. DECLARATION OF IN-COMPARTMENT

In the first line there is

>IN-COMPARTMENT i comment

i is the order number of the declared in-compartment; in the comment, one can give a semantical characteristics of the declared in-
compartment, e.g. its name. Example:

>IN-COMPARTMENT 4 INFUSION

In the second line there is a declaration of Ki:

>ITS FLOW = arithmetic expression

Example: ITS FLOW = 27.5.
It means that in the time interval D, 27.5 units of the substance
came into the modelled system through this in-compartment. If it

cannot be declared by an arithmetic expression, we use a declarative program:

ITS FLOW: declarative program

Example: ITS FLOW: READ X
It means that the values corresponding to the considered term Ki
are punched in the input medium of the computer. Another example:

ITS FLOW: GO TO 7 8 8 IF $K3$ = 7
7: $X = K3 + 0.7$
GO TO 9
8: $X = 7$
9: GO TO 0

(We assume that this declaration concerns the in-compartment 3).

It means that the measure of the substance transported through
the incompartment 3 into the modelled system increases 0.7 in the
first step and the following steps until it reaches for the value 7
and then it is constant.

Ki is declared, however it needs not occur in the declaration.
If it occurs it means the value in the preceding step. In the declarative program the value of Ki is determined by the last value of
the identifyer X, which must occur in the program.

If the transport of a tracer is performed through the declared
incompartment we have to express it in the following line (lines) of
the declaration:

LABELLED = arithmetic expression
or: LABELLED: declarative program

The meaning is similar as in the previous text; numerical information of the tracer is given in the appropriate units.
Examples:

LABELLED = 235. It means the infusion of the tracer of 235
                  units constantly.

LA ELLED: GO TO 0 8 8 IF T = 5
X 0
GO TO 9
8: X = 235
9: GO TO 0

This example means the similar infusion as in the first example but
only since the moment T = 5.

8. COMPARTMENT DECLARATION

It declares a compartment which is not an in-compartment nor an out-compartment. In the first line there is

COMPARTMENT i comment

Its meaning is similar as in the case of the declaration of an in-compartment. In the following lines there are the declarations of the partial input in the compartment: in the second line there is

ITS INPUT comment

In the following line (lines) there is one or more declarations of the components; they have the form

FROM Cj = arithmetic expression
FROM Cj: declarative program

A declaration of a component of an input into a compartment, which comes from the same compartment, is admitted (it concerns the minimal cycles of the system). Declarations of several various components of an input which come all from the same compartment are also admitted: it is not logically necessary but it can simplify the programming and it does not cause any difficulties for the compiler.

Then the declaration of the output from the compiler follows in the new line; it has the following form:

ITS OUTPUT IS CONSTANT
or: ITS OUTPUT IS UNDETERMINED
or: ITS OUTPUT = arithmetic expression
or: ITS OUTPUT: declarative program

The first case is used for expressing that the volume does not depend on the time during the modelling; the actual value of it is determined by the initial conditions (see section 12). The last two cases are similar as in the preceding parts. If the input and the volume of a compartment are declared by such declarations we can use an "implicit declaration" of the output, presented as a second case; the actual value of the output can be determined automatically by the computer from the values of the input, actual value of the volume and the value of the volume in the preceding step. The word UNDETERMINED can be replaced by any word beginning by UN, e.g. UNKNOWN, UNIMPORTANT.

Then the declaration of the volume of the compartment follows. It has the similar form as the declaration of the output into the compartment:

ITS VOLUME IS CONSTANT
or: ITS VOLUME IS UNDETERMINED
or: ITS VOLUME = arithmetic expression
or: ITS VOLUME: declarative program

The implicit declarations of the volume and of the output of the same compartment are not permitted. Example of a compartment declaration:

COMPARTMENT 2: MARROW
ITS INPUT: (C1 IS PLASMA, C3 ARE MATURING ERYTH-
            RONS)
FROM C1 = 32
FROM C3: READ X
ITS OUTPUT IS UNDETERMINED
ITS VOLUME IS CONSTANT

9. DECLARATION OF OUT-COMPARTMENT

In the first line is

OUT-COMPARTMENT i comment

The meaning is similar as for the declaration of the in-compartment. If the out-compartment has only one component it is declared in the following line (lines):

FROM Cj = arithmetic expression
or: FROM Cj: declarative program

The meaning of it is similar as in the previous chapters, specially in the declaration of partial inputs into compartments.

If there are more components, in the following lines there are analogical declarations for other components. For this case similar rules are valid as for the declarations of more components of the partial input into compartment.

Note: the identifier Gi is thus declared (the only value substantial for modelling the out-compartment), however it needs occur in the declaration.

10. TRACER DECLARATION

If the application of a tracer is not modelled or if the tracer is considered as a steady substance no tracer declaration is used in COSMO. If we wish to take fission of the tracer into account, we describe it in the tracer declaration. It has the form:

FISSION OF TRACER = arithmetic expression
or: FISSION OF TRACER: declarative program
or: HALFTIME = unary expression

The first two forms define the fission of the tracer by the form commonly used in COSMO; the fission is the quotient

$$\frac{\text{measure of the tracer at the beginning of the step}}{\text{measure of the tracer at the end of the step}}$$

The recursive definitions are not permitted in the tracer declarations.

11. BODY OF MODEL

The body determines the situation which is valid during the whole modelling. It is a sequence of all necessary declarations which have been described in the preceding chapters. The ordering of declarations is not fixed by COSMO rules but we recommend to put the declaration of the time as the first one, followed by all declarations of in-compartments, by all compartment declarations, by all declarations of out-compartments, by a tracer declaration and finally by the format declaration. Only a compartment declaration and one format declaration must occur in the body, the other ones can be absent if they are not needed. Two declarations of the time, of the format or of the same (in-, out-) compartment have no meaning, two or more tracer declarations are interpreted as they describe more simultaneous effects upon the tracer. At the beginning, at the end and between any declarations, additional programs can be joined; they must be initiated by a line containing the word PRO-GRAM and eventually a comment. They are interpreted as usual in algorithmic programming (thus e.g. the identifier $V1$ means only the volume and does not concern $HV1$). The body must begin by a line containing the word BODY followed eventually by a comment. At the end of the body there must be the information determining the duration of the modelling. It is of the following form: REPEAT WHILE unary expressions IS GREATER THAN another unary expression.
Examples:
REPEAT WHILE 100 IS GREATER THAN T
REPEAT WHILE $HV3$ IS GREATER THAN 100

12. INITIAL CONDITIONS

Before the body a part which determines the initial conditions of the modelling occurs. This part begins by the word INITIAL followed eventually by a comment; in the following lines there is a program which determines the initial values of various terms (identifiers). Of course - in the practice the program contains statement of the type

term = number (i.e. assigning)

or: READ term (i.e. input of a value through the computer input unit)

Examples:

$HV1 = 20000$ READ $K3$ $T = 0$

If a term is used in assigning the initial value to another term, its initial value must be assigned beforehand. E.g. $HV1 = 0.03 * V1$ has meaning only in the case when before it the initial value of $V1$ is assigned. All terms to which the initial values are not assigned begin the modelling at the initial value 0. In order to eliminate the inaccuracy in the first steps (specially in the case of the controlling among the compartments) we must assign the initial values to so much as possible terms. This demand simplifies the compilation substantially and it needs not any more special programming work of the user of the language COSMO: he has only to consider profoundly the properties of the model and transform them more or less mechanically into simple statements of the program.

13. HEADING OF THE MODEL; APPENDIX

Before the word INITIAL there is a part of the COSMO text called Heading. It must always contain at least one line:

NUMBER OF COMPARTMENTS: i

i is the number of all compartments, including the in-compartments and the out-compartments.

Then there are the declarations of identifiers which are not terms, if they are necessary (see section 3). They are of the form:

REAL sequence identifiers

eventually: INTEGER sequence of identifiers

The identifiers in the sequences need not to be distinguished by any sign. The first form means that in the following COSMO text the mentioned identifiers note real decimal numbers (limited only by the floating point hardware of the used computer), and the second from means that the mentioned identifiers will note only integers (often indices).

If two or more identifiers are used being not terms which begin by the same letter followed by different numbers, only one of them - with the highest number - must be presented in the heading.

Note: No texts are permitted in COSMO before the heading. The labels of the tapes and similar identification, usual in various computing centres for all programs, are admitted but they are not included into COSMO texts.

After the end of the body, i.e. after the statements REPEAT etc. there is an appendix. It is always a program, often a single statement STOP.

14. GENERAL PRINCIPLES OF COMPILING

The algorithm of the compiler from COSMO is not exactly described since there could be a lot of modifications depending on the hardware of the used computer. In this chapter, only general principles of the compilation are mentioned, considered by the author as useful ones for any compiler from COSMO.

Let us assume that a system of automatic programming is at disposal and its language L satisfies at least the properties of programs expressed in section 3 †. The COSMO compiler translates the texts in COSMO into the equivalent texts in L and punches them or stores them into the inner memory or magnetic tape. Then the compiler or the interpreting program for L can be applied. Thus, we can describe only translation from COSMO into L. It is purely sequential: during the text in COSMO is read, the target text in L is compiled.

In the following description, the words "to copy the text until. . ." mean that the following symbols of the processed COSMO text are sequentially transferred as the following symbols of the compiled program in L; the words "until. . ." are understood so that the object mentioned after "until" is not copied any more; if the letter H is read so it is omitted and the following letter is transformed in this way: K to I, G to H, V to B. The copied text can be empty, i.e. it can contain no symbols. The key word means any of the following words: COMPARTMENT, IN-COMPARTMENT, OUT-COMPART-MENT, TIME, STEP, FISSION, HALFTIME, FORMAT, PRO-GRAM, REPEAT.

1. The heading is read and the declarations of real arrays K, G, V, I, H, B are compiled. Each of them has one index, the lower bound of which is 1 and the upper bound is the number of all the compartments. The identifiers K, G, V have the same meaning as in COSMO. The other ones correspond to the identifiers with two letters:

---

† More exactly: the identifiers have only one letter; the identifiers followed by a number can be considered as array identifiers with one index.

COSMO: *HK HG HV*
    L: I   H   B

Then the declaration of reals X, D, T, F, K, C is compiled. The letters F, C, L are used for intermediate results, X, T, D have the same meaning as in COSMO.

2. Then the declarations of other identifiers used in COSMO are copied, until the word INITIAL.

  Note: if L has other properties concerning declarations, they are to be interpreted in the compiler (e.g. a vocabulary of identifiers COSMO - L).

3. After the word INITIAL has been read, the reference number 4, the following colon and then the program which assigns zero to all used identifiers are compiled. Then the following program is copied until the word BODY. After the word BODY has been read, the statement GO TO 2 and then a reference number 1: are compiled. The compilation proceeds according to paragraph 4.

4. The compilation is branched according to the key word. See the following paragraphs:

5. If the word PROGRAM is read, the following lines are copied until another key word.

6. If the word STEP has been read the compiling is branched according to following symbol:

  6a. If it is a sign of equality, the sequence D = is compiled and then the following text is copied until another key word.

  6b. If it is a colon, the following text is copied until a key word is read. Then $D = X$ is compiled.

  In both cases, the statement $T = T + D$ is compiled. Then the compilation proceeds as in paragraph 4.

7. If the word TIME is read the compilation is branched according to the following symbol:

  7a. If it is a sign of equality the sequence X = is compiled and then the following text is copied until another key word.

  7b. If it is a colon the following text is copied until a key word is read.

  In both cases the statements $D = X = T$ and $T = X$ are compiled. The compilation proceeds as in paragraph 4.

  7c. If it is I, the statements $T = T + 1$, $D = 1$ are compiled and the compilation proceeds from the following line as in paragraph 4.

8. After the word IN-COMPARTMENT has been read, the following number i is read and stored and the compilation is branched according to the symbol following the words ITS FLOW:

  8a. If it is a sign of equality, Ki = is compiled and the following text is copied until a new-line signal.

8b. If it is a colon, the following text is copied until a key word or a word LABELLED. Then $Ki = X$ is compiled.

In both cases, when the word LABELLED then occurs, the following text is processed similarly as in 8a or 8b (I instead of K) until a key word. Otherwise a statement $Ii = 0$ is compiled. Then, in both of the cases, the statements $Vi = Ki$ and $Bi = Ii$ are compiled and the compilation proceeds as in the paragraph 4.

9. After the word COMPARTMENT has been read the following order number i is read and stored, the statements $C = 0$, $L = 0$ are compiled and the compilation proceeds in the line following the words ITS INPUT:

9a. If the word FROM is read, the following identifier is read and omitted, the following natural number j is read and stored. If the following symbol is a sign of equality, the sequence $X =$ is compiled and then the following text is copied until one of the words FROM or ITS. If the following symbol is colon, the following text is copied until one of the words FROM or ITS. In both cases the following work of the compiler is, that the statements $F = X * Bj$ and $F = F/Vj$ are compiled. Then the other statements $C = C + X$ and $L = L + F$ are compiled. If the word FROM has been read, the work described in this paragraph 9a is repeated until the word ITS is read.

9b. If the word ITS has been read, the compilation proceeds according to the following paragraph.

10. Zero is stored in the address n of the compiler. The statements $Gi = C$ and $Hi = L$ are compiled. The word OUTPUT is read and the compilation is branched according to the following symbols.

10a. If it is I, the compilation is branched according to the initial letter of the following word: if it is U it jumps to the paragraph 12, otherwise the text until the word ITS is read and omitted.

10b. If it is a sign of equality a sequence $Ki =$ is compiled and the following text is copied until the word ITS,

10c. If it is a colon, the following text is read until the word ITS. Then the statement $Ki = X$ is compiled.

In all three cases, the statements $F = Bi * Ki$ and $Ii = F/Vi$ are compiled and the words ITS VOLUME are read. Then:

11. The compilation is branched according to the following symbol:

11a. If it is I the compilation is branched according to the initial letter of the following word: if it is C the following text is read and omitted until a key word; if it is U, the same action is done and then the compilation of the statements $X = Vi - Ki$, $Vi = X + Gi$ is following.

11b. If it is the sign of equality the sequence Vi = is compiled
and the following text is copied until a key word.

11c. If it is a colon, the following text is copied until a key
word; then the statement $Vi = X$ is compiled.

In all these cases, if the contents of the address n is 1, the
compilation jumps to the point 13, otherwise the statements
$X = Bi - Ii$ and $Bi = X + Hi$ are compiled. The compilation proceeds as in paragraph 4.

12. The contents of the address n is changed to 1. The statement
$L = Vi$ is compiled. The text is read and omitted until the word
VOLUME and the compilation proceeds to the point 11.

13. The statements $L = L + Gi$, $Ki = L - Vi$, $F = Bi * Ki$, $Ii = F/Vi$,
$X = Bi - Li$, $Bi = X + Hi$, are compiled. The compilation proceeds as in the paragraph 4.

14. After the word OUT-COMPARTMENT, the following number
is read and stored. The statements $L = 0$ and $C = 0$ are compiled and the compilation proceeds from the following line. It
can be described similarly as in the point 9a, but the word ITS
must be there replaced by any key word. In this case the statements $Gi = L$ and $Hi = C$ are compiled and the compilation continues as in the paragraph 4. Otherwise it is repeated (similarly
as in the paragraph 9a).

15. If the word HALFTIME has been read, the statements $X =$
-0.693147 $X = X * D$ are compiled, then the sequence $X = X/$
followed by the text, which occurs after the word HALFTIME
in the processed COSMO text, is compiled. Then the statement
$X = $ EXP X is compiled and then:

15a. The statements multiplying all Bi, Hi, Ii by X, are compiled. The compilation proceeds as in paragraph 4.

16. If the words FISSION OF TRACER have been read, the compilation is branched similarly as in the points 8a, 8b (X instead of
Ki in 8a). Then the compilation proceeds as in the paragraph
15a.

17. If the word FORMAT has been read, the statement GO TO 3,
then the reference number 2 with a colon and the statement for
a new line in printing are compiled. Then the following line is
read and stored and the corresponding statements for printing
of the heading are compiled. The following line is read and the
corresponding statements for printing are compiled.

18. Since the words REPEAT WHILE have been read, the sequence
GO TO 0 0 1 IF is compiled, the following text is copied until
the word IS, the text IS GREATER THAN is omitted, the sign
of equality is compiled and the following text is copied until a
new-line signal. The following text is copied until the word
STOP, including it. Then it is suitable to compile the instruc-

tion GO TO 4 in order to make it possible the run of several
modelling by the same program with different values on the input of the computer.
Note: if there is the need to model a lot of systems without the use
of tracer, it would be suitable to eliminate the term initiated by H
from the language COSMO and all parts concerning the identifiers
and the tracer from the compiler. Thus, the system would be more
effective for the mentioned cases.

There is a test whether the used numerical parameters of a
model are not rather unsuitable with regard to the accuracy of modelling (specially concerning the time): we can change the order of
compartments and repeat the compilation and the modelling. If the
results do not differ in the bounds of tolerance, we can believe into
the accuracy of the modelling.

The described compiler is programmed but not tested as yet on
the computer ODRA 1013 [167]. This computer has an autocode
MOST 1 which can be considered as FORTRAN very limited [145].
The compiler itself is in MOST 1 and it will compile from COSMO
into MOST 1. (MOST 1 is a concrete representation of the language
L). The author alone has programmed the COSMO compiler within
one month. After having eliminated all the errors from the COSMO
compiler, its translation from MOST 1 into ODRA machine code
will be carried out with the perforation. The perforated compiler
in ODRA machine code will translate from COSMO into MOST 1 and
then the application of the MOST 1 compiler will be used: either by
the system "load and go" or by the system "load and perforate".

15. EXAMPLE

A partial model of incorporation of iron into erythrocytes (according to [118])

NUMBER OF COMPARTMENTS: 7
REAL A
INITIAL:
$V1$ = 100
$HV1$ = 100
$V2$ = 85
$V3$ = 30
$V5$ = 1000
READ $V7$

BODY:

STEP = 2

COMPARTMENT 1: PLASMA
ITS INPUT:
FROM $C2$ = 11
FROM $C6$ = 21
FROM $C5$; $X = 1$
ITS OUTPUT = 33
ITS VOLUME IS CONSTANT
IN COMPARTMENT 6: FROM ERYTHROCYTES
ITS FLOW = 21

COMPARTMENT 2: MARROW
ITS INPUT:
FROM $C1$ = 32
FROM $C3$: READ A
$X = A$
ITS OUTPUT IS UNDETERMINED
ITS VOLUME IS CONSTANT

COMPARTMENT 7: DELAY
ITS INPUT:
FROM $C2$: READ X
ITS OUTPUT = $G7$
ITS VOLUME = $G7$

COMPARTMENT 3: MATURING ERYTHRONS
ITS INPUT:
FROM $C7$ = $G7$
ITS OUTPUT = $A + 21$
ITS VOLUME IS CONSTANT

OUT-COMPARTMENT 4: ERYTHROCYTES
ITS INPUT
FROM $C3$ = 21

COMPARTMENT 5: STORAGE
ITS INPUT:
FROM $C1$ = 1
ITS OUTPUT = 1
ITS VOLUME IS CONSTANT

FORMAT
   T $HV2$ $HV3$ $HG3$ $HG4$
  *** **   **   **   **

REPEAT WHILE 120 IS GREATER THAN T

STOP

16. OTHER FEATURES OF COSMO

It can be observed that the substantial influence of the transport of substance is present only in mixing of tracer and in implicit definitions. In case that we do not use them, we can model by means of COSMO other systems where for example the information is transported and processed. We present some examples:

a. Modelling of differential analyzer.

The semantics of used terms rather differs from their usual semantics in modelling of the transport in compartmental systems; but the language COSMO as well as the compiler COSMO can be used without any modifications.

The parts of a differential analyzer can be described as compartments with one component of its partial input and with its volume as well as its partial output equal to the value of the partial input. The tracers have no importance.

COMPARTMENT i: IT ADDS THE INPUTS FROM Cj AND Ck
ITS INPUT:
FROM $Cj = Gj + Gk$
ITS OUTPUT $= Gi$
ITS VOLUME $= Gi$

COMPARTMENT r: IT PERFORMS THE DERIVATION OF Cj
ITS INPUT:
FROM Cj: $X = Vj - A$ A is an auxiliary identifier
$X = X/D$ declared in the heading
ITS OUTPUT $= Gr$
ITS VOLUME: $X = Gr$
$A = Vj$

The curious relation of equality among the volume, the input and the output of a compartment is not satisfied in (usual) compartmental systems, but it is not in contradiction with COSMO system, if the implicit definitions are not used. Eventual simplifications of the system for these cases are planned at the Biophysical Institute for the future.

b. Modelling of digital systems.

The neuron networks modelled similarly as in the preceding paragraph can be programmed in COSMO, if we perform a small modification in COSMO compiler: instead of declaring all the terms in L as reals, they are declared as integers. As an example a compartment is declared modelling a neuron the input of which is 1 iff all the inputs from $C2$, $C3$, $C4$ are 0 an at least two inputs from $C5$, $C6$, $C7$, $C8$ are 1. An auxiliary identifier Y must be declared.

```
COMPARTMENT 1
ITS INPUT:
FROM C2: X = 0
GO TO 0 5 0 IF K2 = 1
GO TO 0 5 0 IF K3 = 1
GO TO 0 5 0 IF K4 = 1
Y = G5
Y = Y + G6
Y = Y + G7
Y = Y + G8
GO TO 5 0 0 IF Y = 2
X = 1
5: GO TO 0
ITS OUTPUT = G1
ITS VOLUME = G1
```

The programming system modelling Boolean operations can be easily obtained from COSMO: before the initial conditions the compiler puts the subroutines (procedures) for the Boolean operations with the operands N, M (special identifiers), the result is going to the identifier M. The procedures can be called ET, VEL, NON etc.

A compartment which carries out the conjunction of the outputs from Cj, Ck:

```
COMPARTMENT i
ITS INPUT:
FROM Cj: N = Gj
M = Gk
ET
X = M
ITS OUTPUT = Gi
ITS VOLUME = Gi
```

In this case the language L must automatically carry out at least the jumps into procedures without parameters.

ACKNOWLEDGEMENTS

The author has discussed the properties of COSMO with his colleagues in seminaries organized at the Institute of Biophysics of the Charles University (Prague) (Head: Prof. Dr. Z. Dienstbier); the author would like to express his thanks to the colleagues, specially to Mrs. Ph. Mr. J. Pixova for her help in English translation and to MUDr. J. Brousil for the scientific consultations concerning the section 15.

DISCUSSION

Brennan:

I should like to extend my congratulations to the author on doing a very fine job of making a really special-purpose problem oriented language.

I would offer a suggestion that I think he would lose some of the value of the direction he has gone, in making it oriented towards compartmental medical modelling, if he seriously attempted to add to it modelling of analogue computers or neuron networks. I agree it could do these things but I think you would lose the nice medical flavour of your language in trying to do so. I would urge you instead to continue what you have done. I think it is an outstanding attempt.

Molnar:

I think it was a good' idea including tracer facilities in a simulation language and my question would be whether you can deal with more than one tracer.

Kindler:

No - only one tracer because it is usual in the application of COSMO. In our Institute we use only one tracer. I do not know of any case of using two tracers but if we did use two tracers, we could make two models - in COSMO. Of course, it may be uneconomical in this case but on the other hand, the compiler is effective for the usual work in actual medical practice.

PROBLEM-ORIENTED DIAGNOSTICS AND OTHER AIDS TO ANALYSIS AND DESIGN

ROGER A. GASKILL

Advanced Systems Engineering, Martin Marietta Corporation, Orlando, Florida, USA

Abstract: Recent emphasis on ease of simulation has detracted from more important considerations. Attention should be turned to ways of increasing the effectiveness of simulation. This can be done by supplementing simulation with various symbolic and/or numerical analyses controlled by the simulation software. Several useful analyses and approaches to their implementation are suggested in this paper.

1. INTRODUCTION

Digital simulation has become too easy. At least two problems have been created by modern simulation languages and procedures. First, the ease of simulation has encouraged wanton use. Perhaps this problem can be solved by management-imposed restrictions or by better education. The second problem results from the elimination of certain analytical aspects of simulation for the sake of programming ease. Undue attention is thereby focused on the simulation itself, and the problems motivating the simulation are obscured. It must be remembered that simulation, per se, cannot solve design and analysis * problems. Simulation only can simulate. One solution to this second problem is to revert to a procedure that forces the user to do some analysis. But this is not necessary. Analysis and design aids can be incorporated in the simulation software, and programming ease can be retained.

2. BACKGROUND

What analysis and design aids should be provided? In attempting to answer this question, consider first what analyses are by-passed by modern simulation procedures. The user is no longer required

---

* For certain analyses, analyzers can be simulated and added to the basic simulation.

to assign scale factors or draw block diagrams. Although neither of these steps is essential to simulation, both are useful in that they tend to focus attention on the physical system to be simulated. Determination of scale factors involves a rough analysis of system behavior. This analysis is not only instructive by itself, but it also provides a useful guide for interpreting the simulation results. By drawing block diagrams, relationships are made apparent that are impossible to determine by simulation alone. An example of this is provided by the following simple analysis and design problem.

2.1. *Problem*

Assuming that the velocity of an object falling through a fluid medium is governed by the equation

$$M \frac{dV}{dt} + KV^2 = Mg \, , \tag{1}$$

find the relationship between the limiting velocity (V_L), mass (M) and drag factor (K). Also, determine values of M and K to provide a particular limiting velocity (V_{LP}).

2.2. *Solution*

Simulation appears to be an appropriate tool for attacking this problem. The problem is physically oriented, and it is modeled by a nonlinear differential equation. This equation happens to have an analytic solution given by

$$V = \sqrt{\frac{Mg}{K}} \tanh \sqrt{\frac{Kg}{M}} \, t \, , \tag{2}$$

when the initial velocity is zero. Since the maximum value of the hyperbolic tangent is unity, it follows that

$$V_L = \sqrt{\frac{Mg}{K}} \, . \tag{3}$$

Ignoring this solution for the moment, consider the modern simulation approach to the problem.

The differential equation is first rewritten in the form:

$$\frac{dV}{dt} = (Mg - KV^2)/M \tag{4}$$

or

$$\frac{dV}{dt} = g - KV^2/M \, . \tag{5}$$

Using DSL/90 language [144], the mathematical model can now be programmed by the single statement:

$$V = \text{INTGRL } (0.0, G-(K*V*V)/M) \qquad (6)$$

where the number preceding the comma is the initial value of V. A few auxiliary statements are added to this, including one to indicate that V is to be graphed versus time. Next, trial values of M and K are selected, and the solution is evaluated by the computer for each set of values. Assuming that three values are selected for each parameter and all nine sets are used, then the simulation results can be represented by three sets of curves of the form shown in fig. 1. These curves indicate that a limiting velocity does exist, but very little is revealed concerning the relationship between the limiting velocity and the system parameters. This relationship is made somewhat more apparent by plotting V_L versus one of the parameters (fig. 2).

From fig. 2, it is clear that many combinations of M and K can provide any particular limiting velocity, but only a few of these combinations are identified. It appears that a cross-plot of fig. 2 is advisable. Selecting a particular limiting velocity (say, V_{LP1}), all M,K combinations identified for this velocity are plotted in a K,M coordinate system and a curve is sketched through the points (fig. 3). This curve provides additional combinations of M and K for the specified velocity. By carefully repeating this procedure for several velocities, it may be recognized that all curves can be approximated by straight lines through the origin. This suggests that any particular limiting velocity corresponds to a particular ratio between M and K. A plot of V_L versus M/K (fig. 4) supports this hypothesis, since it appears that all of the measured V_L values fall on a smooth curve. Fig. 4 represents a partial solution to the example problem as obtained by a modern simulation procedure and subsequent analysis. Now consider how this problem would be treated by the old-fashioned, "difficult" simulation procedure.

Assuming the procedure requires both a block diagram and scaling, the block diagram would probably be drawn first (fig. 5). Next, the maximum (or limiting) value of V would be estimated. To estimate this value, it would be noted that V must stop increasing when the input to the integrator vanishes. From the block diagram it is clear that the integrator input vanishes when

$$\frac{KV^2}{M} = g . \qquad (7)$$

Thus, the limiting value of V is given by

$$V_L = \sqrt{\frac{Mg}{K}} , \qquad (3)$$

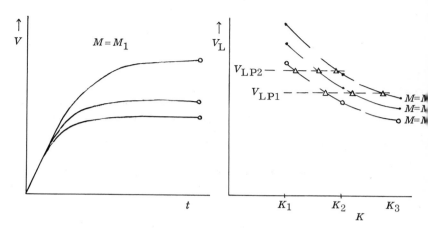

Fig. 1. Simulation outputs for $M = M_1$.   Fig. 2. Plot derived from simulation
                                           outputs for $M = M_1, M_2, M_3$.

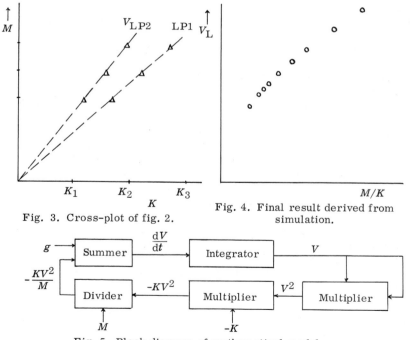

Fig. 3. Cross-plot of fig. 2.   Fig. 4. Final result derived from
                                              simulation.

Fig. 5. Block diagram of mathematical model.

which is the relationship implied, but not proven, by fig. 4. The design part of the problem would be solved by rewriting equation (7) as

$$\frac{K}{M} = \frac{g}{V_{LP}^2} \, . \tag{8}$$

2.3. *Discussion*

It may be argued that block diagrams are not really important because the same solution obtained by inspection of the block diagram could have been obtained by inspection of the mathematical model. But modern digital simulation procedures encourage the user to ignore the mathematical model. The emphasis is placed on achieving a successful simulation as quickly and easily as possible. Perhaps this emphasis is motivated by a belief that the simulation (as a manifestation of the mathematical model) can always provide just as much useful information as the model itself, and do it more readily and vividly. The example problem has shown that this belief is unfounded. Some physical problems are not amenable to solution by simulation, even when simulation appears to be the proper approach. For such problems, taking time to draw and study a block diagram actually saves time and effort.

Should scaling and/or block diagramming be reinstated as a required part of simulation procedure? Probably not, but the answer depends on how often these steps are really useful. The question may be unanswerable for some time. For one reason, people are not likely to advertise costly mistakes resulting from excessive emphasis on ease of simulation. Some of these mistakes may not even be recognized for years.

Most comparative studies of simulation procedures consider only the steps involved in simulating a given mathematical model. More comprehensive studies are required to determine the overall value of a procedure. Such studies should consider how the procedure aids in refining the mathematical model and in minimizing the required number of computer runs. Refinement of the original mathematical model is often advisable, either to make the simulation more realistic or to eliminate unnecessary detail leading to excessive computing time. It seems reasonable to suppose that at least some aspects of block diagram analysis would aid this refinement.

3. ANALYSIS AIDS

In principle, a block diagram could be generated by the com-

puter, using the program statements as a starting point. This
would provide the dual advantage of retaining convenience and
assuring agreement between the block diagram and the program.
But an automatically generated block diagram might not be very
useful, since no one could be forced to study it. As an alternative,
the computer could analyze the block diagram (or equivalently, the
program statements) and report its findings to the user. For
example, from the information contained in fig. 5, the computer
could print out:
1. The equilibrium equation (equation 7).
2. The type of equilibrium (e.g., stable or unstable).
3. The loop gain (KV/M).
Of these three analyses (or problem-oriented diagnostics), the
first is essentially the solution to the example problem, the second
is a check on the validity of the model, and the third is essentially
a time constant. The equilibrium analysis actually provides a two-
way check. If the physical system is known to be stable and the
diagnostic reads "unstable", then the model is wrong. But if the
diagnostic reads "stable" and the simulation is unstable, then the
simulation is wrong. In this case, the loop gain analysis may provide a clue to the trouble. Almost all digital simulation techniques
have difficulty with small time constants (or equivalently, large loop
gains). Because the accuracy, stability and efficiency of digital
simulation depends strongly on loop gains, it would be helpful to
have an additional print-out indicating an allowable upper limit on
loop gain.

How can the suggested aids be implemented? One attractive
possibility is to provide a completely separate program just for
block diagram generation and/or analysis. This program should
be designed to accept the same input deck that the simulation program does. The numerical data cards might be omitted, however,
because the primary purpose of the program would be symbolic
analysis rather than numerical analysis. Use of a separate program would permit a much more complete symbolic analysis than
would be feasible by incorporating this analysis in the basic simulation software. But most of the modern simulation software
already includes a limited amount of symbolic analysis, if only to
sort the program statements into proper order. And MIMIC [125]
for example, checks each loop to determine if any algebraic * loops
are present. It would probably be feasible to extend this analysis so
that loop gains could be determined. Although the symbolic expressions for loop gains would have to be determined by the software,
only the numerical values need be made available to the user.

---

* An algebraic loop is essentially one not containing an integrator.

4. DESIGN AIDS

The discussion so far has centered on aids to analysis. Analysis is almost always an important aspect of simulation, even when the objective is design. The simulation approach to design is sometimes called analytical design. A design is postulated and then analyzed to answer such questions as:
1. Does the designed system perform the desired functions?
2. Is the design feasible?
3. What are the most significant parameters of the system?
4. What are the relationships between design parameters and performance parameters?
5. How can the design be improved?
The first question is answered simply by simulating operating conditions and observing the performance of the simulated system. The other questions are not answered as easily. A proposed design may appear to function beautifully and yet be completely unworkable because of extreme stresses or dependence on precise control of parameter values. Probably most stress analyses are best left to separate specialized programs, but loop gain analyses can provide an indication of potential trouble spots. Just as high loop gains pose problems with accurate and efficient simulation, they also imply possible difficulties with the physical system being simulated. High loop gains indicate the presence of high natural frequencies and small time constants. When these characteristics are present in loops containing large masses or inertias, they also indicate the presence of large stresses.

The dependence of system performance on design parameters is sometimes best studied by symbolic analysis, as in the example problem. When symbolic analysis is not feasible, recourse can be made to numerical evaluation of partial derivatives. The usual evaluation procedure is rather laborious. First, a reference run is made, using nominal values for the design parameters. Then additional runs are made, changing one parameter value at a time, and restoring each parameter to its nominal value between runs. Finally, the change in each performance parameter is noted and divided by the corresponding design parameter change to approximate each partial derivative. Because this procedure is inconvenient, analysis of partial derivation is often restricted to those parameters intuitively felt to be most significant. As a result, important influences of other parameters may remain undetected.

Besides being awkward and subject to human error, the manual procedure for determining partial derivatives leads to excessive round-off error because the performance parameter changes must be determined from the limited number of significant figures in the se, is rarely a useful goal.

print-out. The disadvantages of the manual procedure could be eliminated by an automatic procedure. The user would write a statement indicating what partial derivatives are desired, and the computer would sequence through the required number of runs and calculate the derivatives.

Partial derivatives of performance parameters (or performance indeces) are important to design because they not only reveal how tightly the design parameters must be controlled but they also indicate how the performance can be improved. With the aid of additional software, the design parameters can be automatically optimized. Such software is included in the Dynasar [93] program.

Another important use of partial derivatives is in the approximation of a nonlinear system by a linearized model. Such a model can aid design by permitting the use of standard design techniques. In autopilot design, for example, it is helpful to have the aerodynamics expressed in the form of transfer functions. To obtain these transfer functions from the nonlinear simulation, the nonlinear aerodynamic differential equations must first be approximated by linear differential equations. This is done by expanding the expression for each time derivative in the form of a Taylor series, retaining only the linear terms. The partial derivatives appearing in the Taylor series are evaluated by the method described above, and the linearized differential equations are transformed and combined into various transfer functions.

Certain straightforward designs can be accomplished directly by the simulation software. A notable example is the design of logical controllers. Many large systems include a special-purpose digital computer to control the analog portions of the system. To simulate such a system, it is necessary to simulate the functions of this controller. With the older simulation languages, the controller had to be described in terms of components, using only relays (as in DAS [43]) or perhaps gates and flip-flops (as in COBLOC [68]). Some other languages, such as DSL/90, permit the use of **FORTRAN** logic statements to describe the controller. This amounts to automatic design, since the software determines and assembles the basic operations required to satisfy the functional specification of the controller. By automatic block-diagramming, this design could be made available to the user.

5. CONCLUSIONS

It is probably too soon to recommend a specific set of analysis and design aids for incorporation in simulation software. What is needed at this time is a more thorough study of how simulation is used and how this use can be made more effective. Simulation, per se, is rarely a useful goal.

For design and analysis applications, simulation is best regarded as an information-processing technique. No new information is generated by simulation, but the information provided by the user is returned to him in a different form. Changing the form of information is a basic technique for solving problems. By considering the available information in a sufficient number of different forms, the problem solution should become obvious. Analog simulation exploits this technique by expressing the information in at least three forms: the mathematical model, a block diagram of the model, and the simulation itself. Modern digital simulation procedures de-emphasize the mathematical model and eliminate the block diagram.

By emphasizing simulation rather than problem-solving, simulation software developers have missed an opportunity to make digital simulation even more useful than analog simulation. Digital computers can manipulate the source information in more ways than analog computers can. There is no need to restrict simulation languages to simulation alone. Once a physical system has been described in a simulation language, it should be possible to process this description in many different ways. Since this is a capability not possessed by analog simulation, the potential impact on digital simulation can scarcely be imagined.

DISCUSSION

Editor's note

In his presentation of the paper Mr. Gaskill discussed the properties and uses of simulation methods. He presented the following suggested list of properties of the simulation approach:
1. It is highly deceptive.
2. It is never exact.
3. It cannot solve problems.
4. It generates no new information.
5. It is not sufficiently instructive.
This list is referred to during the following discussion.

Garwick

I want to put one question — I think that one of the purposes of continuous simulation was as a design tool; at least you try something out on the computer before you make it — I do not think you said very much about that.

Gaskill

Well I agree – why does anyone use simulation? We use it as a
temporary substitute for hardware, in which case we are attempting to design the hardware by trial and error methods – testing the
hardware in a simulated environment and if it does not work we
rebuild the hardware and try it again. We can also use the simulation as a design tool where we simulate all the hardware. The
problem there again is that the traditional simulation approach is
strictly trial and error and I think we are putting our heads in the
sand if we continue to use the trial and error approach. I feel that
there is sufficient information available in the description of the
model itself so that we can obtain general analytical relationships
which will tell us how to design the system.

Parslow

The whole point of simulation is that you get an insight into the
problem.

Gaskill

Well – I should say that is just a beginning. That is just the foot
in the door. I think the example problem in my paper illustrates
what too often happens in my experience in industry. Someone uses
simulation because he thinks that this is an automatic key to understanding the problem. He finds that this is just entering a maze
of blind alleys, and he would have been much better off if he had
used just a little bit of commonsense. I believe that simulation is a
foot in the door but I believe that very often, once we have got our
foot in the door, to open the door the rest of the way we should use
a different approach.

So let us use a simulation language to describe the problem of
interest to us – or at least the system of interest to us and then
let us operate on this description in various ways including simulation.

Douglas

I can agree with the first three points in Mr. Gaskills list. I do
not think that the first one is particularly important, because the
probability of mis-use of a tool is not an argument for not having
it. I cannot agree with point four because if you are using simulation at all, then in fact you must use it in the form of generating
information because it is on that information that you are going to
base your analysis. The whole point of simulation for me, particularly in an industrial environment, is in fact to simulate some-

thing that I cannot study otherwise. In part, this is a training of the management and a training of the analyst himself. If you are setting out to deal with a plant, you cannot stop the plant to study it. Each manager has in mind a model of how the plant works, which is actually a simulation in his head and we are trying to improve this by giving him a lot more information about how his plant might behave.

I agree that one has to be very careful that the model we build is a good one and it is perfectly true that we have to use trial and error. What is wrong with trial and error   I have used it for a long time in research and I see no reason why we should not go on doing so. If I understand most of the things that have been done in this field of languages, it has been trial and error and quite a lot of error!

Gaskill

Of course, I hope to stimulate discussion here. Point four I think perhaps is the only point which is indisputable. I think data processing does not generate information – there is no more information available in the output of a data processor than went into it.

Garwick

May I have one word there. You see there is a confusion because the word information is used in two entirely different ways: one in the Shannon sense, in which case you do not create information – it only disappears. There is another sense used by computer people, where you really do create information.

Gaskill

I am a Shannon type.

Dahl

Even in the Shannon sense it would be correct to say that the model itself contains information so there is information in the machine.

Gaskill

I agree – the model itself contains all of the information. The only thing that the simulation can do is to destroy information.

Douglas

This is just a thoroughly unhelpful way of looking at things, if I may say so, and you are now being thoroughly pedantic. You know perfectly well what I mean by this kind of information!

Molnar

Can you deal with probabilistic systems?

Gaskill

I am not sure what you mean by probabilistic systems. Of course, we use Monte Carlo techniques.

Molnar

In which do you have random numbers?

Gaskill

There is no particular problem engendered by the use of random numbers in continuous systems simulation. You see when you ask about specific implementations, I am only qualified to answer in terms of continuous systems simulation.

I feel that I really owe a further answer to Douglas – when I refer to the fact that the computer can provide a new perspective on the problem and this is what you call new information. Now as to whether it is insufficiently instructive or not, as I said before, it is certainly highly instructive. I am just saying that if we restrict ourselves completely to the trial and error approach, we are being satisfied with half a loaf. I think we can get more.

GENERAL DISCUSSION - SESSION 8

Krasnow:

Lackner in the earlier discussion on Brennan's paper raised the question of the relationship between the continuous and discrete simulation activities with the opinion that in some way or another these activities really should be married. I think this is a subject that is worth some more extended consideration during the general discussion, and I would like to inject a few thoughts in this direction.

There was at the computer conference last month in Atlantic City a panel discussion which attempted to explore some of the relationships between the continuous simulation activity and the discrete. As usual with panels, nothing was really resolved, but a number of points were brought out, which I think were relevant. There is an obvious simularity of intention when you consider the relationship of the user to the problems that he has at hand. His approach to resolving these problems is essentially an experimental approach, whether you take the continuous or discrete way. But if you look a little more deeply at the mechanism, there seems to be quite a number of differences which may not be as easy to resolve as they appear. The first and probably foremost difference is in the view of the problem, what we may call the world view, taken by the user. In one case, in the case of the continuous field it is essentially a mathematical viewpoint, based on the concepts of differential equations. In the discrete case it is essentially a descriptive viewpoint, not a mathematical viewpoint. And this imposes some very different approaches to the problems.

A second difference lies in the treatment of the parellelism. In the case of discrete languages I think much of what we have discussed here has dealt with the concept of "quasi-parallel" which stems from a description by the user in discrete terms. The user establishes the interaction points, discretely, and then the system has to find a way of dealing with this description. In the continuous case the user gives what is essentially a continuous description. And the system arbitrarily and automatically establishes the parallelism, through the fixed solution interval of the integration. And furthermore this solution interval is really problem independent; one can state the problem with no reference whatsoever to the solution interval, whereas this is not the case in the discrete situation.

There were other differences that I think are perhaps less fundamental. One of the things that we might note is that in the discrete case complex data structures tend to be very important. In the case of the continuous models one generally finds very simple data structure. One also sometimes finds differences in the time scale of solution, but this would not necessarily seem to be crucial.

One last point has to do with the possibility of some kind of a composite system which can accommodate both forms of modelling. I think a prerequisite to this is the definition by users of applications which require a composite description. It appears that in most cases the engineers dealing with continuous modelling situations are quite content to decompose a large situation, or a large system, into components which are entirely continuous, which limits the scope of the model.

I do not know if this is simply a function of the tools that are available, or a function of the way these problems must be analyzed, but I think that descriptions of applications which require both tools are at least prerequisite to trying to put both tools into a single package.

Caracciolo:

Generally speaking I agree with Krasnow's distinction between continuous systems and discrete type systems. I would perhaps describe the difference a little differently. It seems to me that in both cases we have to deal with an automaton; that is, an input - output - state device, made by a composition of similar smaller devices. However, in the continuous case there is a kind of uniformity in the system which is usually lacking in the discrete case.

In the last case we have in fact much more varied sorts of objects which are not easily identifiable in a mathematical sense, i.e. by means of equations. One usually describes this by saying that a discrete simulation is not a mathematical model, but rather an operational or experimental model.

On the other hand, in the digital simulation of continuous systems the basic problem is how to transform the definition of a continuous automaton, possibly involving partial differential equations, into a discrete one.

Thus generally speaking continuous simulation languages tend to be high level "definitional languages" rather than procedural or algorithmic languages.

Editors' note:

At this point Professor Caracciolo gave a presentation of some recent work. This is described in an Additional Paper in this session of the conference, to be found after the General Discussion, entitled: "On a Research Project on a High Level Simulation Language for Chemical Plants".

Garwick:

It has been stressed that users of these continuous simulation programmes are very unsophisticated as programmers, and efforts are made to produce a way of describing the problem, which is as close as possible to the one that they are used to. I think that Kindler has succeeded very well in this respect. But I am not so certain about the sufficiency of the description given by Brennan.

I have here a report, dated August 1958, on this subject, which I wrote. Brennan was absolutely right in not mentioning it in his survey, because it has not had the slightest influence on anything.

I would like to mention a few things which I said which I think should go into a more modern language. This was written to a large extent for the ears of electro-mechanical engineers, designing servo mechanisms and that sort of thing, an example also given by Brennan. If a servo engineer has a piece of machinery, e.g. a motor, his description of a motor is a simple transfer function, and to force him to use some other notation, or put in intermediate varaibles and so on, I think is more than we can ask of him. We should be able to feed in transfer functions in his form, as new input. That is the way the man who works with the system is accustomed to think.

But there is one second point I would like to bring out, which also was in this paper. One wants to have potentiometers on an analogue computer for two reasons. One is that you are going to set in the constants you know about, and secondly, you want to fiddle with the constants you do not know about. The constants you know about you can enter easily in your system; you do not have to have any special facilities. The "potentiometers" you want to fiddle with were given initial values in this early system and there was some output from the system, which was going to be optimized with respect to these values. So the problem was run several times with different potentiometer settings, until the experimenter had found a good enough solution.

I think that is the sort of facility which should be built into modern systems; because you cannot assume that the user is in any way qualified to add a piece of program performing this optimization in any decent way.

I think that the efforts we have seen today are quite interesting, but I believe that you are not close enough to the user.

Lackner:

I want to go back to the subject that Krasnow was talking about a few minutes ago; the difference between discrete and continuous simulation. I think that the reason there appear to be these differences he outlined so nicely, is in the way of looking into the treatment of parallelism. I believe it has directly to do with the fact that people have an underdeveloped notion of process. In the discrete world you have such things as pure event type simulations, exemplified by SIMSCRIPT, where there is absolutely no notion of continuous action at all; things happen discretely, they schedule other things to happen later, and so on. On the continuous side processes have no beginning and no ending; all processes go on all the time.

The more complex the process notion, the more complex the simulation control algorithm, and that is one reason that the notion remains undeveloped in many of the so-called simulation languages. But the more complex the simulation controller, the more general the simulation scheme must be. On the discrete side processes have nothing but beginnings and endings, and on the continuous side they do not have either; they only have middles.

The process notion should have a beginning which is discrete and an ending - which might be interruption, but it should also have a duration during which time its effects are continuous. The results of both these should be apparent in the outputs generated by the simulation model, whether in hard copy or on the scope.

Douglas:

It seems to me that a lot of the confusion that has arisen on this springs from the analogue background of the one and the digital background of the other. I think the point, of course, is that the digital man knows that in order to solve a continuous process he must digitize it and express it in discrete steps.

We have also, I think, been ridden for a long time by the idea that such discrete steps must necessarily be equal. I have never discovered where this really arose from, except for convenience. As a matter of fact it is far better to solve many differential equations by flexible steps than it is by fixed steps. If you want to introduce this notion, then the question of discretizing a continuous process and fitting it in to an event stream of the type which we are quite accustomed to, does not appear to me to be particularly difficult. I just wonder why everybody finds it so complicated.

I can see also that it is quite simple to have a continuous process feeding the data of a discrete simulation. And moreover, I think that this is going to prove extremely necessary when somebody gets round to realizing that most so-called continuous processes contain a probabilistic element.

When they understand that in fact these things do not actually obey the conditions they have put down, but only to do so with a certain probability, within certain tolerances, they will want in fact to use a discrete form of simulation. I really can not see what all the fuss is about; I do not see there is any difference.

Brennan:

First of all I should like to agree with Garwick on the desirability of having potentiometers and perhaps also transfer functions automatically available as part of the language. This was our hope, and we were unable to put it into the first version of the 360 CSMP programme. It is my personal hope that it will go into a later version.

As far as optimization is concerned it is not clear to me that one can put a good package in that will serve any large variety of users. We try to handle that problem and Lackners problem by segmenting the programs, that is we have an initial section, a dynamic section and a terminal section. In the initial section we are permitted to do some discrete things at time zero, before the run. In the terminal section we have the capability of doing something after the run. It is in that terminal section that we propose to put an optimization routine and in which we are putting in display driver routines. But it is not clear to me that one can actually make a good optimization package that will serve a significant number of applications.

I certainly agree with Douglas that the real world obeys the laws of physics. This is not obvious in discrete modelling, but the laws of physics do hold, and the continuous field emphasizes this, and hopes that the probabilistic effects are minimal. This is more than a hope - we do occasionally put in a noise generator in our models to try to see if there is some effect. Whether or not we will actually couple these two kinds of language remains yet to be seen.

Krasnow made a comment that few people have described any problems that require composite continuous and discrete descriptions. I think it is not just a failure to describe, but a failure to even appreciate the existence of these problems. I think we must first do some kind of contemplation here, before anyone will be willing to spend the time to develop a system to answer a need, when we cannot even prove at this time that the need exists.

On Caracciolo's remarks on partial differential equations, I find that whether one uses a simulation language or FORTRAN, or any other way of programming individual computers, we have today no really polished manner of solving anything that involves partial differential equations. The hybrid computer is really the one other way to do it, and it is at best awkward there also.

Strachey:

Douglas' comment about the differences between discrete and continuous processes reminds me of a quotation from Bertrand Russell in a book on the principles of mathematics, where he is talking about continuity and discreteness. He talks about some mathematicians who, in a typical Hegelian manner, say that everything discrete is continuous and vice versa. But as to the precise nature of continuity and discreteness, they preserve a discreet and continuous silence.

Ross:

I wish to add strong support to the remarks of Garwick and also Caracciolo that one should assist the user in formulating problems in his customary terms, and then the systems should do the chopping up of problem into the terms which it can handle. I think we have discussed it insufficiently here, perhaps because it approaches symbol manipulation rather than modelling.

My other point concerns the method of mapping continuous problems into discrete analyses.

I think there is a very wide untapped area here which starts encroaching on the area of sequencing that we were discussing yesterday. It needs a deeper understanding of the problem class that is being solved. As an example, I refer to the construction of a circuit simulation system by us in AED. The solution was preceded by some true extensions of knowledge in how to go about analyzing these types of non-linear problems.

This analysis then was cast into a form which is particularly suited to discrete digital computation and then all of this was embedded in a system which gave facilities for modelling, graphical input and output, etc. It seems to me that it is not possible for the general purpose simulation systems to take care of all comers and try to cast their problems in your terms. But if we do go to the more specialized areas where a deeper understanding of the physics, if you will, the mathematics of the problem area exists then you have a possiblity of having very exciting solution techniques, done very efficiently.

Caracciolo:

This is in fact a basic question I want to put to Brennan. He has briefly described the source language, and what is the final result of the simulation run. I would like to know something more about the intermediate steps.

Brennan:

First let me comment that the problem is not handled in the way that Caracciolo has previously indicated to be his preference. I gather he would like a language which would take the non-linear model and automatically linearize it, and then solve it as a linear model. That we do not do.

The CSMP program works somewhat as follows: It takes the input statements and converts them to FORTRAN sub-routines which compute the derivative vector. It is an oldfashioned general differential equation solver, which happens to have a number of integrational routines, but conceptually is the same as we used many years ago.

Caracciolo:

I would like to add one comment in order to clarify the difference which I see between the continuous system simulation and discrete system simulation. For continuous system simulation I believe that languages like FORTRAN are quite adequate for running the program. The problem is to get automatically such a FORTRAN program from a more synthetic language. This is essentially a high level symbol manipulation process, I should say.

On the other hand a discrete event system, in which just the basic structure is changing, is not so easily described in FORTRAN.

A similar difficulty however, arises also for continuous simulations if one takes into account that the discretization process can not, at least in general, be uniform in time. It depends in fact on how rapidly things vary in time. If the rate of change varies itself in time then one should have a time dependent discretisation procedure.

Garwick:

It seems to me that some of you are a little misguided when you try to be kind to the user. You will give him an amount of flexibility which I do not think he wants; such as, letting him decide which integration formula he shall use. I believe that most of the users we have in mind are completely unqualified to select between these things. For the same reason I am against permitting the programmer to state his problem in free format. This seems always to a programmer to be the most easy and flexible way of doing it, but I do not think this is the case to an engineer or technician. They are accustomed to have boxes on their drawings, and they label everything with letters, numbers, with a specific style and even a specific sign: in fact they are accustomed to do things in a styl-

ish way. I think it is easier for them to use a stylish way when they
are presenting a program too.

Brennan:

That really gets back to the earlier question: why did IBM choose
to make two rather different types of programs? I certainly agree
with Garwick that there are many engineers and technically trained
people who do like the simple approach: that is why we made the
IBM 1130 system. These people more often than not are beginners
to the field of simulation, they have no or little back-ground, they
want a very simple approach. They do at the same time, because
their problems are simple, expect and need the possibility to change
their models. Their problems are not so complex that they want to
go back to their desk and contemplate for an hour or two, therefore
they are not content with batch model operating.

Because of these combined reasons we felt that we should have a
simple and very primitive language, as Garwick desires, on a
small computer where interaction is possible. On the other hand I
must disagree as to the wish of some other groups of engineers or
technically trained people for a sophisticated language. The only
reason that we could justify the expenditure of time and energy in
making the 360 CSMP programme is the phenomenal success of the
preceding similar systems; particularly DCL 90 and MIMIC. They
did not have these restrictions, they gave a great deal of sophistication and were used by hundreds of facilities (and I presume that
means several thousand individuals). Most of them were not professional programmers but technical people. I think the demand is
clearly there for sophisticated programs and also for primitive
ones. We try to answer both needs.

Gaskill:

The question of whether the users should specify the integration
procedure or whether there should be a fixed integration procedure,
or whether perhaps the simulation software should somehow decide
- this is a question which has been kicking around for a long time.
The approach which I have adopted is to use a very simple integration procedure, the rectangular integration, because it works or at
least can be made to work by selecting the appropriate calculation
area. Incidentally, in our language we basically use a fixed interval and we also provide for making the interval a function of anything the user wants it to be a function of. There is also provision
specifically for making it a stepwise function of time.

I feel there is room for research and it is only reasonable for
the simulation software to select from a library all the possibili-

ties and appropriate integration schemes for whatever simulation problem is presented. I feel that it is possible for the user to select an appropriate integration scheme on the basis of his knowledge of the system. If a description of the system has been placed in the computer, then the computer should be able to do the same: to make its own selection of the integration scheme.

If this is done, I definitely feel that the computer should not keep its decision a secret. I am highly concerned that whenever the software makes a decision it should be printed out. I think that Conway made some relevant remarks a few days ago about a compiler which accepted almost any program and produced running machine code. I think this is probably the direction in which we should go. However, this means that the compiler does have to make somewhat arbitrary decisions. I think it is perfectly all right as long as it tells the user what choices it made.

Caracciolo:

It seems to me that probably one can try to summarize the distinction between a continuous simulation system and discrete simulation system in this way. Continuous simulation languages can really be called problem oriented languages in the sense that what is defined in such a language is not a solving procedure, but just a formal description of the system. This obviously requires that an algorithm is known for transforming the description of the system into a computing algorithm simulating the system. This is just the kind of language which probably was thought of by Strachey yesterday when he said that he would like to have a programming language with just one instruction: "Solve", and it is quite different from other programming languages.

Parslow:

A. P. Herbert, who was a member of the British Parliament, once wrote a speech which he used on three occasions about three separate topics, and nobody noticed. I have been looking at this list of Gaskill's and I find that in the lectures I give in the future, I shall need to have this up on the board on all occasions as a general purpose diagram. I find that it applies to numerical analysis, it certainly applies to computing and to a great extent it applies to thinking.

When I look at this a little further, it seems that I shall have to have it on my office wall. It is my life's story; highly deceptive, never exact, cannot solve problems, cannot generate any information and, speaking as a university lecturer, not sufficiently instructive!

A RESEARCH PROJECT
ON A HIGH LEVEL SIMULATION LANGUAGE
FOR CHEMICAL PLANTS

A. CARACCIOLO DI FORINO

Centro Studi Calcolatrici Elettroniche, C.N.R.
Università degli Studi di Pisa, Pisa, Italy

The following notes describe in a very preliminary fashion a research project, recently initiated in collaboration with Mr. Kardasz and others at the CSCE in Pisa, on a simulation language for continuous systems, particularly directed towards the simulation of chemical plants.

The project consists in developing: i) a "descriptive language" for defining a chemical plant, by specifying its constituent devices, their behaviour, the interconnections, the initial start conditions, etc.... ii) an algorithm for transforming this description into an ordinary computational program, written, for example, in **FORTRAN** or **ALGOL**, for actually performing the simulation by a step by step process.

Generally speaking, a chemical plant will be described by a set of equations of two different types: differential equations (usually partial differential equations) and instantaneous equations establishing instantaneous relations between system variables. Most of them are moreover usually non linear.

The problem then is: first, discretize the system both in time and space, which leads to a set of non linear relations between the set of variables representing the "actual state" of the systems and an analogous set of variables representing the "next state"; second, solve this system with respect to the "next state" variables by linearizing the system, i.e. by developing the given set of equations around the "actual state" variables.

We can briefly illustrate this process by considering a very simplified scheme of a chemical plant for the production of ammonia, as shown in fig. 1. The system appears composed of four devices (I, II, III, IV) and seven pipelines numbered from 1 to 7, of which 1 is an input line, 6 an output line and all the others are internal to the system. For each pipeline let us denote with α the input to the pipeline and with β its output.

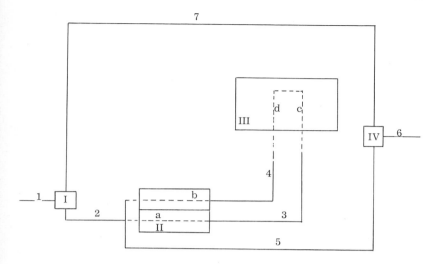

Fig. 1.

Device I is a *mixer*, in which instantaneous mixing of the inputs 1 and 7 is supposed to occur.

Device II is a *heat exchanger* composed of two channels a and b, where the fluid motion goes in opposite directions, essentially exchanging heat from the walls.

Device III is the heart of the system, i.e. the chemical reactor, which can be schematised as an ascending column C, which acts as a column of a heat exchanger, and a descending column, where the actual ammonia producing reaction takes place.

Device IV is a divider, which will be considered here as an instantaneous device separating the final product α_6 from a residual part α_7 which is recirculated. This is obviously a simplification, which however, contains the essential points for the present discussion.

We can mathematically describe the system by giving for each device of the system defining the state of the system, as a time dependent vector V (pressure, temperature, concentration of the components, etc.).

We obtain thus a set of equations:

$$\Phi_I(V_1(t),\, V_{\alpha 2}(t),\, V_{\beta 7}(t)) = 0$$

$$\Phi_{II}(V_a(x, t),\, V_b(x, t)) = 0$$

$$\Phi_{III}(V_c(x, t),\, V_d(x, t)) = 0 \qquad (1)$$

$$\Phi_{IV}(V_{\beta 5}(t),\, V_{\alpha 7}(t),\, V_6(t) = 0$$

$$\Phi_j(V_j(x, t)) = 0 \qquad j = 2,\, 3,\, 4,\, 5,\, 7$$

where Φ_I and Φ_{IV} denote instantaneous non linear relations and the others denote (usually partial) differential equations, which have to satisfy the following boundary conditions:

$$\left.\begin{aligned}
V_a(x_o^H, t) &= V_{\beta 2}(t)\\
V_b(x_o^H, t) &= V_{\beta 4}(t)\\
V_a(x_f^H, t) &= V_{\alpha 3}(t)\\
V_b(x_f^H, t) &= V_{\alpha 5}(t)
\end{aligned}\right\} \text{ for device II}$$

$$\left.\begin{aligned}
V_c(x_o^R, t) &= V_{\beta 3}(t)\\
V_d(x_f^R, t) &= V_c(x_f^R, t)\\
V_d(x_o^R, t) &= V_{\alpha 4}(t)
\end{aligned}\right\} \text{ for device III} \qquad (2)$$

$$\left.\begin{aligned}
V_j(x_{oj}^{pj}, t) &= V_{\alpha j}(t)\\
V(x_f^{pj}, t) &= V_{\beta j}(t)
\end{aligned}\right\} \text{ for pipeline } P_j .$$

Now, for each spatial device one has first to discretize the system, subdividing it into an appropriate number of sequential elementary cells (the number of which should depend on the rate of change of the system state, and therefore is in general time-dependent and introducing a discretized time, by substituting, for instance, each partial derivative $\partial V_p / \partial t$ by $(V_p' - V_p)$, where p is an index enumerating the various cells and where the unprimed variables denote the "actual state" and the primed variables denote the "next state".

A somewhat greater difficulty is posed by the instantaneous devices I and IV, which should be considered as permanent relations, valid both for the actual as well as the next state variables. We cannot discuss here this central point, which is related to consistency conditions and the closed loop character of the system. A simple solution, however, can be obtained by considering the time derivatives, which lead to the substitution of each variable V_p by $V_p' - V_p$. Having done this one finally obtains a set of non linear implicit relations:

$$\psi_p(V_p', V_p, V_1', V_1) = 0 \tag{3}$$

among the "actual state" variables V_p, the "next state" variables V_p' and the "input" variable values V_1' and V_1. These relations can now be developed with respect to V_p' around V_p by assuming

$$\chi_p(V_p', V_p) \simeq \psi_p(V_p', V_p) + \sum_q \left. \frac{\partial V_p}{\partial V_q'} \right|_{V_q} (V_q - V_q) \tag{4}$$

thus obtaining a linear system in V_p':

$$A(V_q, V_1', V_1)V_p' = B(V_p, V_1', V_1) \tag{5}$$

Finally this linear system can be formally solved for V_p', yielding

$$V_p' = H_p(V_q, V_1', V) . \tag{6}$$

In this way one has transformed the set of mathematical equations describing the continuous system, into a kind of sequential automaton, whose "next state" function is exactly given by the functions H_p as above obtained. Given now the initial values V_q^0 for all discretized system variables and the input values V_1 for all times, one immediately obtains a simulation of the system, by simply recursively computing the values of the other system variables by means of (6).

We can then summarize the project in the following terms:

i) to define a "problem oriented language" allowing one to define in a standardized form a chemical (or more generally a complex dynamical system) plant by specifying (a) of what devices the system is composed (for chemical plants one should, for instance, consider, besides those previously mentioned, rectification columns, absorbers, condensers, tanks, etc...., as well as auxiliary equipment like instrumentation and regulators. (b) what are the system's variables and the governing equations, either by giving them explicitly, especially if they are of a particular nature, or by simply referring to them by name and considering them as some sort of primitives whenever they are of a more general or standard type. (c) what will be the inputs (usually as a set of data to be read at run time) and what should be the outputs, i.e. a tabulation of all system variables, or a selection of them, or an elaboration of them (e.g. the average value of some variables, or some correlation coefficients, etc.).

ii) to define an algorithm, which is essentially a symbol manipulation procedure (capable of performing symbolic substitutions, symbolic differentiations, etc.) for discretizing and linearising the system and for solving it formally in the form (6).

This algorithm should then convert the system (6) into an ordinary procedural programming language format, including all input/output operations as well as the additional elaboration which might have been prescribed in the problem specification (see above).

The project here described is still in its early development stage, and is a part of a larger project on the definition and development of "special programming languages" as defined in another paper by the author (English translation through CSCE-CNR-University of Pisa). A preliminary report on the present project is being prepared by Mr. Kardasz.

CLOSING ADDRESS

(delivered at the Conference Dinner, Hotel Bristol, Oslo)

J. N. BUXTON

C-E-I-R, London W1, U.K.

In some ways, delivering the closing speech at this Conference might be thought an unrewarding task. But it is so only in some ways; in others, it puts me in a rather unusual situation.

If we consider your immortal words of the last week, as Editor of the Proceedings those which will be transmitted to posterity are entirely under my control. Now let us consider this contribution of mine; as I am the last speaker at this Conference, I can say what I please and nobody can reply to it!

I had the very enjoyable experience of travelling to Norway - being a Viking country - by ship, and on my journey I read some twenty or so papers. One particular item sticks in my mind which I would like to mention to you and this is the footnote to the efforts of Garwick, due, he says, to Ingerman. To get ahead, and with people like Garwick and Ingerman, to stay ahead in computing, it seems no longer good enough these days to be just an expert in computing. One must have a second string to ones bow; in this case, a fluent and extensive knowledge of ancient Persian. I am considering imitating a sound commercial idea of Knuths; that of selling good names or sets of initials for programming languages. Well, if Knuth acts as a broker of good names for languages, I will do the same in the field of suitable second fields of study for computer men who need to strengthen their positions.

One remark in the Conference which I particularly enjoyed, by the way, was Brennans unconscious exposition of the philosophy of programming a model 360 - you work very hard to try to get your problem into only 128,000 positions of core.

Being Editor of the Proceedings has given me some little difficulty already; particularly with Steele. Initially I said to Steele that I thought the task was really fairly straightforward and two or three weeks should complete it. He seemed a little surprised. One or two of you may have noticed during the last few days that this time estimate has increased every day. At present it stands at about three months, and every time I meet Steele, he sits there waiting for me

to suggest a further advance - after two years I think he will feel
content.

I have in fact already had some entertainment out of the job. The
transcript of the tape recordings is of exceptionally high quality and
everything we said is clearly written down, though in places it
reads rather curiously. I noticed particularly that there seems to
be a new vitamin enriched body-building energy giving food on the
market, known in the transcript as MALTEX. This stuff seems to
be retailed by MIT and it has lots of interesting American religi-
ous-commercial properties. For instance, apparently it descends
from above and however much you use of it, it is never consumed
but eternally renewed. Clearly it is very good for us and we should
all use lots more of it. It seems rather expensive, doubtless due
to the high advertising budget. I was not able to find in the tran-
cript any clear evidence that it is guaranteed fit for human con-
sumption, and I plan to ask the American Medical Association to
investigate this.

As Dahl has said, of course this is a solemn occasion and I
therefore propose to make a solemn speech. I want to discuss, a-
mongst other things, the purpose of holding this sort of conference.
In my time I have attended very many conferences and most of them
are really pretty grim proceedings. Clearly they serve an educational purpose, and they provide a suitable excuse for people to
meet together, if only you could find the people you would like to
talk to amongst the thousands attending. The theory behind this
sort of gathering is entirely different.

The approach is that you should invite some 50 or so people.
Then, you should lock them in a place such as Lysebu or some other delightfully situated prison and the basic intention is just that
they should have the opportunity to meet each other for the week.

Now one of the mechanisms one adopts is to suggest that they
contribute papers. As one of us has said (his name is suppressed
by special request) a principal reason for the existence of papers
is in order that our employers will pay our fares. In certain cases,
the presentation of a paper may even help in obtaining some promo-
tion, and both these facts are undoubtedly true.

The further technical purpose of a paper for this sort of conference is not quite the same as a paper for one of the larger conferences. It is to describe work in progress and to stimulate discussion; not to record one's latest achievement. The organisation
committee endeavours to invite people working in the same general
area but not, you will notice, in identical research fields. There is
an interesting tendency in computing. If you get people working on
just the same problem, - all they will tend to do is pat each other
on the back for the week if they agree, and go through the same old

argument if they do not. The intention was to invite, in this case, language designers in the discrete and continuous areas, simulation users and general purpose language experts as well.

I think that this Conference has been extremely successful and it emphasises many problems of which perhaps some of us were not fully aware. We have talked about general areas such as data structure problems and problems of quasi-parallel programming. We have talked about more specific problems in the simulation field and we have discussed whether or not we need special programming languages in the area at all.

We have had, of course, one or two enthusiastic people who are strongly opposed to special purpose languages, such as the supporters of GPL and CPL; of course, we all know what these initials really stand for though we prefer not to say so. They believe that we should stick to general purpose languages, but we have had many other points of view. Lackner, for example, believes there are some special features about these programming problems which really need a different approach.

An area of particular interest which has cropped up during the week is this question as to whether we are developing software systems for the experienced programmer or whether we are concerned with those few people who have not yet taken their second degrees in computer programming or written their first compiler.

I wish to propose a thesis which I think can throw some light on this problem. I think that, in a technical area of work, research should come first in time. It is carried out by rather few people. It is followed at a later time by development and, later still, by production.

Now on this basis let us compare the discrete and continuous fields. The continuous simulation systems have been in existence a good deal longer than the discrete ones. A lot of the research and development has been done; production work is under way and the users are offered a series of facilities which are well understood and widely accepted. In the discrete field, however, we do not yet understand our problems and we are still working in the areas of language research and development.

Unfortunately, computers are very expensive machines and the users who pay for them need production software systems. I think that in the discrete area, and possibly also in general purpose languages, the designers are trying to persuade the users to accept, as production software, systems which are really by-products of research and development. I think this Conference has emphasised the resulting apparent gap between what the designers provide and what the users need. Meanwhile, the very few production systems around, such as FORTRAN, seem to go on and on.

This Conference was not contended for the presentation of completed work. Its purpose was to bring together a number of people so that they can discuss their current problems, in the hope that the solutions will thereby be a little nearer. As such, I think it has been extremely successful.

In conclusion, I would like to express our gratitude to Ole-Johan Dahl, the man who has done most to bring this Conference about and to make it such a good one.

BIBLIOGRAPHY

[1] Aris, R., Discrete Dynamic Programming (Blaisdell Publising Co.,
A Division of Ginn and Co., New York, 1964), p. 110, 112.

[2] Baldwin, F.R., W.M.Gibson and C.B.Poland, 'A Multi-Processing
Approach to a Large Computer System', IBM Systems Journal, Volume 1, September 1962.

[3] Benyon, R.P., and Henry, W.J., 'SIMTRAN in Australia', SIMULA-
TION, September 1965.

[4] Black, Max, Models and Metaphors (Cornell University Press, Ithaca,
New York, 1962), pp. 235-236.

[5] Blechman, G.E., 'An Enlarged Version of MIDAS', SIMULATION, October 1964.

[6] Blunden, G.P., and Krasnow, H.S., 'The Process Concept is a Bais
for Simulation Modelling', presented at the 28th National Meeting,
ORSA, Houston, Texas, November 4-5, 1965.

[7] Blunden, P., and Krasnow, H.S., 'The Process Concept as a Basis for
Simulation Modelling. IBM ASDD Tech. Rep. 17-181 (November 1965).

[8] Brennan, R.D., 'PACTOLUS - A Simulation Language Which Makes a
Digital Computer Feel Like an Analog Computer', SIMULATION, August 1964.

[9] Brennan, R.D., and Sano, H., 'PACTOLUS - A Digital Analog Simulator Program for the IBM 1620', Proceedings, 1964 Fall Joint Computer
Conference AFIPS, Vol. 26, pp. 299-312.

[10] Brennan, R.D., and Linebarger, R.N., 'A Survey of Digital Simulation:
Digital Analog Simulator Programs', SIMULATION, Vol. 3, No. 6, December 1964, pp. 22-36

[11] Brennan, R.D., and Linebarger, R.N., 'An Evaluation of Digital Analog
Simulator Languages', Proceedings, IFIP Congress 1965, vol. 2, May
14, 1965, New York, N.Y.

[12] Brennan, R.D., and Fahidy, T.Z., 'Digital Simulation', Instruments
and Control Systems, Vol. 39, No. 3, March 1966.

[13] Burgin, G.H., 'MIDAS III - A Compiler Version of MIDAS', SIMULA-
TION, March 1966.

[14] Buslenko, N.P., 'Mathematical Modelling of Production Processes',
M., (1964).

[15] Buxton, J.N. and Laski, J.G., 'Control and Simulation Language',
Esso Petroleum Company, Ltd., and IBM United Kingdom, Ltd., 1962.

[16] Byrne, E.R., 'JANIS, A Program for a General-Purpose Digital Computer to Perform Analog Type Simulations', ACM Nat. Conf., Denver,
Colorado, August 27, 1963.

[17] Caracciolo di Forino, A., 'An Elementary Constructure Theory of Discrete Probabilistic Processes and Parallel Concurrent Processes'.
Paper presented at 'Wiener Memorial Day', Genova (October 1965).

[18] Clancy, John J., and Fineberg, Mark S., 'Digital Simulation Languages:
A Critique and a Guide', Proceedings, FJCC 1965.

[19] Coleman, T.G., "A Time-Delay 'Special Element' for PACTOLUS",
SIMULATION, November 1965.

[20] Conway, R.W., et al., 'CLP - The Cornell List Processor', Communications of the ACM, Vol. 8, No. 4 (April 1965), pp. 215-216.

[21] Corbato, F.J., and Vyssotysky, V.A., 'Introduction and Overview of the Multics System', AFIPS Conference Proceedings, Vol. 27 (1965 FJCC), Spartan Books, Washington, D.C., 1965, pp. 185-196.

[22] Cowley, Percy E.A., 'An Active Filter for the Measurement of Process Dynamics', Proc. 19th Annual Conf. of ISA, New York, October 12, 1964.

[23] Cowley, Percy E.A., 'An Active Filter for the Measurement of Process Dynamics', ISA Trans., Vol. 5, Issue 1, January 1966.

[24] Čulík, K., On Mathematical Models and the Role of the Mathematics in Knowledge of Reality, Kybernetika (Cybernetics) 2 (1966), 1-13.

[25] Dahl, O.J., 'A Plea for Multiprogramming', ALGOL Bulletin (September 1966).

[26] Dahl, O.J., 'Discrete Event Simulation Languages', Lectures delivered at the NATO Summer School, Villard-de-Lans (September 1966).

[27] Dahl, O.J., Myhrhaug, B., and Nygaard, K., 'Simula Tracing System' (Preliminary Version, August, 1966), Norwegian Computing Centre, Forskningsveien 1B, Blindern, Oslo 3, Norway.

[28] Dahl, O.J., and Nygaard, K., 'SIMULA - A Language for Programming and Description of Discrete Event System, Introduction and User's Manual', Third Printing, Norwegian Computing Centre, Forskningsveien 1B, Oslo 3, Norway, May 1966.

[29] Dahl, O.J., and Nygaard, K., 'SIMULA - An ALGOL-Based Simulation Language', Communications of the ACM, Vol. 9, No. 9 (September 1966), pp. 671-678.

[30] Dahlin, E.B., and Linebarger, R.N., 'Digital Simulation Applied to Paper Machine Dryer Studies: Conference Paper, 6th ISA International Pulp and Paper Instrumentation Symposium, Green Bay, Wisconsin, May 4-8, 1965.

[31] Daley, R.C., and Neuman, P.G., 'A General Purpose File System for Secondary Storage', AFIPS Conference Proceedings, Vol. 27 (1965 FJCC), Spartan Books, Washington, D.C., 1965, pp. 213-229.

[32] David, E.E., Jr., and Fano, R.M., 'Some Thoughts About the Social Implications of Accessible Computing', AFIPS Conference Proceedings, Vol. 27 (1965 FJCC), Spartan Books, Washington, D.C., 1965, pp. 243-247.

[33] Dineley, J.L., and Preece, C., 'KALDAS, An Algorithmically Based Digital Simulation of Analogue Computation', The Computer Journal, Vol. 9, No. 2, August 1966.

[34] Durand, H.P., 'DYNASAR Applications', Conference Paper, 1965 Joint Automatic Control Conference, Troy, New York.

[35] Efron, R., Gordon, G., 'A General Purpose Digital Simulator and Examples of its Applications', IBM Systems Journal, Vol. 3, No. 1, 1964.

[36] Fahidy, T.Z., 'Stability Analysis of the Numerical Solution of Partial Differential Equations via Digital Analog Simulation', SIMULATION, July 1965.

[37] Fahidy, T.Z., 'Regions of Asymptotic Stability of Dynamic Systems by the Combination of Lyapunov Techniques and Digital Simulation', SIMULATION, December 1965.

[38] Fahidy, T.Z., Perlmutter, D.D., 'The Application of the MIDAS Digital Simulator of the Study of Kinetic Alternatives in a Chemical Reaction System', SIMULATION, March 1966.

[39] Farris, G.J., and Burkhart, L.E., 'DIAN - A System for Programming a Digital Computer in Terms of Analog Components', Dept. of Chemical Engineering, Iowa State University, Ames, Iowa, 1964.

[40] Farris, G.J., and Burkhart, L.E., 'DIAN Digital Simulation Program', SIMULATION, May 1966.

[41] Forbes, G.F., 'An Engineering Simulator', Proceedings ACM 21st National Conference, August 1966.

[42] Funk, J.E., and Miller, M.B., 'SLASH-3' SRL-66-0007, Frank J. Seiler Research Lab., USAF Academy, Colorado, August 1966.

[43] Gaskill, R.A., Harris, J.W., and McKnight, A.L., 'DAS ' A Digital Analog Simulator', Proc. 1963 Spring Joint Computer Conference.

[44] Gaskill, R.A., 'A Versatile Problem-Oriented Language for Engineers', IEEE Trans. on Electronic Computers, Vol. EC-13, No. 4, August 1964.

[45] Gaskill, R.A., 'Fact and Fallacy in Digital Simulation', SIMULATION, November 1965.

[46] Glaser, E.L., Couleur, J.F., and Oliver, G.A., 'System Design of the GE 645 Computer for Time-Sharing Application', AFIPS Conference Proceedings, Vol. 27 (1965 FJCC), Spartan Books, Washington, D.C., 1965, pp. 197-202.

[47] Glushkov, V.M., 'Two Universal Criteria of Computer Efficiency', Papers of the Ukrainian Academy of Sciences, N4 (1960).

[48] Gordon, G., 'A General Purpose Systems Simulation Program'. Proceedings, 1961 Eastern Joint Computer Conference, New York. The MacMillan Company, December, 1961.

[49] Gordon, G., 'A General Purpose Systems Simulator', IBM Systems Journal, Volume 1, September 1962.

[50] Greenberger, M., Jones, M.M., Morris, J.H., Jr.. and Ness, D.N., On-Line Computation and Simulation: The OPS-3 System, the M.I.T. Press, Cambridge, Mass., 1965.

[51] Greenberger, M., 'A New Methodology for Computer Simulation', Computer Methods in the Analysis of Large-Scale Social Systems, Joint Center for Urban Studies of The Massachusetts Institute of Technology and Harvard University, J.M.Beshers, Ed., Cambridge, Mass., 1965, pp. 147-162.

[52] Greenberger, M. and Jones, M.M., 'On-Line Simulation in the OPS System', Proceedings of the 21st National Conference, ACM, Thompson Book Company, Washington, D.C., 1966, pp. 131-138.

[53] Harnett, R.T., Sansom, F.J., and Warshawsky, L.M., 'MIDAS - An Analog Approach to Digital Computation, SIMULATION, September 1964.

[54] Henry, J.W., 'Some Numerical and Programming Techniques to Allow the Use of a Digital Computer in an Analogue Fashion', Fourth International Conference of AICA.

[55] Herscovitch, R., Schneider, T.H., 'GPSS III - an Expanded General Purpose Simulator', IBM Systems Journal, Vol. 4, No. 3, 1966.

[56] Hills, P.R., 'An Outline of the Simon Simulation System'. Imperial College of Science and Technology, 1966.

[57] Hoare, C.A.R., 'Record Handling', ALGOL Bulletin 21, November 1965.

[58] Hoare, C.A.R., Wirth, N., 'A Contribution to the Development of ALGOL', Comm. of the ACM, June 1966.

[59] Hoare, C.A.R., 'Record Handling'. Lectures delivered at the NATO Summer School, Vilard-de-Lans, September 1966.

[60] D'Hoop, H., Monterosso, R., 'SAHYB - A Program for Simulation of Analog and Hybrid Computer', IEEE Transactions on Electronic Computers, June 1966.

[61] Hughes, F.M., and Brameller, A., 'Digital Simulation of Analogue Methods', The Computer Journal, Vol. 9, No. 1, May 1966.

[62] Hurley, J.R., 'DEPI 4 (Differential Equations Pseudo-Code Interpreter) - An Analog Computer Simulator for the IBM 704', internal memorandum, Allis Chalmers Mfg. Co., January 6, 1960.

[63] Hurley, J.R., 'Digital Simulation I: DYSAC, A Digitally Simulated Analog Computer', AIEE Summer General Meeting, Denver, Colorado, June 17-22, 1962.

[64] Hurley, J.R., Janoski, R.M., Rideout, V.C., Skiles, J.J., and Vebber, W.O., 'Simulation of a Hybrid Computer on a Digital Computer', Fourth International Conference of AICA.

[65] Hurley, J.R., and Skiles, J.J., 'DYSAC - A Digitally Simulated Analog Computer', Proc. 1963 Spring Joint Computer Conference, AFIPS Conference Proc., Vol. 23, p.69.

[66] Hutchinson, G.K., and J.N.Maguire, 'Computer System Design and Analysis Through Simulation', AFIPS Proceedings 1965 Fall Joint Computer Conference, Spartan Books, Washington, D.C. 1965.

[67] James, M.L., Smith, G.M., and Wolford, J.C., Analog and Digital Computer Methods in Engineering Analysis (International Textbook Co.), Scranton, Pennsylvania, 1964, pp. 171-179.

[68] Janoski, R.M., Schaefer, R.L., and Skiles, J.J., 'COBLOC - A Program for All-Digital Simulation of a Hybrid Computer', IEE Trans. on Electronic Computers Vol.EC-15, pp. 74-82, February 1966.

[69] Jones, M.M., 'On-Line Version of GPSS II', Project MAC Memorandum MAC-M-140, March 10, 1964.

[70] Jones, M.M., 'Incremental Simulation on a Time-Shared Computer', unpublished PhD Thesis, Alfred P. Sloan School of Management, Massachusetts Institute of Technology, January 1967.

[71] Kalinchenko, L.A., 'Formal Description of SLANG' (The Collection of Seminar 'Automata Theory', Ukrainian Academy of Sciences, Institute of Cybernetics Edition, the First Issue, 1967, Kiev).

[72] Kantorovich, L.V., 'A Convenient Mathematical Symbolism for Performing Computations with Computers', Doklady Akad. Nauk, 113:738-41, No. 4, April 1957.

[73] Kiviat, P.J., 'Introduction to the SIMSCRIPT II Programming Language', presented at the Symposium on Simulation Techniques and Languages, Brunel College, London, England, May 10-11, 1966.

[74] Kiviat, P.J., 'Simulation Language Report Generators', Brunel University Symposium on 'Simulation Techniques and Languages' 1966.

[75] Knuth, D.E., and McNeley, J.L., 'SOL-A Symbolic Language for General Purpose Systems Simulation', IEEE Transactions on Electronic Computers, Vol. EC-13, No. 4 (August 1964), pp. 401-408.

[76] Knuth, D.E., and McNeley, J.L., 'A Formal Definition of SOL', IEEE Transactions on Electronic Computers, Vol. ED-13, No. 4 (August 1964), pp. 409-414.

[77] Krasnow, H.S., and Merikallio, R.A., 'The Past, Present and Future of General Simulation Languages', Management Science, Vol. 11, No.2 (November 1964), pp. 236-267.

[78] Kribs, Patricia, 'Cycler for the AWAC Simulation'. System Development Corporation Document - TM-1998/000/00. July 20, 1964.

[79] Kurek, Nicholas B., 'Use of the PACTOLUS Program for Simulation of Antenna Servos', SIMULATION, October 1965, pp. 365-368.

[80] Kurek, Nicholas B., 'Digital Simulation of a Servo Tracking System'. Electro-Technology, February 1967.

[81] Lackner, M.R., 'Toward a General Simulation Capability'. Proceedings, 1962 Spring Joint Computer Conference. Palo Alto, California, The National Press, May 1962.

[82] Lackner, M.R., 'A Process Oriented Scheme for Digital Simulation Modelling', Proceedings IFIP Congress 1965, May 25, 1965.

[83] Lackner, M.R., 'Conversational Modelling and Simulation', Proceedings IFIP Congress 1965, May 27, 1965.

[84] Laski, J.G., 'On Time Structure in (Monte Carlo) Simulations'. Operational Research Quarterly, Vol. 16, No. 3 (September 1965), pp. 329-339.

[85] Lavi, A., and Reilley, G., 'ANALOG ALGOL - A Programming Language for Hybrid Computation, 1965 JACC, Troy, New York.

[86] Learonworth, B.M., 'Syntax Macros and Extended Translation', Communications of the ACM, Vol. 9, No. 11 (November 1966).

[87] Lesh, F., 'Methods of Simulating a Differential Analyzer on a Digital Computer', J. of the ACM, Vol. 5, No. 3, 1958.

[88] Licklider, J.C.R., Discussion on Simulation Models, Computer Methods in the Analysis of Large-Scale Social Systems, Joint Center for Urban Studies of the Massachusetts Institute of Technology and Harvard University, J.M.Beshers, Ed., Cambridge, Mass., 1965, pp. 163-165.

[89] Linebarger, R.N., 'Digital Simulation Techniques for Direct Digital Control Studies', Proc. 19th Annual Conf. of ISA, New York, October 12, 1964.

[90] Linebarger, R.N., and Brennan, R.D., 'Digital Simulation for Control System Design', Instruments and Control System, Vol. 38, No. 10, October 1965.

[91] Linebarger, R.N., and Brennan, R.D., 'Digital Simulation for Bio-Medical System Studies', Proceedings, 18th Annual Conference on Engineering in Medicine and Biology, Philadelphia, Pennsylvania, November 10-12, 1965.

[92] Linebarger, R.N., 'DSL/90', SIMULATION, September 1966.

[93] Lucke, V.H., 'Analysis Methods Developed for the Dynamic Systems Analyzer', Conference Paper, 1965 Joint Automatic Control Conference, Troy, New York.

[94] Maclaren, M.D., and Marsaglia, G., 'Uniform Random Number Generators', Journal of ACM, Vol. 12, 1 1965.

[95] Maguire, J.N., Hutchinson, G.K., and Lasser, D.J., 'LOMUSS I, User's Reference Manual', Lockheed Report, LMSC 665784, 1964.

[96] Malenge, J.P., 'Calcul Analogique et Genie Chimique', Genie Chimique, Vol. 96, No. 1, July 1966.

[97] Markowitz, H.M., Hausner, B. and Karr, H.W. 'SIMSCRIPT: A Simulation Programming Language'. The RAND Corporation, Memorandum RM-3310-PR. November, 1962.

[98] Markowitz, H., Hausner, B., and Karr, H., SIMSCRIPT, A Simulation Programming Language, Prentice-Hall, Inc., Englewood Cliffs, New Jersey, 1963.

[99] Matlock, J., 'JANET, Digital Analog Simulation Program', IBM Program Information Department, PID D320 and D3119.

[100] Miyauchi, T., Takata, M., 'Analysis of the Behavior of Salt-Metal Extraction Column for U-Bi Fuel', Chemical Engineering (Japan) Vol. 26, No. 9, 1962.

[101] Molinari, B.P., 'SIMPLE - Simulation Problem Language for Engineers'. The University of Western Australia, September 10, 1965.

[102] Molnar, G., 'SIMULATION Languages SL/I - Supplementary Issue, Vol. 3, CALCOLO (1965).

[103] Morris, J.H., Jr., 'Interpretive System in On-Line Programming', Unpublished Master's Thesis, Alfred P.Sloan School of Management, Massachusetts Institute of Technology, January 1966.

[104] Morris, S.M., and Schiesser, W.E., 'Undergraduate Use of Digital Simulation', SIMULATION, August 1966.

[105] Naur, P., 'The Design of the GIER ALGOL Compiler', BIT. Vol. 3, No. 2,3.

[106] Naur, P., ed.: 'Report on the Algorithmic Language ALGOL 60'.

[107] Newell, A., et al., 'Report on a General Problem-Solving Program', Proceedings, International Conference on Information Processing, Paris, UNESCO House, 1959.

[108] Olaussen, Siving L.K., 'Simulation of an Analogue Computer on the Digital Computer 'FREDERIC', Programming Description', Norwegian Defense Research Establishment, Kjeller, Norway, November 1961.

[109] Ossanna, J.F., Mikus, L.E., and Dunten, S.D., 'Communications and Input/Output Switching in a Multiplex Computing System', AFIPS Conference Proceedings, Vol. 27 (1965 FJCC), Spartan Books, Washington, D.C., 1965, pp. 231-241.

[110] Page, E.S., 'The Generation of Pseudo-Random Numbers', NATO Conference on 'Role of Digital Simulations in O.R.' 1965.

[111] Palevsky, M., and Howell, J.V., 'DES-1', Fall 1963 Joint Computer Conference, Vol. 24, Spartan Books, Inc., Washington, D.C., 1963.

[112] Parente, R.J., 'A Language for Dynamic System Description', IBM Advanced Systems Development Division, TR 17-180, 1965.

[113] Parente, R.J., and Krasnow, H.S., 'An Introduction to a Language for Modelling and Simulating Dynamic Systems', IBM Advanced Systems Development Divn, TR 17-181, November 1965.

[114] Parkhill, S., 'SIMTRAN II Programming Guide (Interim Version)', Tech Memo SAD, Weapons Research Establishment, Adelaide, South Australia, March 1966.

[115] Parslow, R.D., 'AS User's Manual', Brunel University, 1967.

[116] Paynter, H.M., 'Computer Representations of Polyphase Alternating Current Systems for Dynamic Analysis and Control', Proceedings of First International Congress of I.F.A.C., Moscow, 1960.

[117] Peterson, Sansom, Harnett, and Warshawsky, 'MIDAS - How it Works and How It is Worked', 1964 Fall Joint Computer Conference, AFIPS Conference Proc., Vol. 26, October 1964.

[118] Pollycove, M., Mortimer, R., The quantitative determination of iron kinetics and hemoglobin synthesis in human subjects. J. of Clin. Invest. 40, 5, pp. 753-783, 1961.

[119] Pugh, A., III, 'Dynamic User's Manual ', MIT Press (2nd ed, 1963).

[120] Rescigno Aldo, Giorgio Segre: La Cinetica dei Farmaci a dei Traccianti Radioattivi.

[121] Rideout, V.C., and Tavernini, L., 'MADBLOC, A Program for Digital Simulation of a Hybrid Computer', SIMULATION, January 1965, pp. 21-24.

[122] Ross, D.T., and Rodriguez, J.E., 'Theoretical Foundations for the Computer-aided Design System', Proceedings of the SJCC (1963) p. 305.

[123] Saltzer, J.H., 'CTSS Technical Notes', Project MAC Technical Report, MAC-TR-16, March 1965.

[124] Saltzer, J.H., 'TrafficControl in a Multiplexed Computer System', Project MAC Technical Report, MAC-TR-30 (Thesis), July 1966.

[125] Sansom, F.J., and Peterson, H.E., 'MIMIC - Digital Simulator Program', SESCA Internal Memo 65-12, Wright-Patterson Air Force Base, Ohio (May 1965).

[126] Sashkin, L., and Schlesinger, S., 'A Simulation Language and its Use with Analyst-Oriented Consoles', Aerospace Corp. Report, Atr-65 (59990)-5, San Bernardino, California (April 1965).

[127] Scherr, A.L., 'An Analysis of Time-Shared Computer Systems', Dissertation, M.I.T. (1965).

[128] Schlesinger, S.I., and Sashkin, L., "EASL - A Digital Computer Language for 'Hands-On' Simulation", SIMULATION, February 1966.

[129] Schwartz, J.I., 'The SDC Time-Sharing System - Part I and Part II', Datamation, Vol. 10, Nos. 11, 12 (November and December 1964), pp. 28-31 and pp. 51-55.

[130] Selfridge, R.G., 'Coding a General-Purpose Digital Computer to Operate as a Differential Analyzer', Proc. 1955 Western Joint Computer Conference (IRE).

[131] Shah, M.J., James, C., and Duffin, J.M., 'Simulation of an Ammonia Synthesis Reactor', 1966 Conference Proceedings, International Federation of Automatic Control, London.

[132] Sheppard, C.W., Basic Principles of the Tracer Method. Introduction to Mathematical Tracer Kinetics, New York, London, J. Wiley and Son.

[133] Silberberg, Martin, Y., 'Using Digital Computers for Process Simulation', Chemical Engineering, September 26, 1966.

[134] Slagle, J.R., 'A Heuristic Program that Solves Symbolic Integration Problems in Freshman Calculus', Journal of the ACM, Vol. 10, No. 4 (October 1963), pp. 507-520.

[135] Slayton, G.R., 'DIDAS - A Digital Differential Analyzer Simulator', Georgia Div., Lockheed Aircraft Corp., August 1957 (available in SHARE library).

[136] Smith, C.L., Jr., 'All-Digital Simulation for Process Industries', ISA Journal, July 1966.

[137] Smith, H.J., 'Analysis of a Vibrating Heat Engine Using PACTOLUS', SIMULATION, January 1966.

[138] Stein, M.L., and Rose, J., 'Changing from Analog to Digital Programming by Digital Techniques', ACM Journal, Vol. 7, No. 1, January 1960.

[139] Stein, M.L., Rose, J., and Parker, D.B., 'A Compiler with an Analog-Oriented Input Language', Proc. 1959 Western Joint Computer Conference. Reprinted in SIMULATION, March 1965.

[140] Stover, R.F., and Knudtson, H.S., 'H-800 PARTNER - Proof of Analog Results Through a Numerical Equivalent Routine', Doc. No. U-ED 15002, Minneapolis-Honeywell Regulator Co., Aero. Divn., April 30, 1962.

[141] Strachey, C., 'System Analysis and Programming', Information, W.H. Freeman and Co., San Francisco, 1966, pp. 56-75.

[142] Strauss, J.C., and Gilbert, W.L., 'SCADS, a Programming System for the Simulation of Combined Analog Digital Systems', 2nd edition, Carnegie Institute of Technology (March 1964).

[143] Strauss, J.C., 'Basic Hytran Simulation Language-BHSL', Proceedings 1966 FJCC, Vol. 29, November 1966.

[144] Syn, W.M., and Linebarger, R.N., 'DSL/90 – A Digital Simulation Program for Continuous Modelling', Proc. 1966 Spring Joint Computer Conference, AFIPS Conf. Proc. Vol. 28, pp. 165-187, April 1966.

[145] Szczepkowicz: Programowanie w autokodzie MOST1 (Wroclaw, ELWRO Publication 03-VI-1) (Programming in the autocode MOST 1, in Polish).

[146] Takata, Masaru, 'The Programmed Digital Differential Analyzer', Information Processing in Japan, Vol. 1, 1961.

[147] Tocher, K.D., Handbook of the General Simulation Program, Department of O.R. and Cybernetics, United Steel Companies, Ltd., Sheffield, England.

[148] Tocher, K.D., and Owen, D.G., 'The Automatic Programming of Simulation'. Proceedings of the Second International Conference on Operational Research, London, England. English Universities Press, 1960.

[149] Tocher, K.D., 'The Art of Simulation' (English University Press, 1963).

[150] Tocher, K.D., and Hopkins, D.A., 'Handbook of General Simulation Program Mark II', United Steel Companies Ltd., 1964.

[151] Tocher, K.D., 'Review of Simulation Languages', Operational Research Quarterly, Vol. 16, No. 2 (June 1965), pp. 189-217.

[152] Trilling, D.R., 'The Use of a Job Shop Simulator in the Generation of Production Schedules', AFIPS Proceedings 1964 Fall Joint Computer Conference.

[153] Vyssotsky, V.A., Corbato, F.J., and Graham, R.M., 'Structure of the Multics Supervisor', AFIPS Conference Proceedings, Vol. 27 (1965 FJCC), Spartan Books, Washington, D.C., 1965, pp. 203-212.

[154] Watson, J.M., 'DYNASAR Input/Output Concepts', Conference Paper, 1965 Joint Automatic Control Conference, Troy, New York.

[155] Weizenbaum, J., 'Symmetric list Processor' Comm ACM Vol. 6, No. 9 (September 1963).

[156] Weizenbaum, J., 'ELIZA – A Computer for the Study of Natural Language Communication Between Man and Machine', Communications of the ACM, Vol. 9, No. 1 (January 1966), pp. 36-45.

[157] Whitelaw, S., 'An Automated Stock Exchange', Unpublished Master's Thesis, Alfred P. Sloan School of Management, Massachusetts Institute of Technology, June 1965.

[158] Williams, J.W.J., 'The Elliott Simulator Package', Computer Journal, Vol. 6, 4, 1964.

[159] Yershov, A.P., Kozhukhin, G.I., Voloshin, U.V., 'Input Language for Automatic Programming Systems'. Academic Press, London and New York (1963).

[160] Reference Manual, General Purpose Systems Simulator II, International Business Machines Corporation, White Plains, New York, 1963.

[161] Control and Simulation Language. Reference Manual, Esso Petroleum Co., Ltd., and IBM United Kingdom, Ltd., London, England, March 1963.

[162] Anonymous, 'SDS DES-1', Scientific Data Systems Descriptive Brochure, No. 64-42-01C (1964).

[163] MILITRAN Programming Manual, Prepared for the Office of Naval Research, Navy Department, Washington, D.C., by Systems Research Group, Inc., New York, June 1964.

[164] The Compatible Time-Sharing System: A Programmer's Guide, Second Edition, The M.I.T. Computation Center, P.A. Crisman, Ed., The M.I.T. Press, Cambridge, Mass., 1965.

[165] The Michigan Algorithm Decoder, University of Michigan, November 1963 (Rev. ed., March 1965).

[166] IBM Operating System/360/PL/1: Language Specification, Form C28-6571-3, International Business Machines Corporation, 1966.

[167] Samočinný počítač ODRA 1013 (všeobecný popis) in Czech Hradec Králové 1966 (General description of the automatic computer ODRA 1013).

[168] Proceedings of a 'Round Table on Simulation Programming Languages' (Pisa, Calcolo 3, 1, 1966).